MW00761165

DATA COMMUNICATIONS

An Overview

Myron E. Sveum

Metropolitan State College

Prentice Hall
Upper Saddle River, New Jersey   *Columbus, Ohio*

Library of Congress Cataloging-in-Publication Data

Sveum, Myron.
    Data communications : an overview / Myron Sveum.
       p. cm.
    ISBN 0-13-079862-2
    1. Data transmission systems.   I. Title.
   TK5105.S924   2000
   004.6—dc21   99-22958
   CIP

Publisher: Charles E. Stewart, Jr.
Associate Editor: Kate Linsner
Production Editor: Alexandrina Benedicto Wolf
Production Coordination: Carlisle Publishers Services
Cover Design Coordinator: Karrie Converse-Jones
Cover Designer: Alice Shikina
Production Manager: Deidra M. Schwartz
Marketing Manager: Ben Leonard

This book was set in Times Roman by Carlisle Communications, Ltd. and was printed and bound by R. R. Donnelley & Sons Company. The cover was printed by Phoenix Color Corp.

Printed in the United States of America

10 9 8 7 6 5 4 3 2

ISBN: 0-13-079862-2

Prentice-Hall International (UK) Limited, *London*
Prentice-Hall of Australia Pty. Limited, *Sydney*
Prentice-Hall of Canada, Inc., *Toronto*
Prentice-Hall Hispanoamericana, S. A., *Mexico*
Prentice-Hall of India Private Limited, *New Delhi*
Prentice-Hall of Japan, Inc., *Tokyo*
Prentice-Hall (Singapore) Pte. Ltd., *Singapore*
Editora Prentice-Hall do Brasil, Ltda., *Rio de Janeiro*

*This book is dedicated to the loving memory of
my father Glanard Sveum
and
my grandfathers Even Sveum and Alex Honcharoff*

*This book is also dedicated to
my mother Lydia Sveum
and Uncle K. T. "Chief" Sveum
and to the four most wonderful and perfect grandchildren ever to
grace this third rock from our sun:
Shelley Herman, Natalie Harris, Taren Even Beeson, and Anthony Harris
and to my beloved kids
and their significant others:
Brian and Lora, Randy and Tricia, Patty and Chuck,
and Danne and Harry*

PREFACE

This book provides an overview of data communications. It covers a very broad area, including major concepts, with sufficient depth for a one-semester or two-quarter undergraduate course. With a laboratory, the use of this book could extend to two semesters.

The targeted audience are electronic technicians, electrical engineering technology, computer science, and computer information systems students. This book has more technical material than typical business network books. If this book is used for business students, it is hoped the technical information will not overwhelm them. Some higher math and physics portions could be omitted.

Some trigonometry and communications classes are suggested as prerequisites. This will help with the fiber optics area in Chapter 2. Many books completely ignore optical fiber. Section 2.5 can be skipped if the students are deficient in these subjects. However sections 2.5.1 through 2.5.7 do not require any special math or physics. The communications classes should include modulation techniques and the relationship between the time and frequency domains (Fourier analysis).

There are many fine books on data communications, and they are good for their detail and are excellent reference sources. However, they discuss subjects in more detail than is practical to teach in a one-semester or two-quarter survey course. Also they limit discussion of some subjects that are important in the field, or they fail to mention them at all but discuss pet areas in grinding detail. This book is not meant as a reference tool but rather as a teaching book. This is because of the wide-ranging subject area and lack of detailed discussion. When the student actually uses and encounters the telecommunications subject(s), he or she can refer to the other excellent books available.

At Metropolitan State College, we are evolving toward a two-semester course in data communications with extensive laboratories in both semesters. The first semester course will cover Chapters 1 through 9 and Chapter 14 (basics, LANs and some PSTN, and a comparison of Data Link protocols and transport protocols). The second semester will cover the remainder of the book.

In the modem section, biphase modulation is included to introduce Phase Shift Keying and to ease students into this difficult subject. Similarly BiSync is included to ease student transition to modern and widely used protocols.

Several low-cost experiments are possible to enhance learning. Some vendors give away sample programs in network simulation and network monitoring. The amateur radio community has low-cost or free programs on satellite tracking and TCP/IP over AX.25 at tapr@tapr.org. AX.25 is X.25 modified for amateur digital communication (packet) needs. Addresses are included in Appendix A6. An interesting bandwidth experiment can be done with a simulated twisted pair line (12,000 feet equivalent) and an 88-millihenry loading coil. Warren Hioki's fine *Laboratory Manual* to accompany his text, *Telecommunications,* Third Edition, presents many experiments.

Feedback, Inc., has a telecommunications educational test station. The experiments include PCM encoding, noise, error detection and correction, bit error rate, multiplexing, amplitude shift keying, frequency shift keying, phase shift keying, Costas loop demodulator, quadrature phase shift keying, differential phase shift keying, analog to digital conversion, and clock recovery.

Acknowledgments

My thanks to the following people for their inspiration and encouragement. Thanks to Margarete Ralston, a former teaching colleague, for badgering and pestering me into organizing a data communications course on Microsoft PowerPoint. Also Margarete taught me my first data communications course.

I give humble thanks to Dr. Harvey Gates, a part-time teacher at the University of Colorado at Boulder. I had a lot of difficulty organizing my data communications courses because the material was so extensive and no one book was broad enough. Also the books were written for people already in the industry and not for beginning students. Dr. Gates had an extremely well-organized course and in essence showed me how to organize my courses and this book. Dr. Gates is an excellent representative of the fine telecommunications graduate program at CU-Boulder. When one enters their graduate program, it is assumed the student does not know a great deal about telecommunications and data communications, and Dr. Gates takes the student from minimal knowledge to a good understanding of the subject.

I also thank Bill Rinker of Lucent Technologies for his encouragement, his patient advice, and his gentle correction of my errors. Bill has been a friend and an inspiration, and it is very much appreciated.

A student, James Cagel, has done an excellent job proofing the text. James caught errors that both I and the copy editor missed. His help is greatly appreciated.

My colleagues at Metro State—Cliff Cookson, Susan Helms, Gerry Morris, and Dave Cummings—have been most helpful and have encouraged me, and that is also appreciated.

The following individuals provided valuable feedback throughout the various stages of manuscript refinement: Patrick J. Chalmers, ITT Technical Institute; Robert M. Kabanuck, Northwest Technical Institute; Russell H. Myers, El Paso Community College; Patrick Regan, Heald College; and Thomas Young, Rochester Institute of Technology.

My cousin, Al Kaulbaugh of US West, has been a big help with his advice, technical knowledge, and sharp wit.

My friends at Prentice-Hall—Charles E. Stewart, Jr., and Kate Linsner—have been the greatest help in putting this book into print. I thank them sincerely.

My mother, father, grandfather Even, and Uncle K.T. have somehow succeeded in instilling in me their work ethic and love of learning. I know there were many times when success seemed very distant while working with a most recalcitrant child. I now appreciate what they attempted and thank them.

Finally, my sincere thanks to Barb J. Keating, without whose love and encouragement this book could never have been written. In times of discouragement she would shove, prod, and push me onward and back to the computer keyboard.

CONTENTS

DATA COMMUNICATIONS

1

BASICS

OBJECTIVES

In this chapter we will discuss:

    I. Frequently asked questions.
    II. Typical questions students have about this book and data communications.
    III. History of communications, particularly data communications and telecommunications.
    IV. Standards, what they are and why we have them.
        A. Telecommunications and data communications.
        B. Closed standards, advantages and disadvantages.
        C. Open standards, advantages and disadvantages.
        D. Standards organizations.
    V. Networks.
        A. What are networks?
        B. Why do we have and use networks? Advantages of networks.
    VI. Seven Layer Reference Model (RM).
        A. Why do we divide a communications system into layers?
        B. A brief description of the layers and their functions.

1.1 Frequently Asked Questions (FAQs)

Q: What is this book all about?

A: It is about the many different systems that transfer data or digital communications, such as the public telephone system, computer networks, communication satellites, and fiber optics. It includes short distance (Local Area Networks or LANs), long distance (Wide Area Networks or WANs), fiber optics, and satellite systems.

Q: Why could this book be useful to me?

A: The bottom line is *jobs!* The majority of new jobs are with data communications companies and companies that use data communications. Several communications firms in Colorado include IBM, AT&T, US West, Qualcomm, Jones Inter Cable, Hewlett Packard, TCI, and Hughes DirecTV.

Q: What is responsible for this growth?

A: The major factor is the availability of relatively inexpensive, comparatively powerful computers. Much of the workforce in developed countries have computers on their desks and in their homes. The programs and data used and created are *shared!* This requires digital communications. No computer user works in complete isolation!

Q: But I'm not interested in this area. It sounds *boring!* I'm just taking this course because I need the credits and it fits my schedule.

A: You will be using computers in your work, and these computers will be networked together, either locally or wide area. You will be handicapped if you do not have some knowledge of how this is done. If you do not know at least the meaning of the "buzzwords," your career may suffer.

Q: What is the difference between data communications and telecommunications?

A: Simply, telecommunications is voice communications and data communications handles data. With modern technologies the distinction gets very complex and fuzzy. Analog voice signals from the home or office are converted to digital signals for more efficient transmission. Many communications systems handle the data without knowing what type it is. One system, ATM, is designed to handle all types equally well. Some systems, TCP/IP and Frame Relay, were originally designed for only data and can now handle voice.

Q: This seems like a *lot of material.* How much does the book cover and how deep does it go?

A: This is a *survey course* only! There is just too much material to cover in any great depth in one semester, or one or two quarters.

Q: How is this course different from other electronics courses?

A: There are very few design or "number" problems. You will learn about existing systems and protocols. A *protocol* is a set of rules defining how a communication system works. You will not be asked to design your own. The many various protocols, systems, and amount of material can be very confusing. Many students are understandably frustrated by this and ask, "Why not just one (or just a few) protocol(s) or system(s) for everything?" Unfortunately no "golden protocol" or universal system exists. As technology and customer needs changed, new protocols and systems were developed. As the philosopher said, "The only constant is change." Remember, your instructor and this book are just the messengers. *Please don't kill the messengers.*

Q: Acronyms?

A: *Acronym* is defined as a word created from the title of the standard, method, or protocol. This industry probably has the most acronyms of any. Unfortunately knowing what the acronym stands for usually does not convey any useful knowledge. That's why there is a glossary in the back of the book.

1.2 History of Telecommunications

Data communications is different from many other technical areas in that its history is important to understanding the technology, how the communication methods and systems were developed, and how they relate. Communication is closely regulated throughout the world, and an understanding of regulatory and judicial events is also important.

300 B.C.	Greeks invent heliograph.
1605	Francis Bacon develops code for encryption.
1831	Charles Babbage invents "Difference Engine."
1831	Henry invents the telegraph, the first digital (0/1, on/off) communications device. Samuel Morse makes it practical for longer distances.
1845	Western Union Telegraph company is formed.
1854	Philip Reise invents the telephone.
1861	Telegraph lines span the United States from coast to coast. Now messages could be sent from New York to San Francisco in minutes, rather than weeks. This was important is keeping the state of California in the Union during the American Civil War. The Pony Express service (mail service via horseback) immediately ceases, but lives on in the legends of the American West.
1865	First transatlantic telegraph cable is completed. Now messages between the United States and Europe no longer have to wait for ships to carry them.
1870	Tyndall's optical transmission experiment is the basis of optical fiber communications.
1873	Maxwell's equations predict electromagnetic waves. This is the basis of all radio, television, and optical fiber communications.
1875	Emile Baudot develops fixed length code.
1876	Alexander Graham Bell patents the telephone (analog).
1882	First telephone switchboard is developed.
1885	American Telephone & Telegraph is formed.
1888	Hertz demonstrates electromagnetic waves, confirming Maxwell's equations. Communicating over distances without a direct connection (wires) becomes a possibility.
1889–1896	Stowger switch and dial telephone is invented, eliminating the telephone switching operator.
1901	Marconi sends radio communications across the Atlantic Ocean. Now one does not have to rely on expensive cables to send messages long distance. This also opens up the possibility of entertainment broadcasting.
1913	Kingsbury Commitment from AT&T. The U.S. Department of Justice declared that AT&T was violating the Sherman Anti-Trust

Act. In response AT&T issued the *Kingsbury Commitment of 1913* stating that AT&T would not buy out any more independent telephone companies, would allow the independents to be connected to the AT&T network, and would sell its Western Electric stock. About 1,400 independent telephone companies exist in the United States today.

1915   North American transcontinental telephone line is completed.

1928   Nyquist publishes channel capacity formula. This establishes the maximum data capacity of a digital transmission line.

1934   Communications Act creates the U.S. Federal Communications Commission (FCC), a part of the Department of Commerce. The U.S. Congress decreed the airwaves (radio frequency spectrum) are a public commodity and the FCC must be created to best manage this finite resource.

1945   Eniac, the first digital computer, demonstrates the feasibility of digital computing.

1948   Shannon's "Mathematical Theory of Communications" refines the maximum capacity of digital transmission lines.

1948   Bell Laboratories team invents the transistor and later wins the Nobel physics prize. Electronics and computers could now be made smaller, more reliable, and use less power.

1956   AT&T Consent Decree. In 1949 the U.S. Justice Department attempted to break up AT&T by forcing its manufacturing company, Western Electric, to become independent. In 1956 a *Consent Decree* was issued allowing Western Electric to remain part of AT&T, but only to supply common carrier communications equipment.

1957   Soviet Union launches Sputnik I artificial satellite. This set off the "space race" between the Soviet Union and the United States, culminating in the Apollo program, which sent twelve American men to the moon's surface and returned them safely to earth. This race also set in motion satellite development programs, which included communications satellites.

1959   Texas Instruments develops the first integrated circuit. Putting many transistors onto one small piece of silicon made low-cost, small, and low-power electronic systems possible. This eventually led to the development of the affordable personal computer.

1960   The laser is invented. It has many uses, including long distance optical fiber communications systems.

1968   Carterfone Decision allows private devices to be connected to the AT&T telephone system.

1970   Optical fiber losses become less than 20 dB/km, making fiber optic transmission systems practical.

1972	IBM's Systems Network Architecture (SNA) becomes the protocol for the first commercial data network.
1976	X.25 becomes the protocol for the first public networking service.
1978	Ethernet becomes the first Local Area Network (LAN) standard. LANs are used to connect computing equipment together over (local) distances up to 2.5 km.
1984	Judge Harold H. Green decrees the *Modified Final Judgment* (MFJ) and orders the *breakup (divestiture) of AT&T*. The MFJ modifies the Consent Decree of 1956. Microwave Communications, Inc., wanted to build a microwave link for truckers between St. Louis and Chicago, but the existing laws did not allow it to do so. William McGowan, a lawyer for MCI who was quite aware of the biblical story of David and Goliath, filed an anti-trust suit against AT&T. Judge Harold Green issued the Modified Final Judgment (MFJ) of 1984 decreeing a breakup (divestiture) of AT&T into AT&T and seven Regional Bell Operating Companies (RBOC), or "Baby Bells." US West is one of the RBOCs. AT&T still handles the long distance calls. The Baby Bells jointly owned Bellcore, formerly Bell Laboratories, which has since been sold. This divestiture decree allowed independent companies such as Sprint and MCI to compete with AT&T for the very lucrative long distance traffic.
1996	Congress passes a new telecommunications bill opening up competition between local carriers, long distance carriers, and cable television companies. The *Telecommunications Act of 1996* allows RBOCs to compete in long distance service, and the long distance carriers can compete with the RBOCs for local service. The stock of all Regional Bell Operating Companies fell precipitously after this bill passed. At this time (1999) few are willing to make any hard predictions on this bill's ultimate impact, but everyone anticipates that things will be very interesting! As of 1999, the only major action resulting from this bill is that many lawyers are sorting out the legal questions. "Gentlemen, start your lawyers!"

1.3   Standards

1.3.1 Why Do We Have Standards?

To make more $MONEY$! OK, so how does this work? Let's start by looking at some everyday standards. Some mundane standards we have in our everyday life are highway width, automobile tire track widths, paper size (8 1/2 × 11 inches in the United States), rifle bullet caliber, plumbing and electrical fixtures, electrical power voltage and frequency.

In the days of the American Revolution no standard existed for muskets. Each manufacturer had its own very loose standards, and even muskets from the same manufacturer varied considerably. If a musket part broke, it was difficult or even impossible to get a replacement. Often it was necessary to buy a completely new musket. This was obviously inefficient and needlessly expensive.

Today most manufacturers make their products to standards. It would be an inefficient and costly world if we did not have standards within a company or from one manufacturer to another. Developed countries have governmental agencies to create and enforce technical, safety, and environmental standards.

Customers are very reluctant to buy equipment that does not meet a widely accepted standard. Therefore to sell products and make money, companies will make their products according to the prevailing standard. Not to do so can be fiscal suicide.

1.3.2 Types of Standards

A *proprietary (closed) system or standard* is manufactured and controlled by (usually) one company. No other companies are allowed to make equipment or write software using this standard. Examples are ARCnet, a Local Area Network (LAN) system, and the Apple MacIntosh computer.

With an *open system or standard* any company can manufacture equipment or write software. Often a royalty fee is paid to the originating company. An example is IBM's PC (Personal Computer) and also many communication companies using standards we will talk about in later chapters.

1.3.2.1 Proprietary or Closed System

Proprietary or Closed System Advantages
- The advantages are *tighter control, easier consensus,* and a *monopoly* by the controlling company, which can (sometimes) maximize profits. If one company controls the standard, then that company has total control. Subsequent changes are easier than if several companies, each with their own method and ideas, have to hammer out an agreement. Consensus on a proprietary standard proposed within one company is easier than getting several companies, each with different protocols and products to promote, to agree. Each company would tend to push its own product, usually at the expense of the others.

An example is Apple's MacIntosh computer. The MacIntosh was Apple's main source of revenue, and Apple wanted to keep it that way. The MacIntosh was a superior machine to the IBM PC, and Apple reasoned that the world would beat a path to its door to buy MacIntoshes. Therefore Apple wanted to keep its monopoly, and tight control over the MacIntosh manufacturing, and pocket huge profits. Events did not work out this way.

Closed System Disadvantages
- *The customer has no choice of vendors.* An example is the power, gas, and telephone utilities that have monopolies in a given area. Each state has a public service commission to oversee these utilities and to prevent abuses and settle customer disputes. Customers have had little choice in provider, and it is very difficult to be without these basic services. However some customers have opted to install their own solar power and wind power systems, as well as their own propane systems, rather than be bound to the local power and gas utilities.
- *A proprietary standard usually requires deep pockets or control of a niche market.* The companies that successfully market proprietary standard products usually have large financial funding or specialize in niche markets.

- *Often the product is not the best possible or is overpriced.* If a company is making a big profit on its proprietary product, there is little incentive to change, employ new technology, or reduce the price.

- *The customer may go elsewhere.* An example is the IBM PC versus the Apple MacIntosh. Both Apple and IBM underestimated the impact of PCs. Apple found that people beat a path to the doors of the PC clone manufacturers and not to Apple. The PC clone makers were more efficient manufacturers than Apple, and they had a significant price advantage over the MacIntosh. The PC clone makers underpriced the MacIntosh, and Apple's share of the PC market plummeted. Had Apple opened up manufacturing of the MacIntosh to others, the PC business might have evolved quite differently.

- *Sometimes the customer will do without rather than be locked into a closed standard.* A company may decide that the aggravation of a proprietary standard product outweighs the advantages of that system, and simply not buy that product.

- *The controlling company can go out of business,* and support and replacement parts become unavailable. Sometimes when a company goes out of business or stops supporting a product, a third party company will step in to give customer support and manufacture and stock spare parts.

- *The controlling company can cease making the product.* An example is the Texas Instruments TI-99/4L computer, introduced in the late 1970s. This machine, targeting the educational market, was a good 16-bit computer for its time. Other microcomputer companies were reluctant to use the TI-99/4L processor chip, because they feared TI would give priority treatment to its own computer production, putting the other companies using these same chips at a disadvantage. TI realized that greater profits were in chip production rather than computer production, and therefore stopped producing the 99/L4 computer. However, several independent companies supplied parts and software for many years. Even in 1997 a TI-99/L4 club was active in the Denver, Colorado, area.

1.3.2.2 Open System

Open System Advantages

- *The customer has a choice of vendors and is more willing to make an investment.* With an open system several companies can compete for the same market. When a vendor goes out of business or discontinues the product, it is not a catastrophe. The customer is not as likely to be left with unsupported equipment and software and without a source of spare parts. The customer will be able go to other vendors that may support the original vendor under a licensing agreement.

The IBM PC and its descendants opened new markets and encouraged companies to compete in those markets. Microsoft is the most famous and financially successful of those companies, and Microsoft co-founder and CEO Bill Gates, Paul Allen, and other Microsoft cofounders have become billionaires. However, Microsoft has competitors in all its business areas. Each is trying to produce a better product and gain a market advantage. Each market victory or loss is transitory because the technology and markets are changing rapidly. In the personal computer world there is little customer loyalty to any one company. Customers are quite willing to jump quickly from one brand to another. This definitely keeps the competing companies on their collective toes, all to the benefit of the customer.

- *Products from different vendors can operate and communicate with each other.* With open system standards any company can compete. This competition usually results in a less expensive and higher quality product. Often competing companies will solve problems using different methods. Each method may have an advantage for a particular group of customers, or one method proves to be so much better than the competition that it becomes the industry de facto standard. Small companies have become very successful with such innovative products. The only imperative is that the product interface properly with other vendors' products.

- *Smaller companies can compete and may design a better, less expensive product.* Qualcomm is a company that has come up with an innovative and promising solution to radio frequency sharing. Qualcomm has employed ingenious mathematics to develop Code Division Multiple Access (CDMA) for digital radio communications. The "multiple access" means that many users can share the same radio frequency spectrum. We will learn more about this method when we discuss wireless communications in a later chapter.

- *It is often to the advantage of a company to license other companies to manufacture the product.* Datapoint, the makers of the ARCnet LAN, could have gained greatly by allowing other companies to make products to the ARCnet standard. Now ARCnet is a fading technology with static or decreasing sales. The new 100 million bits per second (bps) LANs will probably seal ARCnet's fate.

Open System Disadvantages

- Ah, but the world of open standards is not utopia. *It is harder to get agreement between vendors.* Each company on a standards committee has its own agenda and technology to promote, often at the expense of other members. Yet each company knows that a workable standard for all members must be hammered out, or all members will suffer. Since all companies must agree, control is also more difficult. Historically European and North American companies often disagreed and sometimes even created somewhat differing standards.

- There is also *less control* because each vendor usually manufactures its product without independent monitoring, sometimes leading to product incompatibility.

- *"Standard" items aren't always compatible.* That is, the products from different vendors don't always work with each other. Regardless of what marketing people tell you, "compatible" equipment or software isn't always compatible. One vendor's equipment or software may not work as advertised with another vendor's. This "can of worms" is guaranteed to spawn "finger pointing" (blaming the other guy).

- *A standard can "freeze" a technology, making it difficult to take advantage of innovations.* A standard should be carefully crafted to allow implementation of new technology as it becomes available. For instance, the Futurebus standard (used for computer internal busses) allows up to a 256-bit internal computer bus, well beyond today's largest computer bus sizes.

1.3.3 Standards Are Necessary

Quoting Benjamin Franklin, an American statesman and philosopher, "If we don't hang together, we shall most assuredly hang separately." Of course Franklin was referring to the American Revolutionary War and urging the individual states to put aside their differences (hang together) and cooperate or all would "most assuredly" be hung separately (by the British). Companies must cooperate on standards (hang together), or they will suffer financially (hang separately).

1.3.4 Standards Organizations

Standards organizations create and administer standards. Often competing companies will form a committee to create a standard acceptable to all interested parties. Then the committee will ask a standards organization for formal recognition of that standard. An example is Ethernet, a Local Area Network (LAN) system created by Xerox, Intel, and Digital Equipment Corporation. These companies asked the Institute of Electrical and Electronics Engineers (IEEE) to formalize Ethernet, and this became standard IEEE 802.3.

Many governments have standards organizations. An example is the United States' National Institute of Standards & Technology (NIST), a part of the Department of Commerce.

1.3.4.1 United Nations Standards Organizations
For technical issues affecting many parts of the world the United Nations may be called upon to formalize standards. In the communications area the UN has created the *International Communications Union–Telecommunications-Sector (ITU-T)*. The ITU-T was formerly the CCITT (Consultative Committee for International Telegraphy and Telephone).

1.3.4.2 United States Standards Organizations
The United States has many industrial and governmental standards organizations. The major standards from industry are the *American National Standards Institute (ANSI)*, the *Institute of Electrical and Electronics Engineers (IEEE)*, and the *Electronic Industries Association (EIA)*. The IEEE administers LAN standards. The major governmental standards organization is the *National Institute of Standards and Technology (NIST)*. NIST major standards concerns are the standard volt, standard ampere, time, and critical dimensions for semiconductor manufacture. NIST was formerly the National Bureau of Standards (NBS).

1.3.4.3 Canadian Standards Organizations
Two Canadian standards organizations are the *Canadian Radio and Television Commission*, a governmental agency, and *Industry Canada*, an industrial standards organization.

1.4 Networks

1.4.1 Network Functions

Networks connect data processing equipment, data, and users. Data, images, video, and voice signals are sent over networks. Voice, images, and video begin as analog signals but are converted to digital numbers for better transmission quality through networks.

1.4.2 Network Advantages

Networks connect resources for users to share. Some resources are printers, multiple computers, disk storage, plotters, input/output devices, software, files, and people.

Networks allow better, faster, and mobile communication, such as cellular (mobile telephone service), wireless, and Personal Communications Services (PCS). Network equipment usually has redundancy or backup capability for increased reliability. High-resolution and large color printers and plotters are quite expensive and take up a lot of space in an office or cubicle. Sharing these resources reduces capital equipment and office space costs.

All these advantages add up to more efficient use of resources and greater competitiveness, whether the resources are people, data, or equipment. While "sneakernet" may be more cost-effective for very small companies and small files, it is totally inadequate for most firms. Today's large files, such as graphic files and Computer Aided Design (CAD) files, are best transferred by networks. Often several people will be working on the same project files and efficient file transfers are imperative. Companies have to use networks to be efficient and stay competitive. Traveling executives and salespersons ("road warriors") can keep in touch with the home office, even from cars or airplanes. Networks allow people to do office work from their home in their pajamas, thus reducing commuting time and pollution while increasing efficiency and worker morale.

Some problems are still impractical to solve on a small computer or even a large computer working alone. The Internet allows users to employ mainframe computers or even supercomputers at distant facilities. Multiple machines can be networked together to solve particularly difficult problems. In 1996 mathematicians around the world cooperatively solved a mathematics problem that would have taken about a thousand years on a single mainframe. Each location solved a portion of the problem and then shared files and communicated via the Internet.

In another example Plessey Semiconductor has design centers in the United Kingdom and in California. Since there is an eight- or nine-hour time difference between the two sites, a UK team would work on a project during their day. Then just before the UK crew left work in their evening, they would transfer the necessary files to the California design center. The California team would then begin to work on the project in their morning.

Connecting computers and peripherals together has financial advantages as well. Many software houses offer lower priced versions of their products to be used on networks. Usually the software company limits the number of people using the software simultaneously, but with good planning this limit is rarely reached.

Networks are designed to be more reliable than stand-alone devices (nodes). A failure of several nodes may affect only those nodes and the network will still function, although at a reduced level. The Internet (a very large global network) was designed to function with many of its nodes non-functional. The Internet's huge size makes it virtually impossible for all nodes to be operational simultaneously.

Mobility is increased with networking. One can send and receive electronic mail (e-mail) by using on-line services such as CompuServe or America Online, which have worldwide access. It is possible to be on a business trip away from one's office and yet, by logging onto (connecting with) an e-mail provider, read and answer e-mail. Cellular telephone and Personal Communications Services (PCS) networks increase mobility by allowing quick communication while traveling in an automobile, flying in an airplane, or walking.

1.4.3 Network Disadvantages

Networks are not without their disadvantages. From a basic cost perspective, nothing is cheaper than transferring data on floppy disks via "sneakernet" or "Nikenet." This quickly runs into limits as organizations grow in size and have offices separated by long distances. Companies are then forced to purchase network equipment and software, and to hire trained people to install and maintain the network.

The *capital equipment expenditures* for the network equipment and software operating systems can be considerable. However costs for 10-Mbps (ten million [10 mega] bits per second) Ethernet LANs are relatively low, because the development expenses have been amortized. Costs for the state-of-the-art 1,000-Mbps LANs, though, are still quite expensive. Tying LANs together locally or over long distances can be costly. Designing a network that adequately handles present traffic, and will not be quickly antiquated by future traffic increases, and still at a favorable cost is a challenging task for the network engineer.

The major LAN operating system developers—Banyan, Microsoft, and Novell—have rigorous training and certification for LAN engineers. These *trained people are needed* to design, install, and maintain networks, and they command relatively high salaries. If you are the company comptroller, this is a severe disadvantage; but if you are that trained person, this is a wonderful advantage. It depends on your point of view.

It is possible for people to monitor traffic on networks much more easily than on a stand-alone machine. *Dishonest persons can steal sensitive information* by monitoring network traffic. Credit card numbers can be picked off the Internet by knowledgeable but unscrupulous people. Companies and governments are using *encryption (encoding)* to protect themselves and their customers. Encryption is commonly used when credit card information or other sensitive data is sent on the Internet or other network.

Usually the advantages of networks outweigh the disadvantages. The rapid file transfer and e-mail are more convenient and less expensive than "snail mail" (U.S. postal service).

1.4.4 Network Examples

Local Area Networks (LANs) connect nodes within a room, building, or campus. Examples are Ethernet, Token Ring, and ARCnet. *Wide Area Networks (WANs)* connect cities, countries, and even continents. Examples are T-1, X.25, SNA, BiSync, and SONET. *Metropolitan Area Networks (MANs)* connect nodes in large cities. An example is FDDI.

1.4.5 Why Are There So Many Different Types of Networks?

Each network type was designed to solve a particular networking problem using the existing technology of that time. Technology and customer demand changed, the networking problem changed, and the network designers responded. When we discuss the various protocols, we will see the design philosophy behind each network type (protocol) and why and how each was developed.

Some significant technology improvements that forced changes in network design are high-performance low-cost integrated circuits, fiber optics, digital communications (replacing analog communications), and the microcomputer (distributed processing).

1.5 Open Systems Interconnect Reference Model (OSI RM)

When speaking of how communication systems are organized, one often discusses the Open Systems Interconnect Reference Model. While not every system uses all of the RM's layers, a vendor will often refer to the OSI RM in discussing its system and its relationship to a particular RM layer(s). The Reference Model is based on IBM's *Systems Network Architecture (SNA),* which was introduced in 1972. Even a discussion of the Internet protocol TCP/IP (Transmission Control Protocol/Internet Protocol), whose layers do not correspond exactly to the OSI RM, needs some understanding of the OSI RM.

The widespread use of the OSI RM makes it imperative that we discuss it and learn the function of the various layers. We will get a brief overview of the RM in the next few pages. This first view of the layers may leave the student wanting more detail and specific examples, but a detailed discussion will occur when the various systems and their layer implementations are presented in later chapters.

This *seven-layer model* was developed by the International Standards Organization (ISO). It is a challenge to not mix up the acronyms ISO and OSI, because they use the same letters but in reverse order. *Networks are divided into vertical layers.* An analogy is a multistory building in which the first floor might be for shipping and receiving; the second floor for heating, air conditioning, and plumbing; the third floor for the receptionist; the fourth floor for order filling; and the fifth floor for accounting. Each floor has a distinct function and interfaces with the floor above it and below it.

1.5.1 OSI RM Layers

The International Standards Organization (ISO) has formulated a seven-layer "Reference Model" (RM) for communications networks (see Figure 1.1). The RM divides a source or destination node into seven vertical layers. These layers are sometimes divided into three groups. Each layer performs a specific function. Usually intermediate nodes (nodes between the source and destination used for relaying only) do not need all seven layers. Often only the end users need all layers. Many network protocols do not use all layers or do not divide their layers exactly as per the RM, but we still need an understanding of it.

At the sending source a layer receives the data from the layer above, performs its task, and passes the data to the layer below. At the receiving destination the layer receives the data from the layer below, performs its task, and passes the data to the layer above.

Designing, building, testing, and maintaining networks is a very complex task. By dividing the network into layers or distinct functions we can better define what each layer does. Different groups can work on different layers, and these different groups can be in different companies or even competing companies. The groups working on one layer have a smaller and much more manageable task than the overwhelming job of tackling the "whole enchilada" (system). We thus "divide and conquer." The only imperatives are that each layer perform its function correctly and interface properly with adjacent layers.

Many products have reached the market without proper overall design. Often a product is designed without really understanding what the market actually needs and is willing to pay. The U.S. Department of Defense is famous for designing and having contractors build systems that perform no significantly useful function.

FIGURE 1.1
OSI RM layers.

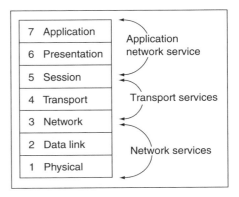

A more homely example happened when two vultures came upon a very large dead elephant. One vulture asked his friend, "How do we eat this big elephant?" To which the other scavenger replied, "One bite at a time!" Moral: Virtually every large project (elephant) can be divided into smaller parts (small bites) to make the entire project manageable.

Another example is the United States' Apollo Project to land men on the moon. This immensely complex task was broken into many parts or layers. Various layers were designed, built, and tested by many different companies. Eventually twelve Americans walked on the moon and returned safely to earth. The Apollo Project was a true "divide and conquer" undertaking.

The problem of reliable and error-free data transfer via a network is very complex. Taken as a whole the task is almost overwhelming; but by dividing the project into several smaller tasks, the job becomes manageable. This preliminary design and project division is also called "top down" design.

1.5.2 Layer Functions and Interface

The function tells what task the layer is to perform, but not how the layer is to perform its task. There is often more than one way to design a system (layer) to perform its job. Technology changes may obsolete a particular method, and the layer specifiers do not want to lock the layer designers into a potentially obsolete technology. Each layer has a particular function or "protocol" and interfaces to adjacent layers, all of which must be specified very carefully.

The interface tells how a particular layer will communicate with the layer above it and the layer below it. For software interfaces, information may be passed in a manner similar to parameter passing in subroutines and functions. The information must be in a particular format (that is, length, the order in which individual fields appear within a frame, the bit order within individual frames). The hardware interfaces (physical level) may be voltages, impedances, and mechanical dimensions.

A frame is the bit pattern sent over the physical link. At minimum, a frame has a starting signal (delimiter) and an ending delimiter. A frame can be a bit stream consisting of a start delimiter, address and control fields, data, an error detection field, and an ending signal delimiter. Frame lengths carrying data range from 424 bits to over 15,000 bits.

Often one frame is not long enough to transmit all the data. The data is divided into segments fitting into the frames. Frames are discussed in more detail in Chapter 3.

1.5.3 Layer Descriptions

The seven layers are difficult to remember, so here are two memory aids. From the bottom physical layer to the top application layer "Please Do Not Throw Sausage Pizza Away." From the top application layer to the bottom physical layer "All People Seem To Need Data Processing." Of course the first letter (in capitals) is the first letter of the appropriate layer.

1.5.3.1 Bottom Three Layers   The three bottom layers are called the Communications Subnet. They are the Physical Layer, the Data Link Layer (DLL), and the Network Layer.

The Physical Layer is hardware, and the DLL and Network Layers can be a mixture of hardware, firmware, and software.

▪ *Layer 1: Physical*   The Physical Layer or Layer 1 is the actual medium that conveys the bit stream. This connects the networks together and carries the "ones" and "zeros" (high voltage or high current/low voltage or low current) or light pulses. Usually the bits are sent serially (in a serial bit stream).

The medium can be fiber optics, twisted pair copper wire, coaxial cable, microwaves, satellite, or radio waves. This layer also concerns itself with the transmitters (emitters) sending the data and with the receivers accepting the signal at the destination or termination end of the medium. Layer 1 also includes the antennas, cables, satellites, and connectors.

When transmitting, the Physical Layer accepts a bit stream (frame) from Layer 2 above it and sends the bit stream (frame) over the medium. Layer 1 does not change the frame format. When receiving, the Physical Layer accepts the bit stream (frame) coming through the medium and sends this bit stream up to Layer 2.

▪ *Layer 2: Data Link*   The Data Link Layer (DLL) or Layer 2 does error control and flow control, synchronizes the receiver to the incoming bit stream, and decodes the bit stream. The DLL detects errors at the receiver, but usually does not correct them. Exactly how errors are handled (error control, or error handling) depends on the system used. Most systems use a re-transmission of data, but some mobile digital radio systems use error correction.

The DLL makes sure that data is not transmitted faster than the receiver can handle or store it. This is called *flow control* Memories (buffers) within the receiving DLL can overflow if the data is coming too fast. If the data is coming too slowly, the network may not be operating at top efficiency.

When transmitting, the DLL receives data from Layer 3, adds some housekeeping information in a header field at the beginning of the frame, and adds error control information in a trailer field at the frame end. This added information is the *Protocol Data Unit (PDU)*. See Figure 1.2. The frame is sent to the Physical Level for transmission over the medium.

A frame consists of the proper combination of all the control information bits, information bits, and error control bits. There are maximum and minimum frame sizes for every protocol. Some frame protocols have a fixed size and others have a variable size. Often more than one frame is needed to send all the information bits.

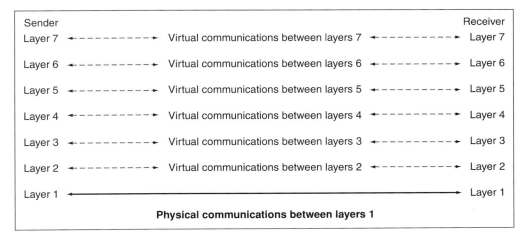

FIGURE 1.2
Virtual communication between layers.

When the DLL receives data from the Physical Layer, it examines the information from the transmitting DLL for errors and flow control information. This information in the PDU is removed from the frame and what is left (a packet) is sent up to Layer 3.

Local Area Networks (LANs) protocols only specify Layers 1 and 2. In LANs the DLL is subdivided into two parts, the Media Access Control (MAC) sublayer and the Logical Link Control (LLC) sublayer.

With Asynchronous Transfer Mode (ATM) the DLL is subdivided into two parts, the Segmentation and Reassembly (SAR) sublayer and the Convergence sublayer.

■ *Layer 3: Network*   Network Layer 3 is concerned with *routing* the frame. The three steps of routing are establishing the connection (set up), maintaining the connection, and terminating the connection (tear down) after the data transfer is complete. In X.25 (an example of a network level protocol), both the Network Level and the DLL perform error control.

1.5.3.2 Upper Four Layers   The upper four layers are the Transport Layer, the Session Layer, the Presentation Layer, and the Application Layer. These upper four layers are called "end-to-end" layers. They are not concerned with what happens with the lower three layers or intermediate nodes. Their concern is only what happens at the initiating (transmitting) node and terminating (receiving) nodes. These layers are usually software.

■ *Layer 4: Transport*   At the transmitting node the Transport Layer divides the data from Layer 5 into smaller units called *packets*. This process is segmentation or disassembly. At the receiving end the Transport Layer puts the packets back together in the proper order to reconstruct the original data and sends it up to Layer 5. This process is *reassembly*.

In some protocols the Transport Layer 4 performs end-to-end error control and recovery. It specifies the security level required and acceptable error rates and delay. It is also concerned about transportation of the data.

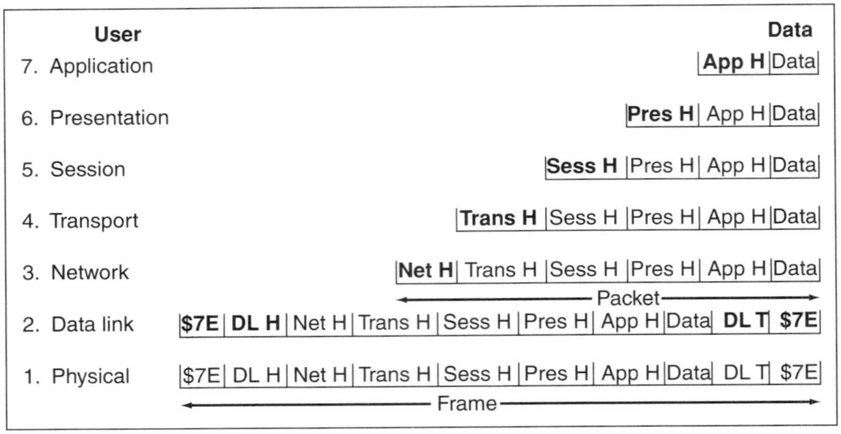

User						Data
7. Application						**App H** Data
6. Presentation						**Pres H** App H Data
5. Session						**Sess H** Pres H App H Data
4. Transport						**Trans H** Sess H Pres H App H Data
3. Network						**Net H** Trans H Sess H Pres H App H Data
						←——————Packet——————→
2. Data link	**$7E** **DL H** Net H Trans H Sess H Pres H App H Data **DL T** **$7E**					
1. Physical	$7E DL H Net H Trans H Sess H Pres H App H Data DL T $7E					
	←——————————— Frame ———————————→					

FIGURE 1.3
Adding a PDU at each layer.

■ *Layer 5: Session*   The Session Layer, or Layer 5, handles login and logout procedures, and tracks time of connection. The time of connection can be thought of as "length of session" and may be used for billing purposes.

■ *Layer 6: Presentation*   The Presentation Layer, or Layer 6, converts the data from Layer 5 into a form understandable to the user. The data from Layer 5 is just bits. Layer 6 converts the bit stream into ASCII (plain text), EBCIDIC (IBM plain text), video, audio, or data as required. The Presentation Layer *presents* the data in its proper format.

■ *Layer 7: Application*   The Application Layer 7 is concerned with how the network is used or applied. Some uses or applications can be e-mail, Internet functions, data file transfers for spreadsheets or word processing, digitized voice, and video.

1.6   Virtual Communications between Equivalent Layers

The process of adding a PDU at each layer and sending it to the same layer at the receiving node is called *virtual communications*. This is illustrated in Figure 1.3. The same or equivalent layers communicate via the PDUs. The actual communication is via the bits of the Physical Layer, but the virtual communication occurs through the PDUs.

SUMMARY

I. Frequently Asked Questions (FAQs) of students about data communications were answered. Data communications and telecommunications are new areas for many students and are very different from other areas of electronics. Hopefully the FAQs will help and encourage students in this sometimes challenging field.

II. A history of communications may help the student gain a perspective by understanding where we have been and hopefully help he or she to appreciate the reasons for the various protocols and transmission methods.

III. Standards were discussed as well as the reasons for these standards. It is foolish and self-defeating for different companies to have differing standards. Customers will shy away from unusual and differing standards, thereby reducing profits.

IV. Open and closed standards were discussed and compared. Generally open standards have greater advantages because they have wider use.

V. Various standards organizations and their roles were discussed.

VI. Networks make an organization more efficient (make more profit). The proliferation of networks has opened up new, high-paying employment opportunities.

VII. Network layers and the reasons for them were discussed. This is a "divide and conquer" approach making it easier to design and maintain systems. The functions of each layer of the seven-layer model were discussed.

VIII. Virtual communication takes place via Protocol Data Units (PDU). This virtual communication is between the same layer at the transmitting node and receiving node. PDUs are added to the beginning of frames. A PDU and trailer are added to the DLL frame.

QUESTIONS

1. List as many advantages and disadvantages of industrial standards as possible.
2. List the telecommunications standards organizations under the United Nations.
3. List some telecommunications standards organizations in the United States.
4. List two standards organizations in Canada.
5. Why would one want to divide a project into layers?
6. What is "top down design"? What are its advantages?
7. Why would one use a network?
8. What are the disadvantages of a network?
9. The rule set governing how a layer works is called a _____.
10. What layer divides the message into packets?
11. What layer(s) detect(s) and compensate(s) for errors?
12. What layer makes the framing?
13. What is the general term for the lower three OSI RM layers?
14. What is the general term for the upper three OSI RM layers?
15. What are the functions of the Data Link Layer?
16. Give five examples of the Physical Layer.
17. What is the general term for the middle three OSI RM layers?

2

TRANSMISSION MEDIUMS AND THE PHYSICAL LAYER

OBJECTIVES

In this chapter we will discuss:

    I. What is the Physical Layer?
    II. Types of wire transmission media.
        A. Twisted pair.
        B. Coax.
    III. RS-232.
    IV. Optical fiber.
    V. Satellites.
    VI. Capacity of transmission mediums.
        A. Nyquist's law.
        B. Shannon-Hartley law.
    VII. Bit rate versus baud rate.

2.1 What is the Physical Layer?

The Physical Layer transmission medium can be optical fiber, twisted pair (TP) copper wires, coaxial cable, microwaves, or radio waves. The Physical Layer also includes the transmitters, emitters, receivers, connectors, and repeaters, as well as the actual medium.

2.2 Twisted Pair (TP)

Twisted pair (TP) copper wire is used between the telephone company's Central Office (CO) and the telephone handset in the office or home, and in some Local Area Networks (LANs). Usually the TP is two solid or stranded #22 to #26 American Wire Gauge (AWG) copper wires. #22 AWG wire is 0.0201 inch (0.51 mm) in diameter, and #26 AWG wire is 0.0159 inch (0.403 mm) in diameter. Each wire in the twisted pair is insulated. The pair (or several pairs) of wires can be either Shielded Twisted Pair (STP) or Unshielded Twisted Pair (UTP). STP has superior resistance to interference, but UTP is cheaper, and so the bean counters prefer UTP. UTP is also slightly smaller, easier to bend, and thus somewhat easier to install than STP.

Twisted pair is used to connect user telephones to the Central Office (CO) and phones in a home, in a building, or on a campus. Another relatively new use is carrying data on 10BaseT and 100BaseT Local Area Networks (LAN). The "T" means twisted pair, the "10" designates 10 megabits per second (10 Mbps or 10 million bits per second) data rate, and the "100" is 100 megabits per second (100 Mbps) data rate. "Base" means only one signal frequency is present at a time; however there may be more than one signal, but all will be using the same frequency. This will be discussed in the LANs chapter.

2.2.1 Category 3 Unshielded Twisted Pair (UTP)

Category (Cat) 3 UTP is designed for voice transmission and is already present in many older buildings. LAN installers will try to utilize any existing Cat 3 wiring to avoid the high cost of installing new wiring for data transmission.

2.2.2 Category 5 Unshielded Twisted Pair (UTP)

Category (Cat) 5 UTP is designed for data transmissions up to 100 Mbps (100 million bits per second) over short distances. Cat 5 UTP manufacturing specifications are much tighter than for Cat 3 UTP. Closer specifications include uniformity, insulation type, and even the number of turns per inch. Although Cat 5 cable is more expensive than Cat 3 cable, it is a seller's market for Cat 5 UTP.

2.2.3 Data Transmission over Category 3 UTP

An older type of TP is Category 3 (Cat 3), intended for voice transmission. When installed years ago, few people had any thought of data transmission. At that time thoughts of LANs and data transmission were the realm of wild dreamers.

But LAN development and customer demand made people look at the possibility of sending data over Cat 3 voice grade TP. By designing ingenious equipment data could be sent over relatively short distances of 100 meters or less, sufficient for many office buildings. The 10BaseT LAN was developed to utilize Cat 3 UTP. The "T" in 10BaseT means twisted pair. The new 100BaseT LANs have made 100 Mbps data rates possible over Cat 3 (UTP) for short distances.

2.2.4 IBM Type 1 Shielded Twisted Pair (STP)

IBM has somewhat different standards than the "Category" standards. IBM Type 1 Shielded Twisted Pair (STP) is designed for Token Ring Networks (TRN) LANs. Type 1 has two pairs of STP per cable, and the entire cable is shielded.

2.2.5 Plenum Cable

Often TP is placed in ventilation airways or ducts or plenum. The reason cable is installed in plenum is ease of installation. Plenums go to all rooms in a building so fewer holes have to be drilled. Plenum cable is required by the National Electric Code (NEC) to have special insulation that is fire resistant. If the cable cannot catch fire, it will not give off noxious fumes, reducing the possibility of smoke inhalation injuries. Currently the insulation used in the United States is Teflon.

2.2.6 Why the Twist in Twisted Pair?

Why must the wires be twisted? Why is the distance between them so critical? If one wire is the signal and the other the return, couldn't we just use a separate return?

Current flowing in a conductor creates a magnetic field. This magnetic field will enter into adjacent conductors and cause interference. However if we have two wires carrying equal currents in opposite directions, the magnetic fields will tend to cancel beyond the wires, reducing interference to adjacent wires.

Signals can also be coupled through stray capacitance into adjacent wires. Again by using equal but opposite currents, this can be minimized. It is quite easy to transmit equal but opposite direction currents through TP. See Figures 2.1 and 2.2. Also interference from an external source affects both wires equally. At the receiver it is not difficult to separate

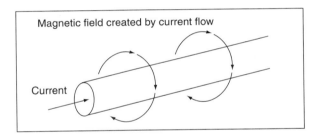

FIGURE 2.1
Why the twist in TP? Why isn't the pair just parallel? Why not a separate ground return? Current flow creates a magnetic field. This magnetic field can enter other nearby signal conductors and cause interference.

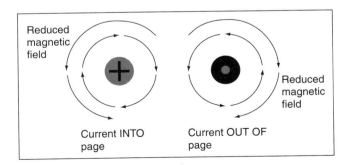

FIGURE 2.2
Twisted pair and magnetic fields. Note that the magnetic fields created by the opposite-direction equal current flows create nearly canceling magnetic fields away from the conductors, thus reducing interference.

the true signal from the interference in both wires with a differential line receiver. We will see this when we discuss RS-232.

Even small changes in the TP twist or capacitance can cause the signal to be corrupted by signal reflections occurring at these changes. These reflections are of little concern for voice, but high-speed data can be corrupted.

2.3 RS-232 and RS-422A

RS-232 and RS-422A are physical level TP protocols standardized by the Electronic Industries Association (EIA). RS is the acronym for "Recommended Standard." The standards include both electrical and mechanical specifications.

2.3.1 RS-232

The 25-pin connector signal specification for RS-232 is indicated in Table 2.1. RS-232 is used for low data rates (19.6 kbps or less) and short distances (less than 15 meters). The specification is for a cable of twenty-five pins, although sometimes only nine pins are used. RS-232 has a separate signal line and return (signal ground) line, increasing noise problems and limiting speed and distance.

The data and control signals of RS-232 are shown in Figure 2.3. The sender has data to transmit, and thus sends (asserts active low) a Request To Send (RTS) signal. The receiver is able to accept data, and thus returns a Clear To Send (CTS) signal. The sender is not allowed to send data until it receives CTS. After receiving CTS the sender sends the data. After the data is sent, the sender unasserts RTS. Thus the receiver knows that no more data is to be sent and unasserts CTS.

If the receiver is unable to accept data, perhaps because of a full buffer, it will not send (assert) CTS. This is an example of flow control.

2.3.1.1 RS-232 Frame Format
RS-232 voltage levels are quite different from the usual logic levels inside a computer (see Figure 2.4a). These computer levels are approximately +5 volts for a logic "1" and zero volts for a logic "0." RS-232 voltage levels are +3 volts to +15 volts for a logic "0," and −3 volts to −15 volts for a logic "1." The zero voltage state is used in logic circuits but not in RS-232. If the receiver is receiving a voltage, either positive or negative, the receiver knows the line is not broken.

The RS-232 frame is asynchronous, meaning that the receiver clock is not synchronized to the transmitter clock, and the receiver does not know when the frame is coming.

An RS-232 frame includes a start bit, data bits, possibly a parity bit, and one or two stop bits. The RS-232 frame is "character oriented," meaning that only one character is sent in each frame. Seven or eight bits make up the data bits, with the least significant bit (lsb) first and the most significant bit (msb) last. In some systems data bit eight is a parity bit, used for error control. A negative going start bit begins the frame, and one or two positive going stop bits terminate the frame.

A common code used to send data between computers is ASCII (American National Standard for Information Exchange). It is shown in Table 2.2. Figure 2.4b shows the

TABLE 2.1

EIA-232-D (DTE Connectors)

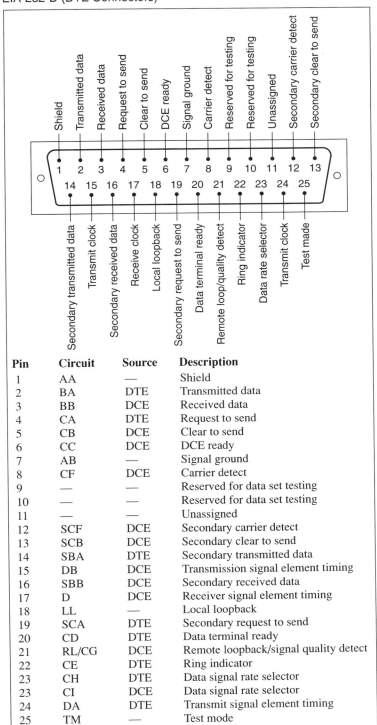

Pin	Circuit	Source	Description
1	AA	—	Shield
2	BA	DTE	Transmitted data
3	BB	DCE	Received data
4	CA	DTE	Request to send
5	CB	DCE	Clear to send
6	CC	DCE	DCE ready
7	AB	—	Signal ground
8	CF	DCE	Carrier detect
9	—	—	Reserved for data set testing
10	—	—	Reserved for data set testing
11	—	—	Unassigned
12	SCF	DCE	Secondary carrier detect
13	SCB	DCE	Secondary clear to send
14	SBA	DTE	Secondary transmitted data
15	DB	DCE	Transmission signal element timing
16	SBB	DCE	Secondary received data
17	D	DCE	Receiver signal element timing
18	LL	—	Local loopback
19	SCA	DTE	Secondary request to send
20	CD	DTE	Data terminal ready
21	RL/CG	DCE	Remote loopback/signal quality detect
22	CE	DTE	Ring indicator
23	CH	DTE	Data signal rate selector
23	CI	DCE	Data signal rate selector
24	DA	DTE	Transmit signal element timing
25	TM	—	Test mode

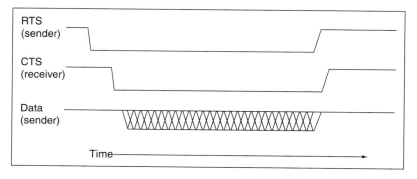

FIGURE 2.3
RS-232 data transfer

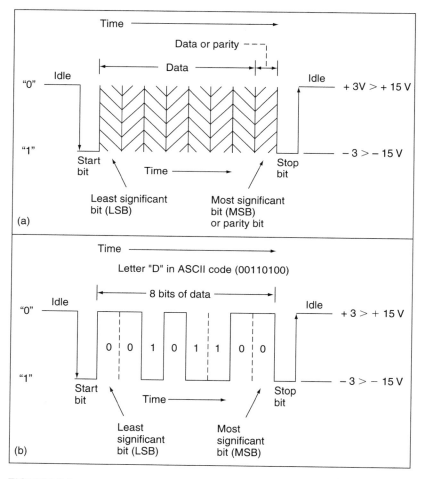

FIGURE 2.4
RS-232 frame format (a) and sending ASCII "D" over RS-232 (b). Oscilloscope trace (voltage (vertical) versus time (horizontal)). The left part of the trace occurs first.

waveform of the letter "D" being transmitted over RS-232. Referring to Table 2.1 we see that the letter "D" is binary "00110100." Originally ASCII was a seven-bit code with the eighth used as a parity bit for error checking. Now the eighth bit is used to create the "extended" ASCII code. The extended code is used for non-English language letters such as the Greek π.

2.3.1.2 RS-232 and Noise

RS-232 is an unbalanced system; that is, the signal wire carries the signal voltage and the signal ground wire is at or near zero volts (ground) (see Figure 2.5). A disadvantage of an unbalanced system is that electrical noise can be coupled onto the signal wire, and the line receiver cannot separate the signal from the noise. Another disadvantage is that the transmitter and receiver may be at different ground potentials. A fast voltmeter (oscilloscope) measuring the difference in ground voltages at the transmitter and the receiver can, and usually does, measure a significant voltage difference. Again the line receiver has no way of separating this ground potential difference from the real signal. These problems limit the data rate to 19.6 kbps and a maximum transmission distance of 15 meters. See Figure 2.6.

Noise affects the signal wire more than the signal ground wire. In Figure 2.6 the digital signal sent is the top trace, the second trace is the external noise, and the third trace is the signal plus the noise. The digital receiver cannot separate the signal from the noise.

2.3.2 RS-422A

RS-422A is a balanced or differential transmission system. The data transmitter has two data output lines. One data line Td transmits the data, and the second data line Td transmits the complement, or differential, of the Figure 2.7 data.

At the differential line receiver a voltage Vsig is developed across the line terminating resistor Rt. The differential line receiver has two inputs, an inverting input and a non-inverting input, similar to an operational amplifier. The inverting input inverts the negative input voltage and adds it to the positive input voltage. External noise affects both lines equally, and the differential line receiver cancels out the noise voltage.

2.3.2.1 Noise on RS-422A

External noise will add equally to the signal and the signal complement (see Figure 2.8). A differential line receiver will invert the signal complement and add the signal and the signal complement, effectively removing the noise. Also ground potential (voltage) between transmitter and receiver can be quite different. Ground potential differences are a form of noise that will be subtracted out.

Equation 2.1 is the differential receiver equation:

$$(S + N + G) - (-S + N + G) = 2S + 0N + 0G \quad \textbf{(Equation 2.1)}$$

where S is the signal, N is the noise, and G is the ground potential difference. This noise canceling feature allows RS-422A to transmit data a hundred times faster than unbalanced RS-232.

TABLE 2.2
ASCII Chart

Ctrl	Dec	Hex	Code	Dec	Hex	Char	Dec	Hex	Char	Dec	Hex	Char
@	0	00	NUL	32	20	SP	64	40	@	96	60	`
A	1	01	SOH	33	21	!	65	41	A	97	61	a
B	2	02	STX	34	22	"	66	42	B	98	62	b
C	3	03	ETX	36	23	#	67	43	C	99	63	c
D	4	04	EOT	36	24	$	68	44	D	100	64	d
E	5	05	ENQ	37	25	%	69	45	E	101	65	e
F	6	06	ACK	38	26	&	70	46	F	102	66	f
G	7	07	BEL	39	27	'	71	47	G	103	67	g
H	8	08	BS	40	28	(	72	48	H	104	68	h
I	9	09	HT	41	29	)	73	49	I	105	69	i
J	10	0A	LF	42	2A	*	74	4A	J	106	6A	j
K	11	0B	VT	43	2B	+	75	4B	K	107	6B	k
L	12	0C	FF	44	2C	,	76	4C	L	108	6C	l
M	13	0D	CR	45	2D	-	77	4D	M	109	6D	m
N	14	0E	SO	46	2E	.	78	4E	N	110	6E	n
O	15	0F	SI	47	2F	/	79	4F	O	111	6F	o
P	16	10	DLE	48	30	0	80	50	P	112	70	p
Q	17	11	DC1	49	31	1	81	51	Q	113	71	q
R	18	12	DC2	50	32	2	82	52	R	114	72	r
S	19	13	DC3	51	33	3	83	53	S	115	73	s
T	20	14	DC4	52	34	4	84	54	T	116	74	t
U	21	15	NAK	53	35	5	85	55	U	117	75	u
V	22	16	SYN	54	36	6	86	56	V	118	76	v
W	23	17	ETB	55	37	7	87	57	W	119	77	w
X	24	18	CAN	56	38	8	88	58	X	120	78	x
Y	25	19	EM	57	39	9	89	59	Y	121	79	y
Z	26	1A	SUB	58	3A	:	90	5A	Z	122	7A	z
[	27	1B	ESC	59	3B	;	91	5B	[	123	7B	{
/	28	1C	FS	60	3C	<	92	5C	\	124	7C	|
]	29	1D	GS	61	3D	=	93	5D	]	125	7D	}
^	30	1E	RS	62	3E	>	94	5E	^	126	7E	~
_	31	1F	US	63	3F	?	95	5F	_	127	7F	DEL

EXAMPLE 2.1

Assume a signal amplitude of 1 volt, a noise level of 5 volts, and a ground potential difference of 1.2 volts. What is the signal level at the line receiver?

$$(S + N + G) - (-S + N + G) = 2S + 0N + 0G$$
$$(1 \text{ volt} + 5 \text{ volts} + 1.2 \text{ volts}) - (-1 \text{ volt} + 5 \text{ volts} + 1.2 \text{ volts})$$
$$= 2 \text{ volts signal} + 0 \text{ volt noise} + 0 \text{ volt ground potential difference}$$

Dec	Hex	Dec	Hex	Dec	Hex	Dec	Hex
128	80	160	A0	192	C0	224	E0
129	81	161	A1	193	C1	225	E1
130	82	162	A2	194	C2	226	E2
131	83	163	A3	195	C3	227	E3
132	84	164	A4	196	C4	228	E4
133	85	165	A5	197	C5	229	E5
134	86	166	A6	198	C6	230	E6
135	87	167	A7	199	C7	231	E7
136	88	168	A8	200	C8	232	E8
137	89	169	A9	201	C9	233	E9
138	8A	170	AA	202	CA	234	EA
139	8B	171	AB	203	CB	235	EB
140	8C	172	AC	204	CC	236	EC
141	8D	173	AD	205	CD	237	ED
142	8E	174	AE	206	CE	238	EE
143	8F	175	AF	207	CF	239	EF
144	90	186	B0	208	D0	240	F0
145	91	177	B1	209	D1	241	F1
146	92	178	B2	210	D2	242	F2
147	93	179	B3	211	D3	243	F3
148	94	180	B4	212	D4	244	F4
149	95	181	B5	213	D5	245	F5
150	96	182	B6	214	D6	246	F6
151	97	183	B7	215	D7	247	F7
152	98	184	B8	216	D8	248	F8
153	99	185	B9	217	D9	249	F9
154	9A	186	BA	218	DA	250	FA
155	9B	187	BB	219	DB	251	FB
156	9C	188	BC	220	DC	252	FC
157	9D	189	BD	221	DD	253	FD
158	9E	190	BE	222	DE	254	FE
159	9F	191	BF	223	DF	255	FF

The noise and ground potential difference are canceled out by the differential line receiver. Yes, equipment can have a voltage difference between the respective grounds! And this voltage increases as the signal frequency goes up, because of inductance in the ground wires connecting the equipment. This can even happen in adjacent Printed Circuit Boards (PCB), in adjacent Integrated Circuits (IC), or even inside an IC!

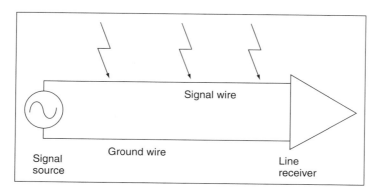

FIGURE 2.5
RS-232 and noise. External noise affects only signal wire.

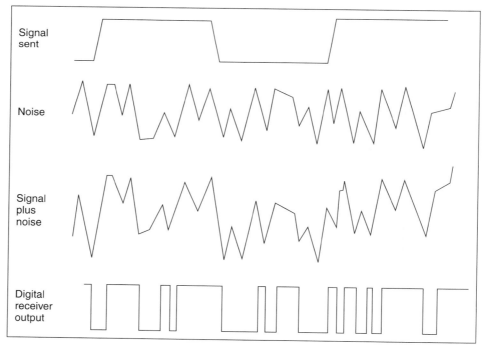

FIGURE 2.6
Effect of noise on RS-232.

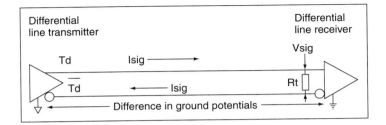

FIGURE 2.7
RS-422A.

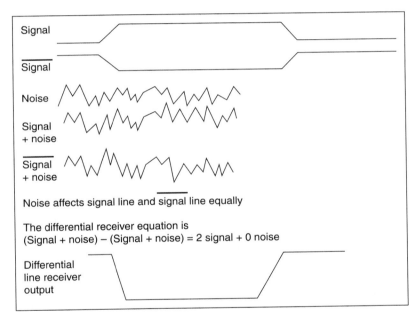

FIGURE 2.8
Noise on RS-422A, a balanced system. RS-422A can send data 100 times faster than RS-232.

2.4 Coaxial Cable

Coax (pronounced "koh-acks") is a single center conductor surrounded by an insulator or dielectric, a copper braid or shield, and finally a rubber environmental protection jacket (see Figure 2.9). The center conductor is the signal conductor, and the braid is the signal return. The dielectric or insulator separates the center conductor and the braid return. The braid shielding provides good protection from external noise sources.

Coax can carry a much higher bandwidth (frequencies) than twisted pair, but it is much more expensive and difficult to install than TP.

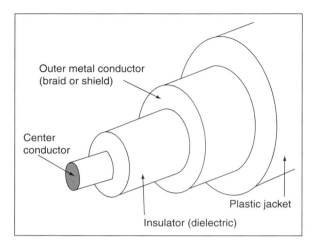

FIGURE 2.9
Coaxial cable.

Coax is used in two types of LANs. Ethernet 10Base5 LANs use RG-8 coax with 50 ohms impedance and a 10-millimeter diameter. Ethernet 10Base2 LANs use RG-58 coax with 50 ohms impedance and a 7-millimeter diameter. RG-58 is cheaper and easier to install than RG-8, and hence is called "cheapernet" or "thinnet" because of its smaller diameter. However RG-8 10Base5 system segments have almost three times the range of RG-58 10Base2 systems (500 meters versus 185 meters). The "RG" means Radio Grade.

Because of coax's high-frequency capability, it is also used in cable television. Flexible coax is used up to about 1 gHz, or 1 billion hertz. Semi-rigid coax is used above 1 gHz and up to frequencies where wave guides are feasible, or approximately 2 to 3 gHz. Semi-rigid coax can be bent permanently into pretzel-like shapes.

A major user of coax is the cable television industry. Many television channels are sent simultaneously down coaxial cables. Each channel occupies a different frequency band, and this technique is called Frequency Division Multiplexing (FDM). RG-6 is usually used and has a characteristic impedance of 75 ohms.

The increasing use of the Internet in homes has spawned a demand for faster data rates than possible over telephone lines. Cable television has a very high bandwidth, allowing great data rates. Very high speed modems for the existing cable television infrastructure are entering the market and are discussed in a later chapter.

2.4.1 Characteristic Impedance

To minimize signal reflections from the end of the coax transmission line, one must attach a resistor to the coax end. That resistor must have a value equal to the transmission line characteristic impedance. Equation 2.2 describes this.

$$\text{Source } Z = \text{line } Z = \text{load } Z^* \qquad \textbf{(Equation 2.2)}$$

where Z is the impedance and Z^* is the complex conjugate of the impedance. The units of Z are ohms, the same as resistance.

The transmission line impedance depends on the inductance and capacitance per unit length and is given by Equation 2.3.

$$\text{line } Z = \sqrt{\frac{L}{C}} \qquad \textbf{(Equation 2.3)}$$

where $\qquad L = \dfrac{\text{inductance}}{\text{unit length}}$

and $\qquad C = \dfrac{\text{capacitance}}{\text{unit length}}$

Note that the line impedance is a function of L and C. These cannot be measured with an ohmmeter, even though the units of impedance are ohms, the same as resistance.

EXAMPLE 2.2 Given a coaxial cable with inductance of 0.4 μH per meter and a capacitance of 66 pF per meter, what is the characteristic impedance?

$$Z = \sqrt{\frac{0.4 \times 10^{-6}}{66 \times 10^{-12}}} = \sqrt{6 \times 10^3} = 77.8 \text{ ohms}$$

The characteristic impedance of the twisted pair is about 75 to 90 ohms. The characteristic impedance of cable television coax RG-6 is 75 ohms.

2.5 Fiber Optics

Light traveling through optically transparent materials travels slower than light in a vacuum. The index of refraction n is a measure of this phenomenon. The speed of light in a transparent material is given by

$$V = \frac{C}{n} \qquad \textbf{(Equation 2.4)}$$

where V is the velocity of light in the material, C is the speed of light in a vacuum, $3 \times 10^8 \frac{meters}{second}$, and n is the index of refraction. n is unitless. The index of refraction n in a vacuum is 1.000. For all transparent substances n is greater than 1.0, and thus light travels slower in that substance than in a vacuum.

Optical fiber is not coated with a shiny metal to reflect the light back into the core. Instead optical fiber uses slight differences in the index of refraction to cause light to be reflected from the cladding and stay in the center (core) of the optical fiber. This is similar to being underwater in a pool and trying to look at objects in the air as in Figure 2.10.

Referring to Figure 2.11, the light enters the optical fiber core and reflects off the core-cladding interface, staying within the core. The index of refraction in the core is

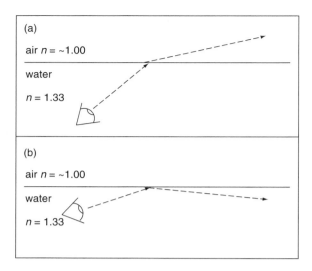

FIGURE 2.10
Fiber optic principles. Fiber optics, similar to light, (a) being bent at a water/air boundary and (b) bouncing off a water/air boundary.

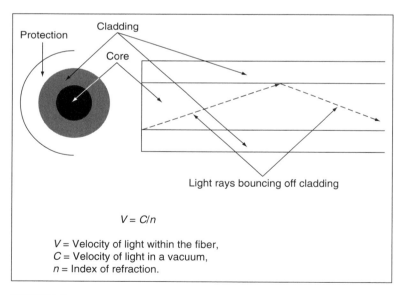

$$V = C/n$$

V = Velocity of light within the fiber,
C = Velocity of light in a vacuum,
n = Index of refraction.

FIGURE 2.11
Fiber optic principles. Index of refraction is greater, and the light travels slower, in the core compared to the cladding.

slightly higher than in the cladding. Referring to Equation 2.4, one can see that the speed of light in the core is slower than in the cladding.

Snell's law, Equation 2.5, relates the angles of a light ray passing from a material with index of refraction n_1 to a material with index of refraction n_2.

$$n_1 \sin \theta_1 = n_2 \sin \theta_2 \qquad \textbf{(Equation 2.5)}$$

Referring to Figure 2.12, if the angle of incident light θ_1 is too small, the light will not be reflected but rather pass into the cladding and be lost.

Referring to Figure 2.13, if θ_1 is large enough, Snell's equation will require a sine greater than 1.000, which is quite impossible. This means the ray will not enter the cladding but be totally reflected. Then θ_1, the angle of incidence, will equal the angle of reflection. The light will bounce down the core, all the while reflecting off the core-

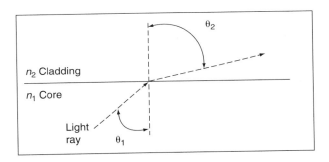

FIGURE 2.12
Fiber optic principles, By Snell's law, $n_1 \, \text{Sin} \, \theta_1 = n_2 \, \text{Sin} \, \theta_1$. If θ_2 is too small, light will enter the cladding (shown above) and not be reflected back into the core, but will be lost into the cladding.

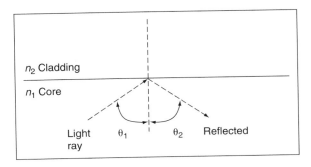

FIGURE 2.13
Fiber optic principles. By Snell's law, $n_1 \, \text{Sin} \, \theta_1 = n_2 \, \text{Sin} \, \theta_1$. If θ_2 is large enough, the equation will require a sine greater than 1.0. Of course this is impossible, meaning the ray is no longer refracted into the cladding but totally reflected. Thus, the angle of incidence equals the angle of reflection ($\theta_1 = \theta_2$).

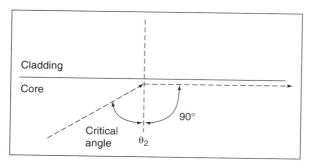

FIGURE 2.14
The light ray travels parallel to the water surface. This is the "critical angle."

cladding interface. If θ_1 in the fiber core is large enough, the light wave will not pass into the cladding, but rather be totally reflected.

In Figure 2.14 it can be seen that at a certain angle it is possible for the light to be reflected parallel along the water surface. This angle is called the *critical angle* θ_C. The critical angle θ_C is the angle the incident (incoming) ray travels for the reflected ray to travel exactly parallel to the core axis. To find the critical angle θ_C, set $\theta_2 = 90$ degrees and therefore $\sin \theta_2 = 1.0$, implying the refracted ray travels parallel to the core axis. Then

$$\theta_C = \sin^{-1}\left(\frac{n_2}{n_1}\right) = \sin^{-1}\left(\frac{n_{\text{cladding}}}{n_{\text{core}}}\right) \qquad \textbf{(Equation 2.6)}$$

EXAMPLE 2.3   Given $n_1 = n_{\text{core}} = 1.495$ and $n_2 = n_{\text{cladding}} = 1.491$

$$\text{then} \quad \theta_C = \sin^{-1}\left(\frac{1.481}{1.495}\right) = 85.8078 \text{ degrees}$$

In Figure 2.15 we see an incoming light ray reflecting off the cladding at the critical angle θ_C. The angle that ray makes at the core-air interface is the angle of acceptance. By Snell's law

$$n_0 \sin \theta_a = n_1 \sin (90^0 - \theta_C) = n_1 \cos \theta_C \qquad \textbf{(Equation 2.7)}$$
$$\text{or}$$
$$\theta_a = \sin^{-1}(n_1 \cos \theta_C)$$

The index of refraction for air n_0 is approximately 1.0000. The angle of acceptance θ_a is the limiting angle that a light source can be off axis (away from the center line) of an optical fiber. The greater the angle of acceptance, the easier it is to get (couple) light into the core.

EXAMPLE 2.4   Given the results of Example 2.3 in which $\theta_C = 85.8078$ and $n_1 = 1.495$,

$$\theta_a = \sin^{-1}(1.495 \cos \theta_C) = \sin^{-1}(1.495 \cos 85.8078^0) = 6.274^0$$

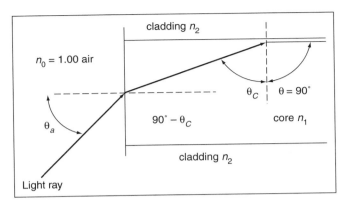

FIGURE 2.15
Angle of Acceptance.

An example of relative indices of refraction is the Archer fish, which lives in Southeast Asia. This little fellow swims to the surface and spots an insect sitting on a tree leaf or branch. The fish, compensating for the different indices of refraction for water and air, expels a series of water droplets from its mouth. The droplets hit the insect, knocking it into the water. Our little Archer fish friend has a meal.

2.5.1 Step Index Multi-Mode Optical Fiber

In **step index optical fiber** there is a sharp (step) change between the indices of refraction of the fiber core and the fiber cladding. Typical values are $n_{core} = 1.500$ and $n_{cladding} = 1.495$. The changes in refractive index are made by adding germanium to the glass. Optical fiber for communications is made of glass, silicon dioxide SiO_2. This is the same chemical formula as sand and quartz. Glass is made from high-purity sand. Sand and quartz have a crystal structure, but glass does not. Surprisingly glass is not considered a solid but rather a liquid! It can change its shape slowly over several years.

The core diameter of step index **multiple-mode** optical fiber is quite large compared with the light wavelength. Typical core diameter is 62.5 μm (micrometers, or 10^{-6} meters), and usual light wavelengths used in multi-mode fiber are 1.31 μm and 0.85 μm. These wavelengths are in the near infrared portion of the optical spectrum. Visible red light is about 0.65 μm. See Figure 2.16.

Because of the large ratio of core diameter to light wavelength in multi-mode optical fiber, the light ray is not constrained to a single path. It can take an infinite number of paths through the optical fiber, and some of these paths are longer than others. Light traveling longer paths will take longer to reach the fiber end than light traveling shorter paths. Light traveling down the fiber core will reach the end first; light bouncing down the fiber at the critical angle will arrive last.

At the receiving end the light from the many paths will combine, sometimes constructively (additive—bright spots) or sometimes destructively (subtractive or cancel— dark spots). This addition and cancellation process will give modes or patterns of light

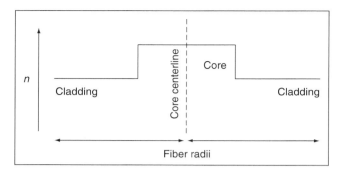

FIGURE 2.16
Step index—Multi-mode. Sharp change (step index) in indices of refraction between core and cladding. Typical n_{core} = 1,500, typical $n_{cladding}$ = 1.495.

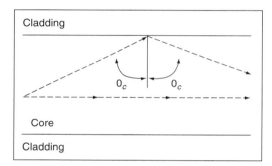

FIGURE 2.17
Step index—Multi-mode fiber. Light rays can take more than one path through the fiber. At the receiving end, light rays can combine constructively (in phase) or destructively (out of phase). Each of these combinings can be considered a "mode," hence the term "multi-mode."

and dark. The speckled appearance of a laser beam is due to monochromatic (one wavelength [color] or frequency) light combining additively (constructive interference—bright spots) and subtractively (destructive interference—dark spots). See Figure 2.17. Because the light arrives at the end at different times depending on the path taken, a rectangular input light pulse will be distorted and broadened (see Figure 2.18). If a series of closely spaced rectangular pulses were sent down the fiber, the differing light delay times would make it impossible for the receiver to distinguish the individual light pulses.

Step index or multi-mode optical fiber is the cheapest glass optical fiber but has the least bandwidth. The many modes (possible paths of travel) of light traveling within the fiber interfere with each other and take different times to travel through the fiber, thus limiting the data rate and maximum possible length. Contrary to popular belief, optical fiber bandwidth is not virtually infinite but is limited by multi-path (multi-mode) light travel and other factors. There is an upper limit to the pulse rate. Typical values for multi-mode optical fiber are 20 Mbps * km. See Figure 2.19.

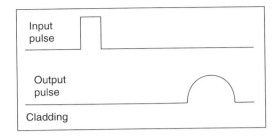

FIGURE 2.18
Multi-mode fiber with a pulse input. Rectangular input light pulse will be distorted and widened at the receiver due to light rays taking different paths through the fiber.

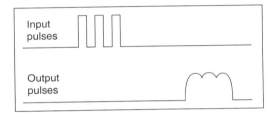

FIGURE 2.19
Multi-mode fiber with multiple pulses. What happens when a fast bit stream is transmitted down a long multi-mode optical fiber? At the receiver it is impossible to separate the individual pulses.

EXAMPLE 2.5   What is the maximum bit rate possible for a multimode step index fiber of 5 km length?

$$\text{Bit rate} = \frac{20 \text{ Mbps} \times \text{km}}{5 \text{ km}} = 4 \text{ Mbps}$$

A major advantage of multi-mode fiber is its low cost and relatively large diameter core of 62.5 micrometers, or 0.00246 inch. This diameter allows easy handling and attaching connectors (connectorization). The total diameter of the core plus cladding is 125 micrometers, or 0.00492 inch.

2.5.2 Single-Mode Optical Fiber

Single-mode optical fiber has a core diameter of about 7 or 8 micrometers, or about 0.000296 inch (see Figure 2.20). This small diameter, about four times the wavelength of the light, allows only one mode (single mode) to exist in the core. No bouncing, destructive or constructive interference occurs. Typical bandwidth is 100 gbps * km. This is 5,000 times the bandwidth of multi-mode fiber. Single mode is the highest bandwidth optical

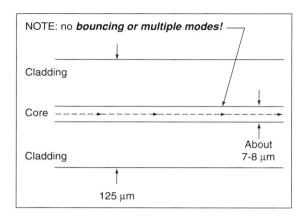

FIGURE 2.20
Single mode step index optical fiber.

fiber and is used for long distance communications. The single-mode fiber bandwidth limitation is due to different light colors (wavelengths) traveling at slightly different speeds. This phenomenon is called *chromatic dispersion.*

EXAMPLE 2.6 A 100-km distance between repeaters is desired. Using single-mode optical fiber, what bandwidth (data rate) can be expected?

$$\left(\frac{100 \text{ gbps} * \text{km}}{100 \text{ km}}\right) = 1.0 \text{ gbps}$$

Single-mode optical fiber is used in long haul (distance) applications such as Wide Area Networks (WANs), Metropolitan Area Networks (MANs), intercity and undersea applications. Many miles of fiber are installed in unused pipelines. The big advantages of pipelines are that the land easement is already in place, no burying has to be done, and the fiber cable has some protection provided by the steel pipeline. Fiber is also laid in railroad right-of-ways. Sprint, which touts its fiber optic network, is largely owned by railroad companies. When burying cable in new paths, horizontal drilling techniques are often used for minimal surface disturbance and lowest cost.

Undersea cables have galvanized steel armor and a copper conductor passing electrical current to the repeaters. This current seems to attract sharks, and "fish bite" protection is mandatory. Surprisingly undersea cables usually have only four optical fibers. Because of the tremendous bandwidth of single-mode optical fiber and clever multiplexing schemes, only a few optical fibers are necessary. Also light passes in both directions in each fiber and is separated at each end. The bandwidth of single-mode optical fiber is astounding. Each undersea optical fiber cable currently being installed has more bandwidth than all operational communication satellites in orbit. Copper cable is no longer being installed in undersea applications.

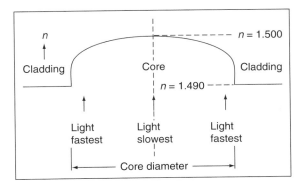

FIGURE 2.21
GRaded INdex (GRIN) optical fiber.

The disadvantage of single-mode optical fiber is its small core. This makes splicing and attaching connectors difficult, and it is difficult to get (couple) light into the small core.

2.5.3 GRaded INdex Optical Fiber

With **GRaded INdex (GRIN)** optical fiber (Figure 2.21) the light travels many paths to the receiver like multi-mode fiber, but nevertheless all the light arrives at the same time. This is done with special fabrication techniques that make the index of refraction vary across the core radius. The index of refraction is greatest at the core center and becomes least at the core edge. Paths down the core center are the slowest but the shortest. Paths away from the core center travel faster, but over longer distances. The net result is that all light, regardless of path, arrives at the same time at the receiver.

Referring to Figure 2.22, the light rays passing straight through the core center and those passing along the curved paths will arrive at the same time at the fiber end. The curved paths are longer than the straight center core path, but the light speed on the curved paths is greater because of the smaller index of refraction. Careful control of the index of refraction across the core radius is required. Since all the rays arrive at the same time at the fiber end, pulse widening is greatly reduced and the bandwidth is much greater than for step index multi-mode fiber. Typical bandwidth-distance specifications for GRIN fiber are 1.0 gbps * km.

EXAMPLE 2.7 Given a graded index fiber 25 km long, what is the maximum bit rate possible?

$$\left(\frac{1.0 \text{ gpbs * km}}{25 \text{ km}}\right) = 40 \text{ Mbps}$$

This is 50 times greater than for multi-mode fiber, but 100 times slower than single-mode optical fiber.

The sophisticated manufacturing techniques needed to control the index of refraction n across the core radius make GRIN fiber the most expensive optical fiber. However GRIN's core diameter is the same as multi-mode (62.5 micrometers), and connectorization

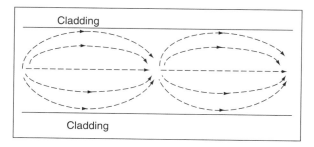

FIGURE 2.22
Light path in GRIN optical fiber. The longer paths travel faster than the shorter paths, so each ray arrives at the receiver at the same time regardless of the path taken. The index profile across the fiber core is carefully controlled to minimize modal dispersion. The output pulse has minimum spreading and the same shape as the input pulse.

(attaching connectors) is much easier than with single-mode. Also the large core diameter gives a wide angle of acceptance.

2.5.4 Optical Fiber Construction

All optical fiber is surrounded by protective coatings. A popular coating is Kevlar. Often a "strength member," a plastic Kevlar wire, is put into the completed cable to allow pulling of the cable without actually putting strain on the optical fibers, only on the strength member.

Optical fiber for data communications is almost always made from glass. The glass is manufactured with such astounding purity that if we could build an optical fiber to view into the deepest oceanic trench, the image would appear perfectly clear all the way to the bottom of the ocean. This makes for extremely low loss optical single mode fiber with best case losses about 0.2 to 0.3 dB per kilometer when used at 1.55-μm light wavelength. This allows repeaters to be spaced up to 100 kilometers apart at 622 Mbps SONET rates. The decibel (dB) is discussed in Appendix A2. SONET, an optical fiber transmission standard, is discussed in Chapter 17.

2.5.5 Plastic Optical Fiber

Plastic optical fiber is cheap and easy to work with, but its losses are very high, up to 400 dB per kilometer. For short distances, low data rates, and cost-sensitive applications, plastic optical fiber may be the best choice. Typical uses might be in automobiles as well as small- and medium-sized aircraft. For cars it could be used for detection of automobile headlight or taillight illumination. Plastic optical fiber has a very large core diameter and thus is multi-mode.

2.5.6 Glass Optical Fiber Comparison

Step index multi-mode optical fiber is the cheapest glass fiber, but it has the lowest bandwidth. Multi-mode is used for relatively short distance transmissions, such as LANs. Its large core diameter makes it relatively easy to work with, making connectorization and splicing less difficult. The large diameter core gives it a wide angle of acceptance, and it is easy to couple light into the core. LEDs (see the emitters section below) are often used as sources.

Single-mode fiber has the highest bandwidth of all optical fibers, but its small core (7 μm) makes it the most difficult to work with. Splicing and connectorization are difficult and require expensive equipment and highly trained personnel. The small diameter core gives it a narrow angle of acceptance, and it is difficult to couple light into the core. LASERs (see the emitters section below), are the usual sources. Lasers are used for long haul such as intercity Wide Area Networks (WANs) and undersea. Automated fusion splicing machines have reduced splice losses to about 0.2 dB per splice. Fusion splicers actually melt the two fibers at the splice point, push the two cables together, and then allow the splice to cool. Losses of less than 0.2 dB are possible.

GRaded INdex (GRIN) is the hardest fiber to manufacture because of the tight control needed for the precise index of refraction gradient across the core radius. Of course that means it has the highest cost. It does have a fairly high bandwidth and is much easier to work with than single-mode fiber. It is used in high bandwidth LANs and in Metropolitan Area Networks (MANs). GRIN's large diameter core gives it a wide angle of acceptance, and it is easy to couple light into the core. LEDs are often used as sources.

2.5.7 Emitters

2.5.7.1 Light Emitting Diodes (LEDs)   Light Emitting Diodes (LEDs) are cheap, emit a wide spectrum (many colors), emit over a wide angle, and are used for low (10 Mbps) data rates. They are used with plastic, multi-mode, and GRIN optical fiber, all having a wide angle of acceptance.

2.5.7.2 LASER Diodes   LASER diodes are much more expensive than LEDs, but their much faster data rates (in excess of 2.5 gbps), narrow spectral band (just a few closely spaced colors), higher power, and narrow angular output make them the emitter of choice for high data rate, long haul, single-mode optical fiber systems. The narrow angular output makes it easier to get more light into single-mode fiber even with its very small 7-mm diameter core and narrow angle of acceptance (see Figure 2.23).

2.5.8 Detectors

2.5.8.1 Photodiodes   A **diode** is an electronic device that allows a large electric current to travel through it in one direction, but almost none in the opposite direction. However if the diode is connected backwards (back biased or reversed biased), only a very small current (leakage) will flow. Photodiodes are used in this reverse biased (electrically connected in reverse) manner.

The photodiode is back biased with about 10 volts. A photon of light knocks an electron out of orbit, and this electron goes to amplifiers and further signal processing. Photodiode detectors are cheap but have a gain less than 1.0. *Gain* is defined as electrons to the amplifier per photons arriving at the diode.

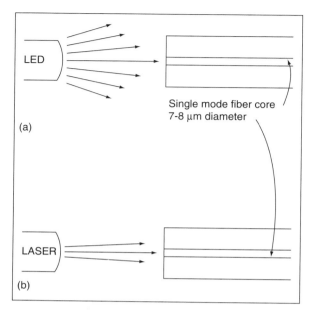

FIGURE 2.23
LED and LASER output angles. The wide radiation angle of the LED (a) makes it difficult to get much light into the single mode fiber. The relatively narrow radiation angle of the LASER (b) gets much more light into the single mode fiber.

$$\text{Gain} = \frac{\text{electrons at amplifier}}{\text{photons arriving at detector}} < 1.0 \qquad \textbf{(Equation 2.8)}$$

2.5.8.2 Avalanche Photodiodes (APD)

Avalanche photodiodes (APDs) are back biased with about 100 volts, creating a high electric field in the depletion region. See Figure 2.24. A photon of light knocks an electron out of orbit. This electron is accelerated by the strong electric field and knocks an electron in another atom out of orbit. Both electrons continue to knock other electrons out of their orbits. This avalanche, or chain reaction, continues until all electrons are collected and sent to amplifiers. Because of this random knocking of electrons out of orbits, APDs are significantly noisier than photodiodes. Avalanche photodiodes also cost more than photodiodes but have a gain between 10 and 100. They require a much higher voltage power supply (and more expensive) than for photodiodes.

$$\text{Gain} = 10 < \frac{\text{electrons at amplifier}}{\text{photons arriving at detector}} < 100 \qquad \textbf{(Equation 2.9)}$$

2.6 Satellites

There are two major categories of communication satellite: the Geosynchronous Earth Orbit Satellite (GEOS) and Low Earth Orbit Satellite (LEOS).

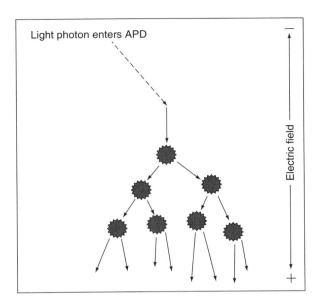

FIGURE 2.24
Electrons avalanching in an APD. An electron is knocked out of its orbit around a silicon atom. The electric field accelerates the electron, and this electron knocks a second electron out of orbit. Both electrons are then accelerated by the electric field. The process continues and more electrons are knocked out of their orbits and accelerated toward the positive voltage.

2.6.1 Geosynchronous Earth Orbit Satellite (GEOS)

A GEOS orbits the earth once per day and remains directly over a point on the earth's equator (Figure 2.25). Thus to a ground observer the GEOS appears to be stationary in the sky, and a ground antenna can be pointed in the same direction at all times. One GEOS can constantly "see" or service about one-third of the earth. Because of the long distance between a GEOS and the earth, both the satellite and ground stations need large high-gain antennas and powerful transmitters.

A GEOS orbit is 35,860 kilometers (22,400 statute miles) above the earth's equator. If the distance were greater, the satellite would drift to the west (slower than the earth's rotation, e.g., the moon), and if the distance were less, the satellite would drift to the east (faster than the earth's rotation).

A "constellation" of three GEOSs spaced above the equator 120 degrees apart can "see" all of the earth at all times, except for the polar regions above 82 degrees of latitude. There are a limited number of places or "slots" in this exact orbit, known as the Clark belt.

The radio signal delay for an earth-GEOS-earth transmission is about 300 milliseconds. This long delay can cause echoes and flow control problems. Digital echo cancelers are used to cancel echoes on voice communications. The digitized voice information is held in a memory and compared with the return signal. If there is a match between the return signal and the original signal, an echo is assumed and the offending echo is digitally canceled or subtracted out. While this method is fine for voice or video, it would be

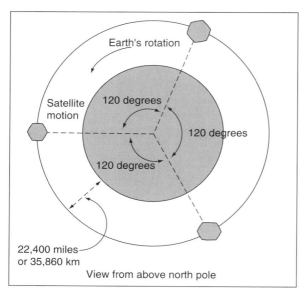

FIGURE 2.25
GEOS.

a disaster for data. Long identical patterns are rare in voice and video, but common in data. True data would be subtracted from the signal and corrupt the information. A special signaling tone is used to alert voice circuits that data is to be sent and the echo cancellation circuitry should be disabled.

The long distance between a GEOS and the earth causes a large signal strength loss that must be made up by high-gain antennas, high-power transmitters, and sensitive receivers.

After launch into low earth orbit the GEOS is maneuvered into the right height and over the desired point above the equator. This point is measured in degrees of longitude. The maneuvering requires a lot of fuel to get the GEOS from a low earth orbit of 125 miles to 22,400 miles. The fuel is a significant portion of the GEOS's launch weight and adds greatly to the launch costs.

GEOS strengths are the ability to use non-steerable antennas at the ground stations and simplex broadcasting to multiple receivers, like the Direct Satellite Service (DSS) in remote areas such as northern Canada, Indonesia's many remote islands, and India's rural villages.

The military appreciates GEOSs because of their reliability, high immunity to destruction in battle, ability to communicate with mobile forces, and lack of dependence on terrestrial facilities. The U.S. military used GEOSs when deployed to Bosnia and Somalia, which have poor communications capability. The military's reconnaissance GEOS satellites can monitor one region continuously, such as Iraq.

Telecommunications companies use GEOSs as backup transcontinental or transoceanic systems for their optical fiber systems. News organizations use GEOS for its ability to communicate from remote locations. **Inmarsat** is a consortium of seventy-nine countries providing communications to ships at sea via GEOS.

2.6.2 Low Earth Orbiting Satellites (LEOSs)

LEOSs are much closer to the earth than GEOSs and do not need large antennas or powerful transmitters in either the satellite or the ground station. This means that both the LEOS and the ground station can be cheaper and the ground station more portable. The disadvantages are that a LEOS is constantly moving relative to a ground observer and may need steerable antennas. Many LEOSs are needed for continuous coverage.

LEOSs orbit between 600 and 1,800 kilometers above ground level (agl). To a ground observer a LEOS will always appear to be moving through the sky and therefore may need steerable ground antennas. However the short range for LEOS compared with GEOS means that 400 times less system power is needed. This allows cheaper antennas and earth stations, less battery drain for portable units, as well as cheaper satellites and lower launch costs. All of these factors translate to lower subscriber costs. Much less maneuvering fuel is required and launch weight is less than for GEOS. Often several LEOSs are launched from the same rocket.

A major disadvantage of LEOS is that many must be launched to provide continuous coverage. The many satellites used to create continuous coverage are called a *constellation* (of satellites). Sixty-six LEOSs are used for Motorola's Iridium project, and twenty-four are used for the U.S. military's Global Positioning System (GPS).

2.6.2.1 Big LEOS and Little LEOS
There are two categories of LEOSs: big LEOSs and little LEOSs. Little LEOSs have orbits lower than 1,000 km agl, and big LEOSs have orbits higher than 1,000 km agl. Some LEOS vendors are Orbital Communications Corporation, Motorola, TRW, Orbital Science Corporation, Loral Aerospace, Qualcomm, McCaw Cellular, and Microsoft.

- *Little LEOS* Little LEOSs are less expensive than big LEOSs, only handle data, and operate at frequencies less than 1.0 gHz. Ground transceiver power ranges between 1 and 8 watts.
- *Big LEOS* Big LEOSs are more expensive than small LEOSs. Their orbits are greater than 1,000 km agl, they support both voice and data, and they operate at frequencies greater than 1.0 gHz. Vendors are Motorola with its Iridium project, TRW with Odyssey, Hughes with Space Way, and Loral/Qualcomm with its GlobalStar.

By September 1997, Motorola had launched thirty-four Iridium satellites, and the sixty-six-satellite system was operational in the fall of 1998. The satellites operate at 1.6 gHz, a frequency important to radio astronomers, who are quite concerned about potential interference.

2.6.3 Elliptical (Molniya) Orbit Satellites

Satellites can be put into elliptical orbits rather than circular ones. By careful choice of the orbit, the satellite can be in view for a much longer time than for a circular orbit LEOS. When the elliptical orbit satellite is near the high point of its orbit (apogee), it appears to be moving very slowly across the sky. At apogee the satellite "sees" a large part of the earth. Typical orbits are 580 (perigee, or low point) by 7,800 km (apogee, or high point).

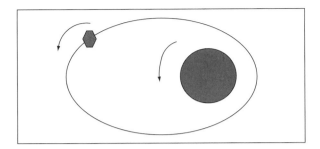

FIGURE 2.26
Elliptical (Molniya) orbit satellites. At apogee (high point) the satellite moves very slowly and, with a carefully planned orbit, appears to be almost stationary to a ground station. The satellite will remain in view for a relatively long time.

The U.S. Air Force has launched an elliptical orbit reconnaissance satellite with an apogee at a high latitude over the former Soviet Union to monitor its nuclear submarine fleet operating in the Arctic Ocean. The satellite will be able to "hover" at the necessary high latitudes (at least for several hours at a time), something a GEOS cannot do. The GEOS must remain over the equator. See Figure 2.26.

Fewer elliptical orbit satellites are needed to make up a constellation than for a LEOS, but somewhat higher system power will be needed than for a circular orbit satellite at a lower altitude. However antenna pointing may be easier. Ground stations may have lower power and be simpler than for a GEOS. Less fuel is needed for an elliptical orbit than for a GEOS orbit, translating into lower satellite and launch costs.

2.6.4 Very Small Aperture Terminal Satellites (VSATs)

With Very Small Aperture Terminal satellites (**VSATs**) the communication is from a host computer and satellite terminal to remote receiving stations via satellite (see Figure 2.27). The system topology may be considered a "star" with the host at the star center. VSATs are often used in remote areas where terrestrial links are expensive or not in place. They are also used for credit card authorization, news services, motel reservations, financial houses, news organizations, and retail stores for inventory control.

The remote sites may use a terrestrial link to communicate back to the host. The daily newspaper *USA Today* uses high data rate VSATs to send the newspaper's text to printing houses around the United States. The receiving stations send back acknowledgment signals to the host via low bandwidth, inexpensive terrestrial links.

The antennas are relatively small, 1.2 to 2.4 meters in diameter (Very Small Aperture). The frequencies used are mostly Ka band at 27.5 to 30.0 gHz (1.05 cm wavelength) for the uplink (ground station to satellite) and 17.7 to 20.2 gHz (1.5 cm wavelength) for the downlink (satellite to ground station). These short wavelengths allow use of small antennas with high gain.

Vendors are Contel ASC, AT&T, Integrated Satellite Business Network (ISBN), and Hughes Network System.

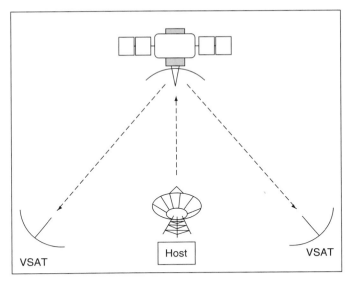

FIGURE 2.27
Very Small Aperture Terminal Satellite (VSAT).

2.7 Nyquist Channel Capacity Law

The *data rate* is the number of bits per second that can be successfully sent through a channel. That channel may be any medium.

Dr. Harry Nyquist found the theoretical limit to the channel capacity C (bits per second, or bps) for a noiseless channel:

$$C = 2 \, BW \log_2 L \qquad \textbf{(Equation 2.10)}$$

where BW is the bandwidth in Hertz (Hz) or $\frac{cycles}{second}$, and L is the number of signaling levels.

EXAMPLE 2.8 For a binary system the number of levels is $L = 2$ ("0" and "1," or two voltage levels of, say, 0 and $+ 5$ volts) with a bandwidth of 3,000 Hz. $\log_2 (2) = 1$.

$$C = 2 \times 3000 * \log_2 (2) = 2 \times 3000 \times 1 = 6{,}000 \text{ bps}$$

EXAMPLE 2.9 Given a four-level system encoding two bits

$$L = 4 \text{ levels} = 2^2 = \text{base } 2^{(\text{number of bits encoded})}$$

The voltage levels might be as shown below:

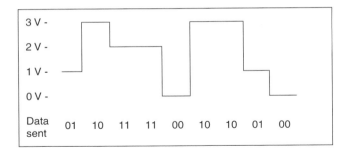

FIGURE 2.28
Bit vs. Baud example. This example uses the four voltage system of the previous slide

Voltage Level		Bits Encoded
3.0 volts	->	"1 0"
2.0 volts	->	"1 1"
1.0 volt	->	"0 1"
0.0 volt	->	"0 0"

and $BW = 3$ kHz

$C = 2\ BW \log_2 (4) = 2 \times 3000 \times 2 = 12$ kbps

A typical four-level transmission is shown in Figure 2.28. The basic formula can be rewritten as follows:

$$C = 2\ BW \log_2 (L) = \frac{2\ BW \log_{10} (L)}{\log_{10} (2)} \qquad \textbf{(Equation 2.11)}$$

$$= \frac{2\ BW \log_{10} (L)}{(0.301)}$$

2.8 Shannon-Hartley Channel Capacity Law

Noise is always present in any real system and limits the transmission rate. The Shannon-Hartley law gives maximum channel capacity for systems with noise.

$$C = BW \log_2 \left(1 + \frac{S}{N}\right) \qquad \textbf{(Equation 2.12)}$$

$$C = BW \left[\frac{\log_{10}\left(1 + \frac{S}{N}\right)}{\log_{10} (2)}\right] = BW \left[\frac{\log_{10}\left(1 + \frac{S}{N}\right)}{0.301}\right]$$

where $\left(\frac{S}{N}\right)$ is the signal-to-noise ratio.

EXAMPLE 2.10 With a 3-kHz bandwidth (as in the telephone system) and a $\left(\dfrac{S}{N}\right)$ ratio of 10

$$C = 3 \text{ kHz} \left(\frac{\log_{10}(1 + 10)}{0.301} \right) = 10.37 \text{ kbps}$$

2.9 Bit Rate versus Baud Rate

Bit rate (bits per second, or bps) and baud rate (hertz [Hz], or cycles per second) are not the same thing. The units (per second) are the same, but nevertheless the two are different. The bit rate and Baud rate were the same in the early days of modems and data transmission. The demand for higher bit rates has spawned clever encoding schemes to get higher bit rates without increasing the Baud rate and bandwidth. However, some still use the terms interchangeably.

Bit rate in bits per second is how much data is actually sent, and the units are bits per second (bps), kilobits (1,000) per second (kbps), megabits (million) per second (Mbps), or even gigabits (billion) per second (gbps).

Baud rate is the rate at which the signal changes in changes per second. The term *baud* honors M. Baudot, a French pioneer in telegraphy. Since Baud is derived from a proper name, it is sometimes capitalized. M. Baudot is known for developing the Baudot code in telegraphy.

EXAMPLE 2.11 We see that by using four levels ($L = 2^{\text{[bits encoded]}} = 2^2 = 4$) it is possible to send two bits in one signal change.

Voltage Level		Bits Encoded
3.0 volts	->	"1 0"
2.0 volts	->	"1 1"
1.0 volt	->	"0 1"
0.0 volt	->	"0 0"

We thus send two bits per baud (signal change, or signal state). Refer back to Figure 2.28 for an example.

EXAMPLE 2.12 We use sixteen levels and can encode four bits ($L = 2^4 = 16$ levels).

Voltage Level		Bits Encoded		
		Binary		Hexadecimal
3.75 volts	=	%1111	=	$F
3.50 volts	=	%1110	=	$E
3.25 volts	=	%1101	=	$D
....				
0.50 volt	=	%0010	=	$2
0.25 volt	=	%0001	=	$1
0.00 volt	=	%0000	=	$0

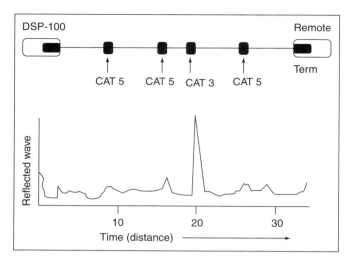

FIGURE 2.29
DSP-100 TDR test results. A CAT 3 connector has been installed 20 meters from the tester.

We send four bits per baud, or signal change or signal state. This is similar to 1B2Q signaling used with ISDN.

When we study modems, we will see examples of sophisticated systems using more than simple voltage differences for signal states.

2.10 Troubleshooting

2.10.1 Twisted Pair (TP) and Coax Testing

A state-of-the-art test instrument for Category 5 TP testing is the DSP-100© Cable Meter from Fluke Corporation. This handheld tester performs **cross talk** (NEXT [Near End Cross Talk]) measurements and tells the users how far down the cable a fault lies. The DSP-100 sends signal pulses down the cable and measures the return signal.

The user can switch to the Time Domain Reflectometry (TDR) test. A pulse is sent down the cable. The reflections from the pulse are analyzed and can show impedance, cable loss, and any variations in impedance. These variations can be caused by poor installation of connectors, pinching of the cable (changing cable dimension), or sharp bends in the cable. These variations in impedance cause reflections and potentially high data errors.

Figure 2.29 shows a TDR trace indicating a Cat 3 connector installed when a Cat 5 connector should have been. The trace also shows how far from the test the fault is located. The DSP-100 actually shows time on the horizontal trace. However if the user enters the velocity of propagation of signals (how fast the signal travels) on the cable into the tester, the DSP-100 will convert time to distance and display the distance. Figure 2.30 shows a TDR trace with a cable open at 27 meters.

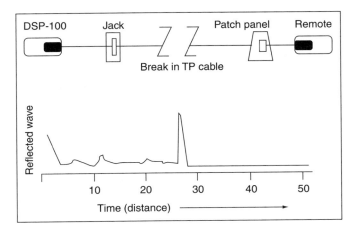

FIGURE 2.30
DSP-100 TDR test results.

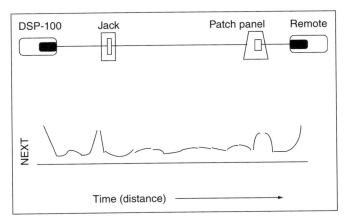

FIGURE 2.31
DSP-100 NEXT test results.

For a cross talk test the DSP-100 sends pulses down the TP under test. The pulses closely resemble 100-Mbps LAN signals. The pulses are coupled from the pair under test onto the other pair, and these coupled signals are analyzed by the DSP-100 using Digital Signal Processing (DSP) techniques. These cross talk tests are called Near End Cross Talk (NEXT).

If the cross talk level is too high, the user needs to know where the fault is located. The unit will display the cross talk amplitude versus distance, showing where the excess cross talk is occurring. A common offender is the eight-pin modular plug (RJ-45). Typical test results are shown in Figure 2.31.

2.10.2 Optical Fiber Testing

Optical fiber cable losses can easily be measured by sending a light source with a known power into the cable and then measuring its output. The difference between the measurements is the cable loss. Also see Appendix A2 for an example.

A very useful instrument for finding faults in an optical cable is the Optical Time Domain Reflectometer (OTDR). The OTDR sends a laser pulse down the optical cable. Reflections are displayed on the screen's vertical scale, and distance is displayed on the horizontal scale. Reflections occur at changes (discontinuities) along the cable, such as splice connectors, bends that are too tight (too small a radius of curvature), and terminations. Figure 2.32 shows a typical display from a Tektronix Ranger TFS 3031 OTDR. A splice is shown at 47.16 km. Figure 2.32c is an enlarged view of a reflection at 35.77 km. This instrument is portable and designed for servicing use in the field.

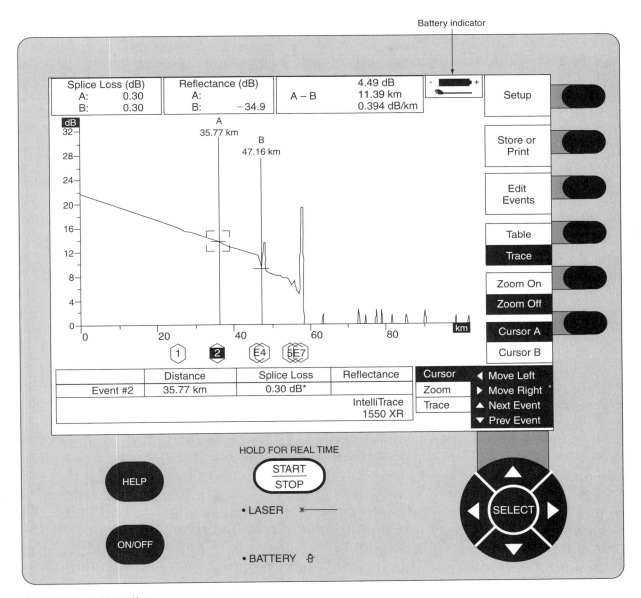

FIGURE 2.32A
OTDR test result.

SELECT Button and Arrow Keys

Use the SELECT button and arrow keys to move the cursors, manipulate the waveform, edit events in the wave form/table display, and select and change instrument setups.

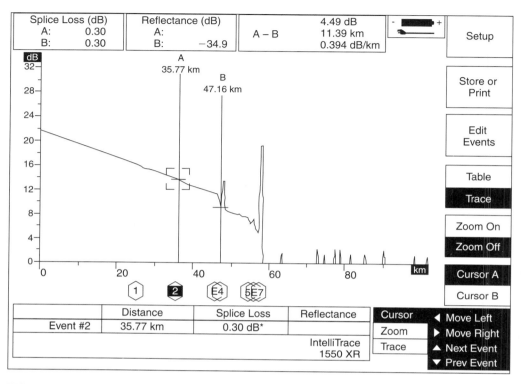

FIGURE 2.32B

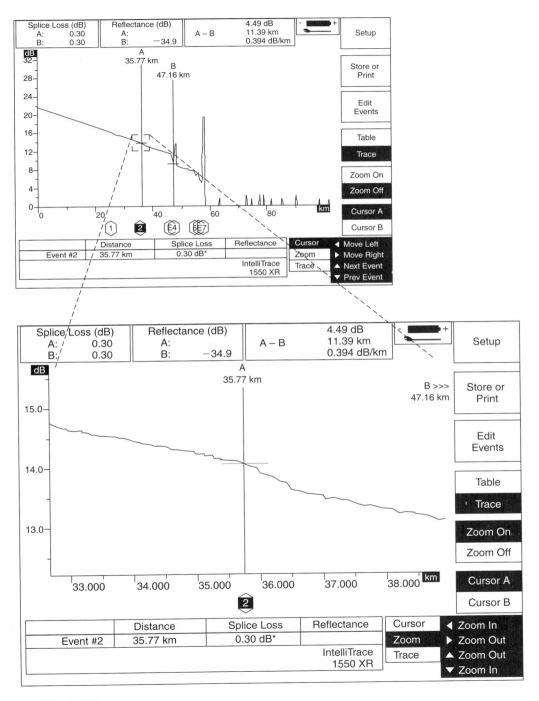

FIGURE 2.32C

SUMMARY

I. The Physical Layer is the layer that conveys the information bit stream. The bits are sent via light pulses, varying voltages or currents, microwaves, or radio waves. The Physical Layer is the bottom layer of the seven-layer Reference Model (RM).

II. The two wire (copper) transmission media are twisted pair and coax. Twisted pair (TP) is merely two insulated wires twisted together. This simplicity makes TP the cheapest media, but it has the least bandwidth. Some types (categories) of TP have higher bandwidth (and higher cost) than others.

III. Coax has a center conductor surrounded by an insulating layer and then a braided shield. Coax has a much higher bandwidth than TP but also costs more. Coax is also less susceptible to interference. The cable television industry uses coax for virtually all its installations.

IV. RS-232 is a Physical Layer protocol, that is, a set of standards. RS-232 usually uses wire (copper) for short distance, low speed, serial data transmission.

V. Noise affects electrical transmission systems. RS-232 and RS-422 are compared for noise resistance. RS-422, with its balanced configuration, is much more noise resistant and has a greater bandwidth.

VI. The index of refraction principle is discussed, as well as how this principle is used to keep the light inside the optical fiber. The three types of optical fiber (single step multi-mode, graded index, and single-mode) are considered relative to cost, bandwidth, and ease of handling. The characteristics of photodiode detectors, and LED and LASER emitters are compared.

VII. The three types of satellite orbits, (low earth, geosynchronous, and Molniya) are compared as to their advantages and disadvantages.

VIII. Nyquist's and Shannon-Hartley's capacity versus bandwidth laws are compared. Nyquist's law is for a noiseless channel, and the Shannon-Hartley law takes into account channel noise.

IX. Baud rate and bit rate, often a confusing topic, are clarified. *Baud rate* is the rate the signal changes, or modulation rate. The *bit rate* is the rate of data transfer. The two are not necessarily the same. Often people (even authors of books) tend to equate the two, but they are most certainly different.

QUESTIONS

1. What is the main advantage of Category 5 UTP over Category 3 UTP?
2. What gives TP some interference reducing capability?
3. Your boss has ordered a 100-Mbps LAN system for your building. The building has Category 3 TP wiring available. Do you go with the Category 3 TP or choose another option? What other medium possibilities do you have?
4. You are to design a fiber optics communications system with a data rate of 55 Mbps and a distance of 10 km. What type of fiber would you use? Justify your answer.
5. Which of the following are UTP characteristics?
   a. Better shielding than coax.
   b. Better shielding than STP.

   c. Better interference characteristics than a single wire.

   d. Category 3 is designed for voice transmission.

   e. Category 5 is designed for data transmission.

   f. Category 5 is more expensive than Category 3.

   g. Category 5 is present in many older buildings.

   h. Used for cable television.

   i. More expensive than coax.

   j. Used for some LANs.

6. Which of the following are coaxial cable characteristics?

   a. Better shielding than UTP.

   b. Used for some LANs.

   c. Used for cable television.

   d. Always cheaper than TP.

   e. Has resistor terminations to maximize reflections.

   f. The characteristic impedance is measured in ohms.

   g. The characteristic impedance is measured by an ohmmeter.

7. Match the optical fiber type (multi-mode, single-mode, or graded index) with the proper characteristic. There may be more than one answer.

   a. Cheapest

   b. Most expensive

   c. Highest bandwidth

   d. Smallest core

   e. Hardest to work with

   f. Very long distance transmission

   g. Highest data rate

   h. Lowest data rate

   i. Biggest core

8. Match the emitter (LED or LASER diode) with the proper characteristics.

   a. Cheapest

   b. Lowest data rate

   c. Suitable for multi-mode

   d. Suitable for single-mode

9. You are to design a fiber optics communications system with a data rate of 622 Mbps and a desired distance between repeaters of 110 km. What type of optical fiber and emitter would you use? Justify your answer.

10. Why are GEOSs more expensive than LEOSs?

11. Why would echoes be a problem with GEOS and not with LEOS?

12. Why would flow control be a problem with a GEOS and not with a LEOS?

13. Why would one want to put a satellite into an elliptical orbit?

14. What is the difference between bit rate and baud rate? Can they be the same rate? Can the baud rate be greater than the bit rate?

15. Can the bit rate be greater than the baud rate?

16. Given a three-bit encoding and a bit rate of 8,000 bps, what is the baud rate?

17. Given an eight-level system and a bandwidth of 3 KHz, what is the maximum theoretical bit rate?

18. Given a system with a 12-kHz bandwidth and a signal-to-noise ratio of 49:1, what is the theoretical bit rate?

19. Given an optical fiber with a core index or refraction of 1.490 and a cladding index of refraction of 1.484, what is the critical angle? What is the angle of acceptance?

3

THE DATA LINK LAYER (DLL)

OBJECTIVES

In this chapter we will discuss:

I. What does the Data Link Layer (level 2) do?
    A. It synchronizes the receiver to the frame.
    B. It does error control.
    C. It does flow control to prevent the data from being transmitted too fast or too slow.
    D. It does routing (finding the best route) for the frame.
        1. *Connection oriented* means the connection is maintained throughout the data transfer.
        2. *Connectionless* means no connection is maintained through the data transfer. Rather, data is sent via independently routed datagrams.
    E. The relationship between the DLL and upper level protocols—such as X.25, SNA, and TCP/IP—is discussed.
II. The control field's function is discussed.
    A. The control field specifies the type of frame or packet, sequence in the total transmission, error control, and housekeeping.
III. Virtual communications between the same layers is examined.

As a review Figure 3.1 shows that the DLL is at level 2 of the OSI RM. A summary of the various DLL protocols is shown in Table 3.1 and Figure 3.1. Use these to compare DLL systems as we study them.

The term *bursty* or *burstyness* means the data comes in bursts, or intermittently, not continuously. Data must be received continuously for real-time voice or video. Data may be received in bursts or not continuously. See Figure 3.2.

3.1 Data Link Layer Duties

The functions of the DLL are summarized in Table 3.1.

TABLE 3.1

Date link layer functions

Synchronizes receiver to bit stream
    Finds start of frame
    Finds fields within frame
Error detection
    Error control
    If error is detected, the message is repeated
Flow control
    Receiver gets data at right speed, not too fast, not too slow
Destination/Source Addresses
    Connectionless, datagrams
Path specified
    Setup/teardown needed
    Connection oriented

Data link layer functions

Frame sequence numbers
    Frames may arrive out of order
    Need sequence number to put frames back into proper order
Priority
Allowable delay
Can this frame be discarded?
    Network congestion
Type of encryption
Upper level protocol type
    Where is frame to go after being received?
    More than one upper level protocol may be used

FIGURE 3.1

OSI RM layers.

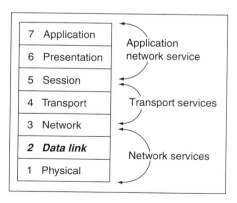

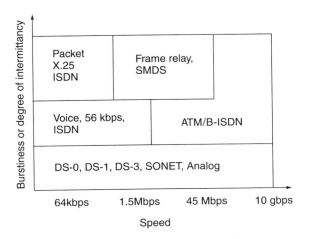

FIGURE 3.2
DLL protocols—speeds & burstiness

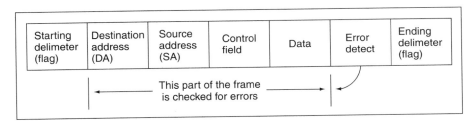

FIGURE 3.3
DLL frame structure. Though each field is shown to be about the same length, they usually have different lengths

3.1.1 Synchronization

Data and housekeeping information are sent in a bit stream called a **frame.** If data is to be received correctly, the receiver must know when the frame starts, ends, and the beginning and end of each frame part. The frame structure (for most DLL protocols) is in Figure 3.3. The various frame parts are called *fields*.

The starting and ending delimiters or start and end flags tell the DLL where the frame begins and ends. Thus the DLL can synchronize to the frame. Typically the flag is a binary "0 1 1 1 1 1 1 0" bit pattern or a hexadecimal "7E." This pattern could also appear elsewhere within the frame. Techniques are used to prevent the DLL from mistaking this data pattern from the flag.

It should be noted that the **Physical Layer** synchronizes to the individual bits, whereas the DLL synchronizes to the frame.

3.1.2 Error Control

The last portion of the frame before the ending flag (ending delimiter) is for error checking. The technique is called Cyclic Redundant Code (CRC) or Frame Check Sequence (FRC) and is discussed in Appendix A1 to this book.

The frame is checked for errors from the end of the starting delimiter to the end of the data. It is pointless to error-check parts of the frame that never change, such as the **flags.** If an error is detected, the sending node DLL is notified via a supervisory REJ (REJect) control frame. Usually the sending node will resend the frame in error and all subsequent frames. This technique is called "go back N" frames. Some frames that had arrived without error may be retransmitted unnecessarily. The reason for this apparent inefficiency was the high cost of memory when these protocols were developed. It cost too much to buy a lot of memory for the receiving node.

3.1.3 Flow Control

Flow control is sending the data to the receiver at the right speed; not too fast or too slow. If the network is congested or has failures, switching nodes can get more data than they can handle. The sending node must be told to slow down the data rate. If the transmitting node is not sending the data fast enough, the network efficiency will be reduced. The sending node must be informed to speed up the data transmission rate. This is done in the control field via a supervisory RNR (Receiver Not Ready) frame.

3.1.4 Addresses or Route

Depending on the protocol type, the second field is either the **Destination Address (DA)** or path routing information. Immediately following the DA field is the Source Address (SA) denoting the origin or source of the frame. If a Destination Address (DA) is used, the system is connectionless. If routing or path information is used, the system is connection oriented.

3.1.4.1 Connection Oriented
If a connection (path) is set up (established) before data transfer occurs, this type of connection is called *connection oriented*. Then the second field of the frame is usually path (route) information. Thus a switching node will know as soon as possible the proper route to send the data. At the end of the session the path is "torn down," and the equipment becomes available for another user.

Equipment is not added or taken away physically during teardown, but rather switched (connected) into the circuit by a special computer. During the setup phase switching equipment is reserved but is not actually in the circuit. After the connection is established, the equipment is actually switched into the data transfer network. The equipment is not actually used until needed, in case the connection is not established, increasing network efficiency.

The third field of the frame is usually the Source Address (SA). The end user often needs to know where the frame is coming from.

3.1.4.2 Connectionless
If a connection does not need to be set up (established) before data transfer, the protocol is called **connectionless.** The second frame is the Destina-

tion Address (DA), and the third field is the Source Address (SA). The switching nodes in the network have the intelligence to route the frame to its proper destination by just knowing the DA. The needed information is kept in a routing table. If the network conditions change, the route may be changed. Possible changes are equipment failure or congestion (too much traffic).

A humorist has referred to connectionless systems as "spray and pray!"

3.1.4.3 Upper Levels, and Connectionless and Connection Oriented   In many systems the DLL is connectionless, but the upper level protocols are connection oriented. (As if this isn't confusing enough already!) The upper levels set up a session, and the DLL does not need to know about the connection. A good example is TCP/IP, covered in Chapter 18. IP is connectionless, and TCP is connection oriented.

3.1.5 Priority

Some traffic is more urgent than other, and some protocols allow these frames to pass through the network before non-urgent frames.

3.1.6 Encryption

Sensitive information—such as credit card data, financial information, and military strategies—is encoded (encrypted).

3.1.7 Allowable Delay

Some frames, such as real-time audio and video, must have a constant delay through the network. Also voice delayed over about 0.3 second becomes annoying to users. Data usually is not sensitive to delay, meaning the frame delay can vary.

3.1.8 Discard Eligibility

If the network becomes extremely congested, frames may be lost or discarded. Voice and video can tolerate some degree of frame loss. Data usually cannot tolerate any losses.

3.2   Control Field

The **control field** handles flow control, housekeeping, and assists in error control. The most used DLLs have three types of frames. Certain bits in the control identify which frame type is being sent. The types and their uses are summarized in Table 3.2.

The *data or information frame* transmits user information as well as housekeeping information, such as the sequence number of the frame that has been sent and the sequence number of the frame that is expected to be received, and is a response expected from the other end. The *supervisory frame* is used for flow control and error notification.

TABLE 3.2
DLL information frame

Information
Send user information (data)
Send flow control
Send frame sequence number
Send sequence number of next frame expected to be received

DLL supervisory frame
RR (Receiver Ready)
"I'm ready to receive frames"
Received last frame correctly
REJ (REJect)
Something is wrong with the received frame
Error
Frame format is wrong
RNR (Receiver Not Ready)
Flow control, receiver can't handle more frames at this time
Next Frame Expected F(r)

DLL unnumbered frames
Set up connection
Tear down connection
Test network nodes
Identify nodes
Initialize nodes

The unnumbered frames are used for housekeeping functions, such as setting up and tearing down connections and status information.

Chapter 20 on SNA covers the use of SDLC, a DLL protocol, with examples of its use. SDLC was the first DLL protocol as described previously. It replaced the inefficient Binary Synchronous Control (BSC), or BiSync.

3.3 Upper Level Protocols

The DLL is transparent to the end user. The end user normally is completely unaware of the intricacies of the lower levels. The user is usually interested only in what happens in the top level (application, or why we are using the darn network in the first place). The packets contain the address of each protocol to be used in each layer above the DLL. The upper layer often has more than one available protocol.

Some of the upper level protocols are TCP/IP, IPX/SPX, and NetBUEI. These will be discussed in later chapters.

SUMMARY

I. "Bursty" or intermittent was defined. Voice and video are constant rate not bursty, but data may be.

II. What the DLL does.

 A. Synchronizes the receiver to the frame (finds the start, end, and individual fields within the frame). Remember the physical level synchronizes to the individual bits.

 B. Error detection and error control; a few DLLs correct errors, but most only detect them and initiate a frame repeat.

 C. Flow control is preventing the receiver from getting data too fast and losing it, or preventing the receiver from getting data too slowly and reducing system efficiency.

III. Frame types are data, supervisory, and unnumbered.

QUESTIONS

1. What is the purpose of DLL synchronization? What is the difference between synchronization at the physical level and at the DLL?
2. What is the starting delimiter and its purpose? What is the ending delimiter and its purpose?
3. What is the method used for error detection? What is the method for error control? How does it work?
4. What is the purpose of flow control?
5. Depending on the DLL protocol, the frame will have either a Destination Address (DA) or routing information. Why? What is each type called?
6. What is the difference between connection oriented and connectionless?
7. Why would one be concerned about delay through the network?
8. Why would discard eligibility be important? Why would any data be discarded?
9. Why would upper level protocol addresses be carried in a frame?
10. What are the three types of frames as determined by the control field? What are their purposes?

4

LOCAL AREA NETWORKS (LANs)

OBJECTIVES

In this chapter we will discuss:

    I. What LANs are and Why they are used.

    II. LAN topology (how they are connected).

        A. Bus.

        B. Star.

        C. Ring.

    III. The types of LANs using each topology.

        A. Ethernet using bus.

        B. Token Ring using ring.

        C. Token Bus using bus.

    IV. The advantages and disadvantages of each type.

    V. The frame structures of each LAN type.

    VI. The coding or modulation type used by each LAN type.

    VII. Frame collisions (two frames from different senders arriving at the receiving node at the same time) and how they are handled.

    VIII. Why frame collisions cannot occur in certain LANs.

    IX. Modulation or coding techniques.

        A. Manchester.

        B. Differential Manchester.

    X. High-speed LANS.

        A. 100 Mbps.

        B. 1,000 Mbps (1 gbps).

4.1 Introduction to LANs

A **Local Area Network (LAN)** is a network of computing resources connected together in a relatively small area such as a room, building, or campus. The computing resources are computers (supercomputers, mainframes, mini-computers, workstations, personal computers), peripherals (modems, printers, plotters), and terminals. The shared computers can be mini-computers, workstations, mainframes, and even supercomputers.

LANs are used to share resources. Resources are computers, programs, files, workstations, terminals, printers, plotters, Wide Area Network (WAN) access, modems, and various input/output devices.

Cost can be reduced by sharing resources. Comptrollers want to reduce capital expenses such as hardware and software. These can be shared over a LAN. Printers can be expensive if everyone in the office needs one, and they take up space in a cubicle. Plotters are still quite pricey. Usually a business needs only a few modems and WAN access ports, and it does not make economic sense for everyone to have one. All these peripherals can be shared on a LAN more cheaply than for all employees to have one of each type.

Many software vendors have special networking prices for their software. The software is on a network file server hard disc drive, and the server sends that required part of the software to the user as needed. A **file server** is a computer with a large hard drive, whose purpose is to send (transfer) data and program files to and from the users on the LAN as requested.

With e-mail better communications are possible between workers, and between supervisors and workers. Our faculty and staff use the LAN to communicate efficiently and quickly with each other via e-mail. Our college president communicates with faculty and staff regularly via e-mail on our LAN. Our athletic department communicates upcoming events over LAN e-mail. For some reason they seem to be reluctant to tell us the scores of the games!

Design teams can be working on the same shared file via a LAN. This eliminates the inefficient "sneakernet" or "Nikenet," the file transfer via floppy disk or magnetic tape. By having several people work on the same project simultaneously, the project can be finished much faster than if only one person works on it. This will allow the company to hit the "market window" for getting a product to the market, thus beating the competition and remaining competitive and profitable. Remember in Chapter 1 we talked about having several people work on a project simultaneously with a "divide and conquer" attack.

4.1.1 LAN Topologies

Topologies are the physical connection or configuration of a LAN. The three common topologies are ring, bus, and star. The LAN types are summarized in Table 4.1.

4.1.1.1 Bus In the bus topology shown in Figure 4.1a the nodes are connected to a continuous conducting medium. The medium is either twisted pair (TP), coax, or optical fiber. Ethernet and ARCnet are two LAN types that use bus topology.

4.1.1.2 Ring Figure 4.1b shows a ring topology. In a ring topology the token, a specific bit pattern, is passed from an upstream node to a downstream node. When the token contains data, it becomes a frame. Tokens and frames pass in one direction only around the ring, except in FDD1 which has dual rings. In FDD1, the frames and tokens travel in different directions on each ring.

TABLE 4.1
Low-Speed LAN Baseband Comparison

Parameter	10Base5	10Base2	10BaseT	Token Ring	Token Bus
Data rate	10 Mbps	10 Mbps	10 Mbps	4 or 16 Mbps	1.5, 10 Mbps
Max segment length	500 m	185 m	100 m		
Total network length	2,500 m	925 m	500 m		
Max nodes per segment	100	30			
Min node spacing	2.5 m	0.5 m			
Physical medium	10-mm coax	7-mm coax	0.6 mm	UTP or STP	Coax, fiber
Coax impedance	50 ohms	50 ohms			
IEEE spec	802.3	802.3	802.3	802.5	802.4
Topology	Bus	Bus	Star, bus	Ring	Bus
Signaling	Manchester	Manchester	Manchester	Diff Manchester	
Collision detection	Excess current	Excess current	Rcvr, trans activ	NA	NA
					ARCnet

4.1.1.3 Star The star topology of Figure 4.1c is used to connect a mini-computer, mainframe computer, or supercomputer to peripherals. Non-LAN examples are IBM's System Network Architecture (SNA) and VSATs, where a host computer transmits via satellite to many ground stations.

4.2 Ethernet

4.2.1 Carrier Sense Multiple Access with Collision Detection

Carrier Sense Multiple Access with Collision Detection (CSMA/CD) is used on all Ethernet LANs. Ethernet uses a bus topology, as shown in Figure 4.2, Node A has a frame to transmit. Node A listens to see if there are any messages being sent by other nodes (Carrier Sense). If Node A does not hear any activity, it will transmit its frame. Nodes B and C hear the frame, and if the frame is addressed to them, Nodes B and C will read the frame. Nodes B and C, hearing activity on the bus, will not transmit. This is Carrier Sense (CS).

What happens if two nodes transmit at nearly the same time and cause interference (collision) on the bus? In Figure 4.2b Node A has a frame to transmit. Node A listens for activity on the bus. Node A does not hear any activity on the bus and transmits its frame. Node C has a frame to transmit and listens for activity on the bus. Node C, thinking there is no activity on the bus, transmits its frame. Node C does not hear any activity because the frame from Node A has not reached Node C. A frame does not travel the length of the bus instantly. It takes a frame about 13 microseconds to travel the 2,500 meters of the potentially largest CSMA/CD 10Base5 LAN. Nodes A, B, and C all detect the two frames in collision (Collision Detection) and ignore the corrupted frames. Nodes A and C transmit until it is certain that all nodes have noted the frames are corrupted.

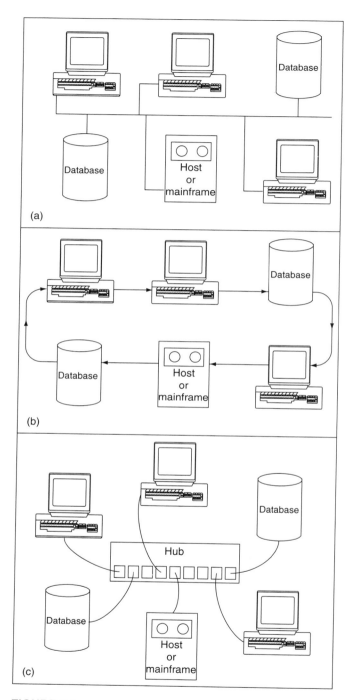

FIGURE 4.1
(a) Bus topology, (b) ring topology, and (c) star topology.

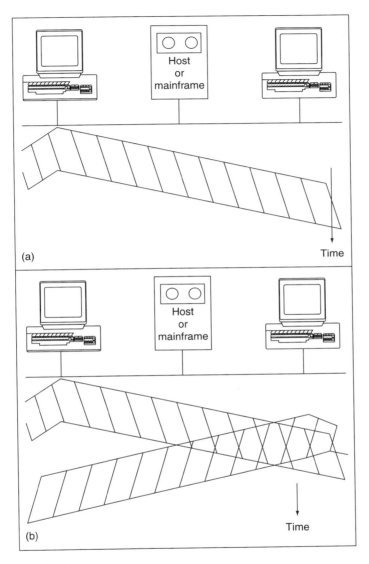

FIGURE 4.2

Carrier sense multiple access with collision detection (CSMA/CD). (a) "A" listens for activity (a signal) on the bus (carrier sense). Hearing no signal, "A" transmits a frame. "B" and "C" receive the frame. (b) "A" listens for signals (activity) on the bus. Hearing none, "A" transmits a frame. A short time later, "C" listens for activity on the bus. Hearing none, "C" transmits a frame. "A", "B", and "C" all detect the two frames in collision (collision detection) and do not read the corrupted frame. "A" and "C" stop transmitting after the frames have reached the coax end.

Both Node A and Node C wait a random time to re-transmit. The times each node must wait before a re-transmission are determined by a random number generator. Thus the wait times are random, virtually guaranteeing them to be different. If the wait times were nearly the same, both nodes would re-transmit at nearly identical times, and the system would be in constant frame collision. Data throughput would plummet to zero.

Frames in collision are detected in two ways. One method is sensing excessive bus current, and the other is the error control system detecting an error via the Frame Check Sequence (FRC) field at the end of the frame. FRC, also called CRC, is discussed in Appendix A1.

4.2.2 10Base5

10Base5 was the first Ethernet system and uses 10-mm diameter coax. Ethernet was developed by Xerox, Intel, and Digital Equipment Corporation (DEC), and became IEEE standard 802.3 in 1985.

To attach a node to a 10Base5 LAN one cuts the coax, adds a special connector into the open coax, and inserts a transceiver or **Media Access Unit (MAU).** This is not the MAU (Multiple Access Unit) of a token ring LAN. The 10Base5 MAU uses a "vampire tap" to couple the energy from the coax center conductor to the transceiver. This works somewhat like an antenna (see Figure 4.3). The MAU connects via copper wire cable to the Network Interface Card (NIC) on the computer or peripheral. Other types of vampire taps penetrate the coax shield, avoiding cutting the coax and attaching expensive connectors. A **NIC** is a circuit card in the computer or peripheral attaching (interfacing) the computer or peripheral to the LAN.

The maximum length of a 10Base5 segment without repeaters is 500 meters, hence the "5." With repeaters the maximum length is five segments, or 2.5 km. The length limitation is due to the propagation time needed for a frame from one end to reach the other. This propagation time is about 13 microseconds, and the frame must be less than this propagation time. The "10" means a 10-Mbps bit rate.

4.2.3 10Base2

10Base2 uses 7-mm diameter coax rather than the 10-mm diameter coax of 10Base5, and this has several advantages. The 7-mm coax is less expensive and more flexible than 10Base5's 10-mm coax, making installation cheaper and easier. 10Base2 is colloquially called "cheapernet" or "thinnet." For 10Base2 the maximum segment length without repeaters is 185 meters or approximately 200 meters, hence the "2." The "10" signifies a 10-Mbps bit rate. 10Base2 can handle only 30 nodes on one segment versus 100 nodes on one segment for 10Base5.

The coax is attached to the Network Interface Card (NIC) by a BNC "tee" or "T" connector, a much cheaper method than the "vampire tap" of 10Base5. BNC is a type of coaxial connector, and no one is certain of the origin of the acronym "BNC."

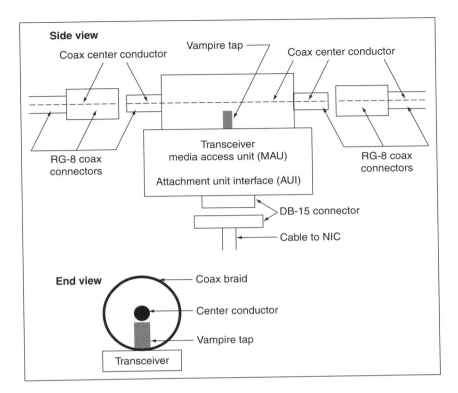

FIGURE 4.3
10Base5 vampire tap.

4.2.4 10BaseT

10BaseT uses #24 AWG (American Wire Gauge) Unshielded Twisted Pair (UTP), which is cheaper and easier to install than coax. The "T" means "twisted pair," and the "10" means a 10-Mbps bit rate. In many buildings the existing voice grade (Category 3) UTP, originally used for telephone circuits, may be used, thus saving the considerable installation costs.

The maximum segment length for 10BaseT is 100 meters, and with repeaters or hubs the total maximum length is 500 meters. The TP is connected to the hub and the NIC by an RJ-45 telephone connector, which has proved more reliable than coax Ethernets.

The topology of 10BaseT is a **bus,** with all nodes connected to a hub (Figure 4.4). This hub-centered design is sometimes incorrectly called a star topology. A hub can be placed in a telephone "wiring closet," where a building's telephone lines converge. This could simplify 10BaseT installation by using the existing TP that had been used for telephones. The hub receives the signal from a node and re-transmits it to all the other nodes; hence the hub is also called a *multiport repeater*. The hub continually sends out test signals checking to see if the node is functioning properly.

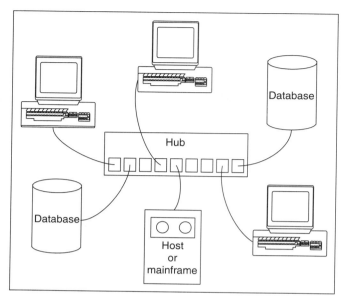

FIGURE 4.4
10BaseT topology.

The hub is the critical element in a 10BaseT LAN. If the hub fails, the entire net goes down. A single point of failure is not necessarily a bad thing. Electronics systems have become quite reliable, and if the entire network fails, the technician usually has to test only one item (the hub) in the network. If a single node fails, the technician will check that node and the cabling between the failed node and the hub. In the past it was considered a bad thing to have one point of failure (the hub). However troubleshooting 10BaseT systems is easier because the technician knows where to start looking for the problem.

4.2.5 Ethernet versus IEEE 802.3 Frames

The **IEEE** is the standards body for LANs. The standard was first begun in February (2nd month) 19(80); hence we have 802.X standards. Ethernet was developed before the 802.3 standard.

Ethernet and 802.3 frames are slightly different (see Figure 4.5). The preamble for 802.3 is divided into the seven-byte preamble and the one-byte SFD (Start Frame Delimiter). If the preamble and the SFD are added together, they are identical to the eight-byte Ethernet preamble. The Ethernet type field, sometimes called the Ethertype, specifies the higher level (level 3 and above) protocol used in the data field. Some Ethertypes are $0080 (TCP/IP) and $0600 (XNS, Xerox Network System). The 802.3 networks have been deployed for a considerable time, and this is what one will most likely encounter. The frame differences will only be a factor when an older Ethernet system needs expansion.

Both frame types have Source and Destination Addresses, each six bytes long. The data field's length ranges from 46 bytes to 1,500 bytes. If the data is less than 46 bytes,

Ethernet Frame					
8 bytes	6 bytes	6 bytes	2	min = 46 max = 1500	4
Preamble	Destination	Source	Type	Data/Pad	FCS

802.3 Frame						
7	1	6	6	2	min = 46 max = 1500	4
Preamble	SFD	Dest	Source	Length	Data/Pad	FCS

FIGURE 4.5
Ethernet frame versus 802.3 frame. These are the bit streams formatted by the DLL and sent over the physical layer. Ethernet preamble = "1010 . . . 101011." 802.3 preamble = "1010 . . . 1010." SFD 5 start frame delimiter = "10101011."

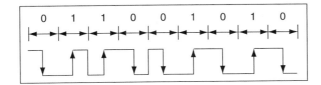

FIGURE 4.6
Manchester encoding in 802.3 and Ethernet. Transition in every bit used for synchronization. "0" = negative-going transition, "1" = positive-going transition.

padding bits are used to bring the field length to 46 bytes. At the end of the frame is the Frame Check Sequence (FRC), used for error detection. This is a Cyclic Redundancy Check 32 bits long (CRC32).

4.2.6 Manchester Encoding

Manchester encoding is used in all 10BaseX IEEE 802.3 Ethernet systems. See Figure 4.6. There is a high-to-low or low-to-high transition in the middle of every bit time at a 10-megabit rate. These regular transitions make it very easy for the receiver clock to synchronize to the bit stream. The disadvantage is that some bits have two transitions in every bit time, doubling the bandwidth required to a 20-megabit rate, but this is not a significant limitation on coax or TP medium. Two transitions per bit are needed when two consecutive 1's or 0's are transmitted. This is a case where the baud rate is twice the data rate. Many systems try to get the data rate greater than the baud rate to conserve radio spectrum space, but with wired LANs the signal is kept within the coax or TP and does not interfere with other users. Thus we can have this apparent "waste" of spectrum space.

When a logic "0" is sent, there is a negative transition, and when a logic "1" is sent, there is a positive transition.

4.3 Token Ring Network (TRN)

A **Token Ring** LAN's topology is a ring as shown in Figure 4.7. A token is passed from one node to another. A *token* is a unique bit pattern passed from one node to its next downstream neighbor node. Whichever node has the token may modify it by adding Source and Destination Addresses, and data and control information. When data is put into the token the token becomes a **frame.**

The frame is passed around the ring until it reaches the destination node. The destination node copies the data, sets the A (Address noted) bit and C (Copied successful) bit. The frame passes back to the sending node, which generates a new token.

Two Token Ring LANs are Token Ring Network (TRN) from IBM and Fiber Distributed Data Interface (FDDI). TRN uses one ring, but FDDI has two counter-rotating rings. The data in FDDI travels in opposite directions. FDDI has many similarities to TRN. In both TRN and FDDI delays between data transmission and data reception can be accurately determined, making these deterministic systems. This is particularly useful for process control (control systems).

Token Ring Network was developed by IBM in the early 1980s. The original data rate was 4 Mbps, but in 1988 IBM announced a 16-Mbps rate. The maximum distance is 300 meters between devices using coax, and with a maximum of 260 devices. If Unshielded Twisted Pair (UTP) is used, only 72 devices at a maximum distance of 100 meters are possible.

4.3.1 Multistation Access Unit (MAU)

A Token Ring Network (TRN) is logically connected in a ring; however, all the nodes are connected to a **Multistation Access Unit (MAU)** or concentrator so that the connection looks like a star as per Figure 4.8.

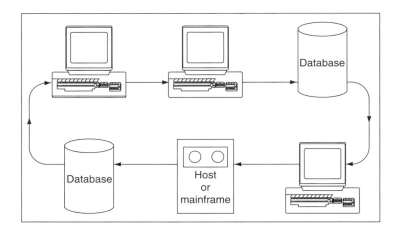

FIGURE 4.7
Token ring logical topology.

TRN is called a star wired ring. This TRN MAU is not the MAU (Media Access Unit) of 10Base5 Ethernet systems (see Figure 4.9).

The Token Ring MAU is a passive device, having no amplifiers, only relays. Each working node sends a +5 volts control signal to the MAU. The +5 volts control signal closes a relay and connects that working node into the ring. If a node is not functioning, it will not send the +5 volts control signal to the MAU, the relay will not be energized, and the node will be disconnected from the ring. MAUs are usually designed for eight nodes but can be expanded through the Ring In (RI) and Ring Out (RO) connectors.

4.3.2 Basic TRN Operation

When the TRN is first turned on, it must determine which node is the "boss" or Active Monitor for all nodes. The Active Monitor is usually the node with the highest address. The Active Monitor provides synchronization. After an Active Monitor is selected, it will purge the ring of all tokens or frames, generate a new token, and monitor ring activity at least every 10 milliseconds. If no activity is detected, the Active Monitor generates a new token, making the system "fail-safe."

An analogy is a freight train on a circular track with a sign on the engine signifying whether the train is carrying freight (data) and a coal tender stating the names of the destination and sending stations. If the train is carrying freight (data), it is a frame. If the train does not have any freight (data), it is a token. If the train is carrying freight (data), the addressed station will unload the freight as the train is passing through. The addressed station

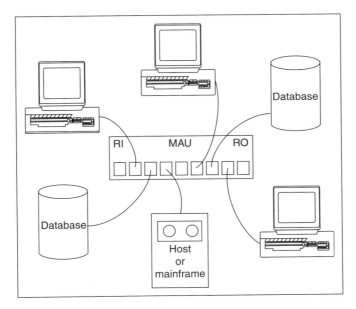

FIGURE 4.8
TRN physical topology.

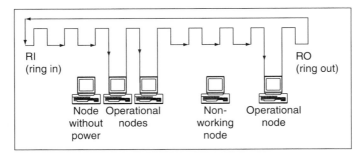

FIGURE 4.9
Multistation access unit (MAU) for token ring, connected as a star wired ring. The operational nodes send +5 volts to the MAU, opening a relay and connecting that working node into the token ring network (TRN).

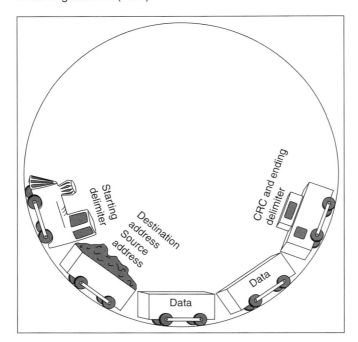

FIGURE 4.10
Token ring.

will put a flag on the engine telling the sending station that the freight was delivered. The CRC or FRC error detection field can be considered the train's caboose. See Figure 4.10.

4.3.3 Differential Manchester

Differential Manchester encoding, shown in Figure 4.11, has at least one transition in every bit for easy receiver synchronization. *Differential* means the transition direction (0 to 1, or 1 to 0) depends on the previous state.

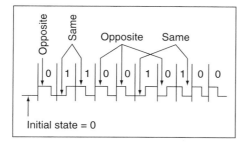

FIGURE 4.11
Differential Manchester encoding for TRN. Requires at least one transition in each bit for synchronization. Next bit level depends on previous bit level: "1" starts same as previous bit ended, "0" starts opposite from previous bit ending.

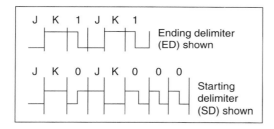

FIGURE 4.12
Differential Manchester violations. Violations used for special signaling (called "J" and "K" bits), no mid-bit transitions, and same level for entire bit length. "J" starts at same level as previous bit, "K" starts at opposite level from previous bit.

In a bit time, a logic "1" starts at the same level as the previous bit ends. A logic "0" starts the bit time in an opposite state than the previous bit. Note that a logic "1" or "0" does not have a fixed state like logic circuitry or RS-232, nor a certain direction transition as in Manchester encoding. In Figure 4.11 note that the initial level is low. The first "0" forces the level to change to high. There is a transition in the middle of this "0" bit (transition in every bit time). Next is a "1" with no transition at the bit start, but a low-to-high transition at the middle of the bit time. The next "1" also has no transition at the bit start, but a high-to-low transition in the middle of the bit time. The next "0" has a transition at the bit start and opposite transition at the middle of the bit time.

TRN uses violations or exceptions in the differential Manchester encoding for signaling in the Starting Delimiter (SD) and Ending Delimiter (ED) as shown in Figure 4.12. These signaling bits are designated "J" and "K" and do not have mid-bit transitions; hence they are "violations." A "J" starts at the same level as the previous bit. A "K" starts at the opposite level as the previous bit.

FIGURE 4.13

Token format. SD = starting delimiter, AC = access control (T bit–"0" for token, "1" for frame), ED = Ending delimiter (E–error bit is set if any node detects an error, I–intermediate frame means more frames are coming).

SD	AC	ED
JK0JK000	PPPTMRRR	JK1JK1 I E

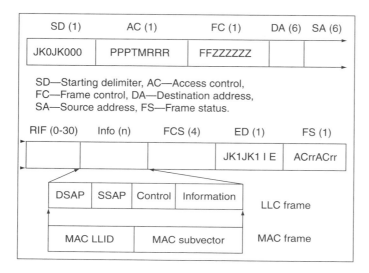

SD—Starting delimiter, AC—Access control,
FC—Frame control, DA—Destination address,
SA—Source address, FS—Frame status.

FIGURE 4.14

TRN frame format. FC = frame control, DA = destination address, SA = source address, FS = frame status, RIF = routing information field, FCS = frame check sequence, A = address recognized, C = frame copied, R = reserved bits, DSAP = destination service access point, SSAP = source service access point, LLID = MAC length ID.

4.3.4 TRN Token and Frame Format

A token, shown in Figure 4.13, has only the SD, AC, and ED fields. There is no need for address fields since no data is being sent. Remember that tokens do not carry data, but frames carry data. The Starting Delimiter (SD) "JK0JK000" field synchronizes and alerts the downstream node that a token or frame is arriving. The AC field is a control field and will be discussed shortly. The Ending Delimiter (ED) "JK1JKIE" field denotes the end of the token. If the "E" bit in the ED is set, it means that a node has discovered an error, and if the "I" bit is set, it means there are more frames coming.

A frame format is shown in Figure 4.14 and is described in Table 4.2. The Access Control (AC) field has three "P" priority bits, a "T" bit (which is "1" for a frame and "0" for a token), and three reservation bits for a node to reserve use of a token to send data. It is possible for a frame or token to keep circulating forever in the ring, and the "M" bit prevents this from happening.

TABLE 4.2
TRN Format

1. Starting Delimiter (SD)   "JK0JK000"
2. Access Control (AC)   "PPPTMRRR"
   Priority P—three bits, 0 to 7 encoded priority
   Token T Bit—"1" for frames, "0" for tokens
   Monitor M bit—used to detect persistently circulating frames
   Reservation bits—to reserve use of a token
3. Frame Control (FC)   "FFZZZZZZ"
   If "FF" is "01," it is an LLC frame
   If "FF" is "00," it is a MAC frame
   "Z"s are coding various types of MAC frames
4. Destination Address (DA)
5. Source Address (SA)
6. Routing Information Field (RIF)—* used when interconnecting LANs with routers and bridges
7. Info
8. Frame Check Sequence (FCS) or CRC
9. Ending Delimiter (ED)—* includes E bit, a node detected an error in reading the frame
10. Frame Status
    Copy (C) bit—receiving node successfully copied frame
    Address Recognized (A) bit—node recognizes that the frame was meant for itself

In LANs the DLL (Data Link Layer) is subdivided into two parts: the **Medium Access Control (MAC)** and the **Logical Link Control (LLC)** sublayers. TRN frames are one of two types: MAC frames for housekeeping and control, or LLC frames to send data. The Frame Control (FC) field "FFZZZZZZ" tells the frame type. If "FF" is "0 1," the frame is an LLC type. If "FF" is a "0 0," the frame is a MAC type. The "ZZZZZZ" encodes various types of MAC frames.

The Destination Address (DA) and Source Address (SA) fields are each six bytes. The Routing Information Field (RIF) is used when interconnecting LANs with routers and bridges, and is from zero to thirty bytes long.

The Information Field contents will vary depending on whether the frame is an LLC or MAC. If it is a MAC frame, the first subfield is the MAC LLID (MAC Length Identification), and the second subfield is the MAC subvector. If the frame is an LLC, the first field is the Destination Service Access Point (DSAP), and the second field is the Source Service Access Point (SSAP). Next is the control subfield and finally the information. The Service Access Points (SAPs) are the addresses in level 3 that the data is sent from or sent to.

The Frame Check Sequence (FCS) field is a 32-bit Cyclic Redundancy Check (CRC32) for error control.

The Ending Delimiter (ED) field tells the receiving node that the FS field is the only field left to be received. The ED, like the SD, has "J" and "K" control characters. The SD's zeros are replaced with ones in the ED. The ED has an "E" bit indicating when a node has detected an error and an "I" bit telling the receiver that more frames will follow.

The Frame Status (FS) field has the "A" and "C" bits. The "A" bit is set by the receiving node telling that it has recognized that frame was meant for itself. The "C" bit is set by the receiving node telling that it has successfully copied the frame.

4.3.5 TRN Operation

Referring to Figure 4.15 Node 30 has been designated the Active Monitor because it has the highest address. Node 30 generates a token and passes it to Node 10. The "T" bit is not set, indicating a token. Node 10 has no data to transmit but examines the token for errors. Node 10 finds no errors, regenerates the token, and sends it to Node 20.

Node 20 has data to send, so it seizes the token and sets the "T" bit, changing the token to a frame. Node 20 wants to send the data to Node 10 and thus sets the DA (Destination Address) to 10, the SA (Source Address) to 20, and resets the "A" and "C" bits.

The frame goes next to Node 30. Node 30 notes that the frame is not addressed to itself and does not read the data. However Node 30 examines the frame for errors. Finding no errors, Node 30 sends the frame to Node 10.

Node 10 notes that the frame is addressed to itself and therefore sets the "A" bit and checks for errors. Node 10 finds no errors and thus copies the data. Node 10 sets the "C" copy bit and sends the frame to Node 20.

Node 20 examines "A" and "C" bits and notes that they are set, meaning that Node 10 has recognized the address and successfully copied the data. The frame has served its

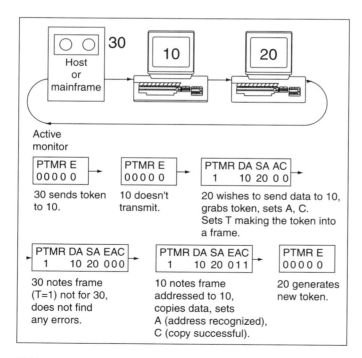

FIGURE 4.15
TRN operation.

purpose, so Node 20 generates a new token. The new or "fresh" token will now be available for any node to seize, create a frame, and transmit data within that frame.

4.3.6 TRN Operation with an Error

Let us examine the procedure when an error occurs as in Figure 4.16. As before, Node 20 has data to send, so it grabs the token and sets the "T" bit, changing the token to a frame. The "A" and "C" bits are reset. Node 20 adds the DA, SA, and data, and sends the frame to Node 30.

An error occurs between Node 20 and Node 30. Node 30 detects the error, sets the "E" bit, and sends the frame to Node 10.

Node 10 notes that the frame is addressed to itself and therefore sets the "A" bit. Since Node 10 also notes the "E" bit is set, it does not copy the frame but resets "C" and transmits the frame back to Node 20.

Node 20 sees that Node 10 has not copied the frame ("C" = 0), even though Node 10 was aware that the frame was addressed to itself ("A" = 1). Node 20 re-transmits the frame, clearing the "E" and "A" bits. The frame passes through Node 30 and finally to Node 10.

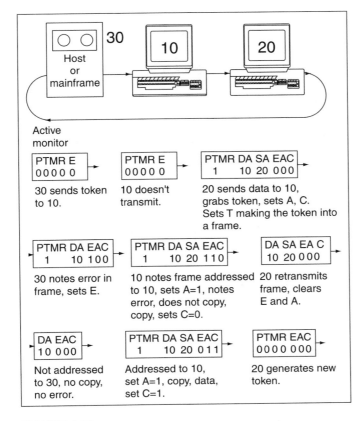

FIGURE 4.16
TRN operation with an error.

4.3.7 TRN Operation with a Reservation

In Figure 4.17 Node 30 wishes to reserve a frame for future data transmission and sets the R (reserve) bits to 2. Node 10 receives the token and sets the P (priority) bits to 2 to prevent lower priority nodes from using the token. Node 20 cannot use the token because Node 20 has a lower priority. The token comes back to Node 30, which grabs the token and puts data onto it, making the token a frame. Node 10 sees that the frame is addressed to itself and sets the A (address recognized) bit, reads the data, and sets the C (copied) bit. Node 20 sends the frame unchanged, and Node 10 resets the P (priority) bits and generates a new token.

4.4 Token Bus

Token Bus is specified in IEEE 802.4 and has three major manufacturers: General Motors with MAP, Datapoint Corporation with ARCnet, and Thomas-Conrad with TCNS. General Motors created Manufacturing Automation Protocol (MAP) as a standard for the factory floor.

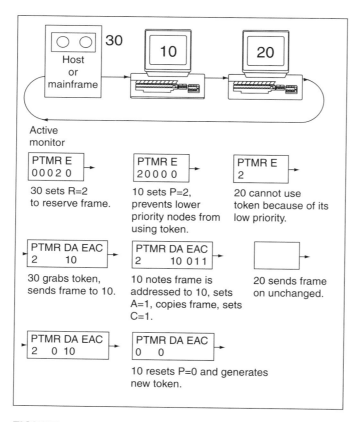

FIGURE 4.17
TRN operation with a reservation.

Datapoint Corporation of San Antonio, Texas, created Attached Resource Computer network (ARCnet) in 1977. Datapoint tried to maintain exclusive control of ARCnet by keeping it a closed standard and thus reap maximum financial return. ARCnet is installed in about 6 million computers worldwide. That is a large base, but if Datapoint had made ARCnet an open standard, they would have benefited much more. ARCnet would be a major LAN architecture today instead of merely a footnote. Nevertheless the telecommunications engineer should be knowledgeable about Token Bus because of the many systems installed.

Thomas-Conrad of San Antonio, Texas, has created TCNS (Thomas Conrad Network System), a 100-Mbps Token Bus system. However Thomas-Conrad has elected not to publicize the specifications, and keeps TCNS a closed standard. The company claims to have sold as many NICs and hubs as there are FDDI equivalents.

4.4.1 ARCnet

The upside of Datapoint's ARCnet is its low cost, and forgiving and flexible cabling system. Segment lengths range from 300 feet to 2,000 feet; with repeaters the total length can reach 20,000 feet, almost 5 miles! The downside of ARCnet is its paltry 2.5-Mbps data rate, one-quarter that of Ethernet and one-half to one-seventh that of Token Ring. ARCnet is not recommended for new installations but only for small existing ones.

The ARCnet topology is either a bus or a star with either active (with amplifiers) or passive hubs. The passive hubs merely extend the network and do not have any amplification. The active hubs amplify and split the signals. ARCnet supports Unshielded Twisted Pair (UTP), coax (RG-62 with 93 ohms characteristic impedance), or optical fiber.

4.4.1.1 Token Passing   The NIC (Network Interface Card) address is not written into a ROM but set by dip switches on the NIC or by software. The addresses determine the token passing order. The token is passed from a high address to the next lowest address. The NIC with the lowest address passes the token back to the highest address. This is called "rollover." Figure 4.18 shows the logical passing of the token on the bus. The token starts at

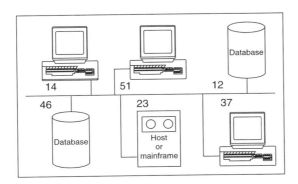

FIGURE 4.18
Token passing. The token is passed from Node 51 to 46 to 37 to 23 to 14 to 12, and rolls over to Node 51.

address 51; continues in turn to addresses 46, 37, 23, 14, and 12; and then rolls back to 51. The token passing is by address and not by location as in Token Ring.

4.5 High-Speed LANs

There are three 100-Mbps LANs: 100BaseT ("fast Ethernet"), 100BaseVG ("AnyLAN"), and Fiber Distributed Data Interface (FDDI). These are summarized in Table 4.3. There are two 1.0-gbps (10^9 bps) LANs: Fibre Channel and Gigabit Ethernet. Only FDDI was very mature in the late 1990's, but its high cost has slowed its acceptance.

4.5.1 100BaseT

The 100BaseT or "fast Ethernet" transmits at 100-Mbps (100 megabits per second, or 10^8 bits per second). It can operate with Category 3, 4, or 5 Unshielded Twisted Pair (UTP) or optical fiber. It is compatible with 10BaseT. 100BaseT uses the existing MAC layer of 10BaseT, meaning it is also a CSMA/CD system. Like 10BaseT it has a bus topology with a maximum segment length of 205 meters.

Like all Ethernet systems, the delays are not constant, so this is a probabilistic system. *Probabilistic* means that probability theory must be used to compute a range of delays, and the delays cannot be determined precisely. 100BaseT is the least costly of the three 100-Mbps LANs.

4.5.2 100BaseVG or "AnyLAN"

The 100BaseVG or "AnyLAN" was developed and is supported by Hewlett-Packard (the "VG" stands for "voice grade."). Not many other vendors have jumped onto this HP bandwagon as of 1999. 100BaseVG supports Category 3, 4, or 5 TP, and optical fiber. 100BaseVG is more expensive than 100BaseT. The "AnyLAN" means that this LAN will support Token Ring tokens and frames, or Ethernet frames.

TABLE 4.3

High-Speed LAN Comparison

Parameter	FDDI	100BaseT	100BaseVG
Data rate	100 Mbps	100 Mbps	100 Mbps
Max segment length		205 m	
Total network length	100 Km		
Max nodes	500		
Max node spacing	2 Km		
Physical medium	Optical fiber	UTP or fiber	UTP or fiber
Coax impedance	NA	NA	NA
IEEE spec	None	TBD	TBD
Topology	Dual ring	Bus, or star	Star
Signaling	NRZI-4B5B	Manchester	
Collision detection	NA, uses tokens	Excess current	NA

This is a *deterministic* (with predictable, determined precisely, constant delays) LAN suitable for voice, video, and control systems data.

4.5.3 Fiber Distributed Data Interface (FDDI)

Figure 4.19 shows the dual ring topology of FDDI. **FDDI** uses a token system allowing many frames to exist simultaneously on the ring. This differs from Token Ring Networks (TRN), which can have only one token on the ring. Also TRN has one Active Monitor. In FDDI control is distributed around the ring, and all nodes have maintenance responsibility.

FDDI can handle synchronous traffic (such as voice and video), control information, and asynchronous traffic (such as data). The synchronous traffic requires guaranteed bandwidth and delay times; delay must be minimal and uniform. Asynchronous is delay-insensitive, allowing variable delays.

FDDI's dual rings allow "self-healing" of faults. Figure 4.20 shows broken cables in the rings. The two nodes nearest the break detect the fault and re-route the token as shown.

FDDI is a standard developed by ANSI (American National Standards Institute). Copper based (TP and coax) standards (CDDI) are being developed, which should help FDDI's acceptance. Thus far FDDI has failed to gain great acceptance because of its high cost.

4.5.3.1 4B/5B Encoding The 4B/5B encoding uses five bits or five light pulses to encode four bits. If too many consecutive zeros are sent over the optical fiber, the receiver may lose synchronization. The 4B/5B coding shown in Table 4.4 illustrates all sixteen possible combinations of four bits being mapped to a five-bit code. Also eight control characters are included in the five-bit code, meaning twenty-four combinations are used out of a possible thirty-two. Each five-bit code has at least two ones. Note that the five-bit code has no more than five consecutive zeros in any two five-bit combinations. The only exception is "quiet," which does not transmit at all. The "idle" state is repetitive pulses.

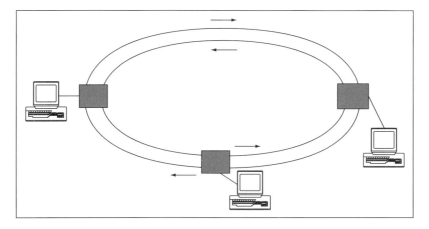

FIGURE 4.19
Fiber distributed data interface (FDDI) topology.

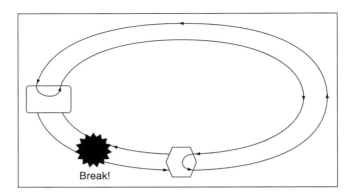

FIGURE 4.20
Break in FDDI is "self-healing."

TABLE 4.4
4B/5B Encoding

Data Bits		Encoded Bits		
Hex	Binary	Light Pulses Sent	Control Symbols	
$0	0000	11110	Halt	00100
$1	0001	01001	Idle	11111
$2	0010	10100	Non-data J	11000
$3	0011	10101	Non-data K	10001
$4	0100	01010	Quiet	00000
$5	0101	01011	Reset	00111
$6	0110	01110	Set	11001
$7	0111	01111	Terminate	01101
$8	1000	10010		
$9	1001	10011		
$A	1010	10110		
$B	1011	10111		
$C	1100	11010		
$D	1101	11011		
$E	1110	11100		
$F	1111	11101		

Why use five bits to send four bits? The fiber optic emitters are either *on* or *off*. If too many consecutive zeros (emitter off) occur, the receiver could lose synchronization. Note that a maximum of three consecutive zeros occur in the encoded bits, even when two 5B encodings are put together.

Note also that the Idle state is consecutive 1's, and the Quiet state is no emission or all 0's.

This apparent "waste" of bandwidth is not a problem because bandwidth is *cheap!*

PA	SD	FC	DA	SA	info	FCS	ED	FS
I symbols	JK	C L FF ZZZZ						

FIGURE 4.21
FDDI frame format.

Why is this apparent "waste" of bandwidth allowed? The problem is synchronization, not bandwidth. High data rates on optical fiber are easily achieved. Bandwidth is cheap on optical fiber. Synchronization is not a trivial problem when an optical pulse can be less than 3 ns (nanoseconds).

4.5.3.2 FDDI Frame The FDDI frame format shown in Figure 4.21 is similar to the format of TRN. The PA (Preamble) field consists of sixteen I(idle) pulses. The SD (Starting Delimiter) field is a "J" and "K" character. The FC (Frame Control) field has eight bits. The first bit indicates the class of service: synchronous (delay-sensitive, for instance, real-time voice or video) or asynchronous (delay-insensitive, for instance, data). The L (Length) bit indicates two- or six-byte address fields. Usually the address fields are six bytes long. The FF and ZZZZ bits indicate tokens, and LLC, MAC, or SMT frames. SMT frames are housekeeping frames.

The FCS (Frame Check Sequence) is used for error control. The ED frame has one "T" for frames and two "T"s for tokens. In the Frame Status (FS) field the "E" bit indicates an error detected, the "A" bit means a node has recognized a frame addressed to itself, and the "C" bit confirms that the addressed node has successfully copied the frame.

4.5.4 Very High-Speed LANs

A new kid on the block is Fibre Channel with data rates from 133 Mbps to 4.25 gbps. In 1999 Fibre Channel was used only for backbone applications because of its high price tag.

In 1999 gigabit Ethernet is being sold for very competitive prices, making it the lowest priced very high-speed LAN. It is likely the low price will make gigabit Ethernet the most popular 1-gbps LAN.

4.6 IEEE 802.2 versus ISO RM

It is helpful to compare the IEEE 802.2 specification to the ISO Reference Model's (RM) Data Link Level (DLL).

The left side of Figure 4.22 shows the ISO Data Link Level (DLL) and the physical level. The control field format generated by the Logical Link Control (LLC) is similar to HDLC's control field. SDLC, used in SNA, and LAP/B, used in X.25, are quite similar. If one understands one format, understanding the other is not difficult. These are discussed in other chapters.

The right side of Figure 4.22 shows how the 802.X DLL is subdivided into two parts: the LLC (Logical Link Control) and the MAC (Medium Access Control). The MAC layer

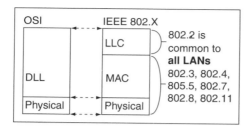

FIGURE 4.22
IEEE 802.2 vs. ISO RM. The ISO DLL frame protocol is HDLC. MAC = medium access control, LLC = logical link control, HDLC = high-level data link control, and DLL = data link level.

TABLE 4.5
IEEE 802.X Standards

802.1 Network Control and Management—common to all LANs
802.2 Logical Link Control—common to all LANs
802.3 Ethernet
802.4 Token Bus
802.5 Token Ring
802.6 SMDS/DQDB
802.8 optical fiber

has the physical address of the Network Interface Card (NIC) in the node. This has nothing to do with the MacIntosh (**MAC**) computer. When asked, "What is your MAC address?" some users will say plaintively, "But I don't have a MAC, I have a PC!"

The LLC is specified by IEEE 802.2 and is common to all LAN types. The MAC and Physical Layer are specified by various IEEE 802 specifications, each unique to the particular LAN type. Figure 4.23 also shows the relevant IEEE 802.X standards. The types are summarized in Table 4.5.

The LLC in layer 2, specified by IEEE 802.2, is common to all types of LANs. Also layers 1 and 2 specifications describe the various types of MAC associated with a particular type of LAN: 802.3 with Ethernet (CSMA/CD), 802.4 with Token Bus (ARCnet), 802.5 with Token Ring, 802.6 with SMDS, and 802.8 with optical fiber LANs. The NIC address is encoded at the Medium Access Control (MAC) sublayer of the DLL. The address is occasionally two bytes long, but usually six bytes long.

The first three bytes are unique to each Ethernet manufacturer and are assigned by the IEEE. The last three bytes are administered by each manufacturer and are usually unique to each NIC manufactured. The address is written (burned) into a **ROM** (Read Only Memory) on the NIC. If the NIC fails and the user wishes to keep the same address in the LAN, the ROM from the old NIC must be physically moved to the new NIC.

Figure 4.23 breaks out the LLC portion of the frame. The LLC is specified by IEEE 802.2 and is the same for all LANs. There are three types of frames: information, supervisory, and unnumbered. The Ns field tells the frame number sent, and Nr gives the frame

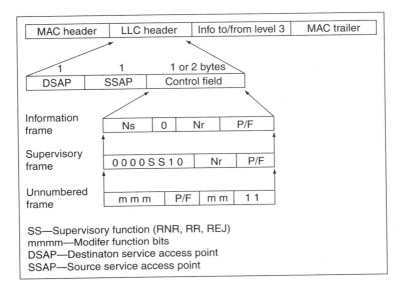

FIGURE 4.23
Logical level control (LLC) frame. SS = supervisory function (RNR, RR, REJ), mmmm = modifier function bits, DSAP = destination service access point, and SSAP = source service access point.

number received, and each Nx field is three bits. The Poll/Final (P/F) bit has a dual use. It is used to ask a question of another node (Poll), or it is used to inform the receiving node that the frame is the last or final frame (Final).

The supervisory frames are of three types: RR (Receiver Ready), RNR (Receiver Not Ready), and REJ (REJect). The RR is similar to the ACKnowledge (frame received correctly), and the RNR is used for flow control. The RNR is used by the receiver to tell the transmitter to slow down because the receiver cannot handle any more data. This might happen if the receiver's data buffers were full. The REJ (REJect) is sent when the receiving node finds something wrong with the frame, such as a wrong format or an error detected by the CRC (FRC).

The Service Access Point (SAP) selects the program or protocol in level 3 and may be considered an address. The SAP is the same for all types of LANs and is defined in IEEE 802.1. The SSAP is the level 3 Source Address, and the DSAP is the level 3 Destination Address.

4.7 Troubleshooting

A good LAN troubleshooting guide is *Pocket Guide to Network Troubleshooting* by Scope Communications of Marlbough, Massachusetts. Their suggestions for troubleshooting are below and use their FrameScope™ portable LAN data analyzer. (The methods will also work using other vendor's analyzers.)

1. Know your network. Benchmark your network in normal operation so that you know what to expect in terms of what protocols are used, what stations generate and receive the most traffic, and what stations have the highest errors. Use the statistics collection option of the FrameScope™ protocol analyzer.

2. When a problem appears, ask yourself these questions:
   a. Who is affected? Is one station affected or many stations?
   b. Is this the first time the problem has appeared, or is it a recurring problem?
   c. What path does the communications (packet or frame) take? Are there possible weak links, such as a bridge, router, long length of cable?
   d. Have there been any hardware or software changes on either the sending or receiving stations, or any on the routers, switches, or bridges?
   e. Can the problem be duplicated?
3. Check the error rates, and localize the problem.
4. Make an educated guess (hypothesis) as to the fault, and develop a test strategy. A sample hypothesis is shown below.

Jack complains to Jill that he is getting slow response from a server. Several possible causes are:

- A server without sufficient capacity
- A misconfigured server
- A router without sufficient capacity
- A misconfigured router
- High network traffic
- High traffic through a router
- Excessive re-transmission
- Excessive broadcasts
- Other error conditions

Jill should check for traffic levels and find any stations generating or receiving a lot of traffic. If there is such a station, find out why the traffic is excessive. If the traffic is normal and the server is not receiving an excess number of requests, the server or the router may be inadequate or misconfigured. Jill will compare the router and server traffic with data she took earlier when the network was functioning properly.

5. If the fault isn't resolved, repeat step 4 with a new hypothesis.
6. Resolve the problem, and test the solution.

Sometimes the problem is in the medium (cabling, twisted pair, optical fiber, etc.). Below are more of Scope's suggestions for Token Ring and Ethernet.

4.7.1 TRN Troubleshooting

1. Check the statistics to find out the error type. Figure 4.24a shows FrameScope™ displays of network statistics. Check overall error types and the station(s) reporting them. The station reporting the error is not necessarily the problem cause. The problem may be in the transmitting node, the upstream station, or the cabling.

2. Isolate the fault domain if possible. Check each station beginning with the station reporting the highest number of errors and working down the ring in order of connection (ring order). Repeating, the problem may be in the cabling or an upstream node.

3. FrameScope™ has the capability to disconnect a node by the REMOVE NODE command. Use this to disconnect the error reporting station, and see if the error has disappeared. If the error persists, repeat the process with the next upstream node.

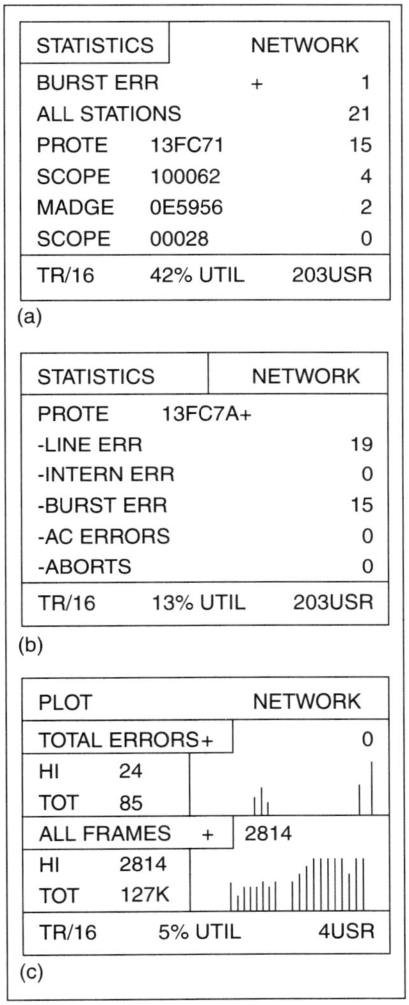

```
┌─────────────────────────────────────┐
│  ┌──────────────┬────────────────┐  │
│  │ STATISTICS   │    NETWORK     │  │
│  ├──────────────┴────────────────┤  │
│  │ BURST ERR      +         1    │  │
│  │ ALL STATIONS            21    │  │
│  │ PROTE    13FC71         15    │  │
│  │ SCOPE    100062          4    │  │
│  │ MADGE    0E5956          2    │  │
│  │ SCOPE    00028           0    │  │
│  ├───────────────────────────────┤  │
│  │ TR/16    42% UTIL    203USR   │  │
│  └───────────────────────────────┘  │
└─────────────────────────────────────┘
```
(a)

```
┌─────────────────────────────────────┐
│  ┌──────────────┬────────────────┐  │
│  │ STATISTICS   │    NETWORK     │  │
│  ├──────────────┴────────────────┤  │
│  │ PROTE      13FC7A+            │  │
│  │ -LINE ERR               19   │  │
│  │ -INTERN ERR              0   │  │
│  │ -BURST ERR              15   │  │
│  │ -AC ERRORS               0   │  │
│  │ -ABORTS                  0   │  │
│  ├──────────────────────────────┤  │
│  │ TR/16    13% UTIL    203USR  │  │
│  └──────────────────────────────┘  │
└─────────────────────────────────────┘
```
(b)

```
┌─────────────────────────────────────┐
│  ┌──────────────┬────────────────┐  │
│  │ PLOT         │    NETWORK     │  │
│  ├──────────────┴────────────────┤  │
│  │ TOTAL ERRORS+           0    │  │
│  │ HI     24                    │  │
│  │ TOT    85                    │  │
│  ├───────────────────────────────┤  │
│  │ ALL FRAMES    +   2814        │  │
│  │ HI    2814                   │  │
│  │ TOT   127K                   │  │
│  ├───────────────────────────────┤  │
│  │ TR/16    5% UTIL      4USR   │  │
│  └───────────────────────────────┘  │
└─────────────────────────────────────┘
```
(c)

FIGURE 4.24
Statistics displays FrameScope™. FrameScope™ can plot two statistics at a time.

4. Determine if the fault is in the cabling. FrameScope™ can act as a station (node) replacement. Use FrameScope™ in place of the offending station. If errors persist, the fault is likely to be in the cabling. If a cabling fault is suspected, run the LOBE TEST and check for error while FrameScope™ is working on the suspected cable run. If errors still occur, run SIGNAL STRENGTH to determine if the signal strength is adequate.

4.7.1.1 Non-Isolating Errors   Non-isolating errors are those that cannot be easily traced to a single station, domain, or node. These types of errors may be due to jitter buildup. FrameScope™ has a JITTER TEST that sends a series of test patterns designed to stress the clock recovery circuits of the stations. After the JITTER TEST has completed, examine the report to see if any stations have reported excess errors.

4.7.1.2 Beacon Frames Beacon frames are generated by stations that have not received any tokens or frames within a specified period of time. They indicate a breakdown between the reporting station and its upstream neighbor. FrameScope™ will signal an alarm if beacon frames are found.

4.7.2 Ethernet Troubleshooting

4.7.2.1 Link Errors Link errors are the most common problem on 10BaseT networks. A link error means there is an improper connection between the station and the concentrator. Scope suggests the following to isolate link errors: Isolate the problem by connecting the FrameScope™ to the concentrator via a known good cable, and see if the problem disappears. If the problem goes away, the problem is in the cable. If the problem persists, it is in the concentrator.

4.7.2.2 CRC Errors CRC errors occur during collisions. If CRC errors occur when there are no collisions, there are three possibilities: the concentrator, the NIC, or the cabling between the NIC and the concentrator. The FrameScope™ TRAFFIC GENERATOR (Figure 4.24c) is used to generate traffic. Use the FrameScope™ to send traffic on one network tap and receive on the other. If CRC errors continue, move the taps closer to isolate the faulty component.

4.7.2.3 Long and Short Frames Long frames are greater than 1,518 bytes. Short frames are less than 64 bytes. Use FrameScope™ STAT BY STATION command to look at a sorted list of stations reporting these errors. A likely cause is incorrect configuration of the NIC or non-standard drivers. Run a NIC diagnostic to check this.

4.7.2.4 Constant Collisions Constant collisions may be due to a missing termination resistor at either cable end. Reflections from unterminated ends can cause collisions. FrameScope's™ TRAFFIC GENERATOR will generate traffic and look at ALL FRAMES and COLLISIONS in the PERFORMANCE PLOTS tool. A missing termination will cause constant collisions and no transmitted frames.

4.7.3 Protocol Related Faults

Protocol related faults occur when stations exchange data frames but the content cannot be interpreted. Usually this is because the network drive configuration is incorrect or the software is incompatible.

4.7.3.1 Server Not Found If a station is on the network and able to successfully initialize the adapter but is unable to access the server, the station will receive the error message "Server Not Found."

On a Netware (Novell) IPX network, FrameScope™ IPX UTILITIES can be used to find the server. If the server is not listed, the problem may be with the medium or the server may not be on line. If the server is on line, there may be a configuration incompatibility.

On an IP (Internet Protocol) network, use IP UTILITIES to PING the server. If there is no response, a medium problem may exist. If the server answers with a PONG protocol, incompatibility may be the problem.

4.7.3.2 Stations Cannot Communicate

On a Netware (Novell) IPX network, FrameScope™'s IPX UTILITIES can be used to see if the station is reachable. If one cannot reach the station, the medium may be at fault. If the station is reachable, the configuration may be incorrect.

On an IP (Internet Protocol) network, use IP UTILITIES to PING and ARP the station. If one cannot reach the station, the medium may be at fault. If the station is reachable, the configuration may be incorrect.

4.7.3.3 Load Related Faults

If the network has traffic overload, the server and print server may have unacceptably slow response. Scope suggests monitoring the traffic to find the "top talkers." Find each node's contribution to the traffic. Analyze the traffic between stations. Generate traffic to the server and print server to see how many frames are received and how many are in error.

Slow Server Response Slow server response could be caused by the network load being too great, the network load being normal but too much traffic is addressed to the server, an overloaded bridge or router, a slow server, or slow NIC.

SUMMARY

I. A Local Area Network (LAN) is a network of computing resources connected together in a relatively small area such as a room, building, or campus.
II. LANs are used to share resources.
III. Cost can be reduced by sharing resources.
IV. LAN topologies.
    A. Ring.
    B. Bus.
    C. Star.
V. Ethernet.
    A. Carrier Sense Multiple Access with Collision Detection (CSMA/CD).
    B. Collisions can occur because of stations transmitting at nearly the same time.
        1. Corrupted data.
        2. Frame needs to be re-transmitted.
    C. 10Base5.
        1. First Ethernet.
        2. 10-mm coax.
    D. 10Base2.
        1. 7-mm coax.
        2. "Cheapernet" or "thinnet"; less expensive than 10Base5.

    E. 10BaseT.
      1. UTP.
      2. Hub based bus; critical element.
      3. Lowest cost LAN.
    F. Manchester encoding used on Ethernet.
      1. Easy for receiver to synchronize onto bits.
      2. Logic "0" is negative transition in middle of bit.
      3. Logic "1" is positive transition in middle of bit.
VI. Token Ring Network (TRN).
    A. Ring topology.
    B. Token is a unique bit pattern passed around the ring.
    C. When data is sent, the token is changed to a frame.
    D. Nodes connected at the top of an MAU hub, but topology is actually a ring and MAU is passive (only relays).
    E. Active Monitor.
      1. Usually highest node number.
      2. Provides synchronization.
      3. At initialization, it purges ring of all tokens, purges ring of all frames, and generates new token.
    F. Differential Manchester encoding.
      1. Transition in every bit time, making it easy for receiver to synchronize to bits.
      2. Transition direction depends on previous state.
      3. "Violations" are:
        a. Bit times without transitions.
        b. Used for signaling beginning of token/frame and end of token/frame.
VII. Frames
    A. Frames are divided into two parts.
      1. Media Access Control (MAC).
        a. Housekeeping.
        b. Control.
        c. Contains MAC address (address within the LAN).
      2. Logical Link Control (LLC).
        a. Transmit data.
        b. Contains Service Access Point (SAP); address in level 3.
VIII. Token Bus.
    A. Token is sent on a bus. Token is passed from highest address to next lower address.
IX. High-speed LANs.
    A. 100BaseT.
      1. "Fast Ethernet."
      2. CSMA/CD.
      3. 100 Mbps.
      4. Medium can be Cat 3 UTP, Cat 4 UTP, Cat 5 UTP, or optical fiber.
      5. Lowest cost 100-Mbps LAN.
    B. 100BaseVG.
      1. "AnyLAN."
        a. Supports TRN.

   b. Supports Ethernet.
   2. Medium can be Cat 3 UTP, Cat 4 UTP, Cat 5 UTP, or optical fiber.
C. Fiber Distributed Data Interface (FDDI).
   1. Medium is optical fiber; will include copper.
   2. "Self-healing" makes FDDI more reliable.
   3. Uses 4B/5B encoding for LASER pulses.
D. Gigabit Ethernet.
   1. 1 gbps bit rate.
   2. Lowest cost gigabit LAN.
X. IEEE 802.X Standards.
A. Specifies LANs.
B. Specifies MAC layer (physical); unique to each type of LAN.
C. Specifies LLC.
   1. IEEE 802.2.
   2. Same for all LAN types.
   3. Service Access Point (SAP); address in level 3.

QUESTIONS

1. Match the LAN type with the appropriate characteristics. There may be more than one correct answer. Place your answer on the line. Characteristics may be appropriate for more than one type of LAN.

   A. 10-mm coax _____   (1) TRN
   B. 7-mm coax _____   (2) 10Base5
   C. UTP _____   (3) 10Base2
   D. Optical fiber _____   (4) 10BaseT
   E. STP _____   (5) FDDI
                                 (6) Fast Ethernet
                                 (7) VG AnyLAN
                                 (8) ARCnet

2. Match the LAN type with the appropriate characteristics. There may be more than one correct answer. Place your answer on the line. Characteristics may be appropriate for more than one type of LAN.

   A. TRN _____   (1) CSMA/CD
   B. 10Base5 _____   (2) Token
   C. 10Base2 _____   (3) Frame
   D. 10BaseT _____   (4) Probabilistic
   E. FDDI _____   (5) Deterministic
   F. Fast Ethernet _____   (6) Designed by IBM
   G. VG AnyLAN _____   (7) Designed by Xerox
   H. ARCnet _____   (8) Designed by Hewlett-Packard
                                (9) Single ring
                                (10) Dual counter-rotation rings

3. Explain CSMA/CD.
4. Explain how TRN handles an error.
5. Given the following bit pattern, show the Manchester coding.

0	1	1	0	0	1	0	1	0	0

6. Given the following bit pattern, show the differential Manchester coding. Assume a zero initial condition.

0	1	1	0	0	1	0	1	0	0

7. Given the following bit pattern, show the differential Manchester coding. Assume a zero initial condition.

J	K	1	1	J	K	0	0	1	0	1

8. What is the difference between an Ethernet MAU and a TRN MAU?
9. What type of TRN frame sends data?
10. What are the violations in TRN called? What is their purpose?
11. What is the purpose of TRN's RIF field?
12. In TRN what are the functions of the Active Monitor?
13. What is the purpose of the 4B/5B coding in FDDI?
14. In an Ethernet NIC, how is the MAC address determined? If the NIC fails and the system administrator wants to keep the same MAC address, how does the administrator proceed?
15. In an ARCnet NIC, how is the MAC address determined? If the NIC fails and the system administrator wants to keep the same MAC address, how does the administrator proceed?
16. What is a MAC? What is a SAP? What is the LLC? It is not sufficient to merely define the acronyms.
17. If you ask someone for their MAC address and they reply, "But I have a PC!" what should be your response?
18. What are five reasons to use LANs?

5

NETWORK OPERATING SYSTEMS (NOSs)

OBJECTIVES

In this chapter we will discuss:

    I. What is a Network Operating System (NOS)?

    II. Compare a computer without a NOS to a computer with a NOS and a Network Interface Card (NIC).

    III. Peer-to-peer LAN.

    IV. Client/Server LAN.

    V. What does a NOS do?

        A. File server.

        B. Print server.

            1. Share printers.

            2. Share plotters.

        C. Network monitoring.

            1. Who is logged into the LAN? Finding hackers and intruders.

            2. What are the traffic rates?

    VI. NOS vendors.

        A. Novell NetWare.

        B. Microsoft NT (New Technology).

        C. Banyan Vines.

        D. Artisoft LANtastic.

        E. Apple AppleTalk.

    VII. Comparison between NetWare and NT.

5.1 Network Operating Systems (NOSs)

Specialized software, called **Network Operating Systems (NOSs),** is needed to control LANs. Before we can discuss NOSs, we must understand how a computer without a NOS is organized.

5.2 PC without a NOS

Figure 5.1 shows the organization of an Operating System (OS) based IBM PC without a NOS. The OS can be DOS or Windows. A command in an application program will call (go to or use) either an OS command, an input device (keyboard) or an output device (printer), or an input/output device (disk drive). If an input, or output, or input/output device is called, the command will be routed to the **Basic Input Output System (BIOS)** and then to the PC hardware. The BIOS is software written or "burned" into a Read Only Memory (ROM) that converts program commands to commands the PC hardware can understand. A ROM stores data even if the power is turned off (this is called *nonvolatile memory*).

5.3 PC with a NOS

When a NOS (LAN Operating System) is added to a computer, a major addition is the Redirector as shown in Figure 5.2. When the Redirector receives a command from the application program, the Redirector determines if the command is intended for the computer Operating System (OS) and BIOS, or for the network. If the command is an OS command, it will be directed to OS, BIOS, and the PC hardware. If the command is a network command, it will be directed to the LAN software and hardware.

A network command will go first to the **NetBIOS (Network Basic Input Output System)** software, then to the LAN protocol software. The LAN protocol software is unique to the type of LAN. Token Ring software will be different from 10Base5 software, and so forth. The LAN protocol software converts the NetBIOS command to a command that the Network Interface Card (NIC) can understand. The NIC is a card that plugs into the computer and is the hardware that connects the computer to the LAN. Generally each type of LAN (10Base5 or Token Ring) requires a different type of NIC, but some NICs can support both 10Base2 and 10BaseT. Newer NICs translate between 10BaseT and 100BaseT.

5.4 Peer-to-Peer versus Client/Server

Peer-to-peer means there is no dedicated server, yet all workstations within the workgroup can communicate with each other via the network. No workstation is a server, and all workstations are considered equals or peers. All workstations share resources. A **server** is a computer dedicated to sending files (serving) to workstations requesting those files; the server allows other computers on the network to use its resources. A client is the computer requesting files from the server.

5.5 NOS Functions

What does a NOS do? It transfers files between computers, and between computers and print servers. Often when a user is using a program, such as a word processor, and requests a file, the user is not aware that the file was not residing on his or her machine's hard drive. When a user commands his or her word processor to print a file, the user also is unaware of the file transfer to a print server. The file transfers are "transparent" to the user.

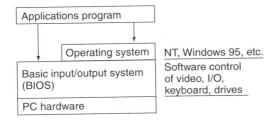

FIGURE 5.1
PC software without LAN software.

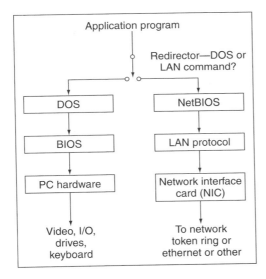

FIGURE 5.2
PC software and LAN software.

5.5.1 Print Server

A **print server** receives files from users on the net and puts the files into a queue to be printed. Some files may get a higher priority in the queue. The print server handles the printer driver and printer queues.

5.5.2 Network Monitoring

The NOS monitors who logs in and that the user employs the correct password. The latest NOS versions have elaborate methods of hacker/intruder detection, monitoring, and disabling (shutting out) the hacker.

NOSs will monitor and log the users for their time on the net. It is possible to monitor a user's e-mail, and the U.S. courts have ruled that an employee's e-mail may be read by the employer. The reasoning is that since the employer provides the equipment and connection to the Internet, the company has the right to monitor what is being sent over the net.

NOSs monitor traffic and are useful to find traffic bottleneck and equipment failures. In an actual case, a very irate customer called the network engineer to find the cause of extremely slow file transfers. The customer raged about paying a lot of money for a poorly performing system and berated the network engineer and his company. The network engineer found that there was a lot of traffic on the net and traced it to one machine. That machine user was sending compact disk (CD) music to his friend several states away! This little antic brought the network to its knees. The customer apologized profusely to the network engineer!

5.6 NOS Vendors

The five major vendors of NOSs are NetWare by Novell, NT by Microsoft, Vines by Banyan, LANtastic by Artisoft, and AppleTalk by Apple.

5.6.1 Novell NetWare

Novell NetWare NOS software for the workstation consists of the Redirector and the NIC driver. Originally NetWare was intended for smaller installations of 100 nodes or less, but version 4.x can support up to 1,000 nodes. The original customers were small- to medium-sized companies. Novell has been very successful selling to these customers and has sold more NOS systems than any other company in the world.

5.6.2 Banyan Vines

Banyan Vines was intended for large companies and organizations. Our college uses Vines, and the U.S. government is Banyan's largest customer. Banyan has not sold as many systems as Novell, but since each Banyan system can support many nodes, the total number of nodes supported by Vines is greater than for NetWare. One of the reasons for Banyan's success was its "Streettalk" directory, or naming service.

5.6.3 AppleTalk

AppleTalk is designed for Apple computers and peripherals to talk to each other.

5.6.4 Microsoft NT Server and Windows for Workgroups

Microsoft has entered the NOS market with Windows for Workgroups and **NT (New Technology) Server.** These products are designed to compete directly with NetWare and Vines. NT has overcome many of the complaints about NetWare and is easier to install and more user friendly. However some Novell veterans are reluctant to leave installation configuration largely to the installation program. Also NT Server has a flat directory structure, a major disadvantage for enterprise networking. An **enterprise network** consists of several (or even many) interconnected LANs and WANs. Novell has a hierarchical directory structure, considered superior for enterprise networking. *Hierarchical* means layered and will be discussed later in this chapter.

5.6.5 Artisoft LANtastic

A low-cost NOS for smaller systems is LANtastic by Artisoft, Inc., of Tucson, Arizona. LANtastic is a peer-to-peer system introduced in 1987. The software is less complicated, easier to manage, and therefore cheaper than its competitors. In peer-to-peer networks, any computer can make its resources available to any other computer on the network. In a server based network, one computer is designated as the server, and usually only the server provides its resources to other computers on the network.

5.7 LAN Protocols

Figure 5.3 shows the various NOS protocols and how they compare to the OSI Reference Model and to TCP/IP. We have discussed the OSI RM and will study TCP/IP in Chapter 18. A detailed description of each vendor's layer is well beyond the scope of this book.

5.8 NT Server versus NetWare

The two big players in the NOS arena are Microsoft NT and Novell's NetWare. How do these two compare? What are their strengths and weaknesses?

OSI RM	Novell netware	Banyan vines	Microsoft NT	TCP/IP	
7	Application				
6 Presentation	NetBIOS		NetBEUI	FTP, Telnet	
5 Session					
4 Transport	SPX	VIP	NWLink	TCP, UDP	
3 Network	IPX	VIPC		IP	
2 Data link	IEEE 802.2 LLC				
1 Physical	802.3 Ethernet CSMA/CD	802.4 Token bus	802.5 Token ring	802.6 SMDS	802.8 Optical fiber	Mac & physical

FIGURE 5.3
NOS protocols. BIOS = basic input output system, IPX = internetwork packet exchange, LLC = logical link control, Net BIOS = Network BIOS, NetBEUI = NetBIOS extended user interface, NWLink = NetWare link, SMDS = Switched multi-megabit data service, SPX = Sequenced packet exchange, VINES = Virtual network system, VIP = Vines internet protocol, and VIPC = Vines interprocess communications protocol.

Novell's strengths are its directory, print, and file services. These run faster than with Microsoft's NT. A *directory* is a list of all users, nodes, and resources. Novell's NDS (Network Directory Service) directory is hierarchical, meaning it has levels like a telephone number. A telephone number hierarchy has a two-digit country code, a three-digit area code, a three-digit Central Office code, and finally a four-digit user code. The system will search through the directory's levels to find the correct user. The hierarchical system is considered superior to Microsoft's flat directory system and will work much better in an enterprise system. An enterprise system is one combining LANs and WANs.

NT's strengths are application support and integration. These run faster than with NetWare. However NT has a flat directory, which is slower and less efficient than Novell's NDS. Using a flat directory has been likened to finding the proverbial needle in a haystack. Microsoft intends to add a hierarchical directory in version 5.0, due out in 1999. NT also uses more resources than NetWare. NT 4.0 has about 30 million lines of code, versus 10 million for NetWare 4.11.

5.9 Testing and Troubleshooting

Novell's LANalyzer is a LAN monitoring, analysis, and troubleshooting part of NetWare. It can work with either Ethernet or TRN. The user can employ either a Network Dashboard display, a tabular display (Figure 5.4), or a graphical display. These displays tell what user is generating packets, how many packets per second, the type of packet, and what percentage of utilization the network is at. The packets can be "captured" for detailed analysis.

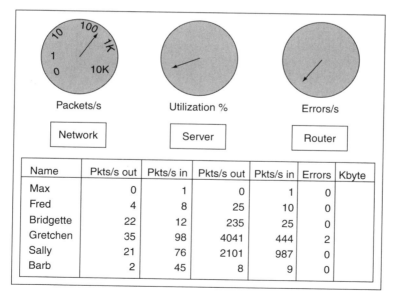

Name	Pkts/s out	Pkts/s in	Pkts/s out	Pkts/s in	Errors	Kbyte
Max	0	1	0	1	0	
Fred	4	8	25	10	0	
Bridgette	22	12	235	25	0	
Gretchen	35	98	4041	444	2	
Sally	21	76	2101	987	0	
Barb	2	45	8	9	0	

FIGURE 5.4
LANalyzer displays.

LANalyzer supports Novel's own IPX/SPX, NCP, RIP, and SAP protocols, as well as AppleTalk, SNA, and TCP/IP.

SUMMARY

I. The redirector is the key piece of software in a computer with a NOS.
  A. The Redirector examines a command to see if it is part of the normal Operating System or a network command.
  B. If the command is an Operating System command, the computer operates as usual.
  C. If the command is a network command, the command will go to the NOS. The NOS will perform the proper network function.
II. A NOS does file serving, print serving, and network monitoring.
  A. The file server shares files among the users.
  B. The print server allows network users to share the printer(s).
III. Network monitoring monitoring keeps track of traffic levels, types of traffic, sources and destinations, what users are logged in, what users will be allowed to log in, and hackers and intruders.
IV. The major NOS vendors are:
  A. Novell and its NetWare.
  B. Microsoft and its NT.
  C. Banyan and its Vines.
  D. Artisoft with its LANtastic.
  E. Apple with its AppleTalk.
V. NetWare's strengths are its directory, print, and file services. Its directory is hierarchical.
VI. NT's strengths are its application support and integration. Its flat directory is considered inferior to NetWare's hierarchical directory.

QUESTIONS

1. What is the purpose of a NOS?
2. What determines if a command is for the PC itself or for the network?
3. What is a NIC? It is not sufficient to merely define the acronym. What does it do?
4. What are the differences between a peer-to-peer LAN and a client/server based LAN?
5. What is the difference between a hierarchical directory and a flat directory? What are the advantages of each?

6

LAN INTERCONNECTION

OBJECTIVES

In this chapter we will discuss:

I. Why do we interconnect LANs?

II. How do we interconnect LANs?

    A. Repeaters.

        1. Physical level only.

        2. Amplify signals only.

    B. Bridges.

        1. Data Link Level (DLL).

        2. Examine address to see if frame should be sent to another LAN.

        3. Boost signal strength.

        4. Same protocol on both sides; no protocol conversion.

    C. Routers and switches.

        1. Network level; route frames to destination.

        2. Protocol conversion.

    D. Gateways.

        1. LAN-to-WAN.

        2. Protocol conversion.

        3. All seven layers.

6.1 Why Interconnect LANs?

As an organization grows, its data processing and network needs often increase also. LANs must be expanded, but there are limits to LAN expansion. These limits are those of the LAN itself (each type has a maximum length and number of nodes) and the amount of traffic. If the traffic load becomes too large, few messages will reach their destination. Large LANs must be split into smaller LANs and somehow still be connected. If the length becomes too great or the signal strength too low, measures must be taken. Also

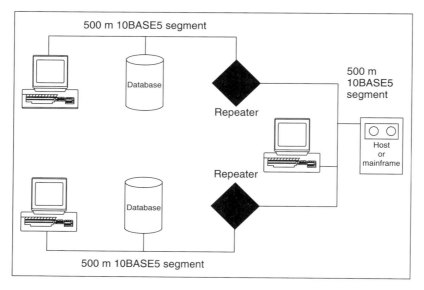

FIGURE 6.1
Repeaters. Total 10BASE5 is 1500 meters in this example, but 2500 meters is possible.

LAN users often want access to the Internet or a Wide Area Network (WAN). There are four devices to connect one LAN to another LAN. These are repeaters, bridges, routes, and gateways.

6.2 Repeater

A repeater merely boosts the signal strength between LANs or segments of a LAN. It can be used to extend the total length of a LAN as shown in Figure 6.1. The maximum segment length of a 10Base5 LAN is 500 meters. By using repeaters, one may connect as many as five segments together, bringing the total LAN length to 2,500 meters. Figure 6.1 shows two repeaters connecting three 500-meter segments of a 10Base5 LAN together into a 1,500-meter total length. Repeaters can extend 10Base5 systems up to 2,500 meters.

A repeater operates at the physical level only as shown in Figure 6.2. It has no intelligence or routing capability. If traffic is heavy and packets (messages) are being lost, it is time to consider installing a bridge.

6.3 Bridge

A **bridge** separates LANs. For instance it may be desirable to have one LAN for engineering, another LAN for sales, and yet another LAN for accounting. We want each group's traffic to remain within its own LAN. But still there are occasions when these different groups will want to communicate with each other via the LANs. Bridges will make this possible. At the DLL (level 2, see Figure 6.3) bridges examine the destination ad-

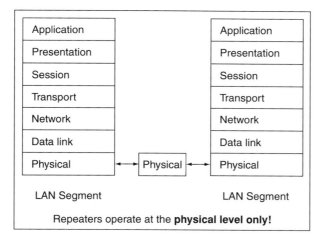

FIGURE 6.2
Repeaters operate at the physical level only.

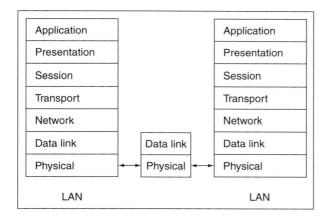

FIGURE 6.3
Bridges operate at the Data Link Level. Bridges examine the frame's destination address and determine if the frame is to be passed to another LAN.

dresses of the frames and determine whether to pass the frame from one LAN to another department's LAN or keep the frame within the originating LAN.

At the physical level the bridge boosts the signal strength like a repeater or completely regenerates the signal. At the Data Link Level (DLL) the bridge checks the frame destination address to see if the frame should be passed on to another LAN.

Bridges usually use the same protocol on either side—for example, Ethernet-to-Ethernet, or Token Ring–to–Token Ring—or convert between different protocols—for example, Ethernet–to–Token Ring. Bridges are fine for medium-sized operations but are totally inadequate for large installations. Enter routers.

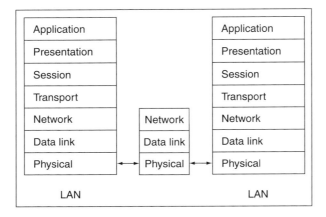

FIGURE 6.4
Routers operate at the network level to find the best route to send a frame to the destination LAN.

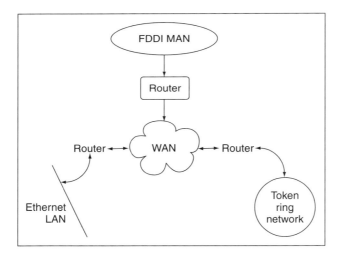

FIGURE 6.5
Connecting LANs via a WAN. The three networks can be separated by thousands of miles, and are connected by a WAN (Wide Area Network).

6.4 Routers and Switches

A **router** does everything a bridge does, but it can connect different types of LANs—for example, Ethernet–to–Token Ring, or Token Ring–to–FDDI, or LAN–to–Wide Area Network (WAN). Therefore routers can be considered Layer 3 protocol converters (see Figure 6.4). By using routers, LANs in widely separated geographical locations can be connected via a WAN as in Figure 6.5. To the users the system behaves like a single LAN.

TABLE 6.1
Switches versus routers

Switches	Routers
WAN	LANs
Telcos	Internet—IP
Connection oriented	Connectionless
Protocols used	Hierarchical routing
X.25	Uses routing protocol
Frame Relay (FR)	
Asynchronous Transfer Mode (ATM)	
Flat address	

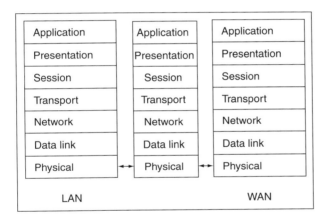

FIGURE 6.6
Gateways can operate at all levels and convert between various protocols. Gateways can provide access to WANs and the Internet.

This is LAN Emulation (LANE), that is, making the entire system appear to be one LAN, even though the different LANs may be oceans apart.

Routers also find the best routing for a frame passing from one LAN to another. Level 3 hardware performs this routing. Of course this makes routers much more expensive than bridges and repeaters. Cisco Systems of San Jose, California, is the world's largest supplier of routers. Their 7000 series can provide connectivity to Asynchronous Transfer Mode (ATM) and T1/E1 systems. With large networks, routers are imperative to prevent lost frames and to deliver frames in a timely manner.

The network nodes are called switches in an ATM network, and they are called routers within the Internet. Routers handle the IP (Internet Protocol) addressing. The differences are summarized in Table 6.1.

6.5 Gateway

A **gateway** is a converter between different protocols. This conversion in level 2 can be between different LAN types (Token Ring–to–Ethernet), different WAN protocols (X.25-to- SNA), or LAN-to-WAN (SNA or X.25). See Figure 6.6. A gateway can make protocol conversions in all seven layers, and it can convert between different network formats.

SUMMARY

I. LANs are interconnected to:
    A. Keep any single LAN from having too much traffic.
    B. Extend the distance or span of a LAN; increase signal strength.
    C. Access to WANs.
II. Repeaters.
    A. Boost signal strength.
    B. Physical level only.
III. Bridges.
    A. Separate various types of users and their traffic.
    B. Will examine the address to see if the frame should pass into another LAN.
    C. Data Link Level (DLL).
    D. Boost signal level.
IV. Routers.
    A. Examine addresses to find best route to send frame to destination.
    B. Sometimes do protocol conversion.
    C. Network level 3.
V. Gateways.
    A. LAN-to-WAN.
    B. Protocol conversion.

QUESTIONS

1. What are routers and bridges used for?
2. What are the differences between routers, repeaters, and bridges?
3. You are the network administrator of an Ethernet LAN of length 1,900 meters. If the network is used only 10 percent of the time and packets are not being lost, should you use a repeater, bridge, or router? Justify your answer.
4. You are the network administrator of an Ethernet LAN of 2,500 meters length. Engineering, marketing, sales, and shipping use this same LAN. The network is becoming congested, and some packets are being lost. What is your recommendation to upper management? Justify your answer.
5. Your company has opened two branch offices in California and Florida. 10BaseT LANs will be used at both branches and your Denver headquarters. What is your recommendation to tie the three offices together? Justify your answer.

7

THE PUBLIC SWITCHED TELEPHONE SYSTEM (PSTN)

OBJECTIVES

In this chapter we will discuss:

IX. What is common channel signaling? It is signaling (control signals) and voice using different channels.
  A. More efficient because signaling used its own circuits, (no expensive voice circuits) and setup and takedown of calls much faster.
  B. Hackers' holiday was over.
X. Signaling System 7 (SS7).
XI. Switching computers.
  A. 4ESS (4 Electronic Switching System).
  B. 5ESS (5 Electronic Switching System).
XII. Packet Switched Networks (PSN).

7.1 Public Switched Telephone System (PSTN)

Figure 7.1 shows an approximate overview of the **Public Switched Telephone System (PSTN)**. The home or small office user is connected to the **Central Office (CO)** via Unshielded Twisted Pair (UTP) cable. This connection is called the local loop. The *local loop* usually carries analog voice signals or audio tones from a modem. The CO is sometimes referred to as the *local exchange*.

The analog signal from the local loop is converted to a digital signal at the CO. This process is called an **Analog to Digital (A/D) conversion** and is done by a Codec. Codecs are discussed in Chapter 8. Digital signals are more efficient to transmit than analog signals. Digital signals are more resistant to electrical interference and are also easier for computers to switch and manipulate.

7.2 How Is a Call Handled?

An "on hook" situation is when the handset is resting on the cradle and no current from the CO flows through the user's telephone. To begin to use the telephone, the end user lifts the handset. This is called an "off hook" condition. The "off hook" starts a 20-milliampere current flowing, which is detected by the CO.

The user dials the number, and the CO begins to route (switch) the call to the final destination. The switching control chooses the first (lowest in Figure 7.1) available trunk, or the path with the fewest switches, in which to route the call. The local CO's switching equipment checks to see if the destination user is served by that CO. If the destination user is indeed served by that CO, the call will be routed without going to other COs or any other facility.

If the destination user is not served by the local CO, the CO looks for a direct connection (trunk) between itself and the destination CO. If a trunk direct connection is found, the call is routed along that trunk. A *trunk* is a connection with many lines capable of handling many conversations.

If no direct truck exists between the two COs, the local CO will send the call routing information to the next level above, a Toll Center. The Toll Center will try to route the call directly, but if it cannot route the call, the Toll Center will send the routing informa-

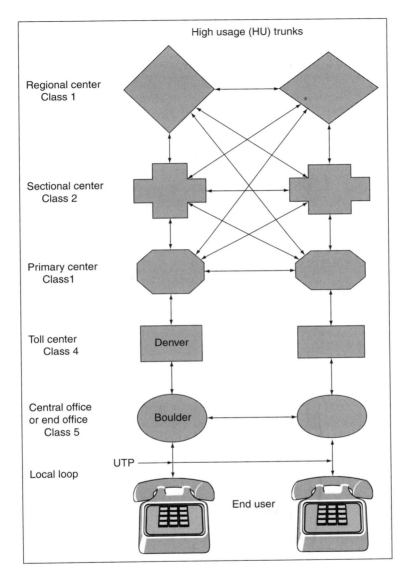

FIGURE 7.1
AT & T system (approximate).

tion to the next level above. This process continues until a route is found. Then the voice circuits will be switched allowing the voice conversation to begin. Note the routing is done before the voice circuits are actually connected. This will be discussed further when we examine Common Channel Interoffice Signaling (CCIS).

The user begins speaking into the handset's microphone. The microphone's resistance varies with the speaker's voice, changing the current. This changing current is the analog voice signal sent to the CO and digitized by the Codec.

7.3 AT&T System

Figure 7.1 is a very approximate diagram of a small portion of the hierarchical AT&T system. Users are connected to the Central Office (CO) by the local loop. Trunks connect the CO to the Toll Center, and the Toll Center to the Primary Center. *Hierarchical* means a layered system. For instance an international telephone call has the country code, the area code or city code, the central office code, and finally the user's last four-digit unique telephone number. The Primary Center is connected by High Usage (HU) trunks to the Sectional Center and then to other Sectional and Regional Centers. In the United States there are ten Regional Centers and about 19,000 Central Offices.

Blocked calls are calls that did not find an available trunk and were forced to go up to a lower class call center. Traffic engineering designs the system to handle most peak traffic periods with only a 2 percent probability of a blocked call. Special holidays and emergency situations can overload the system. Blocked calls are those that cannot be completed because of network congestion or failure.

7.4 LATAs, IECs, IXCs, and LECs

Local Access and Transport Areas (LATAs) usually follow state and area code boundaries. However in large metropolitan areas, different area codes may share the same LATA. The Denver, Colorado, area now has two overlapping area codes. It is even possible to have two different area codes for different lines into an office or home!

The local telephone company is called a **telco.** Another term is Local Exchange Carrier (LEC). The long distance carriers—such as AT&T, Sprint, and MCI—are **InterExchange Carriers (IECs)** or **IntereXchange Carriers (IXCs).**

7.5 CO-to-Telephone Connection

The user is connected to the CO by an Unshielded Twisted Pair (UTP) cable. The cable can be up to 3 miles long. The nominal voltage from the CO is -48 volts. The voltage at the user's phone is less, due to wire resistance in the UTP. The ringing voltage is a 255-peak voltage signal at a frequency of 20 Hz as shown in Figure 7.2. These large voltages were needed for the old electromechanical telephones, but modern solid state telephones could use a mere 5 volts. The old voltages are kept for compatibility with any older phone still in use, and clever circuit designs allow the solid state telephones to use the higher voltages.

When the user picks up the handset, a 20-milliampere current begins to flow from the CO. This current flow is detected and initiates the dial tone and the beginning of the call. The UTP carries conversations from the handset to the CO, and from the CO to the handset. It is a full duplex system over a single pair of wires. A special transformer called a *hybrid* separates the two conversations as illustrated in Figure 7.3.

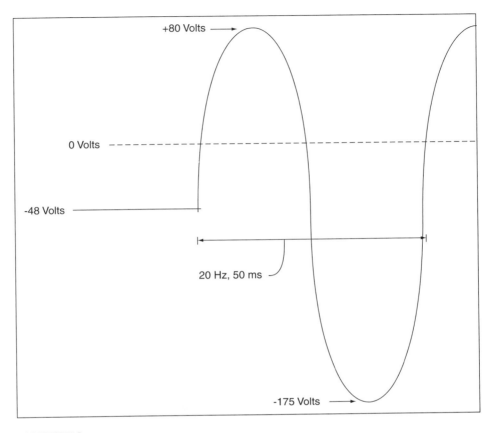

FIGURE 7.2
Telephone voltage levels. The voltage on the red telephone wire with reference to the green wire is a nominal −48 volts. The ringing voltage from the CO is 255 volts peak, at 20 Hz (50 ms period).

7.6 Strowger Switch and the Rotary Dial Telephone

Almon Strowger, a Kansas City mortician, suspected the local human operators were routing customer calls to his competitors. Never mind that his wife, also an operator, was routing competitors' calls to Mr. Strowger's mortuary. In anger, Mr. Strowger invented the Strowger switch, or the "step by step" switch, as it is called today. This switch eliminated many human operators. The Strowger switch is a series of rotary switches. A current pulse will step the switch forward one step.

The rotary dial telephone is designed to activate the step-by-step switch. Each numeric position the dial rotates sends a current pulse to the Central Office with its step-by-step switches. For instance dialing a "8" sends eight current pulses to the Central Office (CO). See Figure 7.4. In the developed world, the rotary pulse telephone and the step-by-step switches have been replaced by the DTMF system, which will be discussed next.

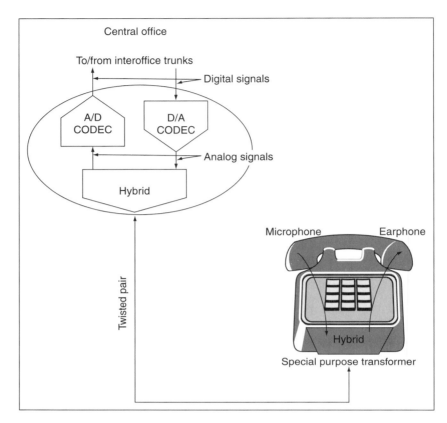

FIGURE 7.3
From the CO to the user.

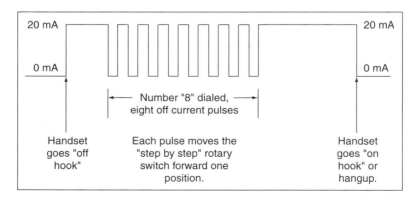

FIGURE 7.4
Rotary-dial phone current pulses.

TABLE 7.1
Dual Tone Multi-Frequency (DTMF)

Frequency (Hz)	1,209	1,336	1,477	1,633
697	1	2	3	A
770	4	5	6	B
852	7	8	9	C
941	*	0	#	D
				Future Expansion

7.7 Dual Tone Multi-Frequency (DTMF)

The **Dual Tone Multi-Frequency (DTMF)** system has replaced the rotary telephone. DTMF is faster and easier to digitize. When one depresses a key on the keypad, two tones (frequencies) are generated and sent to the CO. See Table 7.1 for the frequencies. For instance when one presses a "2," the frequencies 1,336 hertz (Hz) and 697 Hz are sent to signaling equipment at the CO. The signaling equipment decodes the two (dual) tones, enabling the switching equipment to route the call to its destination.

7.8 Why Switch?

We have talked about switching without discussing the need for switching. Now let's find out why we use switching. Without switching, every phone in the world would need a direct connection to every other phone in the world!

The total number of lines needed L would be

$$L = N(N-1) = (N^2 - N) \qquad \textbf{(Equation 7.1)}$$

where N is the number of telephones to be directly connected.

It is impractical to have a direct connection between every telephone in the world. Equation 7.1 tells us that the number of wires would be astronomical! Considering that there are probably over a billion telephones in the world, we see that connecting all telephones together directly is impractical. Also how would the telcos (telephone companies) handle the wireless services? Some other method than direct connection is needed. Switching is how this is done.

The first switches were human operators. The very first telephone operators were young boys, who can be very mischievous and tend to play a lot of pranks. And this is exactly what happened. Bell Telephone quickly realized the error of its management ways and replaced the boys with women.

7.9 Parts of a Switch

There are two parts to a switch: control and fabric. See Table 7.2 to examine the parts of a switch.

TABLE 7.2
Parts of a Switch

Switching control
    Human operator
    Switching computers
Switching fabric—where lines or trunks are connected
    Plubs
    Cords
    Jacks
    Lamps

7.10 Per Trunk Signaling

The original electronic switching was called "per trunk" signaling. The switching signals used the same trunks as the voice path. The switching signals could be heard as the call was being set up. This was the open door hackers slipped through. They would use special tone generators to switch the call as they desired. Also, they sent the tone indicating a toll-free call, allowing a free long-distance call. In an actual instance, a hacker called from a pay phone, routed the call around the world, and rang the pay phone in the next booth, all in about 2 minutes. AT&T wished to make an example of these folks. They pursued them with a vengeance and vigorously prosecuted them to the full extent of the law.

Also per trunk signaling was inefficient. Typical setup times were 20 seconds. Voice grade circuits are expensive, but digital signaling circuits are relatively inexpensive. Setting the call up using expensive voice circuits without knowing if the call could be completed was very inefficient. This would happen if the called party's line was busy or if the traffic was heavy.

7.11 Common Channel Interoffice Signaling (CCIS)

Common Channel Interoffice Signaling (**CCIS**) separates the signaling from the voice. Signaling uses a separate digital circuit than the voice circuits. One signaling circuit can handle many voice circuits. Many voice circuits share the one "common" digital signaling channel, hence the term "common channel." See Figure 7.5.

7.11.1 CCIS Example

After a user dials a number, CCIS checks to see if the destination telephone is busy (Figure 7.5). If the destination is busy, CCIS sends a signal back to the sender CO. The sender CO sends the busy signal back to the originating phone. The busy signal the user hears does not come from the destination CO, but rather from the local CO. No expensive voice circuits were used.

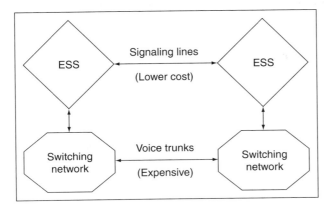

FIGURE 7.5
Common channel signaling path.

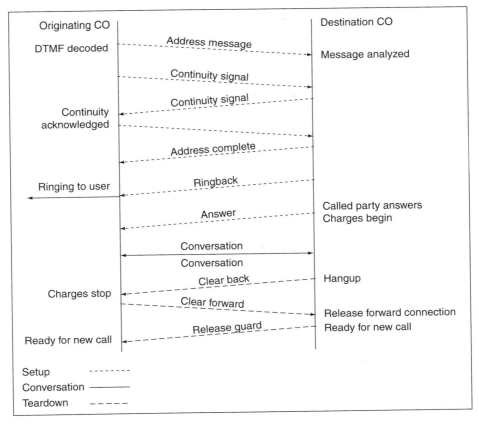

FIGURE 7.6
SS7 call sequence.

If the destination is not busy, CCIS sets up the voice circuits in the necessary voice trunks and sends a ringback signal to the sender CO. The sender CO sends the 20-Hz ringing signal to the originating user's telephone. This ringing signal is not generated at the destination CO but at the call originator's CO. Typical long distance call setup times are 4 to 7 seconds versus about 20 seconds for a per truck call setup.

After one user hangs up, the teardown begins. The teardown is also done over the switching lines. These setup and teardown processes take place over the signaling lines and not the expensive voice trunks. The voice trunks are used only for the conversation itself.

The message on the CCIS signaling circuits is a 28-bit packet with 20 bits of information and 8 bits of error checking. CCIS is based on the UPI-T Signaling System 6 (SS6) standard.

7.11.2 Signaling System 7 (SS7)

Signaling System 7 (SS7) replaces SS6 (See Figure 7.6). The advantages of SS7 are better monitoring, maintenance, and network administration. The major disadvantage of SS7 is its complex coding. In an actual occurrence, an inadequately tested program was installed into an Electronic Switching System (ESS) computer in the New York City area. This program with a serious bug managed to bring down the entire telephone system in the New York City area, including the Federal Aviation Administration's (FAA) Air Traffic Control (ATC) system. No aircraft could land in any of the three New York airports, and all commercial flights were re-routed to Philadelphia or Boston. Yes, tempers flared! The company that wrote the bug quickly admitted its error and revised its software testing procedure.

7.12 Switching Computers

The switching is done by special purpose computers, designed specifically for switching. The software can easily be replaced and updated. The actual switching is handled by the software, or Stored Program Control (SPC).

The "workhorses" of the Lucent Technologies switching computers are the **4ESS (Electronic Switching System)** and the **5ESS.** The 4ESS can handle up to 1,200,000 calls per hour, and the 5ESS can handle up to 200,000 calls per hour. The 4ESS is used in high-demand areas, and the 5ESS is used in lower usage areas. The 4ESS has two processors, one being a backup. There are 136 4ESS machines in the AT&T system in the United States. Nortel, formerly Northern Telecomm, a Canadian company, also makes equivalent machines.

The trunks interconnecting the computers carry voice, data, and video. The signaling is handled by separate SS7 circuits.

7.13 Packet Switched Networks (PSN)

Besides the PSTN voice switching circuits, there are other networks that handle mostly data. These are the Packet Switched Networks (PSN). PSN handle X.25, Frame Relay (FR), Internet Protocol (IP), and other types of data. The same switch can be used for all these data types; it recognizes the type by examining the user's login.

7.14 Echoes

Echoes are unwanted signals sent back to the originating telephone. There are two methods of dealing with echoes: the echo suppressor and the echo canceler.

The **echo suppressor** determines which signal is from the sending telephone and puts an attenuator in the opposite line as shown in Figure 7.7a. The **echo canceler** stores a copy of the signal in digital memory and compares the stored copy with the signals returning. If the returning signal matches the stored signal, the stored signal is digitally subtracted from the returning signal, as shown in Figure 7.7b.

Voice transmissions rarely have repeating bit patterns. However data often has repeating bit patterns that could be mistaken for echoes by an echo canceler. For data transmission the echo cancelers must be disabled. This is done by sending a 2,000- to 2,250-Hz signal for about 400 ms. If the data is not continuous, the tone must be kept on the line to keep the cancelers disabled during the time of no data transmission.

7.15 PSTN Impairments, Testing, and Troubleshooting

7.15.1 Noise

There are several types of noise on the PSTN: thermal noise, electrical noise, and transients.

7.15.1.1 Thermal Noise
Thermal noise is due to random movement of electrons. All electrical components generate thermal or Johnson noise. This noise is given by Equation 7.2.

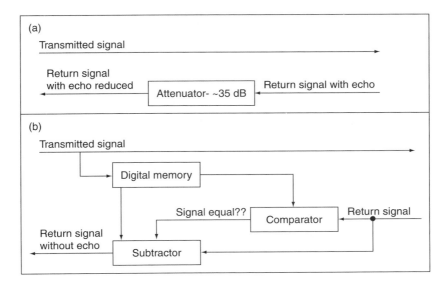

FIGURE 7.7
Echo handling. (a) Echo suppression and (b) echo cancellation.

$$N = k\,T\,BW \qquad \textbf{(Equation 7.2)}$$

where N is the noise power in $\dfrac{\text{joules}}{\text{second}}$ or watts

                k is Boltzman's constant $1.38 \times 10^{-23}\ \dfrac{\text{joules}}{\text{degrees kelvin}}$

                T is the temperature in degrees kelvin
                BW is the bandwidth in hertz

Usually this type of noise is not a great problem for the PSTN in the United States and other developed countries. It is a great concern in weak signal applications such as satellite communication. Using a Codec (compander) to give high amplification to low-level signals and less amplification to high-level signals reduces the effect of Johnson noise.

7.15.1.2 Electrical Noise   Electrical noise is generated by high-voltage interference from power lines, radio, radar, microwave, and television transmitters (Radio Frequency Interference [RFI]), lightning, arc welders, electric motors, computers, television sets, and heating and air-conditioning units.

7.15.1.3 Transients   Transients are caused by changes in power supply outputs, dialing noise, dirty electrical contacts (corrosion), cold solder joints, step-by-step switches, and power line surges. Transients may last only a few milliseconds to 20 milliseconds, but this is plenty of time to corrupt hundreds of bits.

7.15.1.4 Noise Testing   Noise power is measured by the C-message notch filter testing technique (Figure 7.8). A 1,004-hertz signal is sent down the PSTN. A signal is needed to make sure all the switches and connections are properly set up. At the receiver both the noise and the 1,004-hertz tone are present, but we are only interested in the noise. A notch filter removes the 1,004-hertz tone, leaving only the noise. The signal amplitude is measured, and the signal-to-noise ratio computed. A signal-to-noise ratio of 28 dB is considered adequate.

7.15.2 Error Rates

Bit Error Rate (BER, or BERR) is defined as

$$\frac{\text{Bit received in error}}{\text{Total bits in error}}$$

A typical figure might be $1\ e^{-5}$, or 1 bit in error for 10^5 (100,000) bits sent. The Block Error Rate is defined as

$$\frac{\text{Blocks (frames) received containing an error}}{\text{Total blocks (frames) sent}}$$

7.15.2.1 Testing Error Rates   To test BER and Block Error Rates, a pseudo random number (PRN) pattern is sent over the PSTN. This pattern is generated using techniques similar to those used for CRC checking as discussed in Appendix A1. The pattern uses ei-

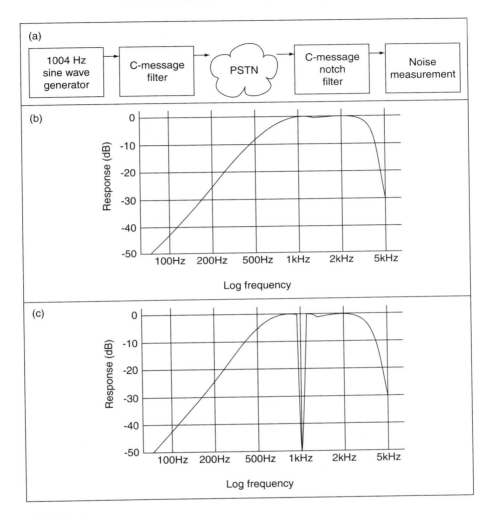

FIGURE 7.8

ther 511 ($2^9 - 1$) bits or 2,023 ($2^{11} - 1$) bits. The exact sequence(s) are known but appear(s) to be random. The receiver test set locks onto the pattern and logs error rates, both Bit Error and Block Error. Error (deviations from the PRN) can be introduced to check the readings. For instance, if the test shows 273 bits in error, a button is pushed and six errors are introduced. The new error rate should be 279 bits in error.

Years ago two technicians were needed to test a system. One would operate the transmitting test set and the other would go to a remote site and operate the receiver test set. Now a technique called **loopback** reduces the workforce needed and allows faster fault isolation.

A technician uses the loopback feature to loop the PRN from the transmitting test set into the receiving test set. If this test passes, the technician enables the loopback feature on the next network node and sends the PRN pattern to that node. If that node checks out properly, the loopback is moved to the next node and that node is checked. This process is repeated until the offending node is found. Then the technician will travel to that site (or inform another technician closer to the bad node) and fix it. Personnel and travel time are reduced. Loopback is also discussed in Chapter 11.

7.15.3 Phase Jitter

Jitter is the short-term change in network delay. An oscilloscope trace will show a fuzzy bit pulse edge. The human ear is not very sensitive to jitter, but modems are very sensitive to phase jitter.

7.15.4 Transmission Monitor

A transmission monitor passively monitors a network and performs these analyses: distortion, noise, delay, delay jitter, signal dropouts, and loss of synchronization. These items are recorded and are available for analysis for troubleshooting.

SUMMARY

    I. The user (home or small office) was connected to a Central Office (CO) via an Unshielded Twisted Pair (UTP) cable; the UTP carried analog audio signals.

    II. The analog signals from the user are converted to digital signals at the CO.

        A. A Codec is used to convert the analog signal to a digital signal.

        B. Digital signals are transmitted and switched (routed) more efficiently than analog signals.

    III. How the call originates.

        A. When the user takes the handset off the telephone cradle, a 20-mA current begins to flow.

        B. The user dials the destination number either by current pulses (rotary dial phone) or by pushing buttons and generating a pair of tones (Dual Tone Multi-Frequency [DTMF]).

        C. The pulses or DTMF tones are converted to digital signals and used to set up the network switching (routing).

        D. After the user is connected to the destination and the user at the destination answers, the users speak into the telephone's microphone. This varies the resistance of the microphone, causing the current to vary.

            1. This varying current is the analog voice signal.

            2. This signal is digitized by a Codec at the CO.

        E. The digital signal is sent through the voice circuits to the destination CO.

            1. A Codec at the destination CO converts the digital voice signal back to an analog signal.

            2. This analog signal is sent to the destination user's telephone via a UTP; this signal goes to the handset's earphone and is converted to sound energy, heard by the destination user.

IV. The AT&T long distance system is a layered, or hierarchical system. The local CO receives a call.
   A. The local CO tries to route the call directly.
   B. If the CO cannot find a direct path for a call to the destination, it sends the call up a level.
   C. The next level up tries to route the call with a direct path.
   D. If this level cannot route the call, it will send the call to the level above. This process is repeated until a route is found and the call completed.
V. LATA (Local Access and Transport Areas approximate area codes).
VI. Local telephone companies are called telcos or Local Exchange Carriers (LEC).
VII. Long distance carriers are called InterExchange Carriers (IECs) or IntereXchange Carriers (IXCs).
VIII. Per trunk signaling uses expensive voice circuits to send switching signals.
   A. Users could hear the switching signals as the circuits were being switched.
   B. Hackers easily broke into the system and made many free long distance calls.
IX. Common Channel Interoffice Signaling (CCIS).
   A. Uses a separate signaling channel than the voice.
   B. "Common" means that all the switching is done on a common channel.
   C. 28-bit packet.
   D. Signaling System 7 (SS7) is the current standard.
X. Packet Switched Networks (PSN) carry data using these protocols:
   A. X.25.
   B. Frame Relay (FR).
   C. Internet Protocol (IP).
XI. PSTN impairments, testing, and troubleshooting.
   A. There are several types of noise on the PSTN.
      1. Thermal noise due to random motion of electrons.
      2. Electrical noise from RFI.
      3. Transients such as corroded contacts, power line surges, and dialing noise.
   B. Noise testing; C-message.
      1. 1,004-Hz tone sent down the line.
      2. 1,004-Hz tone is filtered out at receiver, only the noise remains and is measured.
   C. Error rates.
      1. Bit Error Rate (BER, or BERR); bits received in error divided by total bits sent.
      2. Block (frame) Error Rate; blocks received with error(s) divided by blocks sent.
      3. Test by sending a pseudo random bit pattern; this pattern is known at the receiver.
   D. Loopback tests are used; workforce, time, and travel saving.
   E. Jitter—short-term variations in network delay.
      1. Voice not affected.
      2. Modems are very sensitive to jitter.
   F. Transmission monitor records and analyzes distortion, noise, delay, delay jitter, signal dropouts, and loss of synchronization.

QUESTIONS

1. Why does the PSTN use switching?
2. If you depress the "9" button on a DTMF keypad, what frequencies will be sent to the CO? What will the CO do with these frequencies?
3. What is switching fabric? What is switching control? Give examples of each.
4. What is "in band" or "per trunk" signaling? Why is it no longer used?
5. What does the "common" in *common channel signaling* mean? What are the advantages of common channel signaling?
6. What is SS7? What are its advantages and disadvantages?
7. What is the nominal voltage from the CO to the twisted pair going to the user's telephone? What are the magnitude and frequency of the ringing voltage?

8

MULTIPLEXING AND CODECS

OBJECTIVES

In this chapter we will discuss:

I. Why multiplexing is used.
II. Multiplexing techniques.
   A. Frequency Division Multiplexing (FDM).
   B. Time Division Multiplexing (TDM).
III. Transmission of signals—digital versus analog.
   A. How noise affects analog transmissions.
   B. How noise affects digital transmissions.
IV. Analog to Digital (A/D) and Digital to Analog (D/A) conversion techniques.
   A. Linear conversion; why linear conversion is not used in the PSTN.
   B. Non-linear conversion.
      1. Why non-linear conversion is used in the PSTN.
      2. Codecs; segments.
      3. Codec standards.
   C. Resolution.
   D. Sampling rate; Nyquist limit.

8.1 Multiplexing, Why?

It is less expensive to send more than one conversation over a single transmission path, as shown in Figure 8.1. The technique of sending many conversations over a single transmission medium is called *multiplexing*. The two most used methods are **Time Division Multiplexing (TDM)** and **F/requency Division Multiplexing (FDM)**.

The transmission path medium—whether optical fiber, twisted pair (TP), coaxial cable, satellite, microwave, or radio wave—is usually quite expensive. Satellite and undersea optical fiber cable systems are especially costly. However the multiplexing equipment needed to put many conversations over that medium is usually relatively inexpensive.

129

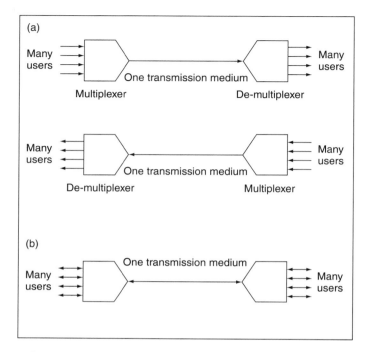

FIGURE 8.1
Full duplex multiplexing systems. (a) Full duplex system with two mediums, and (b) full duplex system with one medium. Data is sent in both directions simultaneously.

There is a relationship between a signal's frequency (how fast it changes) and the bandwidth the signal occupies. This relationship is explained by the Fourier series and is discussed in Appendix A4.

8.1.1 Frequency Division Multiplexing (FDM)

In an FDM system users share the frequency spectrum. The spectrum (available frequencies) is divided among the users. Figure 8.2a illustrates an FDM system as seen on a spectrum analyzer display. A spectrum analyzer displays frequency on the horizontal axis and signal amplitude on the vertical axis. A spectrum analyzer appears to be similar to an oscilloscope, except for the difference in axis. Some digital oscilloscopes can function as either oscilloscopes or spectrum analyzers.

This particular FDM system is used for multiplexing voice conversations and is similar to an older system used in telephone communications. Each conversation uses a different frequency channel. The frequency spectrum is shared among the users.

A voice conversation in a telephone system is limited to 300 to 3,300 hertz by filters. This limited range is sufficient for voice intelligibility but not for good musical or high-fidelity quality. Telephone companies are in the voice transmission business and only rarely transmit music.

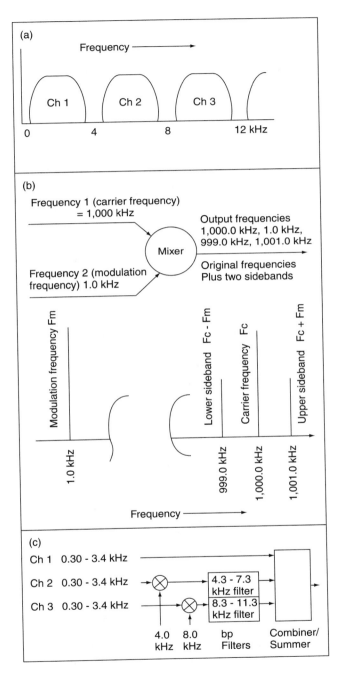

FIGURE 8.2
Frequency division multiplexing (FDM). (a) Spectrum of voice transmission FDM system, (b) Mixing two frequencies, and (c) how the spectrum in (a) is generated.

Mixers and filters are the key ingredients for an FDM system. A mixer combines two signals of different frequencies as in Figure 8.2b The mixer is non-linear, so the output is not only the original frequencies but also the sum and difference of the original frequencies. If signals with frequencies f_1 and f_2 are inputted to the mixer, the output frequencies will be $f_1, f_2, f_1 + f_2$, and $f_1 - f_2$. In Figure 8.2b the carrier frequency Fc of 1,000.0 kHz and the modulation frequency Fm of 1.0 kHz are combined in a mixer. The outputs are the original frequencies of 1,000.0 kHz and 1.0 kHz, and also the upper sideband of 1,001.0 kHz ($Fc + Fm$) and the lower sideband of 999.0 kHz ($Fc - Fm$).

Figure 8.2c shows one method of generating FDM. The channel 1 conversation goes directly to the combiner/summer. The channel 2 conversation enters a mixer. The channel 2 conversation and a 4.0-kHz sine carrier wave signal are mixed. The output is an amplitude modulated signal with two sidebands. The upper sideband is the sum of the 4.0 kHz and any frequency in the channel 2 conversation. The lower sideband is the difference between the 4.0-kHz carrier wave signal and any frequency in the channel 2 conversation. The lower sideband ranges from 700 hertz to 3,700 hertz, and the upper sideband ranges from 4,300 hertz to 7,300 hertz. A band-pass filter removes the lower sideband, and only the upper sideband is passed to the combiner/summer.

Similarly the channel 3 conversation is mixed with an 8.0-kHz sine carrier wave, and again there are two sidebands. A band-pass filter passes only the upper sideband to the combiner. Thus only the upper sidebands enter the combiner/summer and are sent over the medium.

In FDM each channel is given a portion of the frequencies (spectrum) available, or the frequency (spectrum) is divided among the users. One would use a spectrum analyzer to view and troubleshoot an FDM system.

FDM is usually an analog based technique. Cable television uses a similar technique to multiplex the many television channels onto one coaxial cable.

8.1.2 Time Division Multiplexing (TDM)

In a TDM system the users share time. Each user is assigned a small unique unit of time (time slot) in which to transmit the user's data over the medium as shown in Figure 8.3. Users share or divide transmission time (time division).

In Figure 8.3a, a TDM system output is shown as it might appear on an oscilloscope or logic analyzer. A logic analyzer is a special oscilloscope for troubleshooting digital systems. TDM is a digitally based technique.

Usually each data is eight bits or a byte (octet) long. Each data has one place (time slot) in time that it is allowed to pass onto the medium. In Figure 8.3a four data each have their unique slot to be sent over the medium. After all data (four bytes or octets) have been sent in their respective time slots, the sequence repeats.

Figure 8.3b shows how TDM is created. Each data source feeds a storage register. This storage register is a shift register or, more specifically, a First In–First Out (FIFO) shift register. The first bit written into the FIFO will be the first bit read out. The data in these FIFOs is stored until that data's unique time slot (or time to transmit) occurs and the data is read out and sent over the medium.

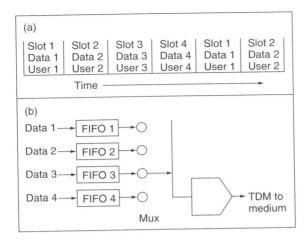

FIGURE 8.3
Time division multiplexing (TDM).

Sometimes the data does not come in at the same rate in all channels. Some channels will have data nearly all the time, and others will have very little data, or slow data, or "bursty" data. Voice, music, or real-time video have data virtually all the time and must have a constant data rate. It is inefficient if all channels are transmitted at the same fast rate when several of the channels have no data. A solution to this dilemma is to transmit only those channels that actually have data. This is done with a statistical multiplexer ("stat-mux"). LANs often have bursty data.

8.1.3 FDM versus TDM

TDM is cheaper than FDM, and thus TDM is used when possible. TDM requires more bandwidth than FDM, but bandwidth is cheap. FDM is an analog method, and TDM is a digitally based method. As our digital data rates increase, the required signal bandwidth increases. See Appendix A4 for a detailed explanation of frequency versus required bandwidth.

One has to qualify the statement that bandwidth is cheap. Bandwidth is cheap when used over a closed medium such as twisted pair (TP), coax, or especially optical fiber. A closed medium is one in which the signal does not escape from the medium and interfere with other users' signals.

Bandwidth is very expensive over the airwaves (radio spectrum). U.S. companies have spent billions of dollars for exclusive rights to certain spectral bands (radio frequency bands) for cellular and wireless communications. Interference can occur between users if careful frequency management is not done. This is one of the tasks of the **Federal Communications Commission (FCC)** and the United Nations. Wireless communications systems must be carefully designed to maximize the number of users while maintaining an acceptable level of interference. The radio spectrum is termed a "limited public resource."

8.2 Analog versus Digital Signal Transmission

Voice and video are analog by nature; that is, they contain an infinite number of possible voltages or amplitudes. The voltages are proportional to the loudness of the voice (or music) signal, or the brightness of the video signal.

The world is analog. However converting an analog signal to an equivalent digital number has many advantages. The obvious advantage is the lower cost and greater efficiency of digital transmission. The digital numbers are easier to manipulate and perform calculations inside a digital computer, as in **Digital Signal Processing (DSP).** A digital number is more easily transmitted over a communications network with fewer errors. Figure 8.4 shows an analog signal converted to a four-bit digital number. Four bits will allow sixteen states:

$$(\text{base } 2)^{4 \text{ bits}} = 16 \text{ states} \qquad \textbf{(Equation 8.1)}$$

When these analog signals are sent over transmission systems, noise and distortion alter the signal. Each amplifier, transformer, transmitter, and receiver adds to the noise and distortion. Compensating for these problems is very difficult. Under poor conditions the signal at the receiving end can become unusable. Some other method had to be found.

Digital signals are subject to the same problems of noise and distortion as analog signals. However digital signals have only two values, either a "one" or a "zero." Electrically a "one" might be approximately 5 volts and a "zero" approximately 0 volt. Special amplifiers at the receiving end (or at a relay station) can easily pick "ones" and "zeros" out of the noise and convert the signal back to clearly definable one's and zero's. These amplifiers are

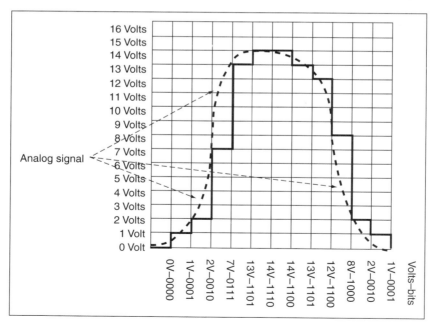

FIGURE 8.4
Analog to Digital Conversion

sometimes called *regenerators* because they "regenerate" the original digital signal. The regenerated signal is an exact copy of the original signal, and no information is lost.

At the receiver the incoming signal may be mixed with a great deal of noise. In Figure 8.5a noise plus signal goes to a simple comparator's input. Simple comparators compare the signal with one reference voltage. If the signal is above the reference, a "one" is outputted. If the signal is below the reference, a "zero" is outputted. As seen in Figure 8.5a, if the signal is near the reference, noise can cause unacceptable spurious outputs. Note that as the input signal jumps about the trip (reference) voltage, the output is very erratic and triggers mostly on noise. The output pulses show very little signal and a lot of noise.

One trick is to use **Schmidt triggers.** These are comparators with positive feedback. The spurious outputs are eliminated by feeding back some of the output to the input. Two different trip points are created, and noise effects are greatly reduced. Note in Figure 8.5b the correct output does indeed regenerate the original digital signal.

Years ago digital transmission was prohibitively expensive, but advances in integrated circuit technology have made digital transmissions preferred. Now digital transmissions are cheaper, more efficient, and more noise resistant than analog. Even analog television signals will be giving way to digital television, allowing **high-definition television (HDTV).**

8.3 Analog to Digital (A/D) and Digital to Analog (D/A) Conversion

8.3.1 Linear A/D and D/A Conversions

In the last section we have seen that a noisy digital signal can be successfully regenerated. However an analog signal will be severely affected and could be rendered unusable. Digital signals are clearly the choice for data communications. Therefore analog signals are usually converted into digital signal for transmission and then converted back to an analog signal at the receiving node. In the telephone system (PSTN) the customers' analog

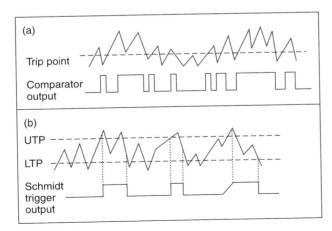

FIGURE 8.5
Schmidt triggers use positive feedback and create hysteresis. UTP = upper trip point, LTP = lower trip point.

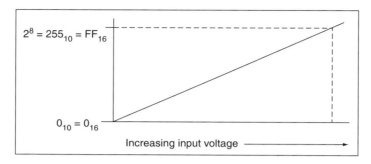

FIGURE 8.6
Conventional A/D converters are linear and feature digital output code that is directly proportional to input.

FIGURE 8.7
Non-linear A/D converters are used in telecommunications because voice intelligibility is most critical and fidelity is not important. Soft sounds (low amplitude) need more amplification than loud sounds, so a logarithmic amplifier is used.

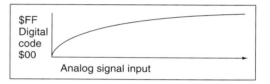

signal from their home or office travels to the Central Office (CO) and is converted to a digital signal (Analog to Digital conversion [A/D]). The digital signal is transmitted to the destination CO and then converted back to an analog signal (Digital to Analog conversion [D/A]) and sent to the receiving customer.

Let's examine the technique used by telephone companies for Analog to Digital (A/D) conversion and Digital to Analog (D/A) conversion. Conventional A/D converters are linear. The digital code output number is directly proportional to the analog input voltage as shown in Figure 8.6. An eight-bit digital code number is shown. The eight-bit output code ranges from 0 to 255_{10} (0 to FF_{16} hexadecimal), or "00000000 to 11111111." These are used in process control, audio compact disks, and most voltage measurements, but not in telephony.

8.3.2 Non-Linear A/D and D/A Conversions

The telecommunications industry uses non-linear A/D and D/A converters to maximize voice intelligibility (Figure 8.7). Voice fidelity is not a crucial issue as it is for audio music compact disks, but voice intelligibility is critical. Soft, low-voltage amplitude signals (whispers between lovers!) need more amplification than loud sounds (your neighbor's kid's drums!). A logarithmic response in the A/D is desired. This method sacrifices some fidelity for voice intelligibility. Gain is defined as

$$\text{Gain} = \frac{\text{Output change}}{\text{Input change}} = \frac{\Delta \text{ output Change}}{\Delta \text{ input change}} = \text{slope} \quad \textbf{(Equation 8.2)}$$

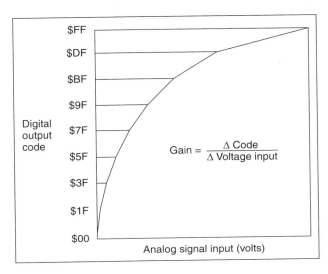

FIGURE 8.8
CODEC gain.

With an A/D converter the output is the digital code and the input is voltage, so the gain is

$$\text{Gain} = \frac{\Delta \text{ output code change}}{\Delta \text{ input voltage change}} = \text{slope} \qquad \textbf{(Equation 8.3)}$$

With the A/D converters used by the telecommunications industry the gain (slope) is highest at low-voltage inputs (soft sounds) and lowest at high-voltage inputs (loud sounds). At the receiving end a special D/A converter changes the digital code back to a linear analog signal. What makes this D/A special is its complementary gain response matching the A/D non-linear response. Used together, this A/D and D/A give a linear system response and are called CODer/DeCoders, or **Codecs.**

Analog signals from the telephone at your home and office are sent over twisted pair (TP) copper wires to the Central Office (CO), where the A/D conversions are made. The digitized signal is sent over the PSTN to the CO at the destination and converted back to an analog signal by the D/A Codec. The D/A Codec output analog signal is sent via TP to the end user's telephone at the home or office.

8.3.3 Codec Segment Gains

The smooth Codec gain graph in Figure 8.7 is actually not a smooth line but rather eight straight-line segments, as shown in Figure 8.8. This type of gain is much easier to manufacture than a smooth line true logarithmic converter. Each of the eight segments covers one-eighth of the total possible digital numbers. Codecs are eight-bit converters, and the total number of possible states is

$$2^8 = 256 \text{ states} \qquad \textbf{(Equation 8.4)}$$

There are eight segments, so

$$\frac{256 \text{ states}}{8 \text{ segments}} = \frac{32 \text{ states}}{\text{segment}} \qquad \textbf{(Equation 8.5)}$$

The slope, or gain, of each segment is different. Together the segments approximate a logarithmic amplifier gain.

8.3.4 Codec Standards

Europe and North America have slightly different Codec standards. North America and Japan use the **μ-law** (pronounced "mu-law" or "meuw-law"), which has a higher gain at low-input voltage signals and less gain at higher input levels. Europeans use the **A-law,** which has a lower gain at low-input voltages and higher gain at higher inputs. The μ-law is considered superior because faint sounds (low-input levels) are reproduced more faithfully.

8.3.5 Codec Resolution

Codecs are A/D converters using eight bits in their digital byte (octet) to represent the input voltage at a point in time. The more bits one uses to represent an audio or video signal, the more faithful the reproduction.

For this example we will use a linear eight-bit converter. With eight bits of resolution the number of possible states is

$$\text{States possible} = 2^{(\text{bits of resolution})} = 2^8 = 256 \text{ possible states} \qquad \textbf{(Equation 8.6)}$$

Assume a maximum input voltage of 10.24 volts. The resolution or difference between two steps or resolution is

$$\text{Resolution} = \text{step size} = \frac{10.24 \text{ volts}}{256 \text{ steps or states}} = \frac{0.040 \text{ volt, or 40 mV}}{\text{step}} \qquad \textbf{(Equation 8.7)}$$

We see that our final output cannot be a continuous wave but a series of steps, each at least 0.040 volt, or 40 millivolts. Figure 8.9 shows what such an output would be with three bits of resolution. Such an output is obviously noisier than one having greater resolution.

Codecs use eight bits in their digital byte (octet) to represent the input voltage at a point in time. The more bits one uses to represent an audio or video signal, the more faithful the reproduction. A smoothing (low-pass) filter is used to smooth out the sharp steps.

While only eight bits are used for Codecs, sixteen bits are used for audio music compact disks (CDs). Let's see what the resolution of sixteen bits is:

$$\text{States possible} = 2^{16} = 65,536$$

$$\text{Resolution} = \text{step size} = \frac{10.24 \text{ volts}}{65,536 \text{ states or steps}} = \frac{0.0001563 \text{ volt}}{\text{step or state}} \qquad \textbf{(Equation 8.8)}$$

$$= \frac{0.1563 \text{ millivolt}}{\text{step or state}} = \frac{156.3 \text{ microvolts}}{\text{state or step}}$$

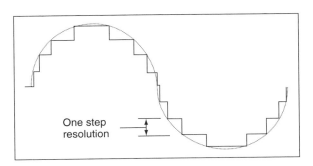

FIGURE 8.9
CODEC resolution. Three bit (8 states = 2^3) resolution digitizing a sine wave (shown by dotted line).

Obviously the smaller steps resulting from sixteen-bit resolution will give a much better reproduction and fidelity than eight bits. However the world's telephone companies are concerned with voice intelligibility, not musical fidelity. Research has shown that eight bits is the minimum possible resolution for adequate civilian voice intelligibility and what paying customers (toll customers) will tolerate. A sixteen-bit Codec is much more expensive to build than an eight-bit Codec, and sixteen bits are twice as expensive to transmit as eight bits.

Military users will tolerate a seven-bit resolution, but these users are trained to understand lower fidelity voice. The listener may not be able to recognize the speaker's voice.

Telephone companies are in the business of transmitting voice digitally, not music. There is no economic reason to use more than eight bits for Codecs for voice transmission over the PSTN.

8.3.6 Codec Conversion Rate

How fast must we sample the Codec input voltage? The faster we sample the input voltage, the better our reproduction. The fewer samples we make, the cheaper our transmission costs. So what is the minimum sample rate possible? Dr. Harry Nyquist determined the lower limit of the sample rate (minimum sample frequency Fs, or $Fs[\min]$), and it is

$$Fs(\text{minimum}) > 2 \times (\text{maximum input frequency}) \quad \textbf{(Equation 8.9)}$$

If we sample at $Fs(\min)$ we get a barely usable reproduction. The arrows in Figure 8.10 show the minimum sample rate.

What happens if we sample at less than $Fs(\text{minimum})$? As seen in Figure 8.10 we will have aliasing, that is, frequencies in our digital sample that are not in the original signal! There is no way to remove these erroneous frequencies. We must prevent them from entering the system by sampling above $Fs(\min)$. An *alias* is using a false name or, in our case, a false frequency.

An analogy is watching a western movie scene with a moving stage coach. The wheel spokes appear to either remain stationary or move backward slowly, or move forward slowly. Motion pictures are a series of photographs (samples) at about a 32 samples/

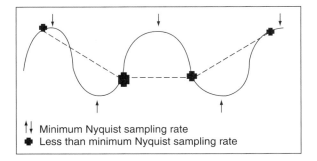

FIGURE 8.10
Aliasing. At the minimum Nyquist rate we can get a reasonable (but not good) reproduction of the input. But below the minimum Nyquist sampling rate, the output signal is NOT an accurate reproduction of the input. This is called "aliasing."

second rate. The rate of motion of the wheel spokes is faster than the 32 sample / second rate, and so we have aliasing, the apparent slow motion of the spokes.

Audio over the PSTN is limited to 3.4 kHz by filters. The minimum sample frequency is 2×3.4 kHz = 6,800 samples / second. Codecs use 8,000 or 8 K samples /second for a slight oversampling.

Eight bits of resolution and 8,000 samples / second have been found to be adequate for voice intelligibility and are the best economic compromise between fidelity and costs. The total sample rate is

$$\text{Sample rate } = \frac{8 \text{ bits} \times 8 \text{ K samples}}{\text{second}} = \frac{64 \text{ K samples}}{\text{second}} \qquad \textbf{(Equation 8.10)}$$

This is the rate of T-1, ISDN, and X.25 systems. Military systems sometimes use only seven-bit sampling.

SUMMARY

   I. Why do we multiplex? Economics.
      A. Transmission medium is often a high-cost part of the system.
      B. Multiplexing and de-multiplexing equipment costs are inexpensive relative to cost of transmission medium.
   II. Methods of multiplexing.
      A. Frequency Division (FDM).
      B. Time Division (TDM).
      C. TDM is usually cheaper than FDM, therefore used more in data communications.
   III. Which is better for transmission, analog or digital?
      A. Digital transmission is more noise tolerant.
      B. Digital transmission is more efficient and lower cost.

IV. Analog to Digital (A/D) and Digital to Analog (D/A) converters.
    A. Linear conversion.
    B. Non-linear conversion is used in the PSTN. Codec and Codec standards.
        1. μ-law.
        2. A-law.
    C. Resolution.
        1. Codecs use eight-bit resolution.
        2. Music uses sixteen-bit resolution.
        3. Military can use seven-bit resolution.
    D. Sampling rate.
        1. Nyquist's limit; sample frequency must be greater than twice the highest frequency to be converted.
        2. 64 kbps is standard for PSTN.

QUESTIONS

1. What is the purpose of multiplexing?
2. What is a Codec?
3. Why do telephone companies digitize the analog telephone conversations?
4. What are the two main types of multiplexing? Explain what each is.
5. Why is bandwidth "cheap" in a closed medium and possibly very expensive over the open airwaves?
6. What is a statistical multiplexer?
7. Given a ten-bit linear A/D and a 6-volt maximum input signal, what is the resolution (minimum step)?
8. What happens if an analog signal is sampled at less than the Nyquist minimum sample rate? How can this effect be eliminated once it is in the system? What can be done to prevent this?
9. What is the Codec type used in North America and Japan? What is the Codec type used in Europe? What are the differences between them?
10. Given a seven-bit system and a sample rate of 7.5 K samples per second, what is the bit rate?

9

MODULATION AND MODEMS

OBJECTIVES

In this chapter we will discuss:

   I. Why do we need a modem to connect a computer to the phone lines?
   II. The relationship between signal frequency and necessary bandwidth.
  III. Modems and why we need modulation.
     A. To put information onto a carrier signal.
     B. The carrier wave and its associated sidebands pass through the PSTN.
  IV. Modulation (putting information onto a signal, or changing a carrier wave [signal]).
     A. Amplitude Modulation (AM).
     B. Frequency Modulation (FM).
     C. Phase Modulation (PM).
     D. Phase Modulation and Frequency Modulation are almost the same thing.
   V. Bit rate and Baud rate are not the same.
     A. Bit rate is how fast the data is transferred.
     B. Baud rate is how fast the signal changes.
  VI. Frequency Shift Keying (FSK); FSK used in first modems.
 VII. Phase Shift Keying (PSK).
     A. Biphase (two-state, one-bit PSK); Two-Phase Differential Phase Shift Keying (DPSK).
     B. Quadrature (four states, two bits) Shift Keying (QPSK).
       1. Four-Phase Shift Keying (Quadrature PSK).
       2. Differential Four-Phase Shift Keying (D Quadrature PSK).
       3. Quadrature Amplitude Modulation (QAM).
VIII. Transmission impairments.
     A. Harmonic distortion.
     B. Phase jitter.
     C. Noise.
  IX. Simplex—one-way (only one direction).
   X. Half duplex—alternate directions; each end takes turns talking.
  XI. Full duplex—both ends talk at the same time.

9.1 Why Can't We Connect Our Computer Directly To The Phone Line?

Computers can transmit logic level voltage 1's (+ 5 volts) and 0's (0 volt) internally because only a wire connects the source and destination. The wire can pass information down to **DC** (**Direct Current** at a frequency of zero hertz) or voltage levels. The telephone system is much more than wires connecting the user's telephone. It has amplifiers, transformers, and capacitors that cannot pass information down to DC or zero hertz. Therefore telephone lines cannot transmit 1's and 0's as voltage levels but can pass **Alternating Current (AC)** signals, such as audio frequencies.

The telephone system was designed for voice transmission at audio frequencies. A **modem** converts the 1's and 0's into modulated audio frequencies that can pass through the telephone system. The telcos even use tones for sending dialing information, namely, the Dual Tone Multi-Frequency (DTMF) system.

9.2 Speed Versus Bandwidth

Voice on the telephone system, or Public Switched Telephone Network (PSTN), is limited to a bandwidth of 300 Hz to 3,400 Hz as shown in Figure 9.1. This bandwidth is sufficient for voice intelligibility but not for high fidelity musical. To send 1's and 0's over the PSTN, the bandwidth would have to go down to 0 Hz or DC (direct current, or not changing). This means that coupling capacitors and transformers could not be used in amplifiers, making amplifier design very difficult. The upper bandwidth end point limits the rate at which data can be sent through the system. We will see that as the data rate increases, the necessary bandwidth also increases. But the 3,400-Hz upper limit of the PSTN limits the data rate. The theoretical relationship between signal frequency and bandwidth is explored in Appendix A4. This relationship is the Fourier series.

Figure 9.2 shows the relationship between signal frequency and required bandwidth. Figure 9.2a shows the oscilloscope (voltage versus time) trace of a low-frequency square wave signal. Figure 9.2b shows the spectrum analyzer (voltage versus frequency) of this low-frequency signal. A spectrum analyzer is an instrument that shows voltage on the vertical axis and frequency on the horizontal axis. Figure 9.2c shows the oscilloscope (voltage versus time) trace of a higher frequency square wave signal. Figure 9.2d shows the spectrum analyzer (voltage versus frequency) of this higher frequency signal.

The greatest amplitude harmonic is at the fundamental frequency f or $1/T$; the next greatest amplitude at $3f = 3/T$; the next highest amplitude at $5f = 5/T$, and so on. Note that in both cases there are multiples (harmonics) of the signal frequency (fundamental). Note also that the higher frequency signal (Figure 9.2c and Figure 9.2d) creates harmonics of a higher frequency. The higher frequency signal needs more bandwidth (frequency space) to adequately transmit its signal.

If we try to increase the data rate (frequency), the period T decreases and therefore the frequency $\left(f = \frac{1}{T}\right)$ increases. Increased frequencies require greater bandwidth. However the telephone system (Public Switched Telephone Network [PSTN])

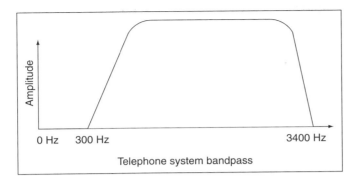

FIGURE 9.1
Limited phone line bandwidth. Lower band limit is 300 Hz, it does not go to 0 Hz or DC. Upper band limit is 3,400 Hz, which limits data rate.

has an upper bandwidth limit of 3,400 hertz. This limits how high the bit stream frequency can be.

9.3 Modulation

Let us examine modulation, first the simple forms and then combinations of modulation techniques to give high data rates through the telephone lines. Modulation combines two or more signals, usually one high frequency (carrier wave, carrier signal, or carrier frequency) and one or more much lower frequency signals (modulation frequency or frequencies). This combination process can be described mathematically, but we will not delve into the math in this book. There are many good books discussing modulation theory. The modulation process modifies or changes the carrier signal as a function of the modulation frequency.

Thus the modulation frequency information is put onto the carrier signal. The carrier signal "carries" or transports the modulation frequency information. Examples are AM and FM broadcast radio. For technical reasons beyond this book's scope, the audio frequencies (voice and music, that is, information) cannot be broadcast (sent or transported) directly over the air or via wireless. The audio frequencies must be put onto the carrier signal via modulation. The carrier frequencies can travel through space from the sender's antenna to the customer's receivers, carrying the audio frequencies.

9.3.1 Modems

Modems convert digital 1's and 0's to an audio frequency that can be sent over the telephone system (Public Switched Telephone System [PSTN]). The PSTN was designed for voice, not data, so modulation techniques are necessary to encode these digital 1's and 0's into an audio waveform compatible with the PSTN. Voice on the PSTN is limited to a bandwidth of 300 Hz to 3,400 Hz as shown in Figure 9.1. To send 1's and 0's over the

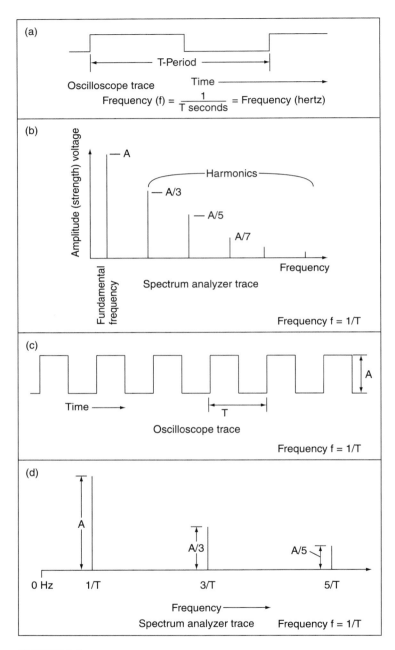

FIGURE 9.2
(a) and (b) Low-frequency binary bit stream, (c) and (d) higher frequency binary bit stream.

PSTN, the bandwidth would have to go down to 0 Hz. This means that capacitors and transformers could not be used in amplifiers, making design very difficult.

Modems are being developed for use over cable television for faster Internet downloading. Cable television has a much greater bandwidth than the PSTN. As of this writing the cable modem standards are still being developed. Slow downloading is one of the major user complaints about the Internet. This is discussed in Chapter 18.

Modems are used to convert between computers and the telephone system. Modems receive digital information from the computer and then use modulation to put the computer information into an audio waveform that can be transmitted over the telephone lines. Modems also receive audio tones from the PSTN and convert them into digital information usable by the computer.

9.3.2 Modulation Types

Modulation combines two waveforms, the carrier frequency Fc and the modulation frequency Fm, in a special way. Mathematically modulation is a type of multiplication.

Modulation is changing or altering a sine wave. In electronics this sine wave is called a *carrier wave*. The carrier wave starts out as a pure single frequency, constant peak voltage sine wave. But this carrier wave does not carry any useful information. With modulation, or altering this carrier sine wave, we change the pure sine wave into something else. Mathematically the sine wave can be described as

$$V(t) = A \sin [(2\pi f t) + \Theta]$$ **(Equation 9.1)**

where A is the peak amplitude in volts or amperes
              f is the frequency in hertz (cycles per second)
              t is instantaneous time
              Θ is the phase shifted angle in degrees or radians

Using modulation we can alter $A, f,$ or Θ, or a combination of A and Θ. See Figure 9.3a.

Three modulation techniques are available for modems. They are Amplitude Modulation (AM), Frequency Modulation (FM), and Phase Modulation (PM). AM is never used alone in modems, but sometimes a combination of AM and PM is used. AM changes the amplitude (A), FM changes the frequency (f), and PM changes the phase (Θ). All these changes in the carrier frequency reflect the modulation frequency or information we wish to put into the carrier frequency.

Figure 9.3a shows what a pure sine wave would look like on an oscilloscope. An oscilloscope shows the waveform voltage on the vertical axis and time on the horizontal axis. Figure 9.3b shows what the pure sine wave looks like on a spectrum analyzer. A spectrum analyzer is an instrument that shows voltage on the vertical axis and frequency on the horizontal axis. Note that the pure sine wave has only one frequency component. The unmodulated wave does not carry any information. To carry any information we must use modulation.

9.3.2.1 Amplitude Modulation In Figure 9.4a we amplitude modulate the carrier wave (the pure sine wave described in the last section with frequency Fc) with a lower

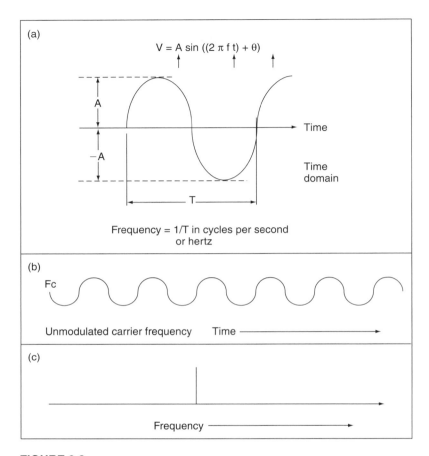

FIGURE 9.3

Modulation (V = **A** sin ((2 π f **t**) + θ). The bold parameters may be varied. These variations are called modulation (a). Modulation is the process of adding information to a carrier signal (frequency) or changing the carrier signal. An unmodulated wave, V = A sin ((2 π f t) + θ), does not change with time (b). Only one frequency is present in the spectrum analyzer trace shown in (c). No information is being sent.

frequency (longer period Fm) wave. This lower frequency wave (modulating frequency Fm) is the information we wish to put onto the carrier wave.

The first three parts of Figure 9.4a are oscilloscope graphs. The modulating frequency Fm is shown in the upper part of the graph. The carrier wave frequency Fc is shown in the second part of the graph. The third part of the graph is the modulated carrier wave. Note that the carrier wave amplitude varies with the modulating frequency waveform. Figure 9.4b is the frequency spectrum of the modulated carrier wave. Note that the carrier frequency is there as before, but there are two other frequencies called *sidebands*. The actual information is in the sidebands. The sideband frequencies are f(sideband) = $Fc \pm Fm$ or $Fc + Fm$, and $Fc - Fm$. The bandwidth is $2\ Fm = [(Fc + Fm) - (Fc - Fm)]$.

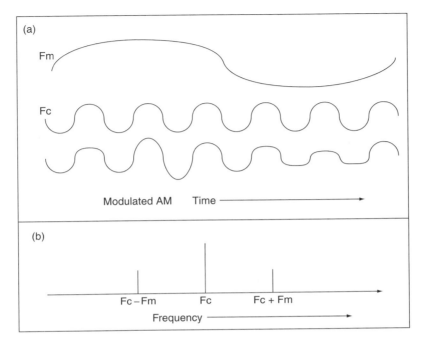

FIGURE 9.4
Amplitude Modulation (V = A sin ((2 π f t) + θ). The carrier amplitude is varied with the modulation frequency.

The AM bandwidth is twice the highest modulation frequency. The higher the modulation frequency, the wider the necessary bandwidth.

Mixers can also perform AM and are discussed in Chapter 8 in the section on Frequency Division Multiplexing (FDM).

9.3.2.2 Frequency Modulation We can change the carrier frequency (*f*) with a lower frequency (longer period *Fm*) wave and create Frequency Modulation (FM). This is used in FM broadcasting and other voice communications systems. This modulation method has the disadvantage of requiring a wide bandwidth but is much less susceptible to noise than AM. Also interference from other weaker FM signals will be ignored. FM is shown in Figure 9.5. *Fm* is the modulating signal, and *Fout* is the FM modulated output signal. The mathematical analysis of FM signals uses Bessel functions. It can be quite involved and not very intuitive. Excellent texts are available for the interested student.

The phase Θ can be changed with a lower frequency (longer period *Fm*) wave and create phase modulation or PM. PM can be considered a special case of FM. The FM diagram is virtually the same for PM.

Note that in Figure 9.5b several frequencies are present in the sidebands, not just one in each sideband like AM. The bandwidth is proportional to the modulating frequency amplitude and can be quite wide.

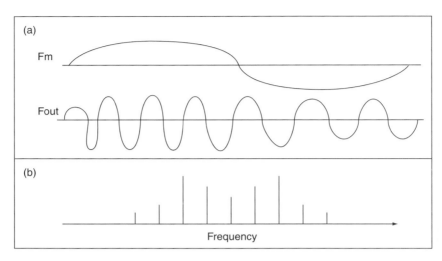

FIGURE 9.5
Frequency Modulation (V = A sin ((2 π ft) + θ). (a) The carrier frequency is varied with the modulation frequency. (b) The frequency spectrum is very complex and is analyzed using Bessel functions.

9.4 Phase Diagrams

A common method of showing phase and amplitude is with a phase diagram or **constellation.** Figure 9.6a illustrates an angular shift or phase shift. If this shows a change in the modulating digital signal, it is called Phase Shift Keying (PSK). Figure 9.6b shows an amplitude shift as a change in radius. If this indicates a change in the modulating digital signal, it is called Amplitude Shift Keying (ASK). Later we will discuss combinations of ASK and PSK.

9.5 Bit Rate and Baud Rate

Bit rate and Baud rate are sometimes used interchangeably. They are not the same! The bit rate (bits per second, or bps) is the rate the data is transferred. The Baud rate is the signaling rate. This can sometimes be considered the carrier frequency. The Baud rate is limited by the upper bandwidth limit of the phone system. If we use clever modulation techniques, it is possible to have bit rates much greater than the Baud rate. Bit rates of 56,600 bps are being successfully transmitted using Baud rates less than the 3,400-Hz bandwidth limit of the phone system. Let us examine methods of getting more bits per baud.

9.6 Frequency Shift Keying (FSK)

The first modem modulation techniques used Frequency Shift Keying (FSK). If the data was a logic "1," a certain audio frequency was transmitted, and if the data was a logic "0," a different audio frequency was transmitted as shown in Figure 9.7. These techniques had a very slow bit rate by today's standards.

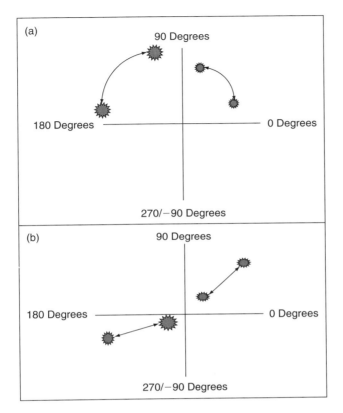

FIGURE 9.6
Constellations. The phase is changed or shifted (a). This a Phase Modulation. It is called Phase Shift Keying if the shift is in response to a digital modulating signal. Constellations show amplitude and phase (b). The angle is the phase, and the distance from the center is the amplitude. This figure shows Amplitude Shift Keying.

The first modem standard was Bell Standard 103, which sent data at a torrid (for that time) 300 bits per second (bps) but did have the advantage of being full duplex (both stations able to transmit simultaneously). The second technique was Bell Standard 202, which ripped along at a whopping 1,200 bps, a big improvement over Bell 103 but very slow by modern standards. However Bell 202 was half duplex (one station transmitting at a time, or both stations alternating transmissions). Both methods quickly ran into the PSTN bandwidth limiting the data rate. For these two protocols the data rate (bits per second) was the same as the baud (signaling rate, or modulation change) rate. The PSTN was designed for voice transmission with its 3,400-Hz upper frequency band limit. This limits the data rate unless we use special techniques.

The frequency spectra of FSK can be quite complicated, and a detailed analysis is beyond the scope of this book. Figure 9.7 illustrates FSK. Figure 9.7a is the digital signal modulating the modem. Figure 9.7b is the modem output (modulated audio frequency) sent to the PSTN. Note that the carrier frequency is higher for a logic "0" and lower for a logic "1." Figure 9.7b is a typical audio spectrum for FSK. The lower

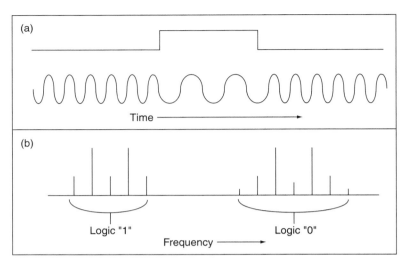

FIGURE 9.7
FSK time and frequency.

grouping of frequencies is for the logic "1," and the upper frequency group is for the logic "0."

For FSK the bit rate is equal to the baud rate.

9.7 Phase Shift Keying (PSK)

9.7.1 Two-Phase Shift Keying

Two-Phase Shift Keying (PSK) is illustrated in Figure 9.8. A sine wave generator output is sent to two buffers, one inverting and the other non-inverting. The buffer outputs are 180 degrees out of phase. An electronic switch switches between the two phases. Which phase is selected depends on whether a logic "1" or logic "0" is to be sent. If a "1" is to be sent, the 180-degree shifted output is selected; if a "0" is to be sent, the zero-degree phase shifted output is selected.

The oscilloscope (voltage versus time) middle trace in Figure 9.8b shows a typical output. The phase diagram of Figure 9.8c shows the two phase states, at zero degrees and 180 degrees. One phase point or dot represents a "1" and the other a "0." For two-phase PSK the bit rate is equal to the Baud rate. Biphase PSK also has the advantage of a narrow bandwidth. Since system noise is proportional to bandwidth, biphase PSK's narrow bandwidth needs can result in lower system noise.

Biphase PSK is not used in any modem telecommunications standard but is found in low signal-to-noise conditions, such as cellular and Personal Communication Service (PCS). It is also used on satellite and deep space probe applications. Biphase was used on the Voyager missions to the outer planets and is on the Galileo mission to Jupiter.

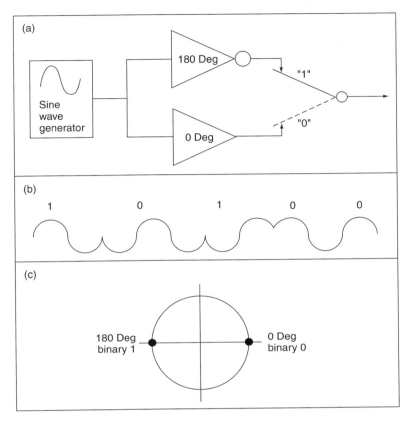

FIGURE 9.8
Binary Phase Shift Keying (BPSK). (a) Binary (two-phase) shift keying, (b) typical two-phase generation, and (c) BPSK phase diagram.

9.7.1.1 Two-Phase Differential Shift Keying (DPSK)   A variation of biphase PSK is illustrated in Figure 9.9. The phase shift of zero degrees or 180 degrees no longer shows a binary one or zero. Instead a phase shift indicates a data change from a zero to a one, or a change from a one to a zero. Synchronization is easier with DPSK. The initial state must be known. Clever synchronization techniques let the receiver know the initial state.

9.7.2 Four-Phase Shift Keying (Quadrature PSK)

Four-Phase Shift Keying, or Quadrature PSK, is used in modems. Bell 212 or V.22 and Bell 201 or V.26 are two such standards. The "Bell" means a North American standard, and the "V" means a European (**CCITT**) standard.

In the block diagram of Figure 9.10 a sine wave generator output is sent to four phase shifters. The buffers shift the phase zero degrees, 90 degrees, 180 degrees, and 270 degrees. An electronic switch selects the proper output and makes the selection, depending

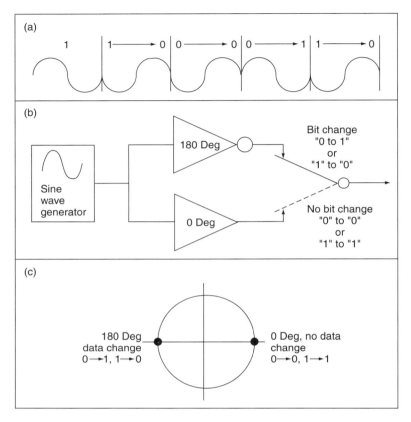

FIGURE 9.9
Differential Binary Phase Shift Keying (DBPSK). (a) Binary Differential (two-phase) Shift Keying, (b) typical differential two-phase generation, and (c) DBPSK phase diagram.

on which two-bit combination is to be sent over the PSTN. For instance a "0 0" bit combination would select zero degrees shifted output; a "0 1" combination would select the 90-degree shifted output; a "1 1" combination would select a 180-degree shifted output; and a "1 0" combination would select the 270-degree shifted output. Each of the four states (0-, 90-, 180-, and 270-degree shifted) represents two bits. Thus for each baud (state or modulation shift) we send two bits. The bit rate (bps) is twice the baud or modulation rate.

Assume an audio carrier frequency of 2,000 Hz used with a Four-Phase Shift Keying system. The data rate is

$$R = 2{,}000 \text{ Hz} \times (2 \text{ bits per state }) = 2{,}000 \times 2 \qquad \textbf{(Equation 9.2)}$$
$$= 4{,}000 \text{ bits per second} = 4{,}000 \text{ bps}$$

Note that the bit rate is greater than the 3,400-Hz upper bandwidth limit of the telephone system.

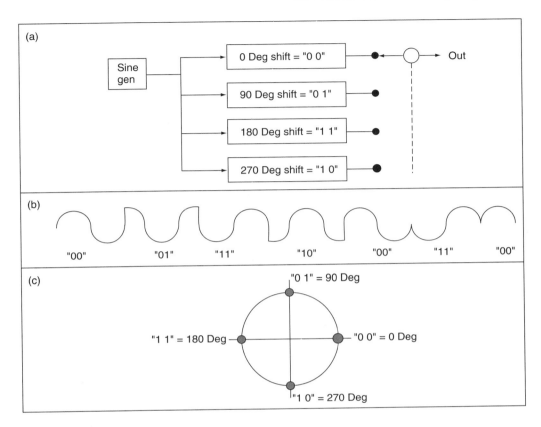

FIGURE 9.10
Quadrature (four phase) Modulation. Bell 212 or V.22 modem = 600 baud/1200 bps; Bell 201 or V.26 modem = 1200 baud/2400 bps. Note that Baud rate and bit rate are not the same. Four states allow two bits to be sent within each state (baud).

9.7.2.1 Differential Four-Phase Shift Keying (D Quadrature PSK) Differential Four-Phase Shift Keying uses the change of data to change the phase. As shown in Figure 9.11, a change of data controls the phase. This is similar to two-phase Differential Phase Shift Keying discussed earlier.

9.7.3 Quadrature Amplitude Modulation (QAM)

In the ever continuing effort to put more bits per second through the limited bandwidth of the PSTN, engineers developed Quadrature Amplitude Modulation (QAM). A typical standard is Bell 209 or CCITT V.32 with sixteen states, a Baud rate of 2,400 Hz, and a bit rate of 9,600 bps. The sixteen states allow four bits to be sent with each state. Each of the sixteen unique states represents a unique four-bit combination.

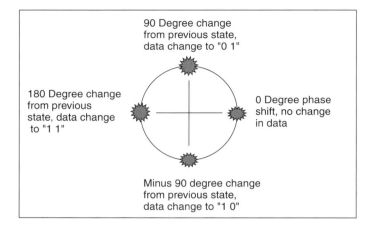

FIGURE 9.11
Differential Quadrature Phase Shift Keying (DQPSK). The phase transmitted depends on the previous state, hence the term *differential*.

In the phase amplitude diagram of Figure 9.12 the phase states are shown progressing counterclockwise from zero degrees at the right horizontal line. Increasing amplitude is represented by increasing radii from the center of the circle. Thus each state is a unique combination of phase and amplitude. This pattern is called a *constellation*.

There are sixteen states, each representing a unique four-bit combination.

$$\text{Number of states} = 2^{\left[\frac{bits}{state}\right]} = 2^{\left[\frac{4\ bits}{state}\right]} = 16 \text{ total states} \quad \textbf{(Equation 9.3)}$$

Table 9.1 shows most of the modem standards. The term *bis* means second in French, that is, the second version of that standard.

The 56.6 Kbps modems have just been standardized. When the modems were introduced, each manufacturer used its own specification. This retarded the acceptance and sales of these newer modems, forcing the manufacturers to find a common standard (V.90). Refer to Chapter 1 for a discussion about the advantages of standards.

9.8 Transmission Impairments

The PSTN distorts the modem constellation in several ways (Figure 9.13). A normal phase diagram is shown in Figure 9.13a. Harmonic distortion (Figure 9.13b) creates harmonics of the transmitted frequencies. *Harmonics* are multiples of the original frequency. For instance, the second harmonic of 1,000 Hz is 2,000 Hz, the third harmonic is 3,000 Hz, and so on. Noise (Figure 9.13c) will expand the constellation points. Phase jitter (the signal being delayed differing times) will cause the constellation points to be widened in the phase directions (Figure 9.13d).

The modem analog signal is converted to digital numbers at the Central Office (CO) of the PSTN. These digital numbers can be delayed differing times during their travels

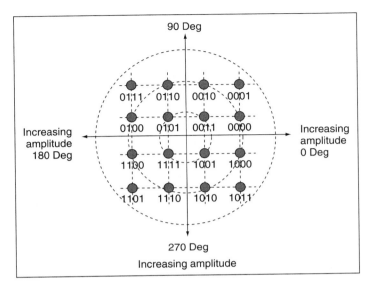

FIGURE 9.12

QAM. Each dot represents a unique four bit combination; i.e., binary "0000_2" to "1111_2" or 0_{16} to F_{16}. There are $2^4 = 16$ dots or states. These states are unique combinations of phase and amplitude because they send a unique four bit combination in one baud (signaling change). This "constellation" could be either Bell 209A at 2400 baud/9600 bps or V.32 modem standard.

TABLE 9.1

Some modem protocols

Type	Data Rate	Baud Rate	Modulation Method	Carrier Frequencies
103	300	300	FSK	1,070/1,270 originate 2,025/2,225 answer
202	1,200	1,200	FSK	1,200/2,200
201	2,400	1,200	DPSK	1,800
V.22bis	2,400	600	QAM	1,200/2,400
	1,200	600	DPSK	1,200/2,400
208	4,800	1,600	PM	1,800
209	9,600	2,400	QAM	1,650
V.29	9,600	2,400	QAM	1,700
	4,800	2,400	DPSK	1,700
V.32	9,600	2,400	QAM	1,800
	4,800	2,400	QAM	1,800
V.33	14,400	2,400	QAM	1,800

FIGURE 9.13
Modem transmission impairments. (a) No impairments, (b) harmonic distortion, (c) noise, and (d) phase jitter.

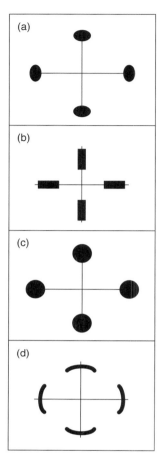

through the PSTN, causing phase jitter. This is rarely a problem in voice transmission but can cause problems for high-speed modems.

9.9 Simplex, Half Duplex, Full Duplex

9.9.1 Simplex

Simplex is one-direction (one-way) transmission. Only the sending node transmits, and only the receiving node receives. Radio and television broadcasting are two examples of simplex.

9.9.2 Half Duplex

Half duplex is one node transmitting while the other node(s) listen. The other node(s) transmit when it is their turn. This is often done because each user shares the spectrum space with the other users. Half duplex examples are some modem standards, such as Bell 212, Kermit, X-Modem, and Y-Modem. Police, taxi, fire, and amateur radio conversations share the same spectrum space and must use half duplex.

The old **BiSync** Wide Area Network protocol uses half duplex. The origination node transmits its entire frame to the destination node. The destination node receives the entire frame and then sends its own frame back to the originating node. The two nodes take turns transmitting and listening. This protocol was dubbed "stop and wait." Never do both nodes transmit at the same time. This obsolete protocol is just too slow for modern needs but originated when transmission facilities were only half duplex.

9.9.3 Full Duplex

Full duplex means both the originating node and the receiving node can transmit at the same time. Both nodes will be able to receive the other's transmission while they themselves are transmitting.

The telephone system is full duplex. The phone system uses the same twisted wire pair to send and receive. The send and receive signals are passing in the opposite direction along the same twisted pair connecting the Central Office to the end user. A device called a *hybrid* separates the two signals and keeps them from interfering with each other. Between Central Offices the receive and transmit signals use separate circuits.

The cellular telephone system is full duplex because the transmitting and receiving signals do not share the same spectrum space. Different frequencies are used for transmitting and receiving. More modern data transmission systems such as optical fiber, Frame Relay, X.25, and SNA are also full duplex.

The Bell 103 modem standard send and receive signal uses separate portions of the telephone voice 300- to 3,400-Hz bandwidth. This is an example of Frequency Division Multiplexing (FDM). Because of the narrow bandwidth used and the simple modulation (FSK) scheme, the data rate is a mere 300 bps.

9.10 Testing and Troubleshooting

Since modems use the PSTN, the imperfections of the PSTN affect modem performance. The impairments include attenuation, noise, delay distortion, harmonic distortion, intermodulation distortion, echoes, amplitude jitter, and phase jitter. Increased data rates need closer distinctions between amplitude and phase of the detected signals.

The signal-to-noise ratio is about 30 dB for a local call in the United States and about 25 dB for a long distance call. For international calls the signal-to-noise ratio may be much lower.

On high-speed systems like V.32 a single error corrupting one state (baud or symbol) will cause four or five bit errors. PSTN noise tends to occur in bursts and corrupt several symbols, resulting in a large number of bit errors. Usual PSTN error testing is for Bit Error Rate (BER), which is the number of bit errors received divided by the total number of bits sent. Modem error control requires re-transmission of a block (group of bits). A block transmission tends to mask individual baud (symbol) errors, so block checking is appropriate.

The Telecommunications Industry Association (TIA) and the Electronics Industries Association (EIA) have formulated RS-496A. RS-496A has six tests for modems, including attenuation and attenuation distortion, delay distortion, phase jitter, frequency offset, intermodulation distortion, and noise. Test results may differ from one time to another, depending on the routing of the call. If a modem is tested on a Monday at 10 A.M. (a high traffic time) and the test is repeated at 11 P.M. (a low traffic time), the results could differ because the call routing was probably different. Even statistics must be called into play to adequately interpret modem test results.

SUMMARY

   I. We cannot put voltage levels directly onto a telephone line; the telephone lines cannot handle direct current signals.
  II. To send data over the telephone system, data must be converted into audio (alternating current) signals; these audio signals must be of a low enough frequency to pass through the phone system.
     A. This limit reduces the maximum data rate, unless we use special techniques.
     B. The faster the data rate, the higher the frequency range (bandwidth) needed.
     C. The PSTN bandwidth is limited to 3,300 Hz, and limits the Baud rate.
 III. In a modem, data is put onto a carrier signal (it "carries" the information); the carrier signal's frequency is low enough so that the signal can pass through the PSTN and still carry the data.
  IV. Amplitude Modulation (AM) changes the signal amplitude or strength voltage.
   V. Frequency Modulation (FM) changes the signal's frequency.
  VI. Phase Modulation (PM) changes the signal's phase.
 VII. Strictly speaking these terms are analog terms; when applied to putting digital information onto the carrier wave, the terms become Amplitude Shift Keying (ASK), Frequency Shift Keying (FSK), and Phase Shift Keying (PSK).
VIII. Early modems used FM.
  IX. Modern modems use a combination of AM and PM to create Quadrature Amplitude Modulation (QAM).
     A. With QAM the data rate is several times the Baud or signaling rate (carrier frequency).
     B. The bit rate (data rate) can be quite higher than the PSTN bandwidth.
   X. Differential keying sends the change in state and is easier for the receiving modem to synchronize.
  XI. Simplex transmission is one-way transmission only.
 XII. In half duplex transmission each end station of the transmission link takes turns transmitting.
XIII. In full duplex transmission systems each end of the link transmits at the same time.

QUESTIONS

1. Explain in your own words AM, FM, and PM.
2. Explain what Baud rate and bit rate are, and how they can be different.
3. How can 9,600 bps be sent through a telephone line with a maximum bandwidth of 3,400 Hz?
4. Explain simplex, half duplex, and full duplex.
5. Why can't computers send digital information directly on the phone lines? Why are modems necessary?
6. What is the general meaning of modulation? What is the purpose of modulation?
7. Explain QAM in your own words.
8. What is Differential Phase Shift Keying? It is not sufficient to merely define the acronym.
9. Given a carrier frequency of 1800 Hz and three bits per state, what is the data rate?

10

T CARRIER

OBJECTIVES

In this chapter we will discuss:.

   I. Why T-1 was created; to increase capacity (number of phone conversations) on existing twisted pair (TP) wire.

  II. What is T and T Carrier?
    A. Time Division Multiplexing (TDM), or time sharing a channel.
    B. T-1 has 24 channels time sharing one TP.
    C. T-3 has 672 channels time sharing one transmission channel.

 III. TDM uses multiplexers and de-multiplexers.

 IV. Basic sample rate from Codecs is 64,000 bits per second.

  V. First In–First Out shift registers are needed to store data until sent out at T-1 bit rate.

 VI. T-1 bit rate is 1,544,000 bits per second.

VII. T-3 is 28 T-1's, and the bit rate is 44,736,000 bits per second.

VIII. T-1 frame contains 24 time slots, or time multiplexes 24 voice conversations onto one T-1 channel; a T-1 frame has one framing bit at its beginning.

 IX. E-1 systems are used in Europe.
    A. 30 eight-bit voice channels at 64 kbps.
    B. One signaling channel.
    C. One framing channel
    D. 32 total channels.

  X. Alternate Mark Inversion (AMI) is used to prevent "DC buildup."
    A. Sending a logic "one"; alternate +3 volts and −3 volts.
    B. Sending a logic "zero"; 0 volt.
    C. Zero substitution is used to keep synchronization at the receiver.
      1. In a long string of logic zeros, two "dummy" ones of the same polarity are sent for receiver synchronization.
      2. This is an AMI "violation," and the receiver ignores this "false" data.

 XI. Synchronization and timing have improved since T-1 was introduced.
    A. D-4 frame (Super Frame, or SF) allows framing bits to send messages.
    B. Extended Super Frame (ESF) is more sophisticated than the SF.

10.1   Why T-1?

AT&T had a problem on Manhattan Island, New York City, in the 1960s. Their twisted pair (TP) lines had reached their maximum capacity, and no more TP lines could be installed. The existing conduits had reached full capacity, and it was totally impractical to add more lines under the skyscrapers of the Wall Street area. Still customer demand dictated that more phone traffic must be accommodated. Something different had to be done to handle the communications needs of the nation's financial district.

Time Domain Multiplexing (TDM) and T-1 were developed to solve this problem. TDM is time sharing of a channel and is discussed in Chapter 8. T-1, T-3, and so on are generically called "T Carrier." Other variations, such at fiber FT and T4M, came about as higher data rates became possible with the introduction of optical fiber. The T Carrier systems are also given the DS-*x* designations. These will be explained as we proceed through this chapter.

TDM was used over the existing twisted pair employing repeaters about one mile apart, or one manhole apart, or about eight city blocks. The manholes were used to gain access to the repeater equipment.

10.2   Multiplexing and De-multiplexing

T-1 systems use an input Time Division Multiplexer (TDM) to time-multiplex 24 inputs onto one T-1 twisted pair (see Figure 10.1). A *multiplexer* is the device that puts the many inputs onto one channel. The student may wish to review TDM in Chapter 8. The inputs may be voice or data. The maximum speed of any one input channel is 64 kbps. See Equation 10.1. Two or more inputs may be combined to get a higher data rate than the 64 kbps of a single channel. The 64-kbps rate is called the **DS-0** rate; 56 kbps is also commonly used. Why 56 kbps is used will be explained later in this chapter.

$$\text{Bit rate } = \frac{8 \text{ bits}}{\text{sample}} \times \frac{8 \text{ k samples}}{\text{second}} = 64 \text{ kbps} \qquad \textbf{(Equation 10.1)}$$

Voice is converted to an eight-bit digital sample at 8,000 samples per second by a Codec. The data rate is 64 kbps. Codecs are discussed in Chapter 8. Twenty-four of these voice channels are multiplexed over one T-1 line.

Twenty-eight T-1 system outputs can be time-multiplexed to create a T-3 system (Figure 10.2). A T-3 system's total channel capacity is

$$\text{T-3 channels } = \frac{24 \text{ channels}}{\text{T-1 system}} \times \frac{28 \text{ T-1 systems}}{\text{T-3 system}} = \frac{672 \text{ channels}}{\text{T-3 system}} \qquad \textbf{(Equation 10.2)}$$

A T-3 system's basic bit rate is 44,736 kbps.

The digital inputs from Codecs or other data sources are stored in a First In–First Out (FIFO) digital storage shift register. The data source's bit rate is usually much slower than the T-1 rate. For instance a single voice channel's data rate is 64 kbps. The FIFO stores the slow input data (e.g., 64 kbps) until it is read out by the multiplexer at 1,544 kbps and sent over the T-1 lines. The data goes into the FIFO slowly at 64 kbps and is read

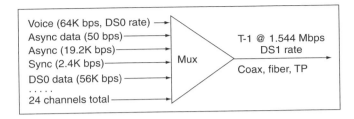

FIGURE 10.1
TDM multiplexer (mux). Twenty-four low-speed channels time share a single high-speed trunk channel.

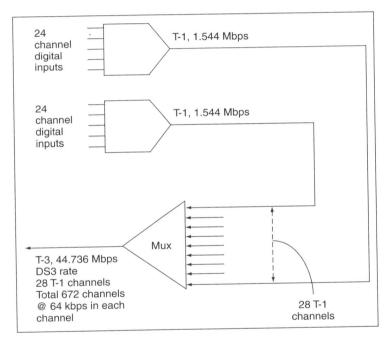

FIGURE 10.2
Multiplexers (continued).

out very quickly at 1,544 kbps. Thus data coming in at various speeds can be handled by the FIFO and multiplexer. Data arriving slower than 64 kbps can also be accommodated; for instance, 56 kbps and 9.6 kbps.

10.2.1 De-multiplexers

At the T-1 receiving end a de-multiplexer (demux) extracts and separates each of the 24 channels and sends each data into 24 FIFOs as shown in Figure 10.3. The data rate into the FIFOs is very fast at 1,544 kbps, and the data rate is read out relatively slowly at 64

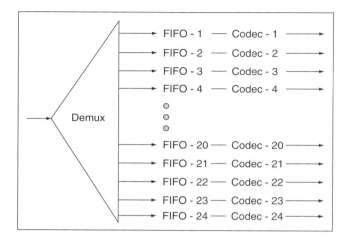

FIGURE 10.3
T-1 demultiplexer.

kbps. Voice information is converted to its equivalent analog signal by a Codec (Digital to Analog converter) at the destination Central Office (CO).

T-1 systems are full duplex; that is, they support simultaneous transmissions in both directions. Usually two separate circuits are used as in Figure 10.4.

10.3 T-1 Frame Format

The T-1 frame format is shown in Figure 10.5. There are 24 channels or time slots, each containing eight bits. Remember that each Codec sample is eight bits. The total frame width is given in Equation 10.3.

$$\frac{24 \text{ channels or time slots}}{\text{T-1 frame}} \times \frac{8 \text{ data bits}}{\text{channel or time slot}} = \frac{192 \text{ data bits}}{\text{T-1 frame}} \qquad \textbf{(Equation 10.3)}$$

A framing bit is added to the beginning of each frame, bringing the total number of bits in one complete frame to 193. A single framing bit signifies the end of one frame and the beginning of the next frame. The framing bit is used to synchronize the receiver to the beginning of the frame.

A Codec samples voice at 8 k samples per second; therefore we have 8,000 frames per second. Each time slot is one digital sample of one voice conversation. The total number of bits per second is

$$\frac{193 \text{ bits}}{\text{frame}} \times \frac{8 \text{ k samples or frames}}{\text{second}} = \frac{1,544 \text{ k bits}}{\text{second}} \qquad \textbf{(Equation 10.4)}$$

This is called the **DS-1** rate.

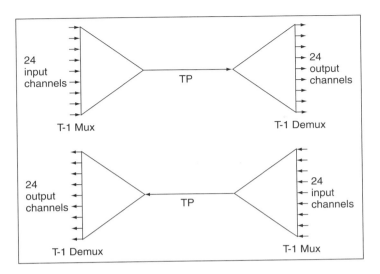

FIGURE 10.4
T-1 duplex.

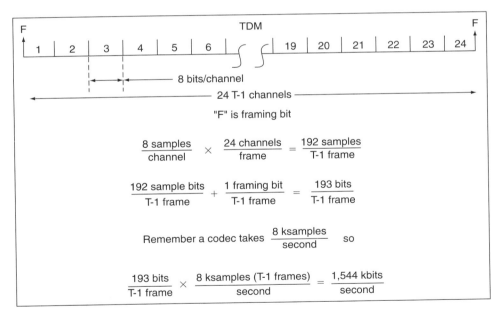

FIGURE 10.5
T-1 frame format.

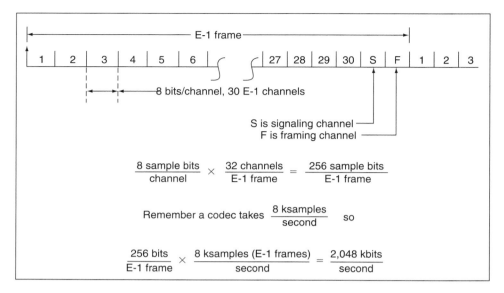

FIGURE 10.6
E-1 format.

10.4 E-1

A similar system, E-1, is used in Europe (see Figure 10.6). The E-1 frame consists of 30 eight-bit time slots. The two time slots at the end of the frame are used for signaling (S slot) and for framing (F slot), so the total number of time slots is 32.

There are 32 time slots of eight bits each for a total of 256 bits per frame. Codecs sample at an $\frac{8\text{ k samples}}{\text{second}}$ rate, or 8,000 frames per second. The total number of bits per second is

$$\frac{8\text{ bits}}{\text{time slot}} \times \frac{32\text{ time slots}}{\text{frame}} \times \frac{8\text{ k samples or frames}}{\text{second}} = \frac{2,048\text{ k bits}}{\text{second}} \qquad \textbf{(Equation 10.5)}$$

Note that no extra framing bits are needed as in T-1. The synchronization and framing are done by the eight-bit framing channel.

10.5 Alternate Mark Inversion (AMI)

T-1 does not send a true binary signal down the physical medium. In Figure 10.7 note the bit stream we wish to send to the T-1 receiver. T-1 uses a three-level system. The three levels are +3 volts, 0 volt, and −3 volts. When a logic zero is sent, 0 volt is sent over the medium. When a logic one, or "mark," is sent, +3 volts or a −3 volts is sent over the medium. Each mark sent has the opposite (alternate) polarity of the previous mark as in Figure 10.7. This system is called **Alternate Mark Inversion (AMI).** The opposite polarity marks prevent "DC buildup," which can saturate inductors and charge capacitors, thus degrading system performance.

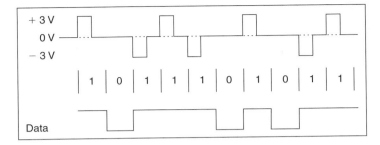

FIGURE 10.7
Alternate Mark Inversion (AMI). T-1 uses a three-level system for transmission, not a binary system. Each "0" is zero volts and no transition. Each "1" has a transition, but in the opposite direction as the previous "1"; i.e., AMI. Thus a "1" can be either a +3V or a −3V. The equal numbers of positive pulses and negative pulses give a net sum of zero volts, preventing "DC buildup"; i.e., charge buildup on capacitors and saturation of iron core transformers. Note that the transition rate of AMI is twice the actual bit rate of the data shown below the AMI. Therefore the bandwidth needed for AMI is twice that needed for the data. This isn't a problem, because bandwidth is cheap (at least on a closed medium).

Note that the AMI waveform has twice as many transitions as the NRZ waveform. This means AMI needs twice the bandwidth of the data. The Baud rate is twice the bit rate. This is not a problem since bandwidth is cheap in a closed medium such as coax, TP, and optical fiber! Closed medium means the signal's radiation energy cannot escape and interfere with other transmissions.

10.6 Zero Substitution

The receiver uses the ones (marks) to synchronize its clock to the transmitter clock. But what happens if a long string of logic zeros is sent? Remember, no voltage pulses are sent for logic zeros. The receiver uses marks (ones) for synchronization. If a long string of zeros is sent, the receiver could lose synchronization, thus losing data. Special provisions are needed.

The Binary 8 Zero Substitution (B8ZS) method is used when there are eight or more consecutive logic zeros. A logical NOR connected to a shift register or FIFO will detect this condition. The transmitted bit stream will contain two AMI violations. The receiver will use these violations only for synchronization and will know that they are not true data.

Figure 10.8a shows the actual data we wish to transmit. The long string of zeros could allow the receiver to lose synchronization. To prevent this, a pulse with the same polarity (an AMI violation) as the last data pulse is sent in bit time 4, immediately followed by an opposite polarity pulse. See Figure 10.8b. In bit time 7, a pulse of the same polarity as the last bit (AMI violation) in bit time 4 is sent. This is immediately followed by an opposite polarity pulse. Note that there is an equal number of positive and negative pulses in these violations, preventing "DC buildup."

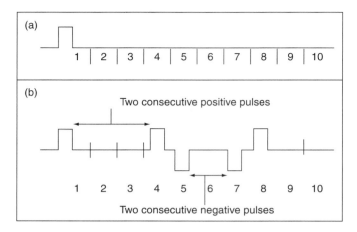

FIGURE 10.8
Binary 8 Zero Substitution (B8ZS). Actual data has eight or more consecutive zeros (a), but the transmitter actually sends the bit stream shown in (b). The consecutive positive and negative pulses are AMI violations, but the receiver will ignore these. Note that there is still an equal number of positive and negative pulses, preventing "DC buildup."

10.7 D-4 Framing Bits

Synchronization and clocking have improved considerably since T-1 was first introduced. Extremely accurate and affordable cesium atomic clocks are used for synchronization, but not every framing bit has to be a logic one. The framing bits can actually be used for signaling and error control! In this instance, signaling is sending maintenance messages.

With **D-4** framing a unique framing bit pattern is sent (Figure 10.9). This is called the "Super Frame," or SF. If the receiver loses sync, synchronization can be regained within three repetitions of the SF.

In a D-4 frame the least significant bits (lsb) in the sixth and twelfth frames are used for signaling as in Figure 10.10. This results in a true 56-kbps rate, also called a DS-0 rate. These "robbed bits" are not discernible to humans for voice and video transmissions.

The data rate is 56 kbps (7 data bits):

$$\frac{7 \text{ bits}}{8 \text{ bits}} \times 64 \text{ kbps} = 56 \text{ kbps} \qquad \textbf{(Equation 10.6)}$$

The Extended Super Frame (ESF) was first proposed in 1978. It consists of 24 T-1 frames. Referring to Figure 10.11, the "F" bits are used for framing and never change, the "D" data bits are used for signaling in the Facilities Data Link (FDL), and the "C" bits are used for error control. Cyclic Redundant Check, or Cyclic Redundant Code (CRC), is the error detection mechanism. See Appendix A1 for more information on CRC.

FIGURE 10.9
D4 framing bits.

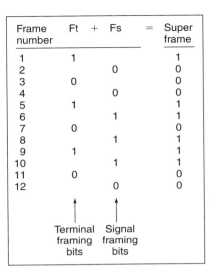

Frame number	Ft	+	Fs	=	Super frame
1	1				1
2			0		0
3	0				0
4			0		0
5	1				1
6			1		1
7	0				0
8			1		1
9	1				1
10			1		1
11	0				0
12			0		0

Terminal framing bits   Signal framing bits

	F	12345678	12345678	....	12345678	12345678
D4 Frame 1	1					
D4 Frame 2	0					
D4 Frame 3	0					
D4 Frame 4	0					
D4 Frame 5	1					
D4 Frame 6	1	S	S	....	S	S
D4 Frame 7	0					
D4 Frame 8	1					
D4 Frame 9	1					
D4 Frame 10	1					
D4 Frame 11	0					
D4 Frame 12	0	S	S	....	S	S
		slot 1	slot 2	....	slot 23	slot 24

"F" is the D4 framing bit. The bits of the time slots are shown. Note that in the 6th and 12th frame the eight bits of every slot or channel are used for signaling, not actual data.

FIGURE 10.10
Robbed bits in D4 frame.

Frame Number	bit use
1	D - data - M bit - 4 Kbps - diagnostics & control.
2	CRC - Cyclic Redundant Check - error control
3	D
4	F = 0 Framing bit
5	D
6	CRC
7	D
8	F = 0
9	D
10	CRC
11	D
12	F = 1
13	D
14	CRC
15	D
16	F = 0
17	D
18	CRC
19	D
20	F = 1
21	D
22	CRC
23	D
24	F = 1

FIGURE 10.11
Extended Super Frame (ESF).

Errors are detected by the CRC bits. A high Bit Error Rate (BER) can indicate a synchronization loss, or a noisy channel. The D bits are used for testing while the system is in use and also for sending messages between end nodes.

ESF also uses the "robbed bit" technique (Figure 10.12). In T-1 the framing bit is not always a "one." In SF and ESF systems the framing bit is also used for signaling. Remember that the frame rate (sample rate) is 8,000 per second. This is an exact multiple of 1,000 Hz.

Before the advent of T-1 systems a 1,000-Hz tone was used to test telephone systems. When this 1,000 Hz was sampled by a Codec, the bit pattern was very repetitive. The T-1 receivers tended to synchronize onto this repeating pattern instead of the framing bits. To get around this problem, the test tone frequency was moved to 1,004 Hz.

10.8 Costs

In the United States in 1999 T-1 costs were about $500 to $600 per month.

Frame Number	bit use	slot 1 12345678	slot 2 12345678	....	slot 23 12345678	slot 24 12345678
1	D					
2	F					
3	D					
4	F					
5	D					
6	C	S	S		S	S
7	D					
8	F					
9	D					
10	C					
11	D					
12	F	S	S		S	S
13	D					
14	C					
15	D					
16	F					
17	D					
18	C	S	S		S	S
19	D					
20	F					
21	D					
22	C					
23	D					
24	F	S	S		S	S

FIGURE 10.12
Robbed bits in Extended Super Frame (ESF).

10.9   Testing and Troubleshooting

The Hewlett-Packard Cerjac Division's T1-Test Advisor is a versatile tester. At first glance the instrument looks like a laptop computer. Figure 10.13a shows a test advisor display for a normally functioning T-1 system. Note the alarm "lights" for signal loss, frame loss, pattern loss, coding type, and density violations. The test summary displays the framing type, status, number of frame errors, and number of bit errors. The technician has the option of introducing errors as a cross-check on the system test.

Repeaters can remotely control from the test set, as shown in Figure 10.13b. Error statistics can be displayed as shown in Figure 10.13c. A telephone number can be dialed

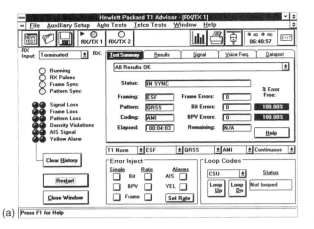

(a)

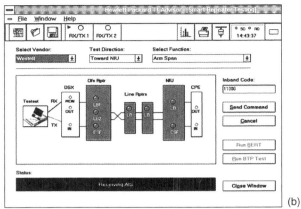

(b)

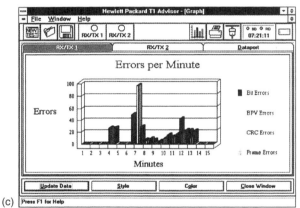

(c)

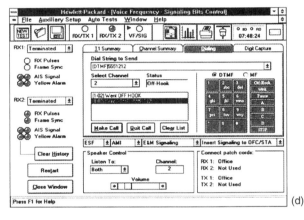

(d)

FIGURE 10.13
T-1 test advisor display-baseline (Courtesy of Hewlett Packard).

from the test set. BERT (Bit Error Rate Test) can be done using Pseudo Random Number (PRN) sequences. The test set has capabilities to find bridges and taps. Signal levels can be monitored (Figure 10.13d) and signals inserted at precise levels and frequencies (Figure 10.13e). Both sides of a voice conversation can be monitored.

SUMMARY

I. T-1 was developed to increase the capacity of twisted pair (TP) cable by using Time Division Multiplexing (TDM).
  A. T-1 has 24 digitized voice channels of eight bits each.
  B. T-1 voice rate is 8,000 samples per second.
  C. Each T-1 voice channel is 64 kbps.
  D. Total T-1 bit rate is 1.544 Mbps.
  E. Each digitized voice input is temporarily stored in a FIFO register.

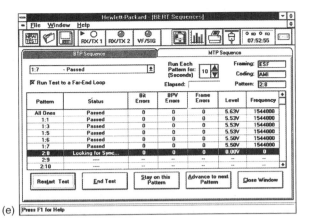

(e)

(f)

(g)

FIGURE 10.13
(continued)

II. T-3 time division multiplexes 28 T-1 lines onto one line for a 44.736-Mbps bit rate.

    A. T-3 is used for long haul (long distance).

    B. T-3 works directly into SONET line rates.

III. E-1 is a similar system used in Europe.

    A. E-1 has 30 eight-bit voice channels.

    B. E-1 has one signaling channel.

    C. E-1 has one synchronization channel.

    D. E-1 has 32 total channels in a frame.

    E. E-1's bit rate is 2.048 Mbps.

IV. T-1 uses Alternate Mark Inversion (AMI).

    A. Logic "ones" are either $+3$-volt or -3-volt pulses.

    B. A $+3$-volt pulse (logic one) will be followed by a -3-volt pulse at the next logic one (alternate mark). The alternating pulses prevent "DC buildup."

    C. Logic zeros are 0 volt.

D. The receiver synchronizes on the marks (pulses); if there is a long string of logic zeros, special AMI "violations" are used to send pulses that the receiver knows are not actual logic ones.

V. T-1 has one synchronization pulse at the beginning of every frame.

    A. As timing capabilities improved, these pulses were used for signaling.

        1. Super Frame (SF) was used for signaling.

        2. Extended Super Frame (ESF) was used for signaling.

    B. Signaling was also done by "robbing" the least significant bits of certain frames.

        1. This resulted in a true 56-kbps bit rate in these frames.

        2. This is not noticeable for voice transmission.

QUESTIONS

1. Why was T-1 developed?
2. Given a digital transmission system similar to T-1 with a digital conversion rate of 10 k samples per second, 22 channels, and a seven-bit sample, what is the total number of information bits per frame and information bits per second? If there are two framing bits per frame, what is the bit rate sent over the medium?
3. A digital transmission system similar to a T-3 has 32 inputs as described in the problem above. What is the total bit rate if this system has four framing bits per frame? T-3's four framing bits are in addition to any from the system in the problem above.
4. What is a FIFO, and how does it work? Can the input bit rate and output bit rate be different?
5. How does an E-1 system differ from a T-1 system?
6. What is AMI, and what is its purpose? It is not sufficient to define the acronym or say that AMI is used to send data over a T-1 system.
7. What are AMI "violations," and what is their purpose? What is done to prevent "DC buildup"?
8. What advantages does the SF have over a T-1 frame with all framing bits being a logic one?
9. How is signaling accomplished in a D-4 frame?
10. What information is conveyed in the ESF framing bits?
11. Why do telcos use a system test frequency different than 1,000 Hz?

11

INTEGRATED SERVICES DIGITAL NETWORK (ISDN)

OBJECTIVES

In this chapter we will discuss:

    I. What is the goal of ISDN? Integrate data transmission.
    II. What is one problem ISDN tries to solve? Limited bandwidth between user and CO.
    III. ISDN types.
        A. Basic Rate Interface (BRI) for home or small office use.
        B. Primary Rate Interface (PRI) for corporate use.
    IV. ISDN equipment.
    V. Signaling; 2 Binary–1 Quaternary (2B1Q).
        A. Four-state, two-bit.
        B. Designed to overcome line losses.
    VI. ISDN superframe.
    VII. LAPD is the Data Link Level (DLL) protocol for ISDN. LAPD frame structure.
        A. Information frame.
        B. Supervisory frame.
        C. Unnumbered frame.
    VIII. Broadband ISDN.

11.1 The Goal of ISDN

In the late 1960s some visionaries realized that data communications would become very important. These people had the foresight to see the advantages of integrating voice and data transmission. The result of their efforts was ISDN. The goal of **ISDN** is the integration of data and voice transmissions, and the integration of packet and circuit switching equipment.

11.2 What is ISDN?

Fast, high-bandwidth trunks connect Central Offices (CO) to Toll Centers, Sectional Centers, and Regional Centers throughout the PSTN. However the "last mile" between the CO and the user residence or business is limited to a 300- to 3,400-Hz bandwidth as shown in Figure 11.1. This is fine for a single voice channel but inadequate for data transmission. Special modem techniques must be used to send data faster than 2,400 bps. Even these special modem techniques are limited to 56 kbps at the time of this writing (1999). These data rates are near the Nyquist and Shannon theoretical limits.

TP has a steady roll off (a decreasing transmission amplitude as the frequency is increased). This roll off is detrimental to voice transmission. Also a phase shift (time delay variation with frequency) occurs, further reducing the voice transmission quality.

When the TP is actually installed between the CO and the user, 88-millihenry loading coils are added. Loading coils, a type of transformer, flatten the frequency transmission out to 3,300 Hz (see Figure 11.2). Above 3,400 Hz the transmission response drops quickly. Also phase shift is reduced in this 300- to 3,400-Hz pass band. Both these factors help voice transmission. This sharp cutoff low-pass filter at 3,400 Hz is needed to prevent aliasing by the 8,000 samples per second of a Codec.

If we wish to transmit data over these lines, we must use modems. Simple modems can transmit data up to 1,200 bps. When we want to transmit data at rates 2,400 bps or

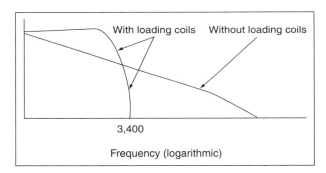

FIGURE 11.1
CO to user TP BW. Bandpass of "last mile" twisted pair (TP) between the CO and user.

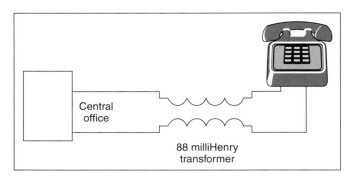

FIGURE 11.2
Loading coil between CO and user.

greater, we must use exotic modem modulation techniques. Modems are discussed in Chapter 9.

11.3 Modifying the TP for ISDN

To use ISDN the loading coils on the TP between the CO and the user must be removed. This widens the TP bandwidth allowing fast data to be transmitted. See Figure 11.1.

11.4 ISDN History

ISDN was first proposed in 1968 and became a CCITT standard in 1984. In those years the average small business or home had little need of high-speed data transfer. Few homes or small offices had computers. Also the computers were expensive, they had small (or no) hard drives, and files were relatively small. The Internet was still the realm of the U.S. military.

ISDN has been used more in Europe than in North America. The North American telcos didn't see much profit in ISDN and never pushed the marketing. Thus the price remained high. Adding ISDN capability to a CO can cost as much as $500,000. However ISDN became popular in the Boston and California Silicon Valley high-tech areas.

Today computers are commonplace in the office and home, and are connected to the Internet. Internet uses require large bandwidths (fast data transfers). With this increased need for fast data transfer, users were screaming for more bandwidth, and finally the U.S. telcos are responding. In late 1997 Colorado's local telco, US West, was offering ISDN for as little as $12 per month, with a nominal installation fee. Of course the ISDN modem was somewhat pricey at $277.

11.5 ISDN Types

There are two types of ISDN: Basic Access and Primary Access. They differ in the data rate, and both are considerably faster than today's fastest modem. A comparison is summarized in Table 11.1.

11.5.1 Basic ISDN

Basic Access, or **Basic Rate Interface (BRI),** ISDN has two 64-kbps Bearer (B) data channels for data and one 16-kbps Delta (D) channel to transmit control information. This is referred to as 2B plus D. The two Bearer channels and the Delta channel total 144 kbps. The two Bearer channels can be combined for a 128-kbps rate.

The 128-kbps rate is used by radio stations to send data (CD quality music) from the studio to the separate transmitter site. The D channel is used to send transmitter data to the studio and control the transmitter from the studio.

Generally the Bearer channels transmit data, and the Delta channel is used for control and signaling.

TABLE 11.1
The Two ISDN Types

Basic Rate	Primary Rate

Two data or "Bearer" ("B") channels of:
    64 kbps each
    128 kbps total
One control or "Delta" ("D") channel of 16 kbps
	23 data or "Bearer" ("B") channels of:
	    64 kbps each
	    1,472 kbps total
	One control or "Delta" ("D") channel of 64 kbps
	Similar to T-1

11.5.2 Primary ISDN in North America

Primary Access, or **Primary Rate Interface (PRI),** ISDN has twenty-three Bearer channels of 64 kbps each, and one Delta channel of 64 kbps. This is referred to as 23B plus D. As in Basic Access the Bearer channels are usually used for data and the Delta channel used for signaling and control. The total data rate for all twenty-three 64-kbps data channels is 1,472 kbps. Note the similarity to T-1 with its twenty-four 64-kbps channels. PRI is designed to interface directly into T-1 systems.

11.5.3 European Primary Access

The European ISDN Primary Access has twenty-nine 64-kbps Bearer channels and one 64-kbps Delta channel (29B plus D), interfacing easily into E-1 systems. Remember from Chapter 10 on T Carrier that the E-1 system has thirty data channels, a framing channel, and a synchronization channel. The total data rate for all twenty-nine 64-kbps ISDN data channels is 1,856 kbps.

11.6   Connecting to ISDN

Figure 11.3 shows a typical connection of an ISDN network. An RJ-45 connector at the customer's premises is the connection to the NT2.

11.6.1 Equipment at the Customer's Premises

Equipment at the customer's premises is categorized in Table 11.2. **Network Termination 1 (NT1)** equipment properly terminates the TP line and gives correct timing, power feed, and error statistics. This can be an ISDN modem on a single **Printed Circuit Board (PCB)** plugged into a computer. **Network Termination 2 (NT2)** equipment gives distribution switching, multiplexing, and concentrating. This may be used in a PBX or LAN server. A PRI system would probably use an NT2, but a BRI system would not.

Terminal Equipment 1 (TE1) is fully ISDN compatible. Terminal Equipment 2 (TE2) is non-ISDN compatible. A Terminal Adapter (TA) is used to connect TE2 equipment to ISDN.

At the CO end of the TP line is the Local Termination (LT). In ISDN jargon the CO is referred to as the Exchange Termination (ET). As if you weren't confused enough already! Within the CO or ET is the Packet Handler (PH), which switches the information packets.

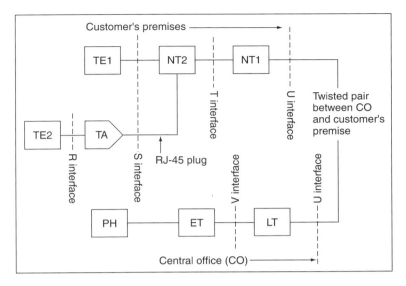

FIGURE 11.3
Connecting to ISDN.

TABLE 11.2
Connecting to ISDN

At the Customer's Premises

NT1 (Network Termination 1) properly terminates the TP line and gives correct timing, power feed, and error statistics. This can be a single Printed Circuit Board (PCB) plugging into a computer.
NT2 gives distribution switching, multiplexing, and concentrating. This may be used in a PBX or LAN server. A PRI system would probably use an NT2, but a BRI system would not.
TE1 (Terminal Equipment 1) is fully ISDN compatible.
TE2 (Terminal Equipment 2) is non-ISDN compatible.
TA (Terminal Adapter) is used to connect TE2 equipment to ISDN.

At the CO

LT (Local Termination)
ET (Exchange Termination)
PH (Packet Handler)

11.7   2 Binary–1 Quaternary (2B1Q)

With the loading coils removed from the TP between the customer and the CO, signal attenuation becomes quite large. Typical values are −15 dB at 3,700 feet, −30 dB at 9,000 feet, and −40 dB at 18,000 feet. About 18,000 feet (approximately three miles) is considered the limit for an ISDN connection.

TABLE 11.3
2B1Q states

Four-state system encodes:
  Two bits
  Similar to modems
"00" → −3 V
"01" → −1 V
"11" → +1 V
"10" → +3 V
This is a Gray code

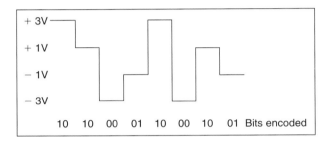

FIGURE 11.4
2B1Q example. Four states (+3V, +1V, −1V, −3V) transmit two bits per state.

This large attenuation necessitates using a special signal transmission technique. ISDN data is not transmitted by a binary level signal, such as RS-232. Rather a four-level, two-binary-state protocol is used. The protocol used is 2 Binary (bits sent using) −1 Quaternary (four states), or **2B1Q.** This protocol reduces the required bandwidth and fights the distortion and attenuation on the lines. Similar techniques are used with modems. 2B1Q uses four states to transmit two bits in each of the four states.

See Table 11.3 for the voltage levels and their corresponding two-bit states. Note the Gray code bit sequence. See Figure 11.4 for an example of a 2B1Q transmission. In the Gray code only one bit changes from one state to the next state.

11.8   ISDN Superframe

Figure 11.5 shows the format of ISDN frames and superframe. A Synchronization Word (SW) begins a frame, except for the first frame of a superframe. A superframe begins with an Inverted Synchronization Word (ISW), which is merely an inverted SW.

Twelve B + B + D (8 bits + 8 bits + 2 bits) groups are in one frame. The M field is used for error statistics, loopback commands, and maintenance.

Loopback is a testing technique wherein a test transmission is sent to the destination, and the destination equipment sends the test transmission back to the sender (see Figure

2B1Q frame	18 bits	8 + 8 + 2	8 + 8 + 2 bits			8 + 8 + 2	6 bits
1	ISW	B1 + B2 + D	B1 + B2 + D	-	- -	B1 + B2 + D	M
2	SW	B1 + B2 + D	B1 + B2 + D	-	- -	B1 + B2 + D	M
3	SW	B1 + B2 + D	B1 + B2 + D	-	- -	B1 + B2 + D	M
4	SW	B1 + B2 + D	B1 + B2 + D	-	- -	B1 + B2 + D	M
5	SW	B1 + B2 + D	B1 + B2 + D	-	- -	B1 + B2 + D	M
6	SW	B1 + B2 + D	B1 + B2 + D	-	- -	B1 + B2 + D	M
7	SW	B1 + B2 + D	B1 + B2 + D	-	- -	B1 + B2 + D	M
8	SW	B1 + B2 + D	B1 + B2 + D	-	- -	B1 + B2 + D	M

$$18 + (18 \times 12) + 6 = 240 \text{ bits per frame}$$

$$12 \times 8 = 1920 \text{ bits per superframe}$$

FIGURE 11.5
2B1Q superframe. SW = synchronizing word (begins a frame), ISW = ~SW = inverted synchronizing word (begins a superframe), M = overhead for maintenance, loopbacks, and error statistics.

11.6). In the past, loopback testing was done by a technician traveling to the destination or repeater equipment and manually enabling the loopback. Now the loopback is done remotely from the originating equipment. Loopback tests are used in all types of data transmission, not only ISDN. When troubleshooting loopback, tests are done first between the technician's local node and the next relay node. If that connection proves good, the loopback is repeated at the next downstream network node, finally reaching and testing the destination node.

11.9 Link Access Protocol over the D channel (LAPD)

The ISDN protocol used at the Data Link Level (DLL) is Link Access Protocol over the D channel (LAPD). This is similar to other DLL protocols such as SDLC, used by SNA, and LAP/B, used in X.25, which we will study in more detail in Chapter 16.

LAPD can be used between an NT and multiple TEs.

11.9.1 LAPD Frame Structure

Figure 11.7 shows the general LAPD frame format. All frames begin with a "flag" denoting the beginning or end of a frame. The flag is a binary "01111110" or hexadecimal "7E."

Next is the address field. The control field contains housekeeping information. The information field is present only in information frames.

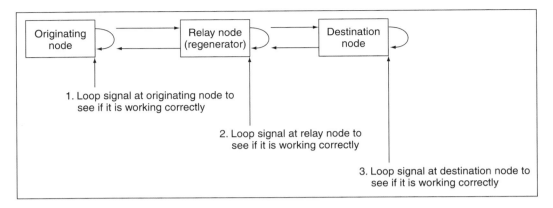

FIGURE 11.6
Loopback. A technician must test a line for performance and failure. Loopback will be used.

Flag	Address	Control	Information	FCS	Flag
← 1 byte →	← 2 bytes →	←1 or 2 bytes→	←—Variable —→	←2 bytes→	←1 bytes→

FIGURE 11.7
LAP-D frame format.

The Frame Check Sequence (FRC) is used to check the frame for errors. Errors are checked between the end of the start flag and the beginning of the FRC. The FRC is another term for Cyclic Redundant Check (CRC), which is discussed in Appendix A1. CRC only determines if an error exists and cannot correct the error. If an error is found, a REJect supervisory frame is sent back to the sender, and an error recovery process is begun. Usually this error recovery process repeats all frames beginning with the frame in error.

There are three types of LAPD frames: information (I-frames), supervisory (S-frames), and unnumbered (U-frames).

11.9.2 Information Frame

If the seventh bit in the control field is a zero, the frame is an information frame (Figure 11.8). The control field is 16 bits. An information frame sends information. But it's not quite as simple as that. All frame types contain certain housekeeping fields, used for flow control and error recovery data. The control field of an information frame contains the Frame number Sent [F(s)] and Frame number Received [F(r)]. F(r) is the number of the next frame expected, not the last frame received correctly. This prevents confusion if the first frame never arrives. The C/R bit in the control field is set to "C = Command" asking for confirmation that the frame was received properly.

$7E	SAPI	C/R	EA(0)	TEI	EA(1)

←—Flag—→|←——————————— Address field ———————————→|

N(s)	0	N(r)	P/F	Information	FCS	$7E

|←———— Control field ————→| —→| Flag |←—
      16 bits

FIGURE 11.8
Information frame. $7E = starting delimiter = binary 01010100, SAPI = service access point identifier—address of network level function (1—packet switching, 16—X.25 functions, 63—OAM—operations, administration, maintenance), C/R = command or response bit, EA(0) = extension address bit = 0, TEI = terminal endpoint identifier, N(s) = number of frame sent, N(r) = number of frame received, P/F = poll/final bit, FCS = frame check sequence (error control).

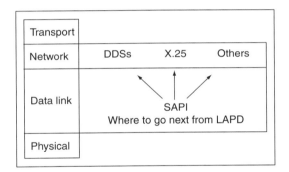

FIGURE 11.9
APB and SAPI. SAPI tells which network-level program or protocol to access. TEI identifies the end terminal that is communicating with the level 3 protocol above. Both the SAPI and the TEI can be thought of as addresses.

Frame number Sent [F(s)] is the number of the frame sent. Frame number Received [F(r)] is the number of the next frame expected. Both F(r) and F(s) are needed for full duplex operation. These frame numbers are needed for flow control and error recovery.

The address field contains the Control/Response (C/R) bit, the Terminal Endpoint Identifier (TEI), and the Service Access Point Identifier (SAPI).

The Service Access Point Identifier (SAPI) designates the network level (level 3) protocol or function that the information is from or is to be sent. The Terminal Endpoint Identifier (TEI) is unique to each user. There are three types of TEIs: broadcast (127 or all bits 1), where the frame is directed to all terminals; non-automatic hardwired into the terminals; and automatic being assigned by the network. The Service Access Point Identifier (SAPI) is the address of the Layer 3 (Network) protocol. See Figure 11.9. A SAPI of 1 is

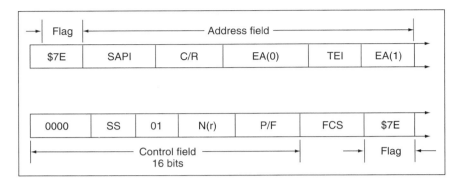

FIGURE 11.10
Supervisory frame. SS = supervisory function (RR = receiver ready, REJ = frame reject,
RNR = receiver not ready).

for packet switching, a SAPI of 16 is for X.25 functions, a SAPI of 32–61 is used for
Frame Relay (FR), and a SAPI of 63 designates DLL management or Administration and
Maintenance (OAM).

The Control/Response (C/R) bit tells if the frame is a command or a response to a
command frame. The Extension bit (EA) tells if there is another byte in the SAPI or TEI
address fields.

Next is the actual information and then the FCS. The Frame Check Sequence (FRC)
is a Cyclic Redundant Code (CRC) used for error detection. A detected error will initiate
an error recovery protocol. Finally the flag field denotes the end of the frame. The end of
field flag is identical to the start of field flag. Both flags are a binary "01111110" or hexadecimal "7E."

11.9.3 Supervisory Frame

Supervisory frames send control information. The control field is 16 bits. If bits 7 and
8 in the control field are a "0 1," the frame is a supervisory frame (Figure 11.10). The
Supervisory (SS) bits tell what type of supervisory frame is being sent. The three types
of supervisory frames are Receiver Ready (RR), Receiver Not Ready (RNR), and frame
REJect. The RR frame confirms error-free reception of a frame and tells the sending
node that the receiving node can accept data. An RNR tells the sending node that the
receiving node cannot accept data (flow control). A REJ frame means that the receiver
has detected an error in the frame. All supervisory frames contain Frame number received [F(r)]. This is actually the number of the last frame received error-free plus one,
or next expected frame.

Frame number Received [F(r)] is the number of the error-free frame that has been
received plus one. Therefore F(r) is the number of the next expected frame. It is necessary
to tell the sender this information if an error has been found and an RNR frame is sent.
The sender will know the last error-free frame received and will re-send data from that
frame onward.

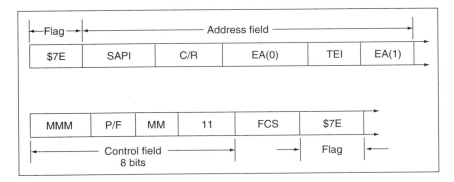

FIGURE 11.11
Unnumbered frame. M = modifier bit.

TABLE 11.4
U-frame types

SABME (Set Asynchronous Balanced Mode)—requests a full duplex (balanced) connection
DISC (DISConnect)—terminate logical connection
FRMR (FRaMe Reject)—unacceptable frame received

11.9.4 Unnumbered Frame

If the last two bits in the control field are a "1 1" the frame is a U-frame. The control field is 8 bits. Unnumbered frames do not need an ACKnowledgment. Unnumbered frames are housekeeping frames (see Figure 11.11). Some U-frame types are listed in Table 11.4.

11.10 Broadband ISDN versus Narrowband ISDN

Just to really confuse the troops, besides BRI and PRI we have Broadband ISDN (B-ISDN). *B-ISDN* is defined as transmission rates greater than PRI. Usually B-ISDN is sent over Asynchronous Transfer Mode (ATM) and Synchronous Optical NETwork (SONET) protocols. Note that this ATM is not the Automatic Teller Machine at which we so terribly abuse our bank accounts! B-ISDN tells what is to be done; ATM tells how it is to be done. ATM and SONET will be discussed in Chapter 17. Narrowband ISDN is BRI and PRI.

B-ISDN uses packet switching techniques, rather than circuit switching methods. B-ISDN supports variable bit rates, including "bursty" data. This is "bandwidth on demand." The user is billed for the actual data sent and not the time of connection. Table 11.5 summarizes the differences between B-ISDN and N-ISDN.

11.11 Testing and Troubleshooting

A good instrument for testing Basic Rate ISDN is the Hewlett-Packard Internet Advisor WAN. It can use the test module HP J2905B for BRI S/T and U Interface.

TABLE 11.5
B-ISDN vs N-ISDN

Broadband ISDN	Narrowband ISDN
Uses high-speed facilities	Uses medium-speed facilities
Packet switching	Circuit switching
Virtual channels	Fixed channels
Variable bit rates:	Fixed bit rates:
Bursting	No bursting
Variable BW on demand	Fixed BW
Only charged for data sent	Charges for time connected
Better throughput per BW:	Less throughput per BW:
Better transport—optical fiber	Poorer transport—cable
Less overhead	More overhead
Less error checking	More error checking

This combination provides LAPD analysis (CCITT Q9.21 specification), S/T and U Interface testing at the customer's premises, SAPI, full X.25, Frame Relay, HDLC decodes on the D channel, and monitor encapsulated LAN traffic. It can log and filter network statistics for troubleshooting and monitor error rates.

SUMMARY

  I. ISDN integrates (ties together) data and voice transmission.
  II. ISDN integrates packet and circuit switching equipment.
 III. ISDN allows fast data transfer between CO and the user over the "last mile." Loading coils are removed from the TP between the user and CO.
    A. Loading coils are in the line for better analog voice transmission.
    B. Not needed and in fact detrimental to data transmission.
    C. Bandwidth is greatly increased for better data transmission.
  IV. Basic Rate ISDN (Basic Rate Interface [BRI]).
    A. Designed for small offices and homes.
    B. Two 64-kbps data channels (2B).
    C. One 16-kbps control channel (1D).
    D. 144-kbps total bit rate (2B plus D).
  V. Primary Rate ISDN in North America (Primary Rate Interface [PRI]).
    A. Twenty-three data channels at 64 kbps per channel.
    B. One 64-kbps control channel.
    C. Similar to T-1.
  VI. Primary Rate ISDN in Europe (Primary Rate Interface [PRI]).
    A. Twenty-nine data channels at 64 kbps per channel.
    B. One control channel at 64 kbps.
    C. Similar to E-1.

VII. Four-state signaling used (2 Binary–1 Quaternary [2B1Q]).
 A. Two bits per state.
 B. Reduces needed bandwidth.
VIII. Link Access Protocol over the D channel (LAPD).
 A. DLL protocol for ISDN.
 B. Similar to other modern DLL protocols such as SDLC and LAP/B.
 C. Has three types of frames.
  1. Information (I-frames); also has flow control data and error detection field.
  2. Supervisory or control (S-frames).
   a. RR (Receiver Ready); similar to an ACKnowledgment (received frame correctly and am ready for the next frame).
   b. RNR (Receiver Not Ready); tells the sender to stop sending frames (flow control).
   c. REJ (REJect); tells the sender there was something wrong with a received frame—error detected (sender begins error recovery) or frame not correct format.
  3. Unnumbered (U-frames) for housekeeping (call setup, call teardown, system testing).
 IX. Broadband ISDN.
  A. Broadly defined as anything faster than PRI.
  B. Designed for sending data over Asynchronous Transfer Mode (ATM) and Synchronous Optical NETwork (SONET) protocols.

QUESTIONS

1. What modification is done to the twisted pair line between the CO and the user for an ISDN installation? Why is this modification needed?
2. What advantage does ISDN have over telephone modems?
3. What are the differences between BRI and PRI? How is PRI different in countries that use E-1?
4. What is the goal of ISDN?
5. What organization standardized ISDN? When?
6. Why was there an initial reluctance to ISDN? What factors are causing this to change?
7. What are the differences between NT1 and NT2 equipment?
8. What are the differences between TE1 and TE2 equipment?
9. What is 2B1Q, and why is it used?
10. Given the following bit sequence, show the correct 2B1Q format.
   110011001010101010001100
11. What is the ISDN superframe?
12. What is loopback, and why is it used? How is it used?
13. What types of LAPD frames are there? How are each used?
14. What is the purpose of the FRC? Does it correct errors?
15. Is the F(r) the number of the frame received? Explain.
16. What is the SAPI? Give several examples. What is the TEI?
17. What is the C/R bit, and why is it used?
18. What are the supervisory frame types, and what are their purposes?
19. Give several examples of U-frames and their uses.
20. What is B-ISDN? What are its advantages?

12

HIGH-SPEED DATA TO OFFICE AND HOME

OBJECTIVES

In this chapter we will discuss:

   I. Why are the data transfer speeds to the home and office so slow over the telephone lines?

   II. Alternative methods of data delivery.

      A. Cable television modem.

      B. High speeds using the telephone twisted pair; Asymmetric Data Subscriber Line (ADSL).

      C. Satellite.

      D. Most of the above have high-speed downlinks but slower uplinks. This is satisfactory for many subscribers.

12.1 Why Are the Data Transfer Speeds to the Office and Home So Slow?

The biggest complaint about the Internet is the slow data transfer speed. Much of the Internet traffic is huge graphical files, which take a long time to download. The speeds between Central Offices (CO) and Internet servers are quite high. These rates range from 1.5 Mbps to 2.4 gbps. The data speed bottleneck is between the CO and the user. This connection between the Central Office (CO) and the home or small office user is called the "final mile." It was designed for voice transmission almost a century ago but has been found to be totally inadequate for today's data transfer demands. This paltry data rate has been described as sending the data through a tiny diameter cocktail straw.

Telephone modems with bit transfer rates of 56 kbps came on the market in 1997, and these modems approach the theoretical data rate limit through the voice grade final mile. These theoretical limits have been formulated by Harry Nyquist and Claude Shannon and were discussed in Chapter 2.

In Chapter 11 on ISDN we saw how the telco could increase the final mile twisted pair bandwidth by removing loading coils. These loading coils were installed to enhance voice transmission, but at the tradeoff of reduced bandwidth. When the loading coils were first installed, the need for data networking was nearly a century in the future. While ISDN is finally getting support from U.S. telcos, it may be leapfrogged by newer technologies.

Television cable modems and Asymmetric Data Subscriber Line (ADSL) are two different technologies that are being defined at the time of this writing (1999). As the name implies, cable modems use the tremendous bandwidth of cable television systems. Community Access TeleVision (CATV) systems use Frequency Division Multiplexing (FDM), as will the cable modems. ASDL will use greater bandwidths and more exotic modulation techniques through the final mile than ISDN, with resulting greater data rates.

An alternative high-speed data transfer is via satellite. Hughes Communications has developed "DirectPC" for fast file downloading from the Internet via the Hughes Galaxy IV geosynchronous satellite (GEOS).

12.2 Cable Television Modems

Originally CATV systems were designed to be only simplex for delivering quality television signals to subscribers. Anticipating customer desire for fully interactive Internet and video services, cable modems will be full duplex. Over 20 percent of the American CATV plants have been converted to full duplex capabilities. Although cable modems will be full duplex, the downstream rate will be as high as 36 Mbps and the upstream rate will be only 10 Mbps. Nevertheless both rates are much faster than the relatively paltry 56 kbps rates of state-of-the-art telephone modems. Most home and small office users download large graphic files from the Internet and rarely upload large files. The "asymmetrical" feature would not be a problem for these users. The Multimedia Cable Network Systems (MCNS) group has issued specifications, and the IEEE 802.14 committee is also developing standards. The DAVIC and DVB standards are being used in Europe.

Analog Devices, Inc., is making a chipset for cable modems. The downstream (forward) data (from the cable/Internet provider to the user) will be in the 42- to 850-MHz band. The upstream (reverse) data (from the user to the cable/Internet provider) will be in the 5- to 42-MHz band in the United States and in the 5- to 65-MHz band in Europe. See Figure 12.1. The forward channel will use a 256-bit Quadrature Amplitude Modulation (QAM) technique. The reverse channel is expected to have a great deal of external noise and will use a noise resistant modulation, Quadrature Phase Shift Keying (QPSK).

Hybrid Networks, Inc., has a cable modem that can be employed over the airwaves. In Colorado, Wantweb, Inc., is using the modem to provide high-speed Internet access in a microwave band.

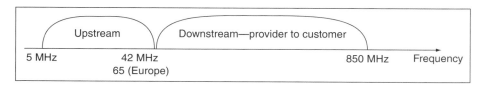

FIGURE 12.1
Cable modem frequencies.

12.3 Asymmetric Data Subscriber Line (ADSL)

Both ADSL and Basic Rate Interface (BRI) ISDN require removing the filter/transformers from the Unshielded Twisted Pair (UTP) between the telco's Central Offices (CO) and the home or small office. Recall from Chapter 11 on ISDN that the filter/transformers are in the TP line to enhance voice transmission, but at the expense of speedy data transmission. ADSL modems use more sophisticated techniques to get much higher data rates than with ISDN.

"Asymmetric" means that the data rates upstream (from the user to the CO) will be different from the downstream (CO to the user) rates. This is because the user will more likely be downloading (receiving) large files, probably from the Internet and the World Wide Web (WWW), but not as likely uploading (sending) huge files.

ADSL allows simultaneous use for data transfer and a telephone on the same line. The telephone service is called **Plain Old Telephone Service (POTS).** That's really true! Just when you had despaired of finding any humor whatsoever in this business! Oh yes, there is PANS (Pretty Amazing New Stuff), but it isn't used as much as POTS!

Figure 12.2 shows how an ADSL system would be connected. Figure 12.3 shows the Frequency Division Multiplexing (FDM) used in one ADSL version. The POTS service uses the same spectrum as before and is easily filtered from the other frequencies using the "POTS splitter." The downstream data uses FDM and Time Division Multiplexing (TDM). An error correction code is appended to the downstream data.

Other xDSL standards are being developed and are summarized in Table 12.1

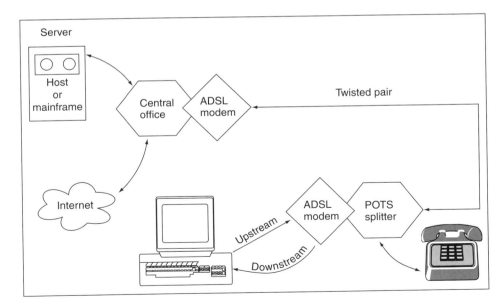

FIGURE 12.2
ADSL connection.

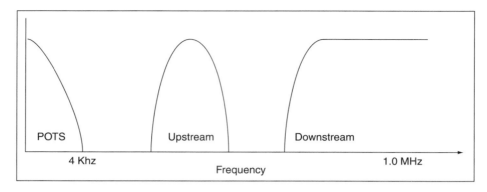

FIGURE 12.3
ADSL FDM.

TABLE 12.1
xDSL standards

Name	Meaning	Data Rate	Mode	Applications
V.221, V.32, V.34	Voice Band Modems	1,200 bps to 28,800 bps	Duplex	Data communications
DSL	Digital Subscriber Line	160 kbps	Duplex	ISDN service, voice and data communications
HDSL	High data Digital Sub-scriber Line	1.544 Mbps 2.048 Mbps	Duplex Duplex	T1 service replacement, E1 service replacement. Feeder plant, WAN access, server access
ADSL	Asymmetric Digital Sub-scriber Line	1.5 to 9 Mbps 16 to 640 kbps	Downstream Upstream	Internet access, LAN access, multimedia
VDSL	Very high data rate Digi-tal Subscriber Line	13 to 52 Mbps 1.5 to 2.3 Mbps	Downstream Upstream	Same as ADSL plus

Source: From the ADSL Forum.

12.4 High-Speed Satellite Internet Transmissions

Hughes Electronics, Inc., is providing high-speed Internet access via Hughes' Galaxy IV geosynchronous satellite. The 400-kbps high-speed data is sent downstream (from satellite to user) only. The user needs to have a conventional modem to access the Internet server at Hughes. The user does not need any radio transmission capabilities to access the satellite. The user to the Hughes Internet server link is via conventional landlines. This precludes use by subscribers in remote locations without telephone or similar access. The system use diagram is shown in Figure 12.4.

The downlink frequencies from Galaxy IV are 11.7 to 12.2 gHz. This service uses only one channel of Galaxy IV. The data is sent using Time Division Multiple Access (TDMA). Other vendors are entering this market.

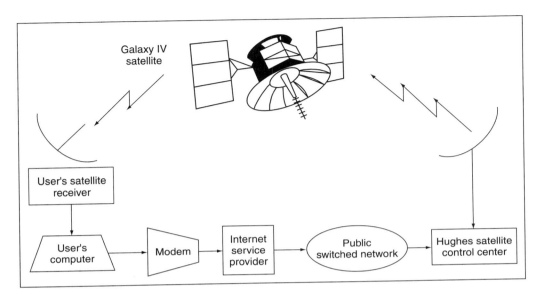

FIGURE 12.4
Hughes DirecPC™ system usage.

12.5 Testing

The Hewlett-Packard 79000 ADSL Test Station is designed for volume testing of ADSL modems coming off the production lines. It can test four modems in parallel to ADSL test standard ANSI T1.433 and POTS standard ITU T0.133. It can test either a Central Office (CO) ADSL transceiver unit (modem) (ATU-C) or a remote end ADSL transceiver unit (modem) (ATU-R).

Tests performed are digital input/output (I/O) functionality, BER, testing the modem's transformer, hybrid and high-pass filter, spurious signals, transmitter power spectral density, Digital to Analog converter, linearity, noise in both the voice (POTS) band and the ADSL band, impulse noise, dynamic range, and edge connector shorts.

It can also test for compatibility with ISDN, POTS, E-1, T-1, pair gain, and HDSL.

SUMMARY

I. Large data files take too long to download to the home or office, for example, Internet files and graphics files.

    A. Too slow for even the fastest telephone modem (56 kbps).

    B. Modems are reaching their theoretical limits.

II. Alternative delivery methods needed.

    A. Cable television modems. Data rates upstream and downstream different (asymmetric). Downstream rates as high as 36 Mbps. Upstream rates as high as 10 Mbps.

    B. Asymmetric Data Subscriber Line (ADSL).
        1. Uses the twisted pair (TP) between the CO and user; loading coils removed as in ISDN.
        2. Frequency Division Multiplexing (FDM); data transmission.
           a. Full duplex.
           b. Upstream (16 to 640 kbps).
           c. Downstream (1.5 to 9 Mbps).
        3. Also has telephone service as before.
    C. HDSL is replacing T-1.
    D. Satellite transmissions giving Internet downloads.
        1. Hughes' Galaxy IV.
        2. 400 kbps.
        3. Still need terrestrial telephone Internet uplink.

QUESTIONS

1. What is the motivation for higher data transfer speeds to the home and office?
2. What is ADSL? It is not sufficient to define the acronym. What multiplexing schemes does it use?
3. What are the upstream and downstream data rates of ADSL? What does the word *asymmetric* mean?
4. Explain how high-speed satellite Internet transmissions, such as DirecPC, work. How does one communicate from the home or office to the satellite? What downstream data rates are possible? How does the user communicate to the host computer?
5. What are the upstream and downstream data rates of cable modems?
6. How is it possible for ADSL to have both modem and POTS simultaneously?
7. Which is faster, Basic ISDN or ADSL? How much faster?

13

CELLULAR COMMUNICATIONS

OBJECTIVES

In this chapter we will discuss:

   I. What are the major problems for mobile telephone systems?
      A. Limited number of users within the allowed frequency band.
      B. Limited data rates within the allowed bandwidth.
      C. Signal fading.
  II. Evolution of analog mobile telephone systems in the United States.
      A. Mobile Telephone Service (MTS).
      B. Improved Mobile Phone Service (IMPS).
         1. Not cellular systems.
         2. Limited user capacity.
      C. Advanced Mobile Phone Service (AMPS).
         1. First cellular system.
         2. Many more users could be accommodated than MTS or IMPS.
         3. Still not enough user capacity.
 III. Frequency Modulation (FM).
      A. "Capture effect."
         1. Signal stronger than fifty times a weaker one (17 dB) will completely ignore the weaker signal.
         2. Allows "frequency reuse"; many more users can employ the same frequency.
      B. Less susceptible to fading than AM; fading caused by hills, mountains, valleys, building shadows, reflections.
  IV. Cells.
      A. Many cells are required to cover the same area as MTS and IMPS.
      B. AMPS is more complex than MTS or IMPS.
      C. Each cell uses lower power than with MTS and IMPS; more customer capacity due to frequency reuse.
      D. Cells are approximately hexagonal shaped.
      E. Cells can be divided into sectors to increase capacity.

    V. Mobile Telephone Switching Office (MTSO).
       A. Computer controlling many cell sites.
       B. MTSO is connected to CO and then to the PSTN.
       C. Keeps track of users.
       D. Controls handoff of mobile unit to other cells and other MTSOs.
       E. Controls mobile unit's transmitter power and frequency.
   VI. The cellular band is 25 MHz wide in the United States; there are 832 channels of 30 kHz each.
  VII. Aloha protocol; slotted Aloha protocol.
 VIII. Interim Standard-54 (IS-54).
       A. Uses the same frequencies and channel widths as AMPS.
       B. Gradually replacing AMPS.
       C. Sometimes referred to as Digital AMPS, or D-AMPS.
       D. Vocoders used to reduce digitized voice bit rate to 13 kbps.
       E. Six time slots per frame.
          1. Voice uses two time slots per frame.
          2. Low data rate usage—one time slot per frame.
          3. Guard time compensates for varying distance of mobile units to cell site.
          4. Ramp time allows the mobile unit to come to full power before transmitting data.
   IX. Global System for Mobile (GSM) communications.
       A. Most used system in the world.
       B. Designed to interface with ISDN.
       C. Fading is compensated by TDMA and interleaving; FDMA using frequency hopping Spread Spectrum.
    X. Interim Standard-95 (IS-95) uses direct sequence Spread Spectrum.
       A. Signal is spread out over 1.23 MHz.
       B. Allows about ten times as many users as AMPS in the same spectrum space.
       C. Uses mathematical Walsh code to separate users (Code Division Multiple Access).
       D. All mobile unit transmitters must be synchronized.
       E. All mobile unit transmitter signal strength must be the same at the cell receiver (near-far problem).

13.1 Mobile Communications Problems

The three major problems faced with mobile telephone and data services are limited number of users within the allowable frequency band, limited data rates within the allowable bandwidth, and signal fading. User numbers and data rates are limited by the very limited radio spectrum available to mobile telephone services. Ingenious methods have been implemented to reduce these problems.

13.2 United States Standards

There are four major cellular standards in the world, summarized in Table 13.1. Note that GSM is not used in North America.

TABLE 13.1
Four major cellular systems

AMPS
    Advanced Mobile Phone Service
    Analog
IS-54
    Interim Standard
    Digital
    TDM and FDM
    Replacing AMPS
GSM
    Global System for Mobile communications
    Most used system in the world except in North America
    Digital
    TDM and FDM
IS-95
    Digital Spread Spectrum—CDMA (Code Division Multiple Access)

FIGURE 13.1
MTS and IMPS system. The transmitter/receiver communicates with uses within a 20-mile radius.

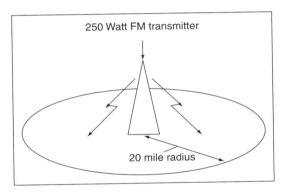

The present analog system used in North America is AMPS, which replaced MPS. We must study MPS to understand the basics of mobile communications and how AMPS evolved from MPS. Both MTS and AMPS use Frequency Division Multiplexing (FDM).

The digital system IS-54 is replacing AMPS on an incremental basis. AMPS and IS-54 must share the same frequency spectrum even while the changeover occurs, which has led to some interesting problems. IS-54 uses both FDM and Time Division Multiplexing (TDM).

13.2.1 Mobile Telephone Service (MTS)

The first major mobile radio system designed to work into the telephone system was Mobile Telephone Service (MTS), inaugurated in 1946 (Figure 13.1). The central transmitter/receiver had a coverage radius of about 20 miles. The transmitter had a 250-watt output, considerably more than today's cellular transmitters. This gave a relatively large coverage area. We will see that this is not an advantage when many customers want to use the system. It ends up limiting the total number of customers and makes expansion very difficult.

Other MTS disadvantages were the need for operators and the fact that the system was half duplex. Most customers had difficulty with half duplex operation. MTS was not a cellular system. We shall define what *cellular* means later in this chapter and discuss how cellular systems are superior to centralized mobile systems.

13.2.2 Improved Mobile Phone Service (IMPS)

Improved Mobile Phone Service replaced MTS. However the improvements were minimal. A user could dial a number, eliminating the operator, and the system was full duplex. However the basic problems of limited channels and difficulty of expansion remained. Many more people wanted mobile telephone service than could possibly be accommodated.

13.2.3 Advanced Mobile Phone Service (AMPS)

AMPS was the first cellular telephone system in North America and was conceptually quite different from MTS and IMPS.

Integrated Circuits (ICs) with powerful features were a major factor in making cellular telephone systems affordable. These ICs are needed in both the cellular base stations and the mobile cell phone to keep the price of cellular down, make the size of the cell phone manageable, and minimize battery drain.

13.3 Frequency Modulation (FM)

Another factor making cellular telephone possible is the "capture effect" of Frequency Modulation (FM). If two FM signals are using the same frequency, they may interfere with each other. However if one signal is fifty or more times stronger (17 dB), the receiver will hear only the stronger signal. The weaker signal will be completely ignored. The stronger signal is "captured," and the weaker signal has no effect at the receiver. This allows frequencies to be reused (frequency reuse) in nearby cells and is the main principle of cellular systems. The signal strength decreases as one moves farther away from the cell transmitter by approximately an inverse fourth power ($1/range^4$, or r^{-4}).

The signal strength varies greatly (fades) because of blockages by buildings, tunnels, hills, and mountains. Mountains, hills, buildings, and utility poles can reflect signals. At the receiver the reflected signal combines with the direct path signal. This also causes fades. While stopped at a traffic light and listening to your favorite FM station, you may have noticed that the signal was in a fade and that the signal was noisy. Merely moving your vehicle a meter or so may have eliminated the fade and the consequent noisiness. This variation can be over 30 dB (1,000 to one) and makes the use of AM impossible. FM is not nearly as sensitive to these great signal strength variations as AM. FM receivers have amplitude limiting circuits that can make signal strength variations almost unnoticeable to most users.

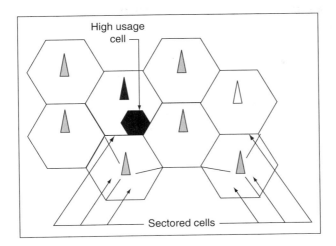

FIGURE 13.2
Cellular system. The cell shape is only approximately hexagonal, since antenna gain patterns do not always follow the ideal. Each cell can be subdivided into three sectors by using three antennas at each cell site. See the lower two cells.

13.4 Cells

MTS used a high-power centralized transmitter/receiver covering a wide area. **Cellular systems** use much lower power and cover considerably less area per cell. Many cells are required to cover the same area. This looks like a disadvantage, but we will see that it isn't. Having many low-powered cells allows frequency reuse; that is, many customers can use the same frequencies. While MTS allowed only a limited number of customers, cellular allows many times more. The relative simplicity of MTS is replaced by the more complicated AMPS system, but many more users can employ AMPS.

A simplified cellular map is shown in Figure 13.2. This map assumes a relatively flat terrain, with users scattered evenly over the map. The borders between cells are the lines at which the signals from two adjacent cells are at equal power levels. This makes the cell shape hexagonal. If buildings, hills, mountains, and non-uniform customer density are considered, the cell shapes may not be an exact hexagon.

13.4.1 Cell Sectorization

A **cell** can be divided into three sectors by three antennas at each cell site to increase the system user capacity. See the lower two cells in Figure 13.2 for an example. Another example is shown in Figure 13.3.

Buildings, high-usage areas such as downtown business districts, and mountains will cause signal fades and may force designers to change the cell shape. In high-usage areas the cells are made smaller to keep the number of users in each cell approximately equal. By using directional antennas aimed over each sector, each cell can be subdivided into three or more sectors as in Figure 13.3. Other cell dividing techniques are to place transmitter/receivers at

FIGURE 13.3
Cell sectorization from cell center. Note the cell is divided into three sectors. This is done by using three antennas with approximately 120 degree horizontal beamwidth. Note also different frequencies are used in each sector. These frequencies are not used in adjacent channels to minimize co-channel interference.

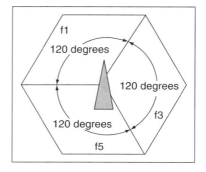

FIGURE 13.4
Cell sectorization from cell indices. Cells can also be sectored from the cell corners or indices. Three cell sites combine to cover a cell. Each site has a 120 degree horizontal beamwidth antenna pointing into the cell. Again, different frequencies are used to prevent interference. Nonadjacent frequencies are used to prevent co-channel interference.

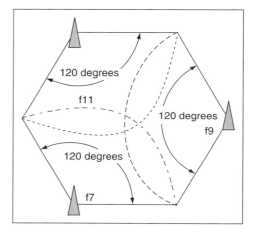

the edge of the cells (Figure 13.4) and to use directional antennas aimed over the individual sectors. Of course different frequencies must be used in each sector (except for Code Division Multiple Access [CDMA], which is discussed later in this chapter).

Many communities consider cellular antennas unsightly and have passed restrictions on their deployment. Cellular providers have found one ingenious solution to this dilemma. The providers lease antenna space in church steeples! This benefits both the providers and the church congregation. Of course the roofing material must be non-conductive to pass the radio waves.

13.5　Frequency Reuse

Frequency reuse, mentioned in Section 13.3, is the key to all cellular systems. It allows many users to employ the same frequency. However the cells using the same frequency must be separated by a sufficient distance. In the case of CDMA the separation is done with a mathematical technique called a Walsh code.

Note that in Figure 13.5, frequency 1 (f_1) is used in the upper left cell and also in the lower center cell. Frequency 3 (f_3) is used in the leftmost cell and also in the upper right

FIGURE 13.5
Frequency reuse. The cells labeled "f1" use the same frequency, the cells labeled "f3" use the same frequency, and so on. The cells are placed far enough apart to keep interfering signals too weak to cause interference. This cell placement is adequate for AMPS.

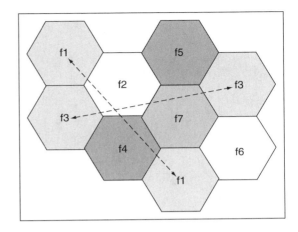

FIGURE 13.6
Frequency reuse (continued). This cell placement is adequate for GSM and IS-54 (D-AMPS).

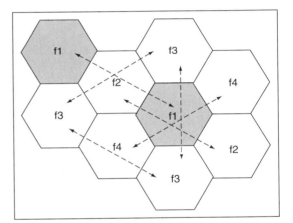

cell. With AMPS the spacing shown is necessary to keep the interfering signals 17 dB or more below the desired signal from the cell central transmitter.

The system designer wants to maximize the number of channels that can be used by each cell. This is done by placing cells using the same frequencies as close together as possible. However there are limits as to how close cells using the same frequencies can be placed. If cells using the same frequency are placed too close together, there will be unacceptable interference. In Figure 13.6 the cells are placed too close together for AMPS but are satisfactory for IS-54, GSM, and IS-95. This correctly implies that these systems have a greater user capacity than AMPS.

13.6 Mobile Telephone Switching Office (MTSO)

Each **Mobile Telephone Switching Office (MTSO)** has a computer controlling a group of cell sites. Each cell site is connected to an MTSO. Each MTSO controls many cell sites.

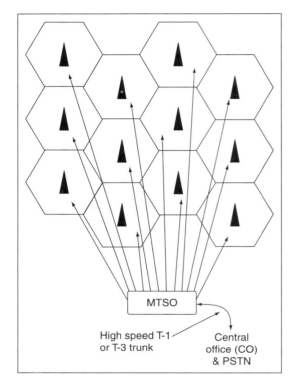

FIGURE 13.7
One MTSO controls many cell sites.

Each MTSO is connected to a Central Office (CO) and other MTSOs. This connection is by coax, twisted pair, optical fiber, or microwave. The MTSOs are connected to the PSTN via a CO. See Figure 13.7.

The MTSO computer handles the cellular calls and keeps track of the mobile users. When a mobile unit travels from one cell into another, the MTSO must transfer the radio connection to the new cell, or even to another MTSO. This transfer is called **"handoff."**

13.6.1 Full Duplex

Cellular systems are full duplex. Different frequencies are used for base-to-mobile (downlink) and mobile-to-base (uplink) transmissions. Full duplex allows the MTSO to send control information to the mobile unit at any time. This control information is piggybacked onto the voice channel, and the user is usually unaware of this transfer. The control information sounds like a "click" to the listener. The MTSO controls the transmitter power and frequency channel of the mobile unit. The MTSO finds an unused frequency channel to use and controls the mobile unit transmitter power to keep all received signals at the base station at the same level.

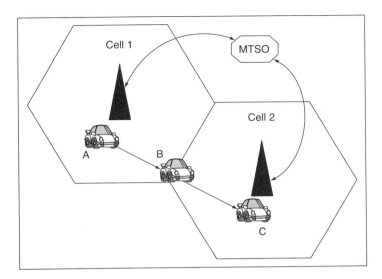

FIGURE 13.8
Handoff. When the mobile unit is at Point A, the signal strength received at Cell 1 is much stronger than that received at Cell 2. When the mobile unit is at Point B, the signals received at Cell 1 and Cell 2 are about equal. The MTSO must decide if the strength at Cell 2 is strong enough to transfer (hand off) the mobile unit to Cell 2. After handoff, the mobile unit is at Point C and communicating with Cell 2. The MTSO switched the operating frequency to prevent interference with mobile units in Cell 1.

13.7 Handoff

We now need definitions. The forward channel, or downlink, is the base transmitter-to-mobile frequency. The reverse channel, or uplink, is the mobile-to-base transmission frequency. See Figure 13.8.

13.7.1 Handoff between Cells

When a mobile leaves one cell and enters another, the following handoff occurs.

1. The MTSO receives signal strength reports from both cells. When the mobile's signal strength is consistently stronger in the new cell, the MTSO begins the handoff procedure.
2. The mobile unit is told to use a new frequency via a data burst on the voice channel. The new frequency is the one assigned to the new cell.
3. The mobile responds with an ACKnowledgment on the reverse setup channel.
4. The conversation continues.

13.7.2 Handoff between MTSOs

The handoff procedure when a mobile unit travels from one MTSO's territory to another MTSO's territory is as follows:

1. The MTSO notes that the signal is getting weaker and asks the new MTSO for a signal strength report from the mobile unit.

2. When the mobile unit's signal strength is significantly greater in the new MTSO's territory, the old MTSO will transfer control to the new MTSO.

3. The new MTSO will assign a new frequency to the mobile unit and adjust its power. This is done via a data burst on the voice channel.

4. The mobile unit responds with an ACKnowledge data word on the reverse channel.

5. The conversation continues.

13.8 Call Setup

13.8.1 Mobile Initiating a Call

When the mobile wishes to initiate a call, the following procedure occurs:

1. Mobile unit is in the idle mode.
2. User enters number and pushes SEND button.
3. Each cell site is constantly transmitting in its one assigned signaling channel. The mobile unit scans through the signaling channels searching for the strongest signal and locks onto it. This is called *self-location.*
4. Some mobile units notify the cell site and MTSO that it has locked onto the cell site. This is called *registration* and makes finding the mobile unit easier for incoming calls.
5. The mobile unit transmits the number called and the Mobile ID Number (MIN) to the cell site.

The MIN can be monitored by a scanner, recorded, and burned into a ROM. The ROM is then installed into a cellular phone and sold on the black market. The guy who buys the black market cell phone makes a bunch of calls to friends around the world. Guess who gets stuck with the telephone bill? You got it! The original initiator of the cellular call! The cellular providers keep detectives busy running down the black marketers. Being such an electronic detective offers excellent job security!

6. The MIN is checked in a database to see if it is a valid number.
7. The cellular phone is connected to the PSTN via a cell site and an MTSO.

13.8.2 A Call from the PSTN to the Mobile Unit

When a call passes through the PSTN to the mobile, the following happens:

1. A unique code is sent out searching for the unregistered mobile phone.
2. When the mobile unit recognizes its own code, it seizes the setup signaling channel.
   *Note:*The mobile unit may have to wait until other units have finished their calls. The number of users could temporarily exceed the available channels.
3. The called mobile unit sends its MIN to the cell site, and the MIN is sent to the MTSO.
4. The MTSO assigns an unused channel to the mobile unit.
5. Talk!

TABLE13.2
Cellular frequencies in the United States

Mobile unit transmit (reverse channel, or uplink)
  824 to 849 MHz, 25 MHz total divided between two providers
Mobile unit receive (forward channel, or downlink)
  869 to 896 MHz, 25 MHz total divided between two providers
Mobile receive frequency = mobile transmit frequency + 45 MHz
Total channels = 25 MHz/0.030 MHz/channel = 832 channels total (416 channels per cellular provider)
  21 signaling channels
  1 signaling channel per cell site
  395 voice channels per provider

13.9   Cellular Frequencies in the United States

The cellular frequencies in the United States are shown in Table 13.2. Note that the frequencies are 824 to 896 MHz. The transmit and receive frequency channels each occupy 25 MHz. The mobile unit's receive frequency (downlink or forward channel) is always 45 MHz above the transmit (uplink or reverse channel) frequency (Figure 13.9).

The uplink always occupies the lower band. This is because radio propagation is slightly better for lower frequencies and system designers want to give the maximum advantage to the mobile transmitter. This saves batteries and allows smaller, less efficient antennas. The base station usually operates from the electric power grid and has higher gain antennas than the mobiles.

Each channel occupies 30 kHz. The total number of channels is

$$\frac{\dfrac{25 \text{ MHz}}{\text{Cellular band}}}{\dfrac{30 \text{ kHz}}{\text{Channel}}} = \frac{832 \text{ channels}}{\text{cellular band}} \qquad \textbf{(Equation 13.1)}$$

The Federal Communications Commission (FCC) of the United States wanted to be sure competition exists in every market area and has made provisions for at least two companies to compete in each cellular market. The two cellular providers will share the cellular frequencies equally. The 25-MHz bands are divided exactly in half. Each provider gets 12.5 MHz of radio spectrum space. The total channels available to one company are 832 / 2 = 416 channels. Of these 416 channels, 21 channels are used for signaling, leaving 395 available for voice use.

A typical cell frequency "reuse" factor value is 7. This means that each cell site has

$$\frac{395 \text{ channels}}{7} \approx \frac{32 \text{ channels}}{\text{site}} \qquad \textbf{(Equation 13.2)}$$

Reuse factors can vary from 1 to 21. In high-use areas we want small reuse factors and many channels per site. Low-reuse values have the possibility of unacceptable frequency

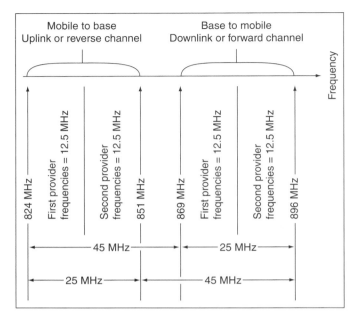

FIGURE 13.9
Cellular frequencies in the United States.

interference. AMPS requires a reuse factor of 7. IS-54, GSM, and other TDM systems can have a reuse factor of 4. A reuse factor of 1 is possible only with CDMA. The lower the reuse factor, the higher the number of channels per site and more potential users.

13.10 N-AMPS (NARROWBAND AMPS)

Better band-pass filters have been developed since the inception of AMPS. This allows the channel width to be reduced to 12 kHz, rather than 30 kHz, giving N-AMPS three times the capacity of AMPS. However this bandwidth reduction comes at the price of reduced system gain.

13.11 Aloha Protocol

We will study the slotted Aloha Time Division Multiplex (TDM) protocol, because IS-54 and GSM use a similar one. The Aloha protocol was developed by the University of Hawaii, based on the island of Oahu. See Figure 13.10. In pure Aloha, if a station on another island wished to transmit data, it did so without listening first. If the receiving station on Oahu received the data successfully, it would respond with an ACKnowledgment transmission. If the data was interfered with and not received successfully, the transmitting station would not get the ACKnowledgment signal. After a wait period, the transmitting station would re-transmit the data until received successfully at Oahu. This system,

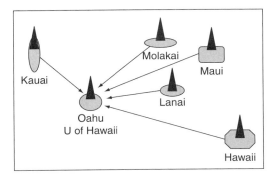

FIGURE 13.10
ALOHA protocol.

although quite simple, suffered from simultaneous transmissions (collisions or contention) and had a maximum theoretical traffic efficiency of only 18 percent.

13.11.1 Slotted Aloha Protocol

Slotted Aloha is a form of Time Division Multiple Access (TDMA). TDMA is used by IS-54 and GSM. Because these important systems use TDMA, we will study slotted Aloha. To overcome the relative inefficiency of Aloha, the University of Hawaii developed the slotted Aloha protocol. Each transmitting station is allotted certain times (time slots) to transmit as in Figure 13.11. Together the five stations' time slots constitute a frame. The stations are synchronized with a timing signal from the main facility on Oahu. The synchronizing signal tells each station when it may transmit its data. The efficiency of slotted Aloha is about 36 percent, twice that of pure Aloha.

13.12   Interim Standard-54 (IS-54)

We have learned that digital transmissions over the PSTN are more efficient than analog. This is also true in the cellular and wireless world. In North America no new frequencies were available for digital cellular systems. The **IS-54** system was developed to provide more user capacity. This digital cellular system had to use the same frequencies and the same 30-kHz channel widths as AMPS. IS-54 is sometimes called "Digital AMPS," or "D-AMPS."

IS-54 is a digital system using digitized voice data (see Table 13.3). Codecs use a 64-kbps data rate. This rate would use too much valuable radio spectrum space, and so some technique had to be found to reduce the data rate and still give good voice-quality transmission. Voice digitizing is done with vocoders, but this very ingenious technique is beyond the scope of this text. The actual bit rate is 13 kbps and is expected to be reduced below that.

13.12.1 IS-54 Frame and Time Slot Structure

Each IS-54 mobile unit is assigned a time slot, somewhat like T-1. However instead of twenty-four time slots as in a T-1 frame, only six time slots are in each IS-54 frame as

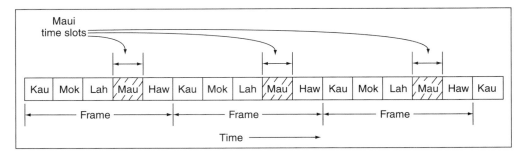

FIGURE 13.11
Slotted ALOHA protocol.

TABLE13.3
IS-54

Digital
TDM
   Six time slots per frame, 1,944 bits in a 40-ms frame length, with 25 frames/second
Replacing AMPS
   Uses same frequencies as AMPS
   Six times capacity of AMPS
   Sometimes called "Digital AMPS"
     D-AMPS
     48.6-Kbps data rate
     Differential Quadrature Phase Shift Keying (D-QPSK) Modulation
   Compression used with voice

shown in Figure 13.12. If the data rate is high, as for voice transmission, the user will have two time slots per frame. If the data rate is low, the user will be assigned one time slot per frame.

Figure 13.13a shows the time slot structure for the IS-54 downlink from the base station to the mobile unit. The first 28 bits are to synchronize the mobile units. Remember that the slotted Aloha format used a synchronization pattern to synchronize the remote transmitters. Next is the Slow Associated Control CHannel (SACCH), a housekeeping and control field. Next is 130 bits of data, followed by 12 bits in the Coded Digital Verification Color Code (CDVCC), another housekeeping and control field. It is analogous to the SAT control signal of AMPS. Finally another 130 bits of data complete the time slot. The housekeeping fields contain data controlling transmitting and receiving frequencies, transmitter power level, signal strength measurement, and handoff information.

The mobile-to-base time slot is shown in Figure 13.13b. The time slot begins with six bits equivalent silent guard time. Radio waves take a finite time to travel from the mobile unit to the base unit. The radio waves from mobile units close to the base unit will ar-

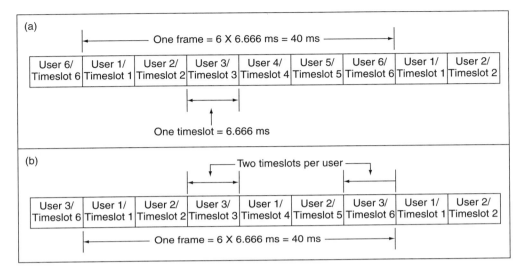

FIGURE 13.12

IS-54 frame structure. (a) Half-rate (data) frame—six users in six time slots. (b) Full-rate (voice or data) frame—three users in six time slots.

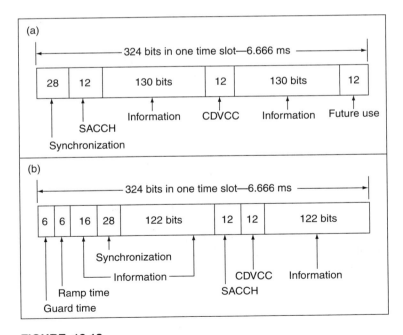

FIGURE 13.13

IS-54 time slot format. (a) Base unit transmitting (downlink)—six time slots in one frame. One frame is 6 × 324 bits = 1944 bits, so six time slots in one frame is 6 × 6.666 ms = 40 ms long. (b) Mobile unit is transmitting (uplink).

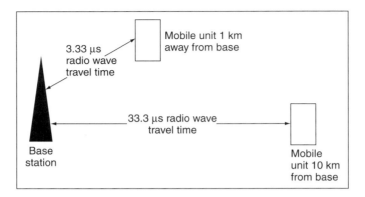

FIGURE 13.14
Why is guard time needed?

FIGURE 13.15
IS-54 π / 4 differential quadrature phase shift keying constellation.

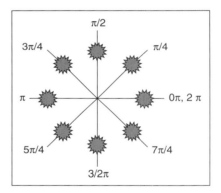

rive much sooner than for mobile units at the cell edge. This **guard time** allows mobile units to be different distances from the base unit as shown in Figure 13.14. These six bits are 123.44 μs long, which is equivalent to 18-km range, longer than shown in Figure 13.14. This 18-km range (123.44 μs) includes both uplink and downlink distances and is greater than any cell radius.

Next is a six-bit 123 μs ramp time. Radio transmitters do not come to full power instantly. The ramp time allows sufficient time for the mobile transmitter to come up to full power before transmitting any data. The data and housekeeping fields follow.

13.12.2 IS-54 Modulation

IS-54 uses π / 4 (180 degrees / 4) Differential Quadrature Phase Shift modulation (π / 4 DQPSK). π / 4 DQPSK is similar to Quadrature Phase Shift modulation, discussed in Chapter 11. The eight-state constellation is shown in Figure 13.15. The word *differential* means that the symbol transmitted is referenced to the previous symbol's phase.

TABLE 13.4
Global System for Mobile (GSM) Communications

Digital—voice at 13 kbps by Linear Predictive Encoding
Most used system in the world
Designed to interface with ISDN
Reduces fading by:
    Frequency hopping Spread Spectrum
    Time Division Multiplexing (TDM)

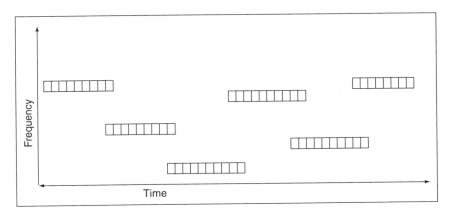

FIGURE 13.16
GSM using FDM and TDM.

13.13   Global System for Mobile (GSM) Communications

GSM is the most popular cellular system in the world (see Table 13.4). It is designed to interface with ISDN. It is a TDMA and FDMA system. There are eight time slots per frame. It uses frequency hopping (Spread Spectrum and FDMA) at a 217-hops-per-second rate, and each time slot is repeated twice. The frequency is changed (hopped) after every frame. These techniques help compensate for signal fading. Figure 13.16 demonstrates both FDM and TDM. Each GSM frame contains eight time slots and is allotted a 200-kHz bandwidth. The frequency bands are 890 to 915 MHz for the uplink and 935 to 960 MHz for the downlink. Each frame is transmitted on one frequency and then hops to a new frequency. Data is repeated in another frame. This is called *interleaving* and reduces fading effects.

    In frequency hopping Spread Spectrum (SS) the transmitted frequency is changed according to a pseudo random code. The code cannot be truly random because the receiver will not know where to listen. The receiver frequency is also frequency hopped using the same code as the transmitter. Each transmission lasts only a short time, usually less than the propagation time to the receiver. This prevents jammers from having enough time to send a jamming signal. Before the jammer can get an interfering signal to the receivers, the use frequency has hopped to a new frequency. GSM changes frequency 217 hops per second, or after every frame. Each frame contains eight time slots.

13.13.1 GSM Frame Structure

Figure 13.17 shows the GSM frame structure. No transmission occurs during the 8.25-bit guard time at the frame end, allowing the transmitter to come up to full power. Each bit is 3.697 μ seconds, and the 8.25-bit time is 30.5 μ seconds long.

Figure 13.18 shows how time slots fit into frames, frames fit into multiframes, and multiframes fit into superframes. GSM is not compatible with IS-54 or AMPS.

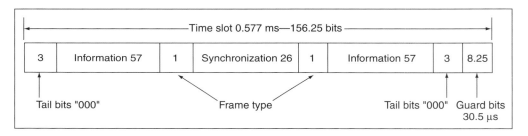

FIGURE 13.17
GSM frame format. Eight time slots comprise one frame of 4.62 ms. Twenty-six frames make up a multiframe of 120 ms. Of these 26 frames, one frame is used for SACCH and another is an idle frame.

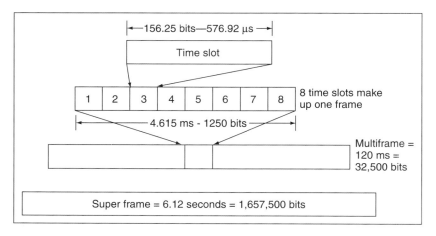

FIGURE 13.18
GSM frame structure.

13.14 Interim Standard-95 (IS-95)

IS-95 uses the interesting means of direct sequence Spread Spectrum to tackle the user capacity problem. Direct sequence Spread Spectrum (SS) techniques do not use a single frequency or two. Rather, the signal is spread out over a much wider spectrum of 1.23 MHz. While this seems like a terrible waste of precious radio spectrum, we will see that it is not. Actually direct sequence SS allows more users than any other method.

Spread Spectrum is difficult to jam or monitor because the signal is spread out over a wide spectrum. The jammer or monitor does not know where the signal will be transmitted, or may be entirely unable to differentiate the signal from noise. To successfully jam the signal a jammer must either know the SS code or put a lot of signal power into the entire used spectrum. Generally this last option is very difficult. Similarly if a monitor does not know the code, he or she must use a separate receiver to monitor all possible frequencies. This is usually quite expensive for average folks, but usually the U.S. military will willingly spend this kind of money to protect its troops.

Table 13.5 compares direct sequence Spread Spectrum and frequency hopping Spread Spectrum.

TABLE 13.5
Spread Spectrum (SS)

Sends transmissions over wide bandwidth
More secure, difficult to monitor or jam
More user & data capacity
Two methods
    Frequency hopping
    Direct sequence—Code Division Multiple Access (CDMA)

Frequency Hopping Spread Spectrum

Signal transmitted on different frequencies
    Each transmission lasts only a short time
    After each transmission the frequency is changed
    Frequency sequence is a pseudo random pattern (code)
    If jammer does not know the code, it is difficult to jam—takes much power in entire band
    If monitor does not know the code, many receivers are needed to cover the entire band

Code Division Multiple Access (CDMA) Spread Spectrum

Transmission constantly spread over wide spectrum
    About 1.23 MHz
    Appears as random noise to eavesdroppers
"Soft" on maximum number of users
Users get privacy by a unique 64-chip "Walsh" code; individual codes are "orthogonal"
    Will not interfere with each other
    "Chip" does *not* mean integrated circuit!

IS-95 uses direct sequence Spread Spectrum or Code Division Multiple Access (CDMA), a clever mathematical technique to address the user limits of other wireless systems. There is no "hard" limit to the number of users as in AMPS, IS-54, and GSM. The practical limit is about ten times as many users as AMPS. Each transmission is spread over 1.23 MHz, one-tenth of the total 12.5-MHz spectrum available. However this spectrum can be shared by 400 or more users.

CDMA assigns each user a unique Walsh code. This code allows many private conversations, each using the same time and frequency. The Walsh code is a 64-"chip" or 64-bit code. The word *chip* has nothing to do with the colloquial term for integrated circuit. A *Walsh code* is a mathematical "orthogonal" code; that is, each signal does not interfere with other signals. Each signal ignores all others. This needs an equal number of "ones" and "zeros" in each chip.

Let's look at a simple example in Figure 13.19 to see how CDMA works. In Figure 13.19a each of the three users has a different Walsh code. In Figure 13.19b user 1 wishes to send data "1 0 1." Each bit is multiplied by user 1's Walsh code chip of "+ − − +" to give the Data 1 transmitted waveform. User 2 and user 3 data is multiplied by their respective Walsh code chips to generate the Data 2 and Data 3 waveforms in Figure 13.18c and Figure 13.19d. This signal is summed together and transmitted over the airways and seen at Figure 13.19e at the base receiver.

At the base receiver the received signal is multiplied by each user's Walsh code. In Figure 13.19f user 3's Walsh code chip and the received signal are multiplied (correlated). The signal is averaged, and Figure 13.19g results. When the average (integral) voltage in the bit time is greater than zero, the output will be interpreted as a logic one. When the voltage average (integral) is approximately zero, the bit will be interpreted as a logic zero. This multiplication of the signal and the Walsh code is a correlation process.

13.14.1 CDMA Caveats

There are two imperatives for a CDMA system. The first is that the base station must receive all frames from each mobile unit at the same time (in synchronism). The base unit sends out a constant synchronizing signal to accomplish this. Also the base station has a special receiver to successfully receive signals with slightly different delay times.

The second imperative is the necessity for the signals from all mobile units to have nearly equal power at the base station. This is called the **"near-far" problem.** A mobile station "near" to the base station must have the same power at the base station as a mobile "far" from the base station. The Walsh code correlation process is based on the received powers being nearly equal. The base station sends out power control signals constantly to each mobile unit for power output adjustment.

13.14.2 Final Thoughts on CDMA

Besides being a clever correlation scheme, there are other advantages to a CDMA system. The number of users can be increased significantly over other cellular systems. When the number of users is increased, the signal-to-interference ratio is reduced and the Bit Error Rate (BER) increases. The capacity of a CDMA system is twelve to thirty times that of an

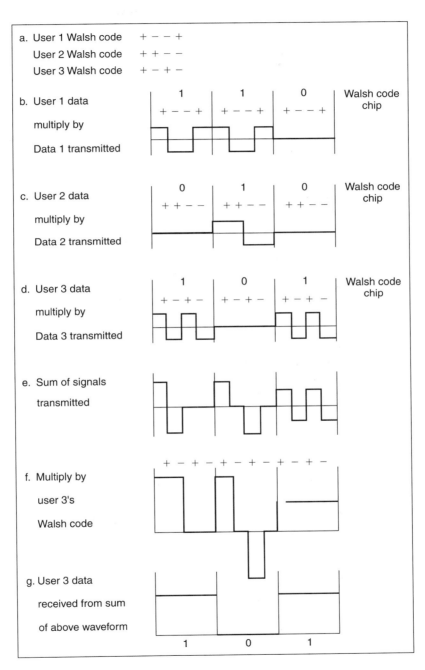

FIGURE 13.19
Walsh code (4 chip).

217

AMPS system. The exact number depends on the acceptable Bit Error Rate (BER). Adjacent CDMA cells can use the same frequency without interference because different Walsh codes prevent interference. Cell location and placement have more tolerance.

In an FM system such as CDMA, the system (processing) gain increases and the transmitted signal bandwidth or frequency deviation increases. Noise also increases and bandwidth increases, but not at as fast a rate. The bandwidth of IS-95 is 1.23 MHz, compared with an IS-54 and AMPS bandwidth of 30 kHz or 0.030 MHz. This wide bandwidth is also helpful in fighting fading. Also handoff is done gradually (soft handoff) and with help from the mobile unit. This is called Mobile Assisted Handoff (MAHO).

13.15 Testing and Troubleshooting

Hewlett-Packard makes a versatile cellular test set for AMPS and N-AMPS in the 8920B Communications Test Set. D-AMPS (IS-54) is covered with the 800 TDMA option. This test set is a spectrum analyzer, digital oscilloscope, power meter, radio frequency and audio frequency generator, and modulation analyzer. With the option 102 adjacent channel power test can be made to ensure minimum interference in adjacent channels. The control signals can be monitored and sent to mobile units. Many types of error measurements can be made. The 1,900-MHz PCS band can be covered with the 83236A interface.

Hewlett-Packard also makes two GSM test sets: the HP 8922S GSM test set for mobile maintenance and the HP 8922M for the manufacturing floor. They can perform transmitter and receiver tests, spectral analysis, error rates, and modulation analysis. They can also emulate a base station with the proper control signals and frequency hopping.

Hewlett-Packard's HP 8924C tests CDMA mobile units. The test set emulates a base station. It measures power over the full 1.23-MHz CDMA bandwidth, transmitted waveform quality, modulation analysis, and error rates.

A base station may have to support AMPS, TDMA (IS-54), PCS, and CDMA (IS-95) protocols. The HP 8921A handles all these protocols with the following adapters. The HP 83204A is the TDMA cellular adapter, the HP 83205A is the CDMA cellular adapter, and the HP 83236A is the PCS interface. This versatile test set performs all the tests mentioned in the paragraphs above.

SUMMARY

    I. Limitations of conventional mobile telephone systems.
        A. Limited number of users possible.
        B. Limited data rates.
        C. Signal fading.
    II. Frequency Modulation (FM).
        A. Allows frequency reuse.
            1. Two signals on the same frequency will not interfere if one is fifty times (17 dB) stronger than the other; AM signals need 1,000 to 1 ratio (30 dB).

      2. Allows transmitters to be closer together.
   B. Much more tolerant of fading than AM.
III. Cells.
   A. Allow frequency reuse.
      1. Transmitters on the same frequency in nearby cells.
      2. Mobile unit's transmitter power is lower than conventional mobile telephone system; saves batteries and allows mobile units to be closer.
   B. May be divided into smaller sectors to increase the number of possible users.
   C. Need a central controller; Mobile Telephone Switching Office (MTSO).
      1. Centralized computer controlling.
         a. Operating frequency of mobile units.
         b. Transmitter power of mobile units.
         c. Handoff when a mobile unit leaves one cell and enters another cell or area controlled by another MTSO.
      2. Connects into the PSTN.
IV. Cellular systems are full duplex and use different frequencies for uplink and downlink.
 V. Cellular frequencies in the United States.
   A. 832 total channels.
      1. 21 control channels.
      2. 395 voice or data channels.
   B. Full duplex.
      1. Upper band is for downlink.
      2. Lower band is for uplink.
      3. Constant 45-MHz difference between uplink and downlink frequencies.
VI. Slotted Aloha is a form of Time Division Multiplexing (TDM).
VII. IS-54 ("Digital AMPS") is replacing the analog AMPS.
   A. Uses TDM.
   B. Three to six times the user capacity.
   C. More difficult to eavesdrop.
   D. Uses Differential Quadrature Phase Shift modulation ($\pi/4$ DQPSK).
VIII. Global System for Mobile (GSM) communications.
   A. The most popular cellular system in the world.
   B. Uses frequency hopping.
   C. Uses TDM.
 IX. Interim Standard-95 (IS-95).
   A. Uses Code Division Multiple Access (CDMA); mathematical division called Walsh code.
   B. Uses direct sequence Spread Spectrum (SS).
   C. Allows more users than any other system.
   D. Very difficult to jam or monitor.
   E. No "hard" limit to maximum number of users; the limit happens when the signal-to-interference ratio becomes too great.
   F. Provides for a "soft" handoff; the mobile unit has intelligence to help in the handoff (called Mobile Assisted Handoff [MAHO]).

QUESTIONS

1. Explain FDM.
2. What is the major disadvantage of MTS?
3. What are the two reasons FM is used in mobile communications instead of AM?
4. What is the "capture effect" of FM? What is the minimum signal-to-interference (S/I) ratio necessary for "capture effect" for an AMPS system?
5. What are the functions of an MTSO?
6. Explain why a handoff is sometimes necessary? Explain the steps in an MTSO-to-MTSO handoff.
7. What is a MIN, and what is its purpose?
8. Why are separate frequencies used for uplink and downlink?
9. List several advantages of a CDMA system over other cellular systems.
10. Using the Walsh code example in Figure 13.19, confirm that user 1 and user 2 receive the correct bit sequence.
11. What are the two methods of Spread Spectrum and the advantages of each?
12. What are two major problems that a CDMA system must overcome?
13. What multiplexing schemes do GSM and IS-54 use?
14. What is the most used cellular system in the world?
15. What are the differences between Aloha and slotted Aloha? Why is slotted Aloha superior?
16. The data rate for cellular systems is usually about 13 kbps. How can voice, usually digitized at 64 kbps for T-1 systems, be sent over a cellular system with much less bit rate?
17. What is orthogonality as applied to CDMA?

14

BINARY SYNCHRONOUS CONTROL (BSC), OR BISYNC

OBJECTIVES

In this chapter we will discuss:

    I. Why BiSync was created.

    II. Why BiSync is still taught.

        A. Obsolete and old but still used.

        B. Forty-five versions exist.

        C. Created before the need for standard realized.

        D. Good teaching tool to see how later standards evolved.

    III. BiSync is byte oriented.

    IV. BiSync frame is asynchronous; the receiver doesn't know when the next frame is coming.

    V. BiSync bits are synchronous; the frame has a unique bit pattern signifying the start of the frame.

    VI. BiSync is a Data Link Level (DLL) protocol.

    VII. BiSync is half duplex; one node transmits while the other listens—"stop and wait."

    VIII. BiSync is similar to several modem protocols.

        A. Kermit.

        B. XMODEM.

        C. YMODEM.

    IX. The parts (fields) of the BiSync frame are discussed; how control or text characters are recognized.

    X. A BiSync transmission example is given.

    XI. A BiSync transmission example with an error is given.

14.1 BiSync Characteristics

Binary Synchronous Control (BiSync or BSC) was developed by IBM in 1962 for host-to-peripheral or host-to-terminal data transfer. This is considered a hierarchical system with a master/slave configuration. The IBM 3270 information display family is based on BSC.

BSC was one of the first data transmission protocols and is somewhat crude compared to newer ones. BSC has been obsoleted by the newer protocols, but we can still learn from it. BSC is a good teaching tool leading into more complex systems and protocols. Despite its age and obsolescence it is still very much in use and about forty-five versions exist. BSC's technology is proven and the development costs have been amortized, making the equipment prices low.

BSC is considered character or byte oriented; that is, special characters are used for control and for the beginning and end of blocks and frames. Also each character transmitted must be decoded at the receiver to see if that character is a control character or a data character. BSC is considered a "transparent" protocol because the receiver could decode data as control characters. Later we will see that special precautions must be taken to decode data and control characters without any ambiguities.

BSC is a Data Link Level protocol and is synchronous; that is, a unique SYN character or bit pattern at the beginning of each frame synchronizes the receiver. The data rate is 2,400 bps and up.

BSC is similar to several modem protocols, namely Kermit (yes, it was named for Kermit the Frog of "Sesame Street" fame), XMODEM, and YMODEM.

BSC is half duplex; that is, only one node transmits at a time while the other node listens. Half duplex is colloquially called "stop and wait," or stop transmitting and wait for confirmation that each block has been received without errors. This process of getting confirmation of an error-free transmission is called *handshaking*.

Error detection is done with a 16-bit Cyclic Redundant Code (CRC-16). This book discusses CRC in Appendix A1.

BSC was quite well received when it was introduced and is still a widely used protocol. It has about forty-five slightly different versions. BSC came about before the need for careful standards design was realized. Succeeding standards such as SNA, with its SDLC DLL protocol, are much better designed.

BiSync supports peer-to-peer, multi-point, or point-to-point operation over private lines or switched facilities.

14.1.1 Synchronous versus Asynchronous

A word about synchronous versus **asynchronous.** The frame has a special character called SYN to synchronize the receiver. Hence the bits are considered synchronous. However the receiver does not know when the frame is coming; hence we say the frame or block is asynchronous. Asynchronous Transmission Mode (ATM) is similar in that respect. We will study ATM in Chapter 16.

14.2 BiSync Frame Format

The SYN character synchronizes the receiver to the incoming bit stream and informs the receiver that the frame information is about to arrive.

The SOH (Start Of Header) byte indicates the header is next. The header is user defined (remember, there are forty-five versions of BSC). The STX (Start of TeXt) indicates

SYN	SYN	SOH	Header	STX	text	ETX or ETB	CRC	SYN

FIGURE 14.1

BiSync frame format. SYN tells receiver that a frame is about to arrive. SOH = start of header, Header = user specified, STX = start of text, ETX = end of text, ETB = end of transmission block, CRC = cyclic redundant code (special code for error control), ACK = acknowledgment that the last frame was received correctly and the sender may send the next frame, NAK = negative acknowledgment (the last frame was received incorrectly), EOT = end of transmission, NUL or NUL1 = filler character to make frame minimum length.

the text or data is next. The ETX (End of TeXt) indicates no more data or text is in the frame. The ETB (End of Transmission Block) indicates that all frames have been sent.

Other control characters are the ACKs. ACK0 from the receiver to the sender confirms correct reception of an *even* numbered block. ACK1 from the receiver to the sender confirms correct reception of an *odd* numbered block. ACKs also tell the sender that the receiver is ready for more data. See Figure 14.1. NAK tells the sender that the last transmission was in error and should be repeated. WACK (Wait ACK before transmit) tells the sender to wait before sending more data. This is used for flow control.

14.2.1 Recognizing Control or Text Characters

Data Line Escape (DLE) is used with STX to indicate that the following text is to be treated as data, until a DLE/ETX or DLE/ETB character pair is encountered.

What happens if a text byte is the same as a control byte? What does the receiver do to differentiate between text and control bytes? After the STX character byte, the receiver treats the bytes as data or text. If the receiver encounters a DLE (Data Line Escape) character, the next bytes are interpreted as control byte(s), until an ETX or ETB character byte is encountered.

14.3 BSC Transmission Example

Let's see how a typical BiSync transmission occurs. The sender (left side of Figure 14.2) sends an ENQuiry frame to the receiver asking, "I have data to send; are you ready?" The receiver (right side of figure) gets the ENQ frame and returns an ACK informing the sender that the receiver is ready to accept data and so please send it. Note that the frames are numbered either odd (ACK1) or even (ACK0). The sender transmits the data. The receiver checks the frame for errors and, finding none, returns an ACK. The ACK includes whether the received frame being acknowledged was odd (ACK 1) or even (ACK 0). This continues until all the data has been sent, and an EOT (End Of Transmission) frame is sent. The receiver responds with an ACK.

It is important to note that this operation is **half duplex (HDX).** Only one node transmits at a time. This is a slower and less efficient method than **full duplex (FDX)** systems. Newer systems use full duplex, and we will study them in later chapters.

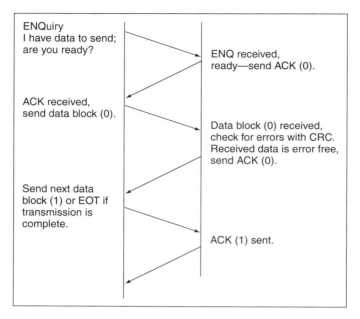

FIGURE 14.2
BiSync "bounce" diagram. Note only one node is transmitting at a time. This is half-duplex (HDX).

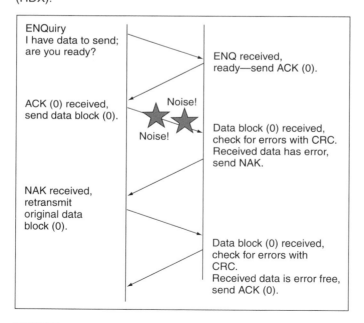

FIGURE 14.3
BiSync "bounce" diagram (continued).

14.4   BSC Transmission with Error Example

What happens if noise corrupts a frame? What is BiSync's error control method? In the "bounce" diagram of Figure 14.3 the transmission is initiated as before. However the receiver detects an error in a frame. The receiver returns a "NAK" (Negative AcKnowledgment). The sender will re-transmit the data.

SUMMARY

    I. SOH; Start Of Header.
    II. STX; Start of TeXt SYN.
   III. ETX; End of TeXt.
   IV. ETB; End of Transmission Block (last frame has been sent).
    V. Error control.
        A. ACK; last frame received OK.
        B. NAK; last frame Not received OK.
        C. Re-send last frame ACK.
   VI. Flow control; WACK (Wait ACK).

QUESTIONS

1. How does BSC handle errors?
2. How are BSC frames numbered?
3. What is DLE used for?
4. How is BSC inefficient compared with full duplex operation systems?
5. In what way is BSC asynchronous?
6. In what way is BSC synchronous?
7. Why was BSC created?

15

X.25 AND FRAME RELAY

OBJECTIVES

In this chapter we will discuss:

I. Why was X.25 developed? Robust error handling was needed to send data over noisy (high Bit Error Rate [BER]) analog lines.

II. The differences between datagrams and virtual connection.
  A. Virtual connection is set up before data transfer takes place.
    1. Routing information is needed in the packet.
    2. Takes the same route to destination.
  B. Datagrams are sent without having a connection set up before data is sent.
    1. Destination Address (DA) is needed in the datagram.
    2. May take different routes to destination.

III. X.25 features are discussed.
  A. Fast select; one packet contains all needed information (good for small data transfers).
  B. Restrict:
    1. Incoming calls.
    2. Outgoing calls.
  C. Closed user groups.

IV. X.25; data transmission between Data Terminal Equipment (DTE) and a PSN.

V. X.75; interface specification between two PSNs.

VI. X.121; DTE addressing specification for international communications.

VII. X.3; Packet Assembler/Disassembler (PAD). PAD is the protocol converter between non-X.25 equipment and an X.25 PSN.

VIII. X.28; used between non-X.25 equipment and the PAD.

IX. X.25 is a Network level (level 3) protocol.
  A. The relationship in the OSI RM is discussed.
  B. Packet encapsulation is discussed.

X. LAP/B is the DLL protocol used by X.25.
  A. Information packets.
    1. Modulo 7.
    2. Modulo 127; used for long delay systems (satellites).

    B. Control packets.
 XI. An example of an X.25 call is given.
    A. Setup.
    B. Data transfer.
    C. Disconnect (teardown).
 XII. An example of an X.25 call with an error is given.
    A. A REJ frame is used to tell the sending node an error was detected.
    B. The "go back N" frames method of error recovery is used.
XIII. Why Frame Relay (FR)?
    A. Lower system error rates allow less error checking.
    B. Error checking done only end-to-end.
    C. Cheaper, faster than X.25.
XIV. FR's relation to X.25 is discussed.
 XV. FR frame structure.
    A. Similar to LAPD.
    B. Has special flow control bits.
        1. Forward Explicit Congestion Notification (FECN).
        2. Backward Explicit Congestion Notification (BECN).

15.1 Why X.25?

In the late 1960s and early 1970s data networking technology was in its infancy, and no standard existed. The transmission circuitry was primitive and noisy with Bit Error Rates (BER) between one error per hundred and one error per thousand bits sent (10^{-2} to 10^{-3} BER). This high error rate meant that an extremely robust error handling system had to be designed. The result was X.25 and its associated protocols. Error checking in X.25 is done between each relay node, and between the sending and receiving nodes.

X.25 was an international effort and thus has worldwide support. It has been around a long time, and many vendors support X.25. X.25 was the basis for the OSI RM and predates SNA.

15.2 Switching

Before we can discuss X.25, we must compare the two types of packet switching: *datagram* and *virtual connection*. In both methods a large message is broken down into smaller units called **packets.** This is known as *segmentation.*

15.2.1 Datagram Switching

The **datagrams** may arrive at the destination out of order. Therefore the datagrams must have a sequence number to put them and their data back into the proper order.

Internet Protocol (IP) is a well-known example of datagram usage. We will study TCP/IP in Chapter 19.

In Figure 15.1a node X is transmitting datagrams Y1, Y2, Y3, Z1, Z2, and Z3 through a Packet Switched Network (PSN). The "Y" datagrams have node Y as their Des-

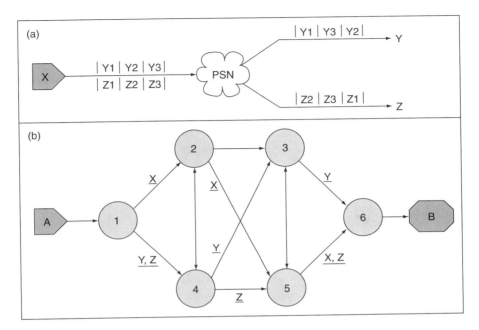

FIGURE 15.1
Datagram path. "Connectionless"—no permanent path, each datagram may take a different
path. Therefore we need destination address (DA), source address (SA), and datagram sequence number. (a) Note that the datagrams may arrive out of order. PSN = packet switching
network. (b) Datagram X path = A, 1, 2, 5, 6, B. Datagram Y path = A, 1, 4, 3, 6, B. Datagram
Z path = A, 1, 4, 5, 6, B.

tination Address (DA). The "Z" datagrams have node Z as their DA. Datagrams can take
different paths through the PSN and may arrive out of order as shown. The receiving
nodes use the datagram sequence numbers to put the data back into the proper order. This
is called *reassembly*. Figure 15.1b shows possible paths within the PSN that datagrams X,
Y, and Z might take traveling from node A to node B.

No setup or teardown of the path is necessary. No connection needs to be established
before data transfer. This type of data transfer is called *connectionless*. A wit has called
datagrams a "spray and pray" method.

Note that each node receives the datagram, stores it, and then forwards it. Each
switching node must decide dynamically where to send each datagram. Factors determining the route include traffic density, equipment availability, line quality, and the particular routing algorithm. The routing algorithm is the switching computer program's
method of determining the route to send the datagram.

15.2.2 Packet Switching and X.25

With virtual call packet switching a path is set up before the data is sent. The same path is
used for sending the entire message. Packets arrive in the same order they were sent, and thus

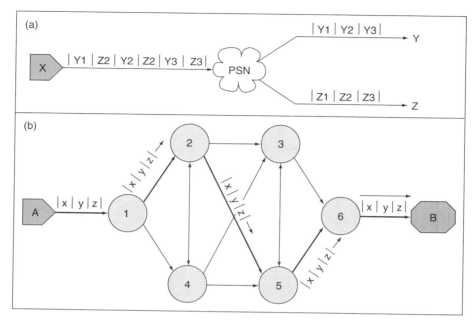

FIGURE 15.2

Packet path. Connection oriented—a route (virtual circuit) is "constructed" before data is actually transferred (a). Logical channel numbers are needed in the headers. Sixteen groups of 256 channels means 4096 available channels. (b) All packets travel this permanent virtual circuit. This circuit is torn down after all data is received and housekeeping done. Packet path = A, 1, 2, 5, 6, B.

no sequence numbers are needed. However the packets must contain routing information. Each packet will contain the same route information. The packet switches examine this routing information and switch the packets according to this information. The route is set up when needed, and the user is billed only for time actually used. A packet sequence number is used for error control, but not for reassembly. Packet routing is shown in Figure 15.2. X.25 is the best-known packet switching protocol.

In Figure 15.2a messages "Y" and "Z" are sent through the PSN from node X to nodes Y and Z. Each message consists of three packets: Y1, Y2, Y3 and Z1, Z2, Z3. All packets of message "Y" and message "Z" arrive in the same order they were sent.

Figure 15.2b show a typical path through a PSN. All packets pass through nodes 1, 2, 5, and 6 before arriving at node B. This path or route is set up before data is sent and torn down after the complete message is received and housekeeping is finished.

Table 15.1 compares datagrams and packets. Both use segmentation to break up the large message into smaller parts. The datagram header must have the Destination Address and sequence number. The destination number is used by the switches to route the datagram, and the route may not be the same from one datagram to the next. The datagram sequence number is needed to reassemble the data into the correct order.

TABLE 15.1
Packet switched vs datagram

Datagram	Packets
Message broken up into smaller parts	Message broken up into smaller parts
Headers contain:	Headers contain:
DA (Destination Address)	Logical Channel Number (route)
SA (Source Address)	Packet number
Sequence number	Travel one route via PVC (Permanent Virtual Circuit)
Can travel different routes	
May arrive out of order	Arrive in same order as sent
Better security—eavesdropper can get only a portion of a message	Security can be a problem—eavesdropper can get the entire message
Error rates: 10^{-6}	Error rates: 10^{-9}

With virtual call switching the circuit is set up before the data is transferred via packet. With X.25 this route is called a **Switched Virtual Channel (SVC).** Each packet contains complete routing information—Logical Channel Number (LCN) and Logical Channel Group Number (LCGN). A Switched Virtual Channel (SVC) has to be set up for each session and torn down at the end of the session. SVCs are created when needed and exist only for the duration of the call.

A **Permanent Virtual Circuit (PVC)** is a dedicated line that does not have to be set up or torn down. The path (logical channel) is part of the packet header. Because no setup or teardown is needed, PVC is cheaper and faster for users needing large data transfers between fixed facilities. A PVC is similar to a leased telephone line. PVCs run counter to X.25's philosophy of bandwidth on demand and are not too popular.

Datagrams may take different routes to the destination node. An eavesdropper can monitor only parts of the message. Packets take the same path allowing eavesdroppers to monitor the complete message. X.25 has options to increase its security.

15.3   X.25 Facilities or Features

X.25 has several features such as fast select, barring incoming or outgoing calls, reverse billing, call redirection, and closed user groups. See Table 15.2.

Fast select is sending one packet containing all necessary information. No setup or teardown phase is necessary. Fast select is often used for credit card verifications. All request data is sent in a 128-byte maximum length setup packet. The host with the database containing the credit card information will return a CLEAR REQUEST packet containing authorization. Just these two packets constitute the entire exchange.

Incoming calls can be restricted from a particular node **DTE (Data Terminal Equipment).** Outgoing calls can be restricted from being made on a particular node (DTE).

TABLE 15.2
X.25 features

Fast packet—one packet with all information
    No setup or teardown
    128 bytes maximum
    CLEAR REQUEST packet is acknowledgment
    Only two packets make up exchange
Restrict
    Incoming calls
    Outgoing calls
Closed user groups

A closed user group is a virtual network within the PSN. DTEs can be restricted from contacting DTEs outside the closed group. DTEs can belong to more than one group. One can see an analogy with Internet chat groups, except that the chat groups have more autonomy.

15.4 X.25 and Related Specifications

X.25 is the CCITT specification for data transmission between Data Terminal Equipment (DTE) and a PSN. DTE is equipment at the ends of the path and could be data terminals, mainframe computers, mini-computers, or peripherals (Figure 15.3).

X.25 is the CCITT interface specification between DTE and the **Data Communications Equipment (DCE)** of a PSN. X.75 is the CCITT interface specification between two PSNs. X.121 is the CCITT DTE addressing specification for international communications (Figure 15.4).

The **Packet Assembler Disassembler (PAD)** is specified by X.3. A PAD is a protocol converter between non-X.25 equipment and an X.25 PSN. The PAD uses the X.3 protocol, and the X.28 protocol is used between the non-X.25 equipment and the PAD (Figure 15.5).

15.5 X.25 and the OSI RM

X.25 is a Network Layer, level 3 protocol and routes the data. X.25 (as do all upper level protocols) must use Layers 2 and 1 to communicate. X.25 receives and sends information from and to the Transport Layer 4 above. Figure 15.6 shows the physical and virtual communications between the bottom three **OSI RM (Open Systems International Reference Model)** layers. The packet is the input or output to or from the X.25 Network Layer. The packet fits into the frame created by the DLL. The frame is passed over the Physical Layer to the receiving node.

Figure 15.7 shows the travel of data from the Transport Layer 4 down to the Network Layer (X.25 is a level 3 Network Layer protocol). The data is received from the Transport Layer, and the X.25 protocol in Layer 3 adds a **Protocol Data Unit (PDU)**. The PDU is

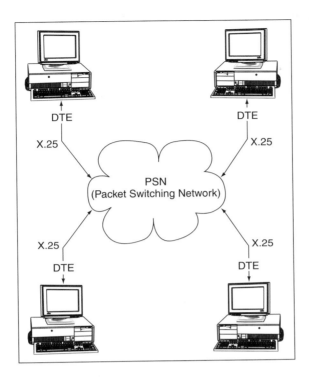

FIGURE 15.3
X.25 network. X.25 is the CCITT (Consultive Committee for International Telephone and Tele-
graph) specification governing the interface between DTE (data terminal equipment) and
DCE (data circuit equipment) of a PSN. The first X.25 specification was issued in 1974.

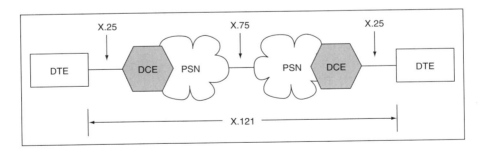

FIGURE 15.4
X.25, X.75, and X.121. X.25 is the CCITT interface specification between DTE and the DCE
of a PSN. X.75 is the CCITT interface specification between two PSNs. X.121 is the CCITT
DTE addressing specification for international communications.

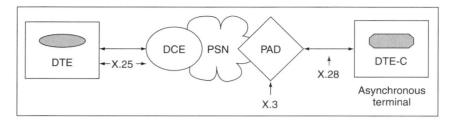

FIGURE 15.5

X.25, X.3, and X.28. PAD = packet assembler disassembler, a protocol converter used to connect non-X.25 packet equipment to an X.25 PSN. X.3 is a PAD protocol between non-X.25 equipment and the PSN. X.28 is a protocol between DTE-C (data terminal equipment, asynchronous) non-X.25 equipment and a PAD.

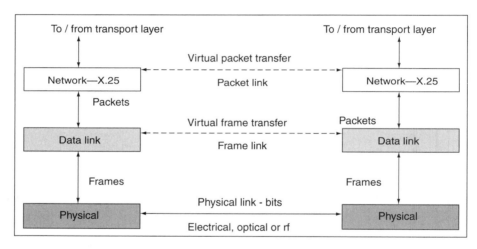

FIGURE 15.6

X.25 and ISO RM, bottom three layers.

housekeeping information, including setup and teardown information and frame sequence numbers. The PDU and the data from the Transport Layer become the X.25 packet. This packet is sent to the Data Link Level (DLL) at Layer 2. The DLL protocol is Link Access Procedure/Balanced (LAP/B) and will be discussed later in this chapter. LAP/B adds its own PDU and a Cyclic Redundancy Code (CRC) for error detection, thus making a frame. The frame is sent to the Physical Layer for actual transmission over the PSN.

Figure 15.8 shows the seven layers of the OSI RM and how they relate to X.25, a Network level 3 protocol. Virtual communication takes place between equivalent layers.

At the relay nodes between the sending and receiving nodes the frame and encapsulated packet are passed to the X.25 Network Layer. Error checking and control are done between each relay node. Error checking is also done between the sending and receiving

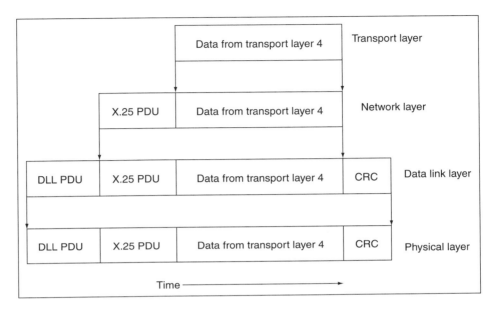

FIGURE 15.7
Packet encapsulation. The physical layer is the layer actually sending bits over a physical medium to other nodes.

node. These two error checking measures give X.25 a very robust error control system. This double error check and control has been referred to as "belt and suspenders" error control. Recall that X.25 was designed to operate over noisy and error prone networks, necessitating a good error handling protocol.

When a relay node sends the packet on to the next node, the first relay node stores a copy of the packet. The first node keeps the copy in case the packet needs to be retransmitted. When the first relay node receives notification that the next node has received the packet successfully, the copy is deleted. This is called "store and forward."

15.6 X.25 Packet and LAP/B Frame

The X.25 Data Link Level (DLL) 2 protocol is **Link Access Protocol / Balanced (LAP/B).** LAP/B is used for link management (setup and teardown and other functions), error control, and flow control. LAP/B is similar to Synchronous Data Link Control (SDLC, used in SNA), LAPD (used in ISDN), and **High Level Data Link Control (HDLC).** All are great improvements over BiSync and have not significantly changed since their inception. Some writers consider LAP/B a subset of HDLC.

Figure 15.9 shows how the Network Layer 3 packet is encapsulated into the DLL frame. The DLL frame has the header flag, virtual communications overhead, CRC, and end flag. The frame information is the Network level packet.

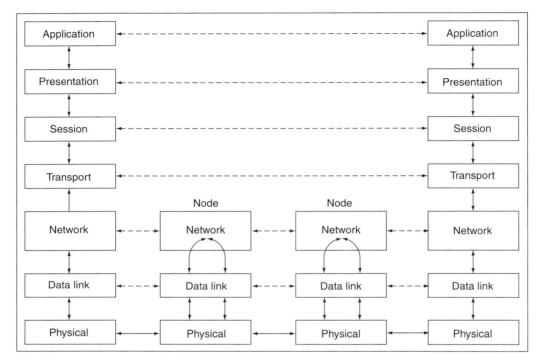

FIGURE 15.8
OSI RM and X.25. Levels 1–3 are "chained layers" used by nodes. Levels 4–7 are "end-to-end layers" used by hosts. Virtual communications - - - - - - - - -, physical communications ——————. X.25 error checking occurs between each node and end-to-end hosts. This as known is "belt and suspenders" error control.

There are two types of packets: information and control. Information frames transmit user information. Control packets are for setup, teardown, and housekeeping, and do not carry any user information. However information packets carry housekeeping information, including packet sequence numbers.

15.7 Packet Headers

15.7.1 X.25 Information (Data) Packet Header

Figure 15.10 shows the detail of an X.25 information packet. This is not the same as the DLL's frame. In the header the Q bit tells if the packet is control or information for the remote DTE or the remote PAD. The D bit tells whether the acknowledgment is end-to-end or merely between local relay nodes.

Bits 6 and 5 are the modulo bits and tell if the **P(s)** and **P(r)** fields are three bits each (modulo 7) or seven bits each (modulo 127). Three bits are sufficient for most terrestrial

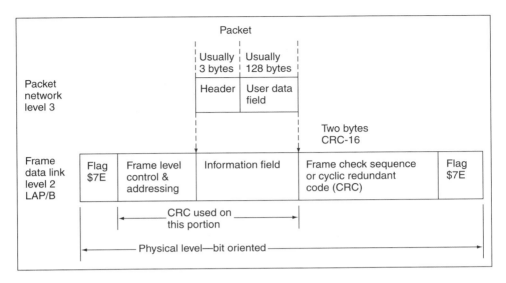

FIGURE 15.9
X.25 frame structure. Remember, the packet is generated at Level 3 (network) and the frame is generated at Level 2 (DLL).

systems, but in satellite systems the delay time can be up to 350 milliseconds. This long delay time allows many frames to be in the system simultaneously, and an acknowledgment will be delayed. With more than seven frames present in the system a modulus greater than seven is needed to keep track of the frames. Figure 15.10a shows seven-bit P(s) and P(r) fields, and Figure 15.10b shows three-bit P(s) and P(r) fields.

Remember that packet switching travels on a virtual circuit. The packets take the same route to the destination. The Logic Channel Group Number (LCGN) and the Logic Channel Number (LCN) tell the packet switches the proper route to send the packets.

The M "more" bit is similar to the Poll/Final (P/F) bit of SDLC and tells the destination if more packets are being sent.

15.7.2 X.25 Control Packet Header

A category I control packet header is shown in Figure 15.11. Note the difference between bits 6 and 5 in this figure and the previous figure. These bits tell the packet type. The packet type tells if the packet is for data or supervisory use. The three common types are RR (Receiver Ready), RNR (Receiver Not Ready), and REJ (Reject).

An RR means that the receiving node is able to accept data (the receiver is ready) or that the last frame was received correctly. This is similar to an ACKnowledgment. The RNR tells the sending node to stop sending data. The receiving node's buffers may be full and unable to receive more data, or a failure has occurred at the receiving node. The LCGN and LCN are the same as before. A REJect indicates an error was found in the

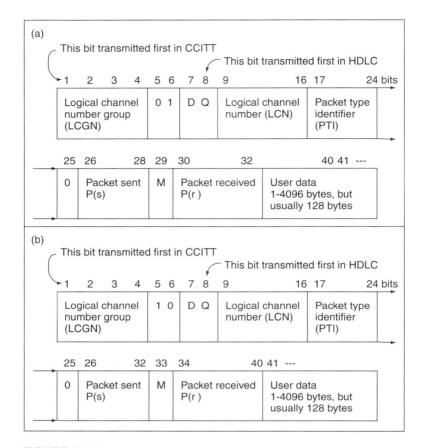

FIGURE 15.10

X.25 packet headers. Bits and six of the first byte are the modulo bits and tell if the frame numbers are three bits (modulo 7) or seven bits (modulo 127). (a) X.25 information packet header (I-packet) with three bit (modulo 7) frame numbers. The modulo bits are "0 1," indicating three bits or modulo 7 in the packet sent and packet received fields. (b) X.25 data packet (D-packet) header with seven bit (modulo 127) frame numbers. The modulo bits are "1 0," indicating seven bits or modulo 127 in the packet sent and packet received fields. LCGN and LCN are used to tell the packet which route to take on the virtual channel. M = similar to P/F (poll/final) bit, Q = control or information packet, D = acknowledgment from PSN or end user, GFI = general format identifier.

packet, and the offending packet should be re-transmitted. Since no data is being sent, no P(s) and P(r) fields are needed.

A category II control packet is used for housekeeping duties such as reset, interrupt, confirmations, call requests, call acceptances, clear requests, clear confirmations, registration, and restart. The packet format is similar to the category I format, except for the packet type.

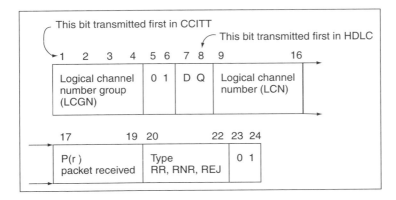

FIGURE 15.11
X.25 Category I control packet header (C-packet). Bits 17 through 24 comprise the control field. The control field consists of the packet received field and the packet type. Bits 23 and 24 are "0 1" and identify this packet as a category I control packet. The packet type is defined by bits 20, 21, and 22. RR = "0 0 0," RNR = "0 0 1," REJ = "0 1 0."

15.8 X.25 Calling Sequence

An X.25 call setup, data transfer, and disconnect are shown in the Figure 15.12 "bounce" diagram. Left node sends a call request RR packet to Right node. Right node is able to take the call and its data and returns an RR packet. Left node sends three frames of data. Right node confirms (RR) all three frames and also adds information on the last (RR) confirmation. Left node has sent all its data and wishes to disconnect. Left node sends a DM (Disconnect) to Right node including the $P(r)$ number confirming correct reception of Right node's data. Right node confirms the disconnect, and the connection is terminated.

Note that $P(r)$ is the packet *expected next,* not the packet already received. There is a possibility that the receiving node will never receive the first packet. In this case it is senseless for $P(r)$ to equal the packet received, since no packet was ever received. The sending node needs to know the packet number next expected.

Note that a timer, T-1, is started on transmissions. When a confirmation of that transmission is received by the originating node, the timer is reset. If a transmission confirmation is not received before the timer times out, the originating node will know a system problem exists. The timer is referred to as "T-1," but there is no relationship between this designation and the T-1 transmission system.

15.8.1 X.25 Calling Sequence with Error

An X.25 session with an error is shown in Figure 15.13. The session is set up as before. However an error occurs during packet 1's $[P(s) = 1]$ transmission. The error is detected at Right node, which sends back a REJ control packet. The packet also tells that Right node is still expecting packet 1 $[P(r) = 1]$. Left node re-transmits packet 1

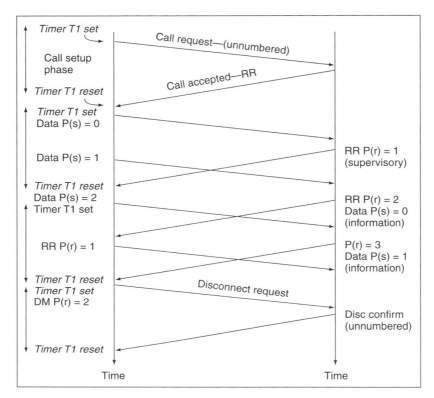

FIGURE 15.12
X.25 call sequence. Note that N(r) is equal to the next expected packet.

[P(s) = 1], and the session continues. Left node also re-transmits packet P(s) = 2 even though this packet had already been transmitted and received successfully. This error control system is called "go back N(umber of packets)" to the packet in error and re-peat all subsequent packets. Early X.25 systems lacked the sophistication to keep track of packets successfully received [P(s) = 2] and opted for the easier-to-implement "go back N" system.

15.9 Link Access Protocol / Balanced (LAP/B)

The DLL protocol is Link Access Protocol / Balanced (LAP/B). It is similar to SDLC used in SNA. As in all DLL protocols LAP/B performs flow control, error control, and management functions. LAP/B is considered by some to be a subset of HDLC. LAP/B and SDLC are similar enough to refer the reader to the SDLC section of Chapter 20 on SNA, rather than repeat almost the same words. The "B" for "Balanced" means both originating node and destination nodes have equal (balanced) call origination capabilities.

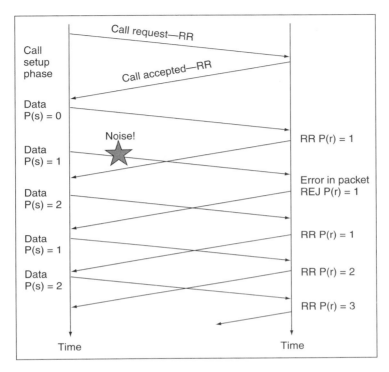

FIGURE 15.13
X.25 call sequence with noise. Again, N(r) is equal to the next expected packet.

15.10 Frame Relay

Improvements in technology have brought much lower Bit Error Rates (BER). BERs of 10^{-15} have been reported on fiber optic systems. This is equivalent to a T-1 system working about 20 years with only one error. Network managers want an answer as to how good the lines are in less than 20 years, so when measuring the BER the signal-to-noise ratio is reduced by optical attenuators, giving some system errors. Mathematical formulas are used to extrapolate these measured errors into the actual BER.

When X.25 was developed, the lines were very noisy and BERs of 10^{-2} to 10^{-3} were the norm. The error checking in X.25 occurred between nodes and between end-to-end nodes. This "belt and suspenders" method was appropriate for these high BERs.

Improvements in BER allowed the development of FR. FR error-checks only between end nodes, that is, end-to-end. FR is more efficient than X.25 because the frames do not have to go through the Network Layer at each relay node. This means faster and cheaper communications and is in contrast to the end-to-end and between node error checking of X.25. This has reduced costs, making FR much less expensive and faster than X.25. X.25 is rarely sold anymore in the United States but FR is very popular. FR asks less of the network and thus is cheaper than X.25. X.25 is still the protocol of choice for data that must arrive at the destination node error-free. FR is much faster than X.25 and has been referred to by wags as "X.25 on steroids." X.25 is simply overkill for today's networks.

FRL's original purpose was to interconnect LANs. FR is particularly good for "bursty" traffic such as LAN data. FR bandwidth can be dynamically changed as the traffic needs change. Recent attempts to send voice over FR have not gotten very favorable reviews, but network managers are salivating at the possible cost savings.

FR can be contrasted with T Carrier. T-1 was developed for predictable, steady-rate voice traffic and is not well-suited for data transfer. Voice is regular, whereas data usually comes in unpredictable bursts. T Carrier's regular time slots work well for voice, but making dynamic bandwidth (data carrying capacity) changes is difficult. FR adapts well to bursty data.

15.10.1 FR and the OSI RM

Figure 15.14 shows the seven layers of the OSI RM and how they relate to FR. Virtual communications take place between equivalent layers. At the relay nodes between the sending and receiving nodes the frame and encapsulated packet are passed to the DLL. Note that error checking takes place only between end nodes, not between every relay node as in X.25 (compare to the X.25 error checking in Figure 15.8).

15.10.2 FR Frame Format

The FR frame is based on LAPD, the ISDN DLL frame, and is shown in Figure 15.15. Flow control is done with the **Forward Explicit Congestion Notification (FECN)** and **Backward Explicit Congestion Notification (BECN)** bits. If the receiving end node is getting data too fast, it will set the BECN bit notifying the sending node to slow down (backward). If the receiving node is asking for data too fast from the sending node, the sending node will set the FECN bit (forward). This informs the receiving node not to ask for data so fast. The slang pronunciations are "freck-en" and "becken." It's really true; network people have a sense of humor. Maybe a bit weird, but nonetheless it exists!

The DLCI is used for routing and is a total of ten bits. It is similar to the LCI of X.25. Its slang pronunciation is "dell see."

If the transmitting node sends frames that could be dropped or discarded, it sets the DE bit in those frames.

The C/R bit is the same as a Poll/Final bit used in other DLL protocols—just another thing to confuse the long-suffering students and promote the fallacy of protocol designers being super smart beings.

15.11   Frame Relay Testing and Troubleshooting

Hewlett-Packard has its Broadband Series Test System (BSTS) modular test set for ATM, Frame Relay, SONET, and LANs. It begins with the HP E4210 mainframe base and the

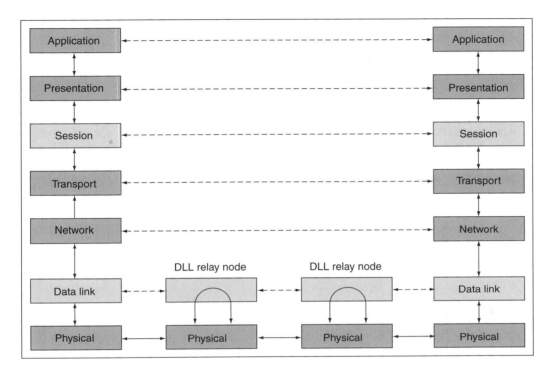

FIGURE 15.14
OSI RM and FR. Levels 4–7 are "end-to-end layers" used by hosts. Virtual communications - - - - - - - - - - - -, physical communications —————. FR error checking occurs between end-to-end hosts only.

FIGURE 15.15
FR frame format. Flags = %01111110 = $7E, DLCI = data link congestion identifier (high order and low order fields separate in frame for a total of ten bits), C/R = command/response or poll/final (P/F) in LAP-D, EA = extended address bits, FECN = forward explicit congestion notification, BECN = backward explicit congestion notification, DE = discard eligibility.

HP E4200B portable base. The bases are UNIX-based machines with plug-in modules for the various protocols.

The Frame Relay hardware plug-in modules are the E4206A T1/E1 Frame Processor module for Frame Relay over T-1 or E-1 systems, and the V-Interface Frame Processor plug-in module. The software modules are the E6278A Frame Relay SVC (Switched Virtual Circuit) Protocol Viewer, the E4215A Frame Relay Test Software, and the E7840A Frame Relay/ATM Interworking Test Suite. Also the E4215B LAN Protocols Test Software can test LAN connected via Frame Relay.

The E4215A Frame Relay Test Software performs frame monitoring and decoding as well as PDU decoding, finds frame errors, tabulates traffic statistics, and generates and monitors test traffic. Filters can be employed to display only the relevant data. The user has a choice of display formats.

The filters include the DLCI, C/R, FECN, BECN, DE bits, frame types, and others. It can check for aborted frames, wrong sized frames, wrong sized address fields, CRC errors, and other items.

SUMMARY

   I. X.25 was developed to send data over noisy analog circuits.
      A. The Bit Error Rate (BER) was very high, about one error per hundred (1e-2) or one error per thousand (1e-3) bits sent.
      B. A robust error recovery system was needed.
         1. The packets were error-checked between every relay node.
         2. The packets were error-checked between the end nodes.
         3. If an error was detected, the packets would be re-transmitted beginning with the corrupted packet; "go back N" method.
         4. The error detection was with a CRC field at the end of the packet.
  II. The difference between a packet and a frame.
      A. A packet is created at the Network level 3.
      B. A frame is created at the Data Link Level (DLL) 2; a frame is a packet plus the DLL PDUs (see Chapter 3).
 III. The difference between datagrams and packets.
      A. Datagrams may take different routes to the destination. "Connectionless" means:
         1. No connection is established (set up) before transferring data.
         2. Datagrams contain the Destination Address but do not contain any routing information.
      B. Packets take the same route from sender to the destination.
         1. "Connection oriented" means a connection must be established (set up) before transferring data.
         2. A Permanent Virtual Circuit (PVC) is a dedicated line that does not have to be set up or torn down for each session.
         3. Packets contain routing information.

   IV. Fast select.

      A. All necessary information is contained in one 128-byte maximum length packet.

      B. No setup or teardown needed.

    V. Various associated specifications.

      A. X.25; specification for data transmission between Data Terminal Equipment (DTE) and a PSN.

      B. X.75; interface specification between two PSNs.

      C. X.121; DTE addressing specification for international communications.

      D. X.3; PAD (Packet Assembler/Disassembler) specification. A PAD is a protocol converter between non-X.25 equipment and an X.25 PSN.

      E. X.28; specification between non-X.25 equipment and a PAD.

  VI. X.25 was the basis for the OSI RM.

      A. X.25 is a level 3 Network Layer specification.

      B. LAP/B is the DLL protocol for X.25.

         1. Similar to SDLC of SNA.

         2. Similar to LAPD of ISDN.

      C. Information packets.

         1. Send data.

         2. Packet sequence numbers for error control and flow control.

            a. Seven packets maximum can be in a system at one time for terrestrial systems.

            b. 127 packets maximum can be in a satellite system at any time.

      D. Control packets.

         1. Receiver Ready (RR).

            a. The receiver node can accept data.

            b. An ACKnowledgment that the data has arrived error-free.

         2. Receiver Not Ready (RNR).

            a. The receiver node cannot accept data.

            b. The data buffers may be full (flow control).

         3. REJect (REJ).

            a. The receiver node has found an error in the packet; error recovery started.

            b. The packet in error must be re-transmitted.

 VII. Frame Relay (FR).

      A. Faster, cheaper than X.25. X.25 rarely sold in the United States, usually Frame Relay.

      B. Does not use the Network level while traversing the PSN.

      C. Much lower BERs allow less error checking.

         1. Error checking done only in DLL, not in any Network level.

         2. Error checking only done end-to-end, not between each relay node.

VIII. Frame Relay is good for data.

      A. "Bursty" traffic (very intermittent).

      B. LAN traffic is "bursty."

  IX. The frame structure is based on LAPD, from ISDN. Flow control done with Forward Explicit Congestion Notification (FECN) and Backward Explicit Congestion Notification (BECN) bits.

QUESTIONS

1. What type of circuits is X.25 designed to operate over? In other words, why was X.25 developed?
2. What improvements in technology have enabled Frame Relay (FR) to be practical?
3. What error checking techniques distinguish Frame Relay from earlier protocols?
4. What is the difference between a frame and a packet?
5. What is an SVC? What is a PVC? What are the differences between them? It is not sufficient to merely define the acronyms.
6. What is one major advantage of Frame Relay over X.25? (Think like a "bean counter"!)
7. What are the two types of packets, and what are their functions?
8. What are the three types of supervisory packets, and what are their functions?
9. What are the differences between packet switching and datagram switching? Give an example of each.
10. What is fast select? Where might it be used?
11. Where in the communications system does the X.25 specification apply?
12. Where do each of the following specifications apply: X.75, X.3, X.121, X.28?
13. Why do some packets have three-bit packet sequence numbers and others have seven-bit packet sequence numbers?
14. What is the purpose of the LCGN and LCN fields in FR?
15. Draw an X.25 "bounce" diagram with information packet P(s) = 2 having an error. Be sure to include the error recovery. Why is this error recovery called "go back N"?
16. Why does P(r) always equal the next expected packet and not the packet actually received?
17. What is the purpose of the T-1 timer in X.25?
18. What are the purposes of each of the Explicit Congestion Notification bits in FR?
19. What are the purposes of the BECN and FECN bits in FR? How do they work?

16

ASYNCHRONOUS TRANSFER MODE (ATM) AND SONET

OBJECTIVES

In this chapter we will discuss:

I. Why ATM?
   A. ATM is designed to be the "all purpose, one size fits all" protocol.
   B. All types of information: voice, video, and data.
II. Asynchronous; the receiver does not know exactly when the cell will arrive.
III. Cells.
   A. 53 bytes in length.
   B. 5 bytes of overhead.
   C. 48 bytes of information.
IV. ATM supports:
   A. Circuit switch.
   B. Packet switch.
V. ATM cell formats.
   A. User-Network Interface (UNI) cell used between the user and the network.
   B. Network-Network Interface (NNI) used between switches within the network.
   C. Cell structure.
      1. Virtual path is specified by the Virtual Path Identifier (VPI) and Virtual Channel Identifier (VCI).
      2. Payload Type (PT) bits tell if the cell is carrying user information or service information.
      3. Cell Loss Priority (CLP) bit indicates if the cell can be discarded when the network becomes congested.
VI. ATM layers. Four sub-layers within OSI RM Physical Layer and Data Link Layer (DLL).
   A. ATM Physical sublayer is usually SONET or DS-3 (T-3).
   B. ATM sublayer manages the transmission between nodes.
   C. ATM Adaptation Layer (AAL).
      1. AAL is concerned about the end-to-end transmission, serving the various types of information, and applications (voice, data, video, images).

2. At the sending end the Segmentation And Reassembly (SAR) segments (divides) the information to be transmitted into 48-byte payloads for the ATM sublayer.
3. At the receiving node the SAR reassembles (puts back together) 48-byte payloads from the ATM sublayer into the proper transmitted information.
4. Convergence Sublayer (CS) formats information from upper levels into correct format for conversion into 48-byte payloads.
5. The CS assigns "class of service" for each type of information.

VII. Classes of service
 A. AAL Class 1 (Class A) is designed for voice and video.
  1. Constant bit rate.
  2. Constant delay through system.
 B. AAL Class 2 (Class B) traffic can be packet video or audio; variable bit rate and delay is acceptable.
 C. AAL Class 3/4 (Class C) traffic is connection oriented but does not require a timing relationship between end points. Class C traffic is data and may use variable bit rates. Loss of data is acceptable.
 D. AAL Class 5 (Class D) traffic is connectionless, may use variable bit rates, and does not need a timing relationship between end users.

VIII. SONET (Synchronous Optical NETwork).
 A. Synchronous Optical NETwork (SONET) is the prevailing standard for long haul optical fiber networks.
 B. It is designed to allow synchronous multiplexing of different data sources. Synchronous multiplexing allows even asynchronous devices to fit into the frame.
 C. SONET is designed to transport many different formats, including ATM, Broadband ISDN (B-ISDN), T-3, E-3, DS-1, and DS-3.
 D. Bit rates are multiples of 51.84 Mbps.

IX. A SONET transmission system is divided into four parts.
 A. Path; end-to-end.
 B. Line; between line termination equipment.
 C. Section; between section termination equipment.
 D. Photonics; the optical portions.

X. SONET frame.
 A. 810 bytes per frame.
 B. 125 μs long at 51.84 Mbps.
 C. Transport OverHead (TOH); TOH does error and alarm monitoring.
 D. Path OverHead (POH); POH is end-to-end information.
 E. Line OverHead (LOH); LOH is processed at each node.
 F. Section OverHead (SOH); SOH is used for framing and performance monitoring.
 G. Synchronous Payload Envelope (SPE) is the payload; using pointers for start of data allows synchronization with data.

16.1 Why Asynchronous Transfer Mode (ATM)?

Good grief! Still another protocol! Well, there is good motive in the designers' madness. **Asynchronous Transfer Mode (ATM)** is designed to be the "all purpose, one size fits all" protocol. ATM can handle all types of information—data, voice, and video—equally well. ATM is the first standard to accomplish this. Hardware has gotten faster, more reliable, and has lower noise than in the days when X.25 was developed. ATM is designed to take advantage of this. T Carrier is still best for voice only and Frame Relay (FR) is best for bursty data, but ATM is the best protocol for mixed data types over a network.

The term *asynchronous* means the receiver does not know exactly when the cell will arrive. The cells contain data as needed by the application. Therefore ATM is a form of statistical multiplexing.

ATM uses small fixed length packets, or "cells," of 53 bytes instead of variable length frames. Because the cell lengths are always the same, the switching can be done in faster hardware rather than software. Frames are variable length and are difficult to process in hardware. Hardware is faster than software, so the ATM switching can be done quicker than for frames. All switches are working in parallel doing the same thing in the same amount of time. A switch must receive the entire frame or cell before re-transmitting. This delay is shorter with short cells rather than large frames.

A cell length of 53 bytes with 48 bytes of payload was agreed upon only after considerable discussion between North American and European standards organizations. Europeans wanted a 32-byte payload. Echo cancelers would not be required for the shorter transmission distances in Europe with a 32-byte payload. The North Americans could not avoid using echo cancelers because the transmission distances are significantly larger than in Europe. Also the traffic in North America has more data than voice, suitable for a longer payload. Therefore the North Americans wanted a 64-byte payload. The European traffic has more voice than data, for which the shorter 32-byte payload would be better. The 48-byte payload became the compromise, pleasing neither camp.

ATM is a form of cell relay. Table 16.1 compares frames to cells. Frames are much longer than cells. One asks if cells are less efficient because they have a higher overhead-to-data ratio. With the very high SONET rates available these differences in overhead become unimportant. ATM is designed to work with SONET at any speed.

TABLE 16.1

Frames versus ATM cells

Frames	Cells
Variable length—up to 9,000 bytes	Constant length—53 bytes;
Traffic type—data	48 bytes of data
LANs	Traffice type
Bursty	Data—bursty
Speeds—45 Mbps	Video
Connection oriented	Voice—constant rate
	Speeds—SONET
	Connection oriented
	Virtual channels
	ATM
	Connectionless—ATM, SMDS

TABLE 16.2
ATM Classes

Four classes:
    A—voice, video; constant bit rate, connection oriented
    B—packet video; variable bit rate, connection oriented
    C—data (FR); connection oriented
    D—data (IP); connectionless

Both frames and ATM are connection oriented. Both set up a virtual circuit at time of establishing the connection. The connection remains in place until the connection termination. The connection does not remain in place as it would with a permanent circuit.

16.2 ATM Supports All Types of Digital Transmissions

ATM is designed to work with bursty data transmissions and constant rate voice and video. ATM is Broadband ISDN's DLL protocol of choice. B-ISDN tells what is to be done; ATM tells how it is to be done. Other protocols work best with either bursty or constant rates, but not both. ATM is the first protocol specifically designed to handle all types of information. Table 16.2 summarizes the capabilities of ATM.

ATM can support circuit switched or packet switched operation. In packet switching, the information is broken down into small units called *packets* and sent to its destination. With ATM the data is broken down into even smaller units called *cells*. Each cell contains identification, control information, and 48 bytes of data. Each node or switch is busy only when the packet is passing through it. All other times it is available for other users and their packets. Multiple routes are available for the packets.

Circuit switching is a setup (switching) of a continuous point-to-point path between sending and receiving nodes. The path can be permanent (leased line) or set up only when in use, as in a telephone call.

Flow control and **error control** are the responsibilities of the end-to-end nodes. The term *unreliable* means the error checking is done only end-to-end, as with Frame Relay, and not between nodes, as in "reliable" X.25. *Reliability* in this context does not refer to the network itself, nor to the equipment or the people running it.

16.3 ATM Cell Formats (Types)

There are two types of ATM cells: the **User-Network Interface (UNI)** cell and the **Network-Network Interface (NNI)** cell. The UNI cell type is used between the user (host) and the first switch into the ATM network. The NNI cell type is used between switches with the ATM network. See Figure 16.1.

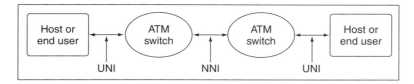

FIGURE 16.1
ATM cell types. User network interface (UNI) between host and switch, and network node interface (NNI) between switches.

FIGURE 16.2
ATM UNI format. VPI = virtual path identifier, VCI = virtual channel identifier, GFC = generic flow control, CLP = cell loss priority, PT = payload type, RES = reserved, HEC = header error control.

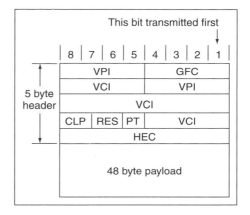

16.3.1 User-Network Interface (UNI) Cell

Figure 16.2 shows the ATM cell format for a User-Network Interface (UNI) cell. The **Generic Flow Control (GFC)** is a four-bit field to customize a local implementation. These bits may be changed by the network. When a high-bandwidth application—such as a **Computer Aided Design (CAD)** or graphics file—wishes to use the network, this field is used to gain proper access to the system. It is also used to handle congestion.

ATM is connection oriented like X.25 and FR. The virtual path is specified by the **Virtual Path Identifier (VPI)** and **Virtual Channel Identifier (VCI).** The VCI is sixteen bits, and the VPI is eight bits.

The **Payload Type (PT)** bits tell if the cell is carrying user information or service information. The Cell Loss Priority (CLP) bit indicates if the cell can be discarded when the network becomes congested. The RES bit is reserved for future use. The Header Error Control (HEC) is an eight-bit CRC used to *check the header only* for errors between switches. The payload is checked at the end nodes (end-to-end) for errors.

16.3.2 Network-Network Interface (NNI) Cell Type

Figure 16.3 shows the ATM cell format for a Network-Network Interface (NNI) cell. The Generic Flow Control (GFC) field is not present in an NNI cell.

FIGURE 16.3
ATM NNI format.

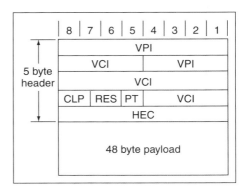

As with UNI, ATM is connection oriented. The virtual path is also specified by the Virtual Path Identifier (VPI) and Virtual Channel Identifier (VCI). The VCI is sixteen bits and the VPI is twelve bits.

As with UNI, the Payload Type (PT) bits tell if the cell is carrying user information or service information and the Cell Loss Priority (CLP) bit indicates if the cell can be discarded if the network becomes congested.

The Header Error Control (HEC) is an eight-bit CRC used to check only the header for errors between switches. The payload will be checked at the end nodes (end-to-end) for errors.

16.4 ATM Layers

The ATM layers do not correspond exactly to the OSI RM DLL and Physical Layer. Both are divided into two sublayers as shown in Figure 16.4 and in Table 16.3.

The ATM Physical sublayer is usually SONET or DS-3 (T-3). However there is talk of ATM to the desktop via LANs. The ATM sublayer manages the transmission between nodes. The VPI and VCI bits in the header control the routing path.

The **ATM Adaptation Layer (AAL)** is somewhat like the DLL of the OSI RM and is divided into the Convergence Sublayer (CS) and the Segmentation And Reassembly (SAR) sublayer. The AAL is concerned about the end-to-end transmission, serving the various types of information, and applications (voice, data, video, images). The AAL may be thought of as an X.25 PAD (Packet Assembler/Disassembler), but with greater flexibility.

16.4.1 Segmentation and Reassembly Sublayer

At the sending end the SAR segments (divides) the information to be transmitted into 48-byte payloads for the ATM sublayer. At the receiving node the SAR reassembles (puts back together) 48-byte payloads from the ATM sublayer into the proper transmitted in-

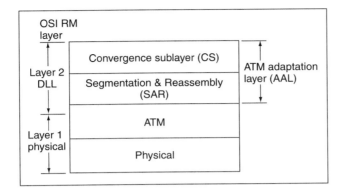

FIGURE 16.4
ATM layers.

TABLE 16.3
Segmentation and reassembly

Segmentation & Reassembly:
   At sending node: divides information into cell payloads
   At receive node: reassembles cell payloads into correct information
Convergence Sublayer:
   Prepares information from higher level for conversion to cells
   Assigns "class of service"

formation. Note that there are no sequence numbers in the ATM header. This is because ATM is connection oriented; that is, the ATM cells take only one path and all cells arrive in the order sent.

16.4.2 Convergence Sublayer

The Convergence Sublayer (CS) formats information from upper levels into correct format for conversion into 48-byte payloads. The CS assigns "class of service" for each type of information.

    The ATM "class of service" is determined by the information's timing, bit rate, and connection mode. There are four AAL classes as shown in Table 16.4.

16.4.2.1 Class 1 (Class A)
AAL Class I, or Class A, is designed for voice and video. These applications need to have the cells arrive with a constant delay time, constant bit rate, and in the same order as sent. The constant delay time means that the timing between end-to-end users must be maintained. Cell arrival in the same order as sent implies

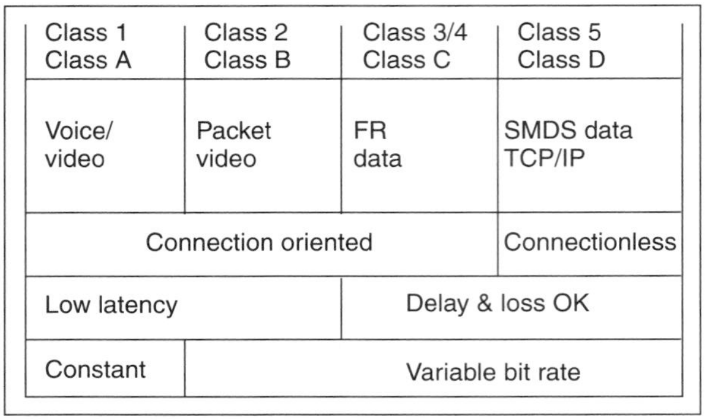

Class 1 Class A	Class 2 Class B	Class 3/4 Class C	Class 5 Class D
Voice/ video	Packet video	FR data	SMDS data TCP/IP
Connection oriented			Connectionless
Low latency	Delay & loss OK		
Constant	Variable bit rate		

FIGURE 16.5
ATM classes of service. FR = frame relay, TCP/IP = transport control protocol/internet protocol, SMDS = switched multi-point digital service.

TABLE 16.4
ATM classes of service

Class 1 (Class A)	Class 2 (Class B)	Class 3/4 (Class C)	Class 5 (Class D)
Connection oriented	Connection oriented	Connection oriented	Connectionless
Constant bit rate isochronous	Variable bit rate OK—isochronous	Variable bit rate non-isochronous	Variable bit rate non-isochronous
User-to-user timing needed	User-to-user timing needed	No user-to-user timing needed	No user- to-user timing needed
Delay unacceptable	Delay acceptable	Delay, loss acceptable	Delay, loss acceptable
Audio	Audio with no data in silences	Data	TCP/IP data; UDP/IP data
Video	Packet video	X.25, LAP/B	SMDS

connection oriented. A constant bit rate ensures that the voice or video will be presented to the end user at the proper speed.

16.4.2.2 Class 2 (Class B) AAL Class 2 (Class B) traffic can be packet video or audio. However the audio must have special techniques to stop data transfer when the speaker is silent. The video must transmit only the parts of the frame that change or are in motion. This works well for low-cost video conferencing. Both these techniques allow a variable bit rate, but some timing must be maintained between end points to allow the audio or video to be re-assembled properly. The cell payloads must be re-assembled into their proper order, so connection orientation is imperative.

16.4.2.3 Class 3/4 (Class C) AAL Class 3/4 (Class C) traffic is connection oriented but does not require a timing relationship between end points. Class C traffic is data and may use variable bit rates. Loss of data is acceptable. This could happen with severe network congestion. Examples of Class C traffic are X.25 data packets and LAP/B frames.

16.4.2.4 Class 5 (Class D)

AAL Class 5 (Class D) traffic is connectionless, may use variable bit rates, and does not need a timing relationship between end users. Variable delays are acceptable, and with User Datagram Protocol (UDP) data losses are acceptable. Examples of Class D traffic are the Internet protocols, TCP/IP and UDP/IP, and SMDS (Switched Megabit Data Service). We will study the Internet protocols in Chapter 19.

SMDS was developed by Bellcore and has been obsoleted by ATM. SMDS was derived from ATM and IEEE 802.6 MAN standards. IEEE 802.6 defines **DQDB (Distributed Queue Dual Bus)**. DQDB is a more robust MAN system than FDDI.

16.5 SONET (Synchronous Optical NETwork)

Synchronous Optical NETwork (SONET) is the prevailing standard for long haul optical fiber networks. It is designed to allow synchronous multiplexing of different data sources. Synchronous multiplexing allows even asynchronous devices to fit into the frame without wasteful "bit stuffing." *Bit stuffing* is putting "place holding" bits into a frame to keep the data in synchronism. Exactly how this is done will be discussed soon.

Oh yes, your spell checker will flag SONET. Shakespeare didn't write sonets; he wrote son*n*ets! My spell checker is not very telecommunications literate!

16.5.1 Protocols Supported by SONET

SONET is designed to transport many different formats, including ATM, Broadband ISDN, T-3, E-3, DS-1, and DS-3.

16.6 SONET and SDH

Both North American and European standards committees have given approval to SONET. However in keeping with the childish tradition of perpetual disagreement between the two continents, the Europeans prefer to use the term Synchronous Data Hierarchy (SDH). The two standards are virtually the same.

The line rates, or bit rates, of SONET are shown in Table 16.5. The **OC-X** rates are for the optical pulses on the optical fiber. The STS-X rates are for the electrical pulses driving the optical emitter and from the optical detector. Note that the base rate is 51.84 Mbps OC-1, and all faster rates are multiples of this rate; 622-Mbps OC-12 systems are in wide use, and 2,488-Mbps OC-48 systems are in the field. OC-192 systems are under development.

16.7 SONET Model

A SONET transmission system is divided into four parts: the path, line, section, and photonics as shown in Figure 16.6. The photonics consists of the optical fiber (usually single-mode for greater bandwidth), emitter (usually a LASER) and detector, relay nodes, and associated electronics. The path, line, and section functions are summarized in Table 16.5 and discussed in the next section.

TABLE 16–5
SONET Line Rates

Synchronous Transport Signal (electrical)	Optical Carrier designation (optical)	Line Rates Mbps
STS-1	OC-1	51.84
STS-3	OC-3	165.52
STS-12	OC-12	622.08
STS-24	OC-24	1244.16
STS-48	OC-48	2488.32
STS-96	OC-96	4976.64
STS-192	OC-192	9953.28

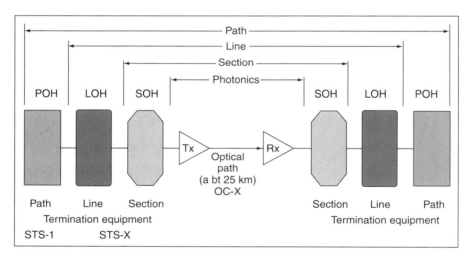

FIGURE 16.6
SONET model. SOH = section overhead, LOH = line overhead, POH = path overhead, Tx = transmitter, Rx = receiver.

16.8   SONET Format and Overhead Portioning

Figure 16.7 shows the SONET frame format. At an STS-1 line speed of 51.84 mbps the frame is 125 μs long. The frame consists of 9 rows of 90 columns (bytes) for a total of $9 \times 90 = 810$ bytes per frame. The frame is transmitted consecutively row by row.

The payload is 9 rows of 86 columns (bytes) for a total of 9×86 bytes payload = 774 bytes per frame. Three columns of overhead are called Transport OverHead (TOH) and are 3 columns (bytes) times 9 rows for a total of 27 bytes of TOH. Within the Transport

TABLE 16.6
Functions of SONET components

Line Overhead:
   Processed at all nodes
   Communicates with higher level components, such as terminals, switches, multiplexers, and digital
      cross connects
   Pointer for frequency justification and Data Communications Channel (DCC)
Section Overhead:
   Between network elements such as regenerators and terminals
   Used for framing and performance monitoring
Transport Overhead (TOH):
   Alarms
   Error monitoring
   Contains Section OverHead (SOH) and Line OverHead (LOH)
Path Overhead
   End-to-end information
   Stays with SPE until the final node

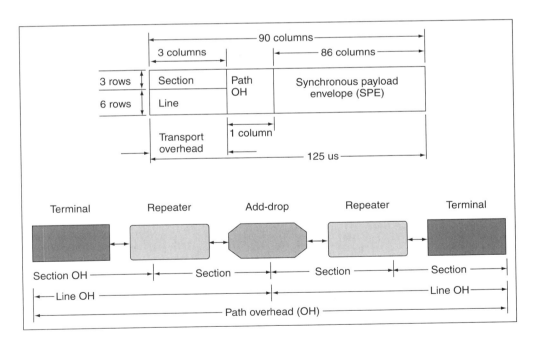

FIGURE 16.7
STS-1 format and overhead portioning. A column equals one byte. Frame size = 90 columns
× 9 rows = 810 bytes/frame. 810 bytes/frame × 8 bits/byte × 1 frame/125 µs = 51.84 Mbps.
Transport overhead is 3 columns (bytes) × 9 rows = 27 bytes. Net payload is 810 bytes − 36
bytes = 774 bytes = >49.536 Mbps.

OverHead is the Section OverHead (SOH) and Line OverHead (LOH). The fourth column in each row is Path OverHead (POH).

16.8.1 Transport OverHead (TOH)

Broadly, the TOH does error and alarm monitoring.

16.8.2 Path OverHead (POH)

The Path OverHead (POH) is end-to-end information and remains with the SPE to the final destination.

16.8.3 Line OverHead (LOH)

The Line OverHead is processed at each node. It is communications for terminals, switches, multiplexers, and digital cross connects.

16.8.4 Section OverHead (SOH)

The Section OverHead (SOH) is processed at each node and also each re-generator. It is used for framing and performance monitoring.

16.9 Synchronous Payload Envelope (SPE) Synchronization

SONET is synchronous, right? Well, virtually all data will *not* be synchronous with the STS line rate. Slight differences are almost certain to exist. So how does SONET handle these differences?

Figure 16.8 shows four consecutive SONET/STS frames. Pointer fields (H H H) are in the first three columns of the first row of the Line OverHead (LOH). The pointer bits tell the receiver where the true data actually starts. Stuffing bits are inserted between the Transport OverHead (TOH) columns and the start of data. These extra bits will count as a sort of overhead. However the data rate is so fast that this extra overhead is inconsequential.

In frame 1 the "H H H" bits tell the start of data. The data in frame 2 is faster than the STS line rate and moves forward in the SPE. The "H H H" bits reflect this, and fewer stuffing bits are needed.

In frame 3 the data is slower than the STS line rate and the data comes later in the SPE. Again the "H H H" bits show the correct start of data. More stuffing bits are necessary.

16.10 ATM Testing and Troubleshooting

There are five parts to ATM testing:

1. Conformance testing to see if the components meet the standards. Conformance testing is specified by the **International Standards Organization (ISO)** standards ISO-9646.

2. Interoperability testing to prove that equipment from different manufacturers works together properly.

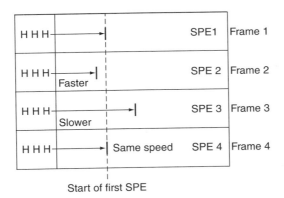

FIGURE 16.8
SPE synchronization. What if the information to be transmitted is not synchronized to the SONET clock? Answer: bit stuffing. STS frame 1 is the reference. The "H H H" pointers give the starting byte of the information. Stuffing bytes are inserted between the transport overhead bytes and the SPE beginning. In frame 2 the clock is faster than the SONET clock and the information comes sooner than in frame 1. Therefore fewer stuffing bytes are needed than in frame 1. In frame 3 the clock is slower than the SONET clock and the information comes later than in frame 1. Therefore more stuffing bytes are needed between the overhead and the SPE beginning.

3. Regression testing to see if new standards and equipment will work with the older versions.

4. Performance testing of the operational network to see if the data transfer and signaling are working properly. Signaling testing answers the question of how much traffic the switch can handle before setup and clears (teardown) start taking longer times, or begins to drop cells.

There are two types of signaling: signaling between customer equipment and signaling between network switches. Data transfer testing tells how much traffic can be handled and the speed at which it can be handled.

5. Diagnostic testing to find and diagnose network operational problems. The International Telecommunication Union—Telecommunications Standardization Sector (ITU-T) has defined the Operations and Maintenance (OAM) protocol. This protocol specifies fault detection and localization as well as performance monitoring.

Tests can be performed either in an out-of-service mode (network not sending live data) or in-service (while the customer sends live data). Of course the in-service testing should not disturb the live data.

Hewlett-Packard has its Broadband Series Test System (BSTS) modular test set for ATM, Frame Relay, SONET, and LANs. It begins with the HP E4210 mainframe base and the HP E4200B portable base. The bases are UNIX-based machines with plug-in modules for the various protocols.

Various plug-in hardware modules and software modules are available. The modules test various portions of conformance, interoperability, and signaling. Other modules test various portions of the ATM four layers. One does not have to buy any more equipment or software than is actually needed.

16.11   SONET Testing and Troubleshooting

SONET has a built-in fault management system. It detects and reports the following faults:

1. *Broken link or broken optical fiber.* This is usually due to the bane of installed cables everywhere, the seemingly ubiquitous backhoe. The **backhoe** is used to dig trenches, and often the operator cuts through a cable. Contractors who dig trenches must check with the local utility company before they dig or face huge legal and damage costs if a cable is cut. However quite often the utility companies' records and prints are not correct and the utility company is at fault. Recently a company was fined $200,000 for tearing up cables. Fortunately this fault is easy to detect. A Loss Of Signal (LOS) is automatically reported to the fault management system. An Optical Time Domain Reflectometer (OTDR) discussed in Chapter 2, can pinpoint the break almost down to the foot.

2. *Degradation of network performance.* This is due to low optical power arriving at the receiver, low emitter transmitted power, optical reflections from poor splices or connections, or excessive jitter. It is detected by excessive errors. The operator sets the error threshold. The number of errors must exceed this threshold for the fault to be reported to the fault management system. Errors can be introduced by inserting an optical attenuator to reduce the signal to the receiver.

3. *Routing errors.* This can be caused by operator error or a software bug. It is detected and reported automatically to the fault management system.

4. *Network element hardware failure.* This is a hardware failure of electronic equipment. It is detected by excessive errors or LOS. The operator sets the error threshold. The number of errors must exceed this threshold for the fault to be reported to the fault management system. This can be difficult to detect without external test equipment, since the failure may prevent useful data from getting to the technician.

The Hewlett-Packard, Cerjac Division's SONET Maintenance Test Station (MTS) Lite is designed for cases where the fault management system is inadequate. The MTS handles speeds up to OC-12.

SUMMARY

I. Asynchronous Transfer Mode (ATM) is the protocol of choice for networks needing to carry all types of information. It is specially designed to carry voice, video, and data under all timing conditions. It is the protocol for Broadband ISDN (B-ISDN).

II. *Asynchronous* means the receiver does not know exactly when the cell will arrive. Nonetheless ATM is designed to interface directly with SONET, a synchronous system.

III. ATM cells are always 53 bytes long. This fixed length allows them to be switched quickly in hardware, rather than slower in software, as was the case for variable length frames. Also the delay traveling through switches is much less and more predictable. The payload is 48 bytes, and the routing and housekeeping information is in the five-byte header.

IV. ATM is connection oriented. The connection must be established (set up) before data transfer can take place. The connection remains in place until all the data has been transferred.

V. There are two types of cells: the User-Network Interface (UNI), to let a user gain access to the network, and the Network-Network Interface (NNI), for use within the network.

VI. The Payload Type (PT) bits tell if the cell is carrying user information or service information.

VII. The Cell Loss Priority (CLP) bit indicates if the cell can be discarded when the network becomes congested.

VIII. The Header Error Control (HEC) is an eight-bit CRC used to check the header only for errors. The HEC is the last byte in the header.

IX. ATM corresponds to the Physical and Data Link Level of the OSI RM. Each of these two layers is subdivided into two layers each.

X. Within the Physical Layer, the ATM Physical sublayer is usually SONET or DS-3 (T-3), and the ATM sublayer manages the transmission between nodes.

XI. In the DLL the ATM Adaptation Layer (AAL) is subdivided into the Convergence Sublayer (CS) and the Segmentation And Reassembly (SAR) sublayer.

XII. The SAR segments (divides) the information to be transmitted into 48-byte payloads for the ATM sublayer.

XIII. The Convergence Sublayer (CS) formats information from upper levels into correct format for conversion into 48-byte payloads. The CS assigns "class of service" for each type of information.

XIV. There are four classes of service, or data types.
  A. Class 1 (Class A) is designed for voice and video; constant delay time, constant bit rate, and in the same order as sent.
  B. Class 2 (Class B) traffic.
    1. Packet video.
    2. Packet audio.
  C. Class 3/4 (Class C) traffic is data.
    1. Connection oriented.
    2. Does not require a timing relationship between end points.
    3. May use variable bit rates.
    4. Loss of data is acceptable.
  D. Class 5 (Class D) traffic is connectionless.
    1. May use variable bit rates.
    2. Does not need a timing relationship between end users.

XV. Synchronous Optical NETwork (SONET).
  A. Prevailing standard for long haul optical fiber networks.
    1. Designed to allow synchronous multiplexing of different data sources.
    2. Synchronous multiplexing allows even asynchronous devices to fit into the frame.
    3. Supports ATM, Broadband ISDN, T-3, E-3, DS-1, and DS-3.

    B. Basic OC-1 rate is 51.84 Mbps.

    C. SONET frame.

       1. 125 μs at 51.84 Mbps.

       2. 810 bytes.

       3. 774 bytes of payload.

       4. Transport OverHead (TOH); does error and alarm monitoring.

       5. Path OverHead (POH); end-to-end information.

       6. Line OverHead (LOH) is processed at each node; communications for terminals, switches, multiplexers, and digital cross connects (DXC).

       7. Section OverHead (SOH); processed at each node and each re-generator. Used for framing and performance monitoring.

QUESTIONS

1. What types of information is ATM designed to handle? Are there any types of data that it will not handle?
2. What was the compromise that resulted in a 48-byte (octet) payload for ATM?
3. Why are fixed-sized cells or packets better than variable-sized frames?
4. What are the differences between circuit switching and packet switching?
5. What are the differences between connection oriented and connectionless?
6. What does *unreliable* versus *reliable* mean, as they relate to data communications?
7. What is the purpose of the CLP bit?
8. What are the VPI and VCI fields used for?
9. What is segmentation? What is re-assembly?
10. Why doesn't the ATM header have cell sequence numbers?
11. Why must Class 1 service have a constant bit rate, constant delay time? Why must the cells arrive in the same order as sent?
12. What are some uses and advantages of Class 2 service?
13. Why can Class 3/4 and Class 5 service tolerate variable bit rates and variable delays?
14. What is the physical medium for SONET?
15. What are the four parts of a SONET system?
16. What is the SONET section, and what does it do?
17. What is the SONET line, and what does it do?
18. What is the SONET path, and what does it do?
19. What is the SOH, and what does it do?
20. What is the LOH, and what does it do?
21. What is the POH, and what does it do?
22. How does SONET synchronize the incoming data?

17

SNA, TCP/IP, AND MURPHY'S LAW

OBJECTIVES

In this chapter we will discuss:

I. The major differences between SNA and TCP/IP.
   - **A.** Data loss.
     - **1.** SNA does not tolerate data loss.
     - **2.** TCP/IP does allow some data loss.
   - **B.** Complexity.
     - **1.** SNA is extremely complex.
     - **2.** TCP/IP is relatively less complex.
   - **C.** SNA needs to know the state of every part of the network.
   - **D.** TCP/IP does not need to know the state of the network nodes.
   - **E.** Architecture.
     - **1.** SNA is centralized star topology with a host machine (usually a mainframe or mini) at the center.
     - **2.** TCP/IP is distributed.
   - **F.** Connection.
     - **1.** SNA is connection oriented; must establish a "logical connection" before data is transferred.
     - **2.** TCP/IP is connectionless; just the Destination Address is needed. The datagram can take many different paths.

17.1 Murphy's Law

Captain Murphy, no doubt in extreme exasperation and frustration over a project having its difficulties, cried the immortal phrase "Whatever can go wrong, will go wrong" and henceforth became a most esteemed member of the pantheon of great American philosophers. Of course the most famous of these august sages is Yogi Berra.

Anyone, and I do mean *anyone*, who has been associated with a technical project knows full well the veracity of Murphy's Law. Most people, even in non-technical fields, know full well the truth of Captain Murphy's bitter lament. Network designers, likewise, are well aware that networks will fail because of either hardware or software bugs.

In the early 1960s **IBM** and the **U.S. Department of Defense (DOD)** were faced with designing data communication networks. Both groups knew full well that network components would eventually fail and that their networks had to circumvent these inevitable failures. How each group approached this problem is interesting and the subject of this chapter. The two very different approaches will help the student understand both systems. Where one group "zigged," the other "zagged."

17.2 TCP/IP Versus SNA

IBM's data network became **System Network Architecture (SNA)** the and the DOD's became **Transport Control Protocol / Internet Protocol (TCP/IP).** Table 17.1 summarizes the differences.

17.2.1 Data Loss

SNA is designed to have essentially no data loss. TCP/IP does allow some data loss. SNA is better-suited for a bank's financial information and similar critical data. TCP/IP does allow dropping some data. This is not a problem with graphic files, and in fact, TCP/IP is quite reliable but may not be suitable for extremely critical data.

17.2.2 SNA Architecture

SNA is a centralized architecture with a host mainframe machine (computer) controlling mini-data-switching computers. The mini-computers use a system called **Network Control Program (NCP).** NCP manages all the peripherals and terminals in branch offices at the network periphery. These machines using NCP do not run any user programs but handle only switching and NCP.

The host computer runs a sub-operating system called **Virtual Telecommunications Access Method (VTAM).** VTAM relieves the operating system of network com-

TABLE 17.1
SNA versus TCP/IP

SNA	TCP/IP
Centralized—tight control	Distributed—loose control
Critical component—host machine	Critical component—network
Any data loss unacceptable	Some data loss acceptable
Connection oriented—"session" must be first established	Connectionless—only Destination Address needed
Extremely complex—only IBM has all source code	Low complexity—source code available
Maintenance difficult—trained teams needed	Maintenance relatively easy

munication responsibilities. VTAM keeps a data base of all machines, peripherals, and communication paths and chooses the routes for the data and any alternate paths. SNA is a very tightly controlled system.

17.2.3 TCP/IP Architecture

TCP/IP uses a very distributed architecture. It was designed to communicate among DOD's widely scattered research computers. A key requirement was to be able to automatically re-route data around failed network parts. This also has use in combat as nodes or terminals may be destroyed by hostile enemy action.

There is no central host machine and no routing tables at any user computer. The routing tables are within the network switching system and are transparent to the TCP/IP user. The datagrams (messages) do not contain any routing information, only the Destination Address and Source Address.

17.3 Connectionless Versus Connection Oriented

SNA must establish a "session" between components before any data can be transferred. A *session* is generally defined as a "logical connection." What this means is that the node desiring to send or receive data must ask if the other node is available for the data transfer and have the path set up by VTAM before the actual data transfer. This is called *connection oriented.*

TCP does establish a connection before actual data transfer. IP and other protocols within TCP/IP do not establish a connection before data transfer. No route setup is done within TCP/IP. This type of operation is called *connectionless.*

17.4 Relative Complexity

TCP/IP is a comparatively simple protocol, and the source code is readily available. SNA is astonishingly complex, and only IBM has all the code. A humorist has dubbed SNA "Satan's Network Architecture." This humorist does not work for IBM.

SNA's extreme complexity necessitates highly trained people to install and maintain it. TCP/IP, being a much simpler protocol, does not require the great depth of training needed for SNA. SNA's learning curve is very steep and long relative to TCP/IP's.

17.5 Advanced Peer-to-Peer Networking (APPN)

The popularity of the personal computer has made the centralized host network very much less used. IBM has responded to this situation with Advanced Peer-to-Peer Networking (APPN). This "New SNA" is truly a new distributed networking system using much of the same terminals and peripherals. IBM's party line declares the two systems are the same, but rather they are compatible and can easily exchange data.

17.6   Final Thoughts

SNA and TCP/IP have very different design philosophies. To reiterate, where TCP/IP developers "zigged," the IBM folks "zagged." While greatly different, the two systems should not be considered incompatible but rather complementary. Using the two systems together an organization can solve any data transfer problem.

TCP/IP is the protocol of the Internet. TCP/IP is one of only a few systems with a military history to find widespread civilian use. This is an extremely rare case of "I'm from the government and I'm here to help you" actually doing just that. History abounds with failed examples of DOD or similar governmental agency decrees and fiats. Two examples are the programming language "Ada," which is hardly ever used except to maintain government computer programs, and VHDL. VHDL is a language the DOD developed to design complex digital circuits. In so doing, it chose to ignore Verilog, a decidedly superior language created by the electronics industry.

QUESTIONS

1. Compare the design philosophies of SNA and TCP/IP. Concentrate on data loss, network failures, and type of architecture.
2. Who created SNA? Who created TCP/IP?
3. Explain "connectionless" and "connection oriented."
4. How does APPN relate to SNA?

18

TCP/IP AND THE INTERNET

OBJECTIVES

In this chapter we will discuss:

I. Who created TCP/IP? The U.S. Department of Defense (DOD).

II. Why was TCP/IP developed? To create a failure resistant network and to connect DOD's research computers.

III. Datagrams.
    A. Connectionless.
    B. Allow dynamic routing change.

IV. TCP/IP four layers.
    A. Network Access 1A; corresponds to OSI Physical Layer 1.
    B. Network Access 1B; corresponds to OSI Data Link Layer 2.
    C. Internet layer; corresponds to OSI Network Layer 3.
        1. Does routing.
        2. Contains these protocols:
            a. Internet Protocol (IP); "unreliable" because IP does not fully error check.
            b. Address Resolution Protocol (ARP); maps an IP address to a LAN address.
            c. Internet Control Message Protocol (ICMP); IP sends housekeeping messages between IP and other machines.
    D. Host-to-Host or Transport Layer. Corresponds to OSI Transport Layer 4; contains these protocols:
        1. Transport Control Protocol (TCP); full error check—"reliable."
        2. User Datagram Protocol (UDP); not full error check therefore "unreliable."
    E. Process/Application Layer contains these protocols:
        1. File Transfer Protocol (FTP); transfers files.
        2. Telnet; log into remote computer.
        3. Domain Name Service (DNS); converts www or e-mail address to IP address.
        4. Routing Information Protocol (RIP).
        5. Simple Mail Transfer Protocol (SMTP); e-mail.

V. What's on the Internet?
    A. World Wide Web.

1. HyperText Markup Language (HTML) is used to program Web sites.
2. JAVA is another Internet programming language.

B. Museums, libraries, data sheets, company advertising, travel information, and the like.

C. Chat rooms.

D. Special interest groups.

18.1   History of TCP/IP and the Internet

In the 1960s the U.S. Department of Defense (DOD) realized that the computers at its research institutions were too centralized. The DOD decided to network these computers together via a failure resistant system.

In 1968 the DOD funded the **Defense Advanced Research Projects Agency (DARPA)** to design a decentralized system, able to withstand multiple failures of DOD's research network and hosts. In 1975 DARPA began work on what would become the Internet, and in 1979 the Internet Control and Configuration Board (ICCB) was formed to guide design of the necessary protocols and the Internet. As a result of efforts by the ICCB, Transport Control Protocol / Internet Protocol (TCP/IP) was implemented.

The history of the Internet is tabulated in Table 18.1. In 1983 the Secretary of Defense mandated TCP/IP for the Internet. There were two networks: ARPANET for the military research organizations and MILNET for military communications. ARPANET became known as the ARPA Internet, or TCP/IP Internet, or just the Internet.

In 1985 the National Science Foundation (NSF), a governmental but non-military organization, was allowed to use TCP/IP to connect its supercomputers. The DOD gradually released the Internet for civilian use.

There is a persistent, but untrue, tale that the DOD wanted nuclear attack survivability for its military computers. The DOD's military facilities are different from the ones we describe here and are protected by means that are quite secret.

18.2   Purpose of the Internet

The major reasons for the Internet and TCP/IP are the ability to log into (connect with) distant or remote computers (hosts) and to transfer files between the user's computer and the remote (distant) computer.

18.3   Datagrams

Table 18.2 summarizes datagrams. TCP/IP sends information using datagrams. The data to be sent is divided (segmented) into datagrams. Each datagram may take a different route to the final destination. The datagrams may arrive out of order at the final destination. If a node or a path segment is not functioning, the network system will route datagrams around the non-working node or path. Even if several portions of the network fail, the datagrams will still get to the desired destination. This is also illustrated in Chapter 15.

TABLE 18.1
TCP/IP History

1968
  Defense Advanced Research Projects Agency (DARPA):
    design survivable system.
1975
  DARPA begins work on Internet.
1977–79
  Protocols begin evolving.
1979
  Internet Control & Configuration Board (ICCB) formed to:
    guide design of protocols & Internet.
1980
  TCP/IP implemented.
1983
  Secretary of DOD mandated TCP/IP.
    ARPANET for research organizations,
    MILNET for military communications.
1985
  National Science Foundation (NSF)
    uses TCP/IP to connect its supercomputers
1990
  Internet has
    3,000 networks,
    200,000 computers.
1993
  Internet has
    over two million computers

TABLE 18.2
Datagrams in TCP/IP

Datagram
  Connectionless:
    message divided into packets,
    packets travel different routes to destination,
      packets may arrive out of order.
    packets are sent without knowing their route,
    packets are sent without setting up connection in advance (connectionless),
    packets routed around nonfunctioning nodes.

OSI RM	TCP/IP Layers	TCP/IP Protocol Suite
7 Application	Process / Application	FTP, Telnet, DNS, RIP
6 Presentation		
5 Session		
4 Transport	Host-to-Host transport	TCP, UDP
3 Network	Internet	IP, ICMP
2 Data Link	Network access	1B - 802.X, X.25
1 Physical		1A

FIGURE 18.1
TCP/IP layers. Network access sublayer 1A includes the physical mediums such as microwave, fiber optic, coax, satellite, twisted pair, and wireless.

18.4 TCP/IP Layers versus the OSI RM

In Figure 18.1 the left column shows the OSI RM (Open Systems International / Reference Model). The middle column shows the TCP/IP layers. The right column shows what constitutes the TCP/IP protocol suite.

The term *TCP/IP* is generally used to include all the various application software shown in the figure. Collectively they are called the *Internet protocols,* or the *TCP/IP protocol suite.* TCP and IP are only two of many protocols, but IP is used in all datagram transfers, and TCP is used in most datagram transfers.

The Internet has four layers, as compared to the seven layers of the OSI Reference Model. At the top is the Process/Application Layer, then the Host-to-Host or Transport Layer, the Internet, and finally the Network Access at the bottom.

18.4.1 Layer Descriptions

18.4.1.1 Network Access Sublayer and the OSI Data Link Layer   The Network Access sublayer 1A, corresponding to the OSI RM Physical Layer 1, is the transmission medium, which can be microwave, optical fiber, coax, satellite, twisted pair, or wireless. The DOD designed TCP/IP to work with any medium, both present and future. This "futureproofing" is one of many reasons for TCP/IP's continued popularity.

The Network Access sublayer 1B is equivalent to the OSI RM Data Link Layer and portions of the Network Layer. It includes the X.25, FDDI, and the 802.X LAN protocols.

18.4.1.2 Internet Layer and the OSI Network Layer   The Internet Layer corresponds to the OSI RM's Network Layer 3. The Internet Layer has three protocols: the In-

ternet Protocol (IP), Address Resolution Protocol (ARP), and Internet Control Message Protocol (ICMP). These will be discussed later in this chapter.

IP is said to be "unreliable" because it does minimal error checking. The only IP error checking is done via a checksum for the header. Full error checking is done with TCP at the next higher level. This "unreliability" in no way reflects on the quality of the overall system.

18.4.1.3 Host-to-Host or Transport Layer

The Host-to-Host Layer corresponds to the OSI RM's Transport Layer and a portion of the Session Layer. Two protocols reside in this layer: Transport Control Protocol (TCP) and User Datagram Protocol (UDP). Data passing through this layer between the Internet Layer and the Process/Application Layer will use either TCP or UDP, but not both.

TCP performs end-to-end error checking and is therefore "reliable." UDP error-checks only its header and is thus considered "unreliable." Remember, these are definitions regarding error control only and not a reflection on the skills of the people designing and maintaining the overall system. Because UDP does not error-check, it is cheaper and faster than TCP. UDP is generally used for applications where an error would not be grievous and for small data transfers.

18.4.1.4 Process/Application Layer

The top layer is the Process/Application Layer consisting of File Transfer Protocol (FTP), Telnet, Domain Name Service (DNS), Routing Information Protocol (RIP), and Simple Mail Transfer Protocol (SMTP).

18.5   Data flow

Referring to Figure 18.2a, the data or request originates at the top Process/Application Layer. The data is passed to the next lower layer, the Host-to-Host Layer. There TCP or UDP adds its header. The data and header are passed to the IP Layer. IP adds its own header and passes the header and data down to the Network Access Layer. The Network Access Layer adds its header, making up a datagram. The Network Access Layer sends the datagram over the Internet.

At the receiving end (Figure 18.2b) the datagram passes up the protocol stack. Each layer examines the particular header addressed to that layer and strips that header off before passing the information to the next level above.

18.6   Layer Description

Figure 18.3 shows more detail of the TCP/IP protocol suite. At the bottom is the Network Access Layer, which can be many different transmission systems. The number associated with each TCP/IP protocol member is the "port" number, or address.

18.6.1 IP Layer

IP sends datagrams between the proper transport protocol, either TCP or UDP, and the Network Access Layer. The Internet Protocol (IP) may be considered a "postal system,"

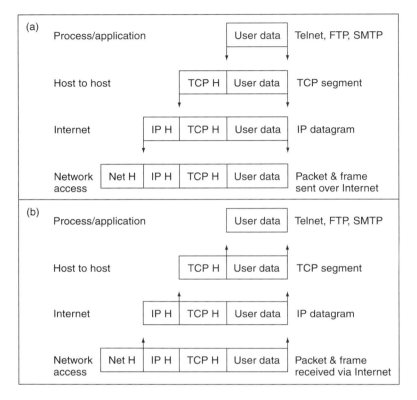

FIGURE 18.2
Data flow. (a) Application to network and (b) network to application. H = header.

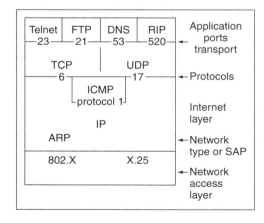

FIGURE 18.3
Layer structure.

meaning that IP sends datagrams (envelopes) without knowing what route they will travel to their final destination. IP does not know, nor does it care, what path the datagrams (envelopes) will take or what the envelope contents are. This is called *connectionless,* meaning that no connection is set up in advance of actual datagram transmissions. No path information is contained within the datagrams, only the final Destination Address.

The datagrams often arrive out of order. Thus a datagram sequence number is needed in each datagram so that the IP at the receiving end can re-assemble the datagrams into their proper order.

18.6.1.1 Internet Control Message Protocol (ICMP)   IP is assisted by the **Internet Control Message Protocol (ICMP)** and the **Address Resolution Protocol (ARP).** IP is connectionless and has no way to send error and status messages back to the sender, so it relies upon ICMP to do these tasks. ICMP sends error and status messages back to the sending host and also handles routing and flow control.

A request through ICMP for information about another IP address is called a **"PING"** (Packet INternet Groper). Really! And you thought network people had no sense of humor! The response with the requested information is called a "PONG." Really again! Another UDP command is "FINGER," which asks the remote host what users are iogged on.

18.6.1.2 Address Resolution Protocol (ARP)   Address Resolution Protocol (ARP) will map, find, or convert an IP address to the Media Access Control (MAC) Layer address (the physical address on the Network Interface Card [NIC] inside the computer or terminal) within the LAN. ARP maintains a table of MAC addresses and their corresponding IP addresses.

18.6.2 Transport Layer Protocols

There are two Transport or Host-to-Host Layers: the Transport Control Protocol (TCP) and the User Datagram Protocol (UDP).

18.6.2.1 Transport Control Protocol (TCP)   At the sending host TCP segments the data into smaller datagrams and adds consecutive sequence numbers. At the receiving host TCP re-assembles the datagrams into their proper order, using the datagram sequence numbers.

When receiving datagrams, IP passes the datagram to the next higher level. The datagram goes to either TCP or UDP. If the protocol number in the datagram is 6, the datagram will go to TCP. If the protocol number is 17, the datagram will be given to UDP.

TCP is a connection oriented protocol, meaning that TCP will set up, maintain, and tear down a connection. TCP keeps track of the status and state of data passing through it. TCP ensures reliable end-to-end (host-to-host) data transmission. Remember that the term *reliable* means that there is end-to-end error checking; it is not any comment on the quality of the nodes or transmission path. TCP can also multiplex data from different applications and is full duplex.

18.6.2.2 User Datagram Protocol (UDP)   UDP also resides in the Host-to-Host Layer with TCP. UDP is "connectionless" and is merely a transport level protocol for the applications in the layer above. *Connectionless* means that the datagram is sent without first setting up a connection.

UDP does not do any end-to-end error checking but uses a checksum in the UDP header. This checks only the correctness of the header. UDP is used for small data transfers where an error is not a serious problem. It is faster and cheaper than TCP because it doesn't have the expensive error checking software, nor does it have to take the extra time to error-check.

Routing Information Protocol (RIP) and **Domain Name Service (DNS)** of the Process/Application Layer use UDP.

18.6.2.3 Application Level Protocols

File Transfer Protocol (FTP)   The purpose of File Transfer Protocol (FTP) is to transfer files. One can log into a remote host and transfer a file to or from that remote host to one's own computer. This is one of the main reasons for TCP/IP and the Internet. FTP is at the Application level. FTP has a Port Address of 21. This is the address in the datagram that TCP recognizes as being intended for FTP.

The UNIX command to enter FTP is "ftp <hostname>." For example:

```
ftp spock
```

where "spock" is the name of the remote host or computer that the user wishes to send files to and receive files from. Note that UNIX almost always uses lowercase text and is very case sensitive. The casual user will log in as user "anonymous" with a password of his or her name or e-mail address.

FTP is used to send to or receive files from a remote computer or server. The original intent was to send programs to run on a remote computer and retrieve the results from running that program. Now programs and their latest updates (binary files) and graphic files can be retrieved (downloaded). The types of files range from scientific to just fun.

The FTP command to retrieve a file is "get," and the command to send a file is "put." For example:

```
get games.html
put response.doc
```

Simple Mail Transfer Protocol (SMTP)   Another major and popular use of the Internet and TCP/IP is **electronic mail,** or **e-mail.** E-mail is handled by **Simple Mail Transfer Protocol (SMTP)** in the Application/Process Layer. E-mail has proved to be one of the most popular uses of the Internet, giving nearly instant text communication almost anywhere in the industrialized world. Because of e-mail's speed, convenience, low cost, and ability to reach large numbers of people, users have dubbed the world's postal services as "snail mail"!

Our college president, academic dean, school deans, and department chairs use e-mail to quickly send pertinent messages to all of their underlings. Faculty and staff are quick to read their e-mail upon coming to work, guaranteeing speedy and sure communications.

E-mail can be used to send or receive files, although in a somewhat different manner than FTP. The files are sent as an attachment to the e-mail message itself. Special software may be required to read the attachment, which may be a graphics, text, or binary file.

Families who are widespread geographically use e-mail to communicate their daily events to each other, something difficult to do with the U.S. Postal Service. The speed of this communication gives a special touch, absent with "snail mail." If the family is large, much less time is spent communicating with e-mail than calling long distance to each member. Also the costs of Internet access are usually much less than for long distance calls, although competition is bringing down long distance phone prices. As of this writing (early 1999) Sprint was offering $0.075 per minute and AT&T was offering $0.15 per minute to anywhere in the continental United States.

Still long distance voice certainly has its advantages over e-mail. Nothing can completely replace voice contact. But companies are now moving into voice communications over the Internet, and they are creating standards for this. With the low Internet access rates and falling long distance prices, competition should be interesting to watch, and the customer will certainly benefit. At the time of this writing (early 1999) Qwest, Inc., was offering less than $0.075 per minute for long distance voice over the Internet.

Telnet Telnet allows the user to log into a remote host (computer) and give commands just as if he or she were seated at a terminal in the same room. This is the second major purpose of the Internet and TCP/IP. Users can log into a remote computer that has more speed or memory than theirs, such as a Cray supercomputer. They might take advantage of lower usage rates on weekends and nights.

The usual UNIX telnet command is "telnet <host name> [port]" or "telnet <computer address> [port]" where the port may be optional. An example is:

```
telnet enterprise
```

The login is either "anonymous" or one assigned by the system administrator at the remote host.

18.7 TCP/IP Frame Structure

Let us examine the TCP/IP frame structure beginning at the bottom Network Access Layer (see Figure 18.4). This frame contains a header and trailer for the Network Access Layer's error control, flow control, and housekeeping. These are not needed by the IP Layer.

Some of the items in the IP Layer header are:

Header length and IP version (L)

Type of service (Y) specifying delay, throughput, reliability, and precedence

Total length (L) of IP datagram

Unique identifier (I) for the datagram

Time to live (TL) prevents datagrams from circulating in the network forever; every time the datagram passes through a node, this number is decremented and the datagram is killed (deleted) when the number reaches zero

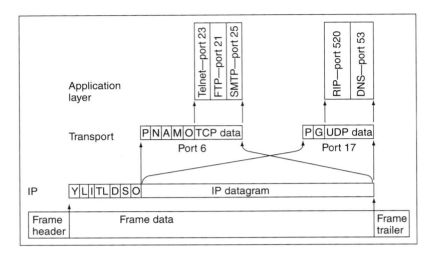

FIGURE 18.4

TCP/IP frame structure. Y = type of service, P = source (destination port), I = identification flags, N = sequence number, L = time to live (protocol, header checksum), A = acknowledgment number, M = ACK, SYN, FIN, D = destination address, O = options, S = source address, G = length (checksum), T = trailer.

Destination Address (D) and Source Address (S)

Options (O) from the sender, for instance, route specification

There is also a checksum in the header for error control. This may be re-computed at each node.

18.8 IP Header

Figure 18.5 shows the structure of the IP header. IP passes its datagram, minus the IP header, up to the next level to either TCP (protocol 6) or UDP (protocol 17).

18.8.1 Sending Data to TCP

When the IP datagram is sent to TCP, the TCP header will have some of the following information:

The source port and the destination port (P)

The sequence number (N) to put the data back into the correct order.

With TCP/IP the datagrams may arrive out of order, and sequence numbers are necessary to re-construct the correct data order

Acknowledgment (A) number telling the next expected TCP datagram, needed for flow control and error control

Sent first					
Version	IML	Type of service	Total length	Identification	Flags
Fragment offset	Time to live	Protocol	Header checksum		
Source address	Destination address	Options	Padding		

FIGURE 18.5

IP header. Version = IP version, IHL = internet header length (the length of header in 32-bit words; also points to beginning of data). "Type of service" giving delay, throughput, reliability, and precedence. Flags—three bits telling whether to fragment or not (fragmentation is sending the data in more than one datagram). "Fragment offset" tells where the fragment starts (if fragmentation has taken place). Time to live—each node that handles the header will decrement this number by one. When the number reaches zero, the datagram is deleted. This prevents datagrams from circulating in the system forever. Protocol = UDP or TCP. Header checksum—for error control. Options allow instant route specification, and padding ensures that the header ends on a 32-bit boundary.

ACKnowledge, NAcKnowledge, FINal flow, and error control characters

Options (O)

The header also has a checksum for error control.

18.8.2 Sending Data to UDP

When the IP datagram is sent to UDP, the UDP header will have the following information:

The source port and the destination port (P)

Length (L) of the datagram

Also the header has a checksum for error control.

18.9 TCP Header

Figure 18.6 shows the details of the TCP header. When the IP datagram is sent to the TCP, the TCP header will have at least the following information:

The source port and the destination port (P)

The sequence number (N) to put the data back into the correct order. With TCP/IP
    the datagrams may arrive out of order and sequence numbers
    are necessary to re-construct the correct datagram order

Acknowledgment (A) number telling the next expected TCP datagram, needed for
    flow control

ACKnowledge, NAcKnowledge, FINal flow, and error control characters

Options (O)

Source Port	Destination Port	Sequence Number		
Acknowledgment Number		Data Offset	Reserved	Urgent
Acknowledgment	Push	Reset	Synchronizer	Finished
Window	Checksum	Urgent Pointer	Options	Padding
DATA		DATA		

FIGURE 18.6
TCP Header. Acknowledgment number—acknowledging data received and used for flow control, gives the next expected TCP octet. Data offset—indicates the data begins here. Urgent—is the urgent pointer being used for urgent data? Acknowledgment—is the acknowledgment field significant? Push—is the push function being used? Reset—Should the connection be reset? Synchronizer—should the sequence numbers be synchronized? Finished—end of data sent. Window (used for flow control)—how much data can receiving host accept? Checksum—for error control. Urgent pointer—indicates urgent data follows. Options—include "end of list," "no operation," and "maximum segment size." Padding—forces the header to end on a 32-bit boundary.

bit	0	8	16	24	31
Class A	0	Network ID	Host ID		
Class B	1 0	Network ID		Host ID	
Class C	1 1 0	Network ID			Host ID
Class D	1 1 1 0	Multicast address			
Class E	1 1 1 1	Reserved			

FIGURE 18.7
IP addressing. The class is assigned as a function of how many hosts are at the site. A Class C address of 1100 0010 0001 0010 1000 0010 0100 0111 binary is given a "dot decimal" address of 194.18.130.71. Each eight bits is given its decimal equivalent.

The header also has a checksum for error control.

18.10 IP Addressing

There are five classes of IP addressing as shown in Figure 18.7.

Class A is for very large networks. Their addresses begin with a "0" and have 7 bits in the Network ID. Thus only 127 Class A addresses are possible, and no more Class A addresses are being issued.

Class B is for medium-sized networks, such as campuses. Their addresses begin with "1 0," and 13 bits are available for the Network ID.

Class C is for small networks, and their addresses begin with "1 1 0" and have 21 bits available for the Network ID.

For readability, addresses are given the "dot decimal" designation. The total address is 32 bits and is divided into four octets. Each **octet** is separated by a "." and each octet is separately converted to its decimal equivalent. A Class B address of:

```
1 0 0 0 0 1 0 0 . 0 1 1 0 0 0 0 0 . 0 0 0 0 0 0 1 1 . 0 0 0 0 0 1 1 1
```

has a dot decimal equivalent of 132.96.3.7. A Class A address can range from 0 to 127, a class B address range is from 128 to 191, and a Class C address can range from 192 to 254.

The Internet is running out of addresses, and a committee is designing the extended address format of 128 bits. This will be able to have several unique Internet addresses for every square centimeter of the earth's surface! Or perhaps they are planning ahead for planetary exploration and colonization!

18.11   IP Connections

The combination of the IP address and the port number is called the *socket*. In Figure 18.8 the Source IP Address and port number (and therefore the socket) are 128.12.20.40 4022. The Destination IP Address and port number (and the socket) are 194.6.22.44 21.

18.12   IP Domains

Domain names denote the type of network: ".mil" for military; ".gov" for government, and the like, or the country. Table 18.3 shows examples.

18.13   Address Resolution Protocol (ARP)

A means of converting or mapping the IP address to the Local Area Network (LAN) is needed, and this is done via Address Resolution Protocol (ARP). When ARP cannot find an IP address, it broadcasts an "ARP REQUEST" to all other hosts on the network asking, "Does anyone have this IP address?" If a host does have this IP address, it will return that information to the requester in an "ARP REPLY." Thus the requester will be able to update its ARP table.

18.14   Domain Name Service (DNS)

A somewhat easy-to-remember e-mail address would be something like "smithjhn@ mscd.edu." DNS converts these e-mail addresses to the binary or dot decimal notation. DNS uses a distributed hierarchical database.

If a local server is requested to find an IP address, it will first check its own table. If it is not able to find that IP address, it will then ask the given host for the IP address. If it

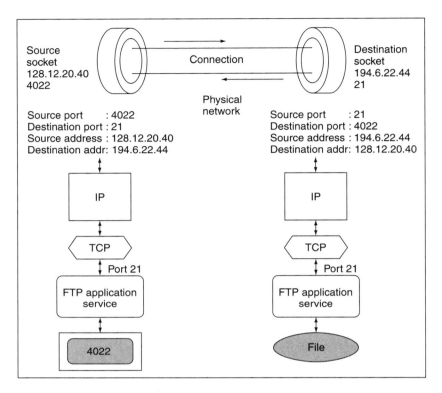

FIGURE 18.8
IP connections.

still cannot find that address, it will then query the root domain server. When the IP address is finally found, it will be stored in the first host memory.

18.15 So What's on the Internet, and How Do We Find It?

The resources available on the Internet are mind-boggling! Libraries and museums are putting their entire collection on the "Net." Finding this information could be overwhelming, but fortunately several tools are available to locate specific information.

Archie (yes, it's named for the cartoon character) uses ftp to access worldwide databases to get file listings, then puts the file listings into a database, and has an easy interface to search that database.

Wide Area Information Server (WAIS) searches databases that have been indexed with key words.

GOPHER originated at the University of Minnesota, home of the Golden Gophers, and is used to "go fer" files and retrieve them. GOPHER is easier to use and friendlier than standard ftp, connects to more resources than ftp, and works from a standard menu. Veronica (also the cartoon character) is the search engine for GOPHER.

TABLE 18.3
Domain Names

.com
   Commercial organization.
.edu
   Educational organization.
.gov
   Government organization.
.mil
   Military organization.
.org
   Organization not included above.
.int
   International organization
.net
   Network support organization.
geographical domains
   .HR (Croatia), .JA (Japan), .CA (Canada)

18.16 World Wide Web (WWW)

The World Wide Web (WWW) is part of the Internet, and Web sites provide information to people accessing the site. Many vendors have their catalogs on their Web sites and allow customers to order merchandise over the Internet using credit cards. Of course strong encryption of the credit card number is used.

Our engineering technology students are taught to access electronic device specification (data) sheets via the manufacturer's Web site.

Our college has general information, its entire catalog, course schedules, faculty biographies and resumes, and departmental news on its Web site. It is possible to register, withdraw from a class, and perform various registration duties via the Web site. Our college will no longer mail final grades but has them available via the Web site. Of course the student must use a password and his or her social security number.

Yahoo and Alta Vista are two search engines to find sites containing the desired information. Netscape's Navigator and Microsoft's Internet Explorer are two commonly used "browsers" to "surf the Web."

The common language that Web sites are written in is HyperText Markup Language (HTML). HTML can make available text, graphic, audio, and video files. JAVA is another language that may be used for Web sites.

18.17 Troubleshooting

TCP/IP network management and troubleshooting differs from packet management. Packet management and troubleshooting worked at the lower levels of the protocol stack: the Physical, Data Link, and Network levels. An IP network may have many Physical networks using many different types of packet switches interconnected by IP gateways.

The IP gateways are what network managers must control. The IP network management must run at the Application level because of the many possible protocols and types of systems within an IP network.

The management and troubleshooting software must be written without regard to the hardware in the IP network. The same protocol must be able to be used for all gateways. However if the problems are at levels beneath the management and troubleshooting software's level, the problem cannot be fixed by the IP administrator. For instance the IP troubleshooter cannot fix a failing operating system or a corrupted routing table or a system needing to be re-booted. The network people must fix these types of problems.

The most popular tool for TCP/IP management is Simple Network Management Protocol (SNMP). Each gateway maintains statistics on its operation in a database called Management Information Base (MIB). Typical gateway data includes:

- The gateway operating system
- Network interfaces
- ARP mappings
- IP software
- ICMP software
- TCP software
- UDP software

Some MIB statistic might include:

- Time since last re-boot
- Number of datagrams received
- Number of datagrams forwarded
- Number of routing failures
- Number of datagrams re-assembled
- Number of datagrams fragmented
- The IP routing table
- Number of messages received and type of message

Many networking systems use a myriad of commands, totally confusing the poor manager. SNMP uses only two: fetch and store. All commands are a variation of these two. For instance, a "get-request" fetches a value from a specific item in MIB. A "get-response" is a reply to a fetch operation. A "set-request" stores a value into MIB.

A *trap* is recording a particular event, such as too many routing failures. When a preset number of routing failures occur, the trap is activated and a message is sent to the network manager.

SUMMARY

I. TCP/IP was created by the U.S. Department of Defense to:
   A. Connect its research computers in a failure resistant network.
   B. Log into remote computers and operate them from hundreds of miles away.

    C. Transfer files between computers.
II. IP uses datagrams.
    A. The data to be sent is divided (segmented) into datagrams.
    B. Each datagram may take a different route to the final destination.
    C. The datagrams may arrive out of order at the final destination.
    D. If a node or a path segment is not functioning, the network system will route datagrams around the non-working node or path.
III. TCP/IP has a four-layer model.
    A. Network Access sublayer 1A.
        1. Corresponds to the OSI RM Physical Layer 1.
        2. Transmission medium can be microwave, optical fiber, coax, satellite, twisted pair, or wireless.
        3. Any medium is therefore "futureproof."
    B. Network Access sublayer 1B.
        1. Equivalent to the OSI RM Data Link Layer and portions of the Network Layer.
        2. Includes X.25, FDDI, and 802.X LAN protocols.
    C. Internet Layer corresponds to the OSI RM's Network Layer 3.
        1. Internet Protocol (IP).
            a. Connectionless, uses datagrams.
                1. Datagrams have Destination Address but no routing information.
                2. Datagrams may take different routes through the network.
                3. Datagrams may arrive out of order; need sequence number to re-assemble them into the proper order.
            b. "Unreliable" because it does minimal error checking.
        2. Address Resolution Protocol (ARP); converts an IP address to a LAN address.
        3. Internet Control Message Protocol (ICMP).
            a. Handles status and error messaging for IP.
            b. "PING" asks for information about an IP address.
            c. "PONG" gives the requested information.
            d. "FINGER" asks what users are logged on.
    D. Transport Layer
        1. Transport Control Protocol (TCP).
            a. Extensive error checking—"reliable."
            b. At the sending host, TCP segments the data into smaller datagrams and adds consecutive sequence numbers.
            c. At the receiving host, TCP re-assembles the datagrams into their proper order, using the datagram sequence numbers.
            d. Connection oriented.
            e. "Reliable"—does end-to-end error checking.
        2. User Datagram Protocol (UDP).
            a. Minimal error checking—"unreliable."
            b. Connectionless
            c. Faster and cheaper than TCP.
    E. Process/Application Layer.
        1. File Transfer Protocol (FTP); transfers files between computers.

2. Telnet; allows the user to log into a remote host (computer) and give commands just as if he or she were seated at a terminal in the same room as the remote host.
3. Domain Name Service (DNS).
   a. IP addresses are 32-bit; each 8-bit portion of the IP address is converted to a decimal number, hence the "dot decimal" notation.
   b. Converts e-mail addresses to the binary or dot decimal notation.
4. Routing Information Protocol (RIP).
5. Simple Mail Transfer Protocol (SMTP); e-mail.

QUESTIONS

1. Why was TCP/IP created? What was TCP/IP's and the Internet's original purpose?
2. What are datagrams? How do they differ from a connection oriented system, such as X.25? Are the datagrams guaranteed to arrive in the same sequence as they were sent? Why or why not? What is the advantage of this?
3. What type of Physical level does TCP/IP always use?
4. What does it mean to say that IP is "unreliable"?
5. What does it mean to say that TCP is "reliable"?
6. What does it mean to say that UDP is "unreliable"? Why would one want to use UDP instead of TCP? What type of error checking does UDP use? What type of error checking does TCP use?
7. What is the "port" number?
8. What are the purposes of "PING" and "PONG," and "FINGER"?
9. What is the purpose of ICMP?
10. What is the purpose of ARP?
11. What does it mean to say that IP is "connectionless" and TCP is "connection oriented"?
12. What is the purpose of FTP?
13. What is the purpose of Telnet?
14. What does SMTP do?
15. What is the purpose of the "time to live" field in IP?
16. Explain the "dot decimal" IP addressing scheme.
17. What is DNS, and what does it do?

19

SYSTEMS NETWORK ARCHITECTURE (SNA)

OBJECTIVES

In this chapter we will discuss:

I. Why was SNA designed? SNA is one of the most widely used network architectures in the world.

II. SNA layers.
  A. SNA was the basis for the OSI RM.
  B. However, it does not correspond exactly to the OSI RM.

III. SNA examples are given.

IV. SNA hardware is discussed.
  A. Front End Processor (FEP) or Front End Controller; offloads communications tasks from the mainframe host.
  B. Cluster Controller; connects between the FEP and peripherals.
  C. Establishment Controller.
     1. Replaces Cluster Controller.
     2. Handles Token Ring LANs, multi-host links, ISDN, APPN, X.21 and X.25, printers, BiSync, and CMIP.

V. SNA operating systems.
  A. Multiple Virtual Systems (MVS).
     1. Not designed or intended for network communications.
     2. Virtual Telecommunications Access Method (VTAM).
        a. Specially designed for communications.
        b. Establishes session.
        c. Needs network defined (full knowledge of network).
        d. System Services Control Point (SSCP) manages the configuration, operation, and sessions of the network.
        e. Performs network management and control.
        f. Physical Units (PUs) and Logical Units (LUs) that VTAM controls are said to be in its "domain."
  B. Network Addressable Unit (NAU). Communications port including:
     1. SSCP.
     2. VTAM.

    3. Logical Units (LUs).
        a. Ports or "windows" providing access to the network.
        b. Controlled by software or firmware in Cluster Controllers or PUs.
        c. Allocate resources to the end users: memory, CPU, databases, sessions, I/O devices.
    4. Physical Units (PUs) are software or firmware.
        a. Actually move the data.
        b. In Cluster Controllers and communications processors.
        c. Do path control; contain node information.
    5. Each Network Addressable Unit (NAU) has a unique network address.
    6. Communications takes place through NAUs.
  C. Network Control Program (NCP); performs routing and flow control between itself and the VTAM, and through the network.
VI. Sessions called Logical Connections.
  A. Between NAUs.
  B. LU-to-LU sessions connect end user application programs.
  C. Control sessions are between two SSCPs, or between SSCPs and PUs and LUs.
VII. Advanced Peer-to-Peer Network (APPN).
  A. Necessitated by the advent of small computers.
  B. Designed to support distributed processing.
  C. Sometimes called "New SNA."
VIII. Bit oriented framing.
  A. Greatly superior to Binary Synchronous Control (BSC).
  B. All types are very similar; if you understand one, you understand all of them.
  C. HDLC (High level Data Link Control).
  D. LAP/B (Link Access Protocol/Balanced) used in X.25 and Frame Relay.
  E. SDLC (Synchronous Data Link Control) developed by IBM for SNA.
    1. Bit oriented.
    2. Full duplex.
    3. Seven frames can be in the transmission system simultaneously.
    4. Acknowledgments, data, and polling can be combined in one frame.
    5. Frame types:
        a. Information.
        b. Supervisory.
        c. Unnumbered.
    6. Frame transmission examples are given:
        a. Without error.
        b. With an error showing error recovery.

19.1   SNA Systems Network Architecture (SNA)

SNA was introduced by IBM in 1974 to connect computing resources over a wide area. The first host machines were IBM 360/70 mainframe computers. The initial use was to provide an airline database for travel agents. There were over 40,000 licensed sites worldwide as of 1994. It is one of the most widely used network architectures in the world.

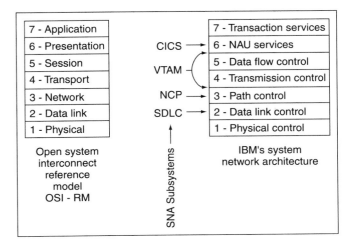

FIGURE 19.1
SNA and the OSI RM.

19.2 SNA Layers

SNA is a layered system with distributed processing and resource sharing. SNA's layers were the basis for the Open System International Reference Model (OSI RM), and of course there is a strong resemblance between the two. There are several Transport Layer protocols available for various applications. Figure 19.1 shows the OSI RM and the corresponding SNA layers. Several parts of SNA are shown in their respective layers. The reader is encouraged to refer to this figure as we discuss the various parts of SNA.

19.3 SNA Network Examples

19.3.1 "Simple" SNA Network

Figure 19.2 shows a very "simple" SNA network with the hardware. At the top is the host mainframe computer. Input / output (I/O) channels connect to local "dumb" terminals and to the Front End Processor (FEP). The FEP can connect to the Public Switched Telephone Network (PSTN) via a modem, then to a Cluster Controller, and finally to peripherals. The FEP will connect to **Digital Service Units (DSU)** interfacing to high-speed communication lines. At the other end of the high-speed link will be another DSU Cluster Controller and finally peripherals and perhaps LANs.

19.3.2 "Typical" SNA System

Figure 19.3 shows another "simple" SNA hardware configuration. Again the host mainframe connects to an I/O channel. The I/O channel connects to a Cluster Controller of the 327X product family and then to local terminals of the 3270 family. The FEP also connects to a DSU and then to a high-speed digital line, such as T-1 or SONET. A 37XX

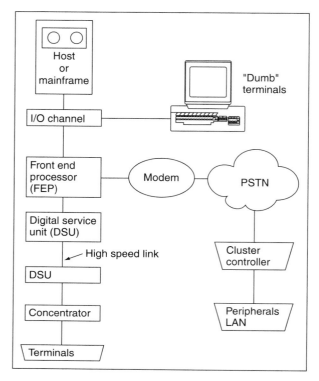

FIGURE 19.2
SNA network (simplified.)

family Concentrator at the digital line destination feeds the data to clustered terminals. The FEP connects to the PSTN via a modem, and hence to many possible end users such as LANs and via Cluster Controllers to peripherals.

19.4 SNA Hardware

Table 19.1 summarizes the hardware functions.

19.4.1 Front End Processor

The **Front End Processor (FEP),** also known as a Communication Controller, is the interface between the mainframe and the communications networks. The FEP offloads communications tasks from the mainframe host. The FEP's functions include routing, flow control, error detection and recovery, buffering of data from slow-speed channels, and disassembly and assembly of packets.

The IBM part numbers for FEPs are 3705, 3720, 3745, and 3725.

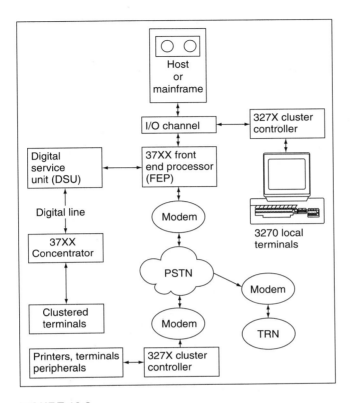

FIGURE 19.3
"Typical" SNA system.

TABLE 19.1
SNA hardware

Host computer offloads communications responsibilities to FEP through I/O channel
Front End Processor (FEP)
    Error control
    Disassemble, re-assemble packets
    Data buffering—high-speed to low-speed; low-speed to high-speed
Cluster Controllers communicate between FEP and peripherals
    Use SDLC to FEP
    Use BiSync to peripherals

19.4.2 Cluster Controller

Cluster Controllers are connected between the FEP and peripherals such as printers and terminals. The Cluster Controller communicates with the terminals via BiSync and with FEP via the more efficient SDLC. We will study SDLC later in this chapter. It is very similar to HDLC (High-level Data Link Control) used in other protocols.

19.4.3 Establishment Controller

The Establishment Controller has replaced the Cluster Controller. The Establishment Controller handles Token Ring LANs, multi-host links, ISDN, APPN, X.21 and X.25, printers, BiSync, CMIP, and many other protocols and systems.

19.5 SNA Operating Systems

Table 19.2 summarizes the SNA operating systems and software, and Figure 19.4 shows where the software is located.

"Multiple Virtual Systems" (MVS) is an often used host operating system. Most operating systems are not designed or intended for network communications. Designing a mainframe operating system for communications would be diluting the power and speed of the machine. The network communications is offloaded to the Virtual Telecommunications Access Method (VTAM), an operating system especially designed for communications.

19.5.1 VTAM

VTAM is a communication operating system that runs under the operating system MVS. VTAM establishes the sessions but needs the **Physical Units (PUs), Logical Units (LUs),** and applications defined. VTAM interfaces with the SNA communications network and a Teleprocessing Monitor (TM). VTAM may be considered to be in Layer 5, the NAU Services Layer, and Layer 4, the Transmission Control (see Figure 19.1). A subset of VTAM is System Services Control Point (SSCP). SSCP manages the configuration, operation, and sessions of the network.

VTAM also performs network management and control. The PUs and LUs that VTAM controls are said to be in its "domain."

19.5.2 SSCP

SSCP is a subset of VTAM. It establishes sessions, de-activates (tears down) sessions, schedules error recovery, and supports devices directly attached to the host.

TABLE 19.2
SNA software

Network Addressable Unit (NAU)—logical input/output port
   Logical Unit (LU)—allocates resources: schedules memory, computer time, session time, I/O devices
   Physical Unit (PU)
      Actually software!—originally patchboards, hence "physical"
      Manages and controls LUs—resource manager; requests downloads; diagnostics; configuration
System Services Control Point (SSCP)
   Network Addressable Unit (NAU)—subset of VTAM; exists in host
   Controls PUs logically attached to itself
   Controls LUs logically attached to itself
   Initializes, de-activates network

19.5.3 Network Addressable Unit (NAU)

A **Network Addressable Unit (NAU)** is a communications port including SSCP, VTAM, Logical Units (LUs), and Physical Units (PUs). Communications takes place through NAUs. Each NAU has a unique network address.

19.5.4 Logical Units

Logical Units (LUs) can be thought of as the ports or "windows" providing access to the network. LUs are controlled by software or firmware in Cluster Controllers or PUs.

LUs allocate resources to the end users. The resources include memory, CPUs, databases, sessions, and I/O devices.

19.5.5 Physical Units (PU)

Physical Units (PUs) are actually software or firmware that move the data. The PUs are in Cluster Controllers and communications processors. PUs do data path control and contain node information for this.

The term *physical* came about because the first device programming was done by patch panels and switches.

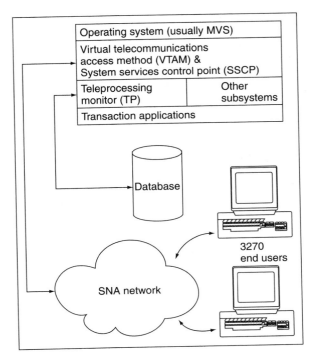

FIGURE 19.4
SNA operating systems and software.

19.5.6 Network Control Program (NCP)

The Network Control Program (NCP) performs routing and flow control between itself and the VTAM, and through the network.

19.6 Sessions

Sessions are called Logical Connections and are between NAUs. LU-to-LU sessions connect end user application programs. Control sessions are between two SSCPs, or between SSCPs on PUs and LUs. See Table 19.3.

19.7 Advanced Peer-to-Peer Network (APPN)

With the advent of affordable small computers, distributed process became practical, and SNA was no longer the only kid on the block. A new network architecture was needed, and the result was **Advanced Peer-to-Peer Network (APPN).** APPN was designed to support distributed processing and is sometimes called "New SNA." Mainframe machines and FEPs are not needed, and this makes SNA much less expensive. APPN supports LANs, PCs, and the IBM AS/400, a distributed processing minicomputer.

19.8 Bit Oriented Framing

There are several types of bit oriented framing: HDLC (High level Data Link Control), LAP/B (Link Access Protocol/Balanced) used in X.25 and Frame Relay, and SDLC (Synchronous Data Link Control) developed by IBM for SNA. These are greatly superior to Binary Synchronous Control (BiSync or BSC), which they have replaced. These Data Link Level 2 protocols are very similar, and we will examine the frame structures in the next figures. BSC was discussed in chapter 15.

19.8.1 Synchronous Data Link Control (SDLC)

The DLL protocol is Synchronous Data Link Control (SDLC). It is bit oriented rather than byte or character oriented, as with BiSync. BiSync is half duplex, but SDLC is full duplex, and as many as seven frames can be in the transmission system simultaneously. Ac-

TABLE 19.3
Sessions

Logical connection between NAUs
LU-to-LU—connect end user application programs
Control sessions
　Between SSCPs
　Between SSCPs and PUs and LUs

knowledgments, data, and polling can be combined in one frame. This makes SDLC more efficient than BiSync.

19.8.1.1 SDLC Frame Figure 19.5 shows the SDLC frame format. The frame begins and ends with a flag, a binary "01111110" or hexadecimal "7E" byte. Special techniques are used to prevent confusion if that particular "7E" flag bit pattern is present in the address or data fields.

The address field identifies the primary and/or secondary transmission or receiving stations. The Frame Check Sequence (FRC) field is a Cyclic Redundant Code (CRC) to error-check the frame from the beginning of the address field. CRC detects errors but cannot correct them. Error recovery methods usually ask for a repeat of the frames containing an error. CRC is discussed in Appendix A1.

19.8.1.2 SDLC Control Field There are three types of SDLC frames: information, supervisory, and unnumbered.

Note that if the last control field bit is a "0," the frame is an information frame. If the last two bits are a "0 1," the frame is a supervisory frame. If the last two bits are a "1 1," the frame is an unnumbered frame. See Figure 19.6.

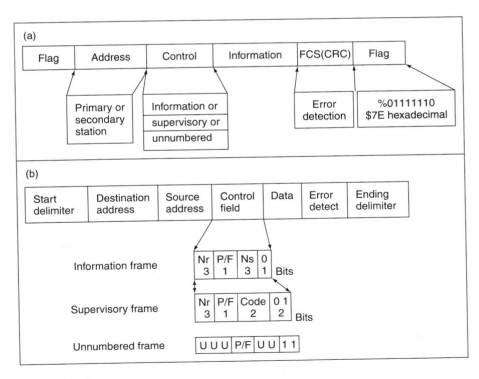

FIGURE 19.5
SDLC frame.

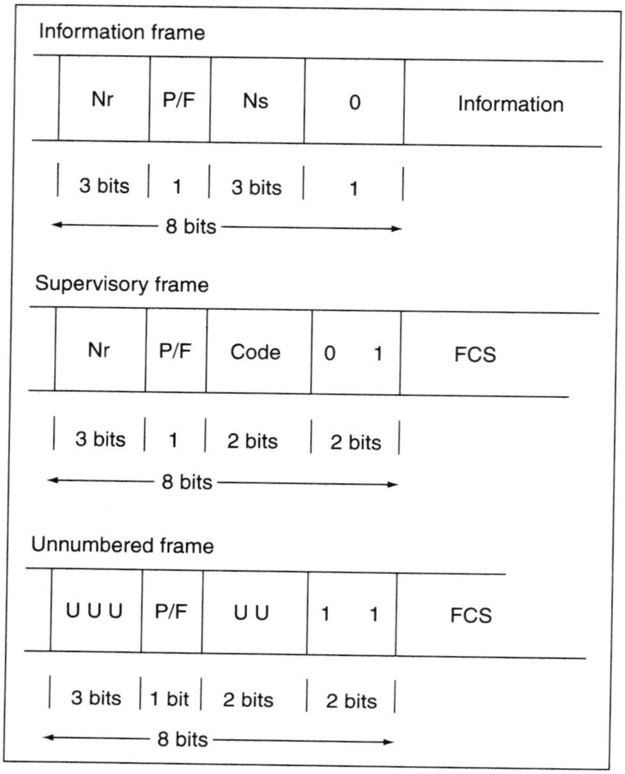

FIGURE 19.6
SDLC control field (three frame types).

Nr is the number of the next frame *expected,* not the frame number already received. Ns is the number of the frame sent. There are 3 bits for the Ns and Nr fields. This implies there can be 8 frames in the system before a receiver response is necessary. Actually only 7 can be accommodated at one time. If there were 8 frames in the system, an ambiguity is possible with the next transmitted frame. Assume there are 8 frames in the system numbered 0 through 7. The next transmitted frame would be numbered 0. The system has no way to distinguish between the first 0 frame and the second 0 frame. For satellite systems with their long delays, the Ns and Nr are 7 bits each, allowing a frame capacity of 127.

The P/F (Poll/Final) bit tells the receiver the frame is making an inquiry (Poll) or is the (F) Final frame in the sequence. If the P/F bit is set to Poll, the sender is asking for a response; i.e., this is not the last frame.

19.8.2 HDLC Examples

Figure 19.7 is an error-free "bounce" diagram showing the Ns and Nr usage.

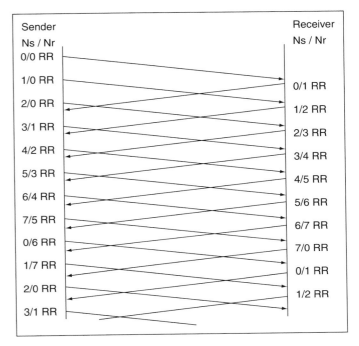

FIGURE 19.7
HDLC (bounce diagram).

The Left sender sends a frame with Ns = 0. Left sender has not received a frame from Right sender. The next frame expected from Right sender to Left sender is number 0, or Ns. Left sender is *expecting* frame number 0, so Nr = 0.

Note that the Ns and Nr numbers are consecutive from 0 through 7 and roll over from 7 to 0. Remember that Nr is the frame number expected, not the frame number actually received. The reason Nr is the next frame expected is to cover the possibility of no response from the receiver. Nr must always have some value. If Nr is the frame actually received, the sender will think that a frame has actually been received. If Nr is the next frame expected and never changes, the sender will stop sending frames after 7 frames have been sent without an acknowledgment. The sender will know that a problem exists with the network or receiver.

In Figure 19.8, frame 4 from Left sender is corrupted by noise. Right receiver notes via the CRC that a frame received is corrupted. Right receiver does not have to know what frame number is corrupted, because Right receiver has been keeping track of Nr = next frame expected and will send the same Nr = 4 again to Left sender.

Left sender will look at the Nr = 4 from Right sender and will re-transmit frame 4 with Ns = 4. The frame numbers will continue as before. All the successive frames will be re-transmitted, even if they had been received without error.

This error control algorithm is called "go back N" frames, and all frames including the corrupted frame and all succeeding frames will be re-transmitted. Note that this is not

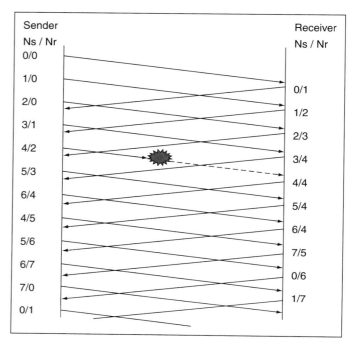

FIGURE 19.8
HDLC (bounce diagram with error).

an error correction method, but rather an error control method. Other error control methods of re-transmitting only the corrupted frame exist but are not used very often.

19.9 Management and Troubleshooting

NetView is used to manage SNA. NetView combines earlier management tools such as Network Communications Control Facility (NCCF) and Network Problem Determination Application (NPDA). Other parts of NetView are Network Logical Data Manager (NLDM), the browse facility, the status monitor, the graphics monitor, and Resource Object Data Manager (RODM).

- *NCCF* provides remote operation. Commands are entered; and VTAM, NetView, and MVS can be controlled at remote sites.
- *NPDA* manages hardware. It collects and maintains data about the network. The troubleshooter can access data from throughout the network.
- *NLDM* is the session monitor. The troubleshooter can determine equipment availability, its configuration, errors, the explicit route, the virtual route, response time, and the session partner, and as well as trace messages.
- The *browse facility* allows the troubleshooter to look at the data log, VTAM device definitions, command lists, and systemwide definitions.

- The *status monitor* collects information about the network. It displays the information in columnar form or graphically.
- The *graphic monitor* is a graphics display of the network operations. Troublesome areas can be highlighted in color to aid the troubleshooter.
- *RODM* is the database for storing and retrieving execution information, configuration information, and status information.
- *NetView* also handles alerts and does response time monitoring. Alerts use *Network Management Vector Transport (NMVT)* protocol.
- The *Response Time Monitor (RTM)* measures the time for data to go to a destination and an Attention Identifier (AID) to return.

SUMMARY

I. SNA was introduced by IBM in 1974 to connect computing resources over a wide area.
   A. The first host machines were IBM 360/70 mainframe computers.
   B. Over 40,000 licensed sites worldwide (1994).
   C. Layered system with distributed processing and resource sharing.
   D. SNA's layers were the basis for the Open System International Reference Model (OSI RM).
II. SNA hardware.
   A. The FEP (Front End Processor) or Communication Controller.
      1. The interface between the mainframe and the communications networks.
      2. Offloads communications tasks from the mainframe host.
      3. Routing.
      4. Flow control.
      5. Error detection and recovery.
      6. Buffering of data from slow-speed channels.
      7. Disassembly and assembly of packets.
   B. Cluster Controllers.
      1. Connected between the FEP and peripherals (printers, terminals).
      2. Communicate with the terminals via BiSync.
      3. Communicate with FEP via the more efficient SDLC.
   C. Establishment Controller.
      1. Replaced the Cluster Controller.
      2. Handles Token Ring LANs, multi-host links, ISDN, APPN, X.21, X.25, printers, BiSync, and CMIP.
III. SNA operating systems.
   A. Multiple Virtual Systems (MVS).
      1. Host operating system.
      2. Not intended for network communications.
      3. Offloads communications to VTAM.
   B. Virtual Telecommunications Access Method (VTAM).
      1. Operating system specially designed for communications.

2. Establishes the sessions.
    a) Needs the Physical Units, Logical Units, and applications defined.
    b) PUs and LUs are said to be in its "domain."
3. Interfaces with the SNA communications network.
4. Performs network management and control.
5. Interfaces with Teleprocessing Monitor (TM).
6. Considered to be in Layer 5 (NAU Services Layer) and Layer 4 (the Transmission Control).
7. A subset.
8. System Services Control Point (SSCP) manages the configuration, operation, and sessions of the network.

C. Network Addressable Unit (NAU).
1. Communications port including SSCP, VTAM, Logical Units (LU), and Physical Units (PU).
2. Communications takes place through NAUs.
3. Each NAU has a unique network address.

D. Logical Units (LUs).
1. Thought of as the ports or "windows" providing access to the network.
2. Controlled by software or firmware in Cluster Controllers or PUs.
3. LUs allocate resources to the end users: memory, CPUs, databases, sessions, and I/O devices.

E. Physical Units (PUs) are software or firmware.
1. Actually move the data.
2. In Cluster Controllers and communications processors.
3. Data path control.
4. Contain node information to do path control.

F. Network Control Program (NCP).
1. Performs routing.
2. Performs flow control between itself and the VTAM, and through the network.

IV. Sessions.
A. Called Logical Connections.
B. Between NAUs.
1. LU-to-LU sessions connect end user application programs.
2. Control sessions are between two SSCPs, or between SSCPs and PUs and LUs.

V. Advanced Peer-to-Peer Network (APPN).
A. Designed to support distributed processing.
B. Sometimes called "New SNA."
C. Mainframe machines and FEPs are not needed.
D. Much less expensive.
E. Supports LANs, PCs, and the AS/400, a distributed processing mini-computer.

VI. SDLC (Synchronous Data Link Control).
A. Developed for SNA.
B. Bit oriented.

C. Acknowledgments, data, and polling can be combined in one frame.
D. Frame types:
  1. Information.
  2. Supervisory.
  3. Unnumbered.

QUESTIONS

1. Who developed SNA? When? Why?
2. What is the relationship between SNA and the OSI RM?
3. How is SDLC different from BiSync? How is this better?
4. What is VTAM, and what does it do? Why is VTAM used for communications and not the host and its operating system?
5. What is SSCP, and what does it do?
6. What is the FEP, and what does it do?
7. What are Cluster Controllers, and what do they do?
8. Give three examples of NAU.
9. What is an LU, and what does it do?
10. What is a PU, and what does it do? Why is it called "physical"?
11. What is the NCP, and what does it do?
12. What is a session? What are the types of sessions?
13. What is APPN, and how does it differ from SNA?
14. Draw an HDLC "bounce" diagram with frame Ns = 2 from the right side being corrupted by noise.
15. What is the purpose of the P/F bit?
16. Is Nr the number of the frame received? Why?
17. Why are Ns and Nr 7 bits each for satellite systems?
18. What is the name of the error control algorithm used by HDLC? How does it work?

A1

CYCLIC REDUNDANT CODE (CRC)

OBJECTIVES

In this appendix we will discuss:

I. The CRC is an error detection method.
II. The CRC is implemented in hardware with shift registers and exclusive ORs (EXORs).
III. We shall see examples of the CRC.
IV. We shall see that the CRC is a very good error detection system.

In the fine tradition of "one-up manship" the **CRC** has been called the Frame Check Sequence (FCS) in various protocols. All these terms still mean the same thing, an error detection scheme. CRC is almost always a hardware implementation, because the hardware is quite simple and faster than software. A shift register is modified by strategically placing exclusive ORs (EXORs) between the flip flops of the shift register. The exact placement of these EXORs is the subject of deep mathematics, which we will studiously avoid.

A1.1 CRC Mathematical Example

Let's look at Figure A1.1 to see a mathematical example of CRC. The data to be sent is

```
1 0 1 1 0 1 0 1 0
```

A polynomial is "divided" into the data. The polynomial describes the placement of the EXORs in the shift register. We'll see how this placement works later in this appendix.

The polynomial does not do a true divide. Where we would normally do a subtraction, we will do an exclusive OR (EXOR). Also the quotient is of no use to us, and therefore we do not use it. We are interested only in the remainder.

Let's go through the example. The first (leftmost) bit of the information is a "1." Therefore the first bit of the quotient is a one. The four-bit polynomial divisor is put below the first four bits of the data and EXORed. The leftmost result is a "0" and is now discarded.

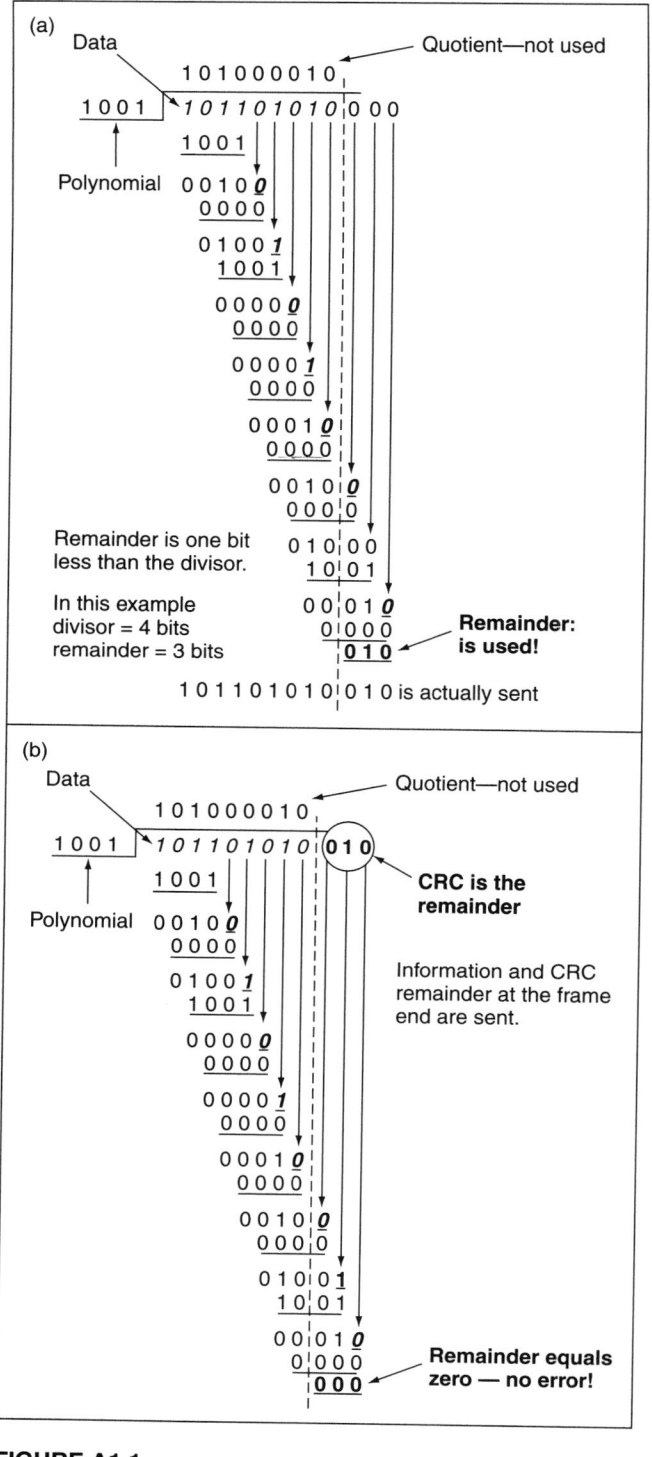

FIGURE A1.1
CRC example (a) at transmitter and (b) at receiver.

The next bit of the data is dropped down into the EXOR result. The process is repeated over and over.

The polynomial divisor is four bits. The remainder we are interested in is one fewer bits than the polynomial divisor, or three bits. We stop when we get the three-bit remainder "0 1 0." The three-bit remainder is the CRC. The remainder is always one bit less than the divisor. Note that this "division" is an EXOR and a shift. The hardware consists of EXORs and flip flops in a modified shift register. What is actually sent is the data, followed by the three-bit CRC remainder.

The data plus the CRC remainder arrive at the receiver. Both are subjected to the same "division" process using the same polynomial divisor. If the remainder is "0 0 0," the entire transmission, data plus CRC, is regarded as error-free. The student is encouraged to place an error or errors into the data and/or the CRC. The remainder will be non-zero, indicating an error. A detected error will initiate the error handling routine, usually the "go back N" method.

A1.2 CRC Hardware Implementation

Figure A1.2 shows the hardware implementation of the CRC example. Each "1" in the polynomial divisor indicates where an EXOR is placed. Table A1.1 gives common polynomial divisions for 8-bit, 12-bit, 16-bit, and 32-bit CRCs.

A1.3 How Good is CRC?

CRC is a very powerful error detection method, yet it is very simple to implement in hardware. But how good is it? Table A1.2 gives us statistics. A 16-bit CRC has the maximum error escape probability of 30 times per million.

A1.4 Problems

A1.4.1 Given data of "1 1 0 0 1 0 1 0" and a divisor of "1 1 0," find the remainder.
A1.4.2 Given data of "1 0 1 1 1 0 1 0" and a divisor of "1 1 0," find the remainder.

FIGURE A1.2
CRC hardware.

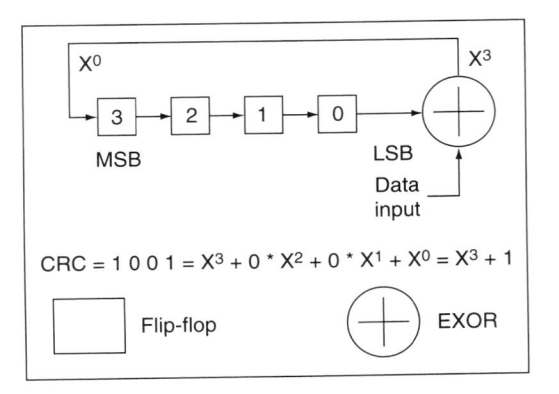

$$CRC = 1\ 0\ 0\ 1 = X^3 + 0 * X^2 + 0 * X^1 + X^0 = X^3 + 1$$

TABLE A1.1
Common polynomials

CRC-8
  $X^8 + X^2 + X^1 + 1$
CRC-12
  $X^{12} + X^{11} + X^3 + X^2 + 1$
CRC-16
  $X^{16} + X^{15} + X^2 + 1$
CRC-CCITT
  $X^{16} + X^{12} + X^5 + 1$
CRC-32
  $X^{32} + X^{26} + X^{23} + X^{22} + X^{16} + X^{12} + X^{11} + X^{10} + X^8 + X^7 + X^5 + X^4 + X^2 + X^1 + 1$

TABLE A1.2

Error Type	16-bit CRC Detection Probability	32-bit CRC Detection Probability
Single bit	1.0	1.0
Two-bit error	1.0	1.0
Odd number of bits in error	1.0	1.0
Error burst < length of CRC (16 or 32 bits)	1.0	1.0
Error burst = length of CRC (16 or 32 bits)	$1.0 - 2^{-15} \sim 3.05 \times 10^{-5}$	$1.0 - 2^{-31} \sim 4.6566 \times 10^{-10}$
Error burst > length of CRC (16 or 32 bits)	$1.0 - 2^{-16} \sim 1.53 \times 10^{-6}$	$1.0 - 2^{-32} \sim 2.3282 \times 10^{-10}$

The Cyclic Redundancy Code (Check) (CRC) is a powerful error detection system. How good is it? According to Stallings' *Local and Metropolitan Area Networks*, 4th Edition McMillan 1996 it is *very good!*

A2

DECIBELS AND POWER

OBJECTIVES

In this appendix we will discuss:

I. Decibels (dB) are ratios; dB can use addition instead of multiplication.
II. Decibels are used to express gains and losses.
III. Power levels referenced to 1 milliwatt are expressed in terms of dBm.
  A. Transmitter, signal generator, or emitter power output can be expressed in dBm.
  B. Receiver and detector sensitivities can be expressed in dBm.
  C. Total system gain can be calculated using dB.
  D. System output power can be calculated using dBm and dB.
  E. System margins can be calculated using dBm and dB.
IV. Decibels can be used to express a voltage ratio.
V. If the input voltage and output voltage are not into the same input resistance and output resistance loads, one should convert the input and output voltages to powers before finding the system gain in dB.

A2.1   Decibels

In communications systems input and output signal levels are usually measured in power. Power is much easier to measure than voltage or current.

Ratios of powers are important for specifying gains and losses. Engineers use **decibels (dB)** to express power gains and losses. Decibels are logarithms of power ratios, and therefore power levels can be multiplied by merely adding decibels. Decibels are a carry-over from pre-calculator days when multiplication and division were difficult but addition and subtraction were relatively easy. Let's look at a few examples.

$$dB \text{ (power)} = 10 \log_{10} \frac{power_{out}}{power_{in}} \qquad \textbf{(Equation A2.1)}$$

EXAMPLE A2.1 If the input power to an amplifier is 0.5 watts and its output is 4 watts, the gain in decibels is

$$\text{dB (power gain)} = 10 \log_{10}\left(\frac{4 \text{ watts}}{0.5 \text{ watt}}\right) = 9.03 \text{ dB} \quad \textbf{(Equation A2.2)}$$

EXAMPLE A2.2 If the power into an attenuator is 12 milliwatts (mW) and the power out was 3 mW, the loss (negative gain) in dB is

$$\text{dB [power gain/loss]} = 10 \log_{10}\left(\frac{3 \text{ mW}}{12 \text{ mW}}\right) = 10 \log_{10}(0.25) = -6.02 \text{ dB} \quad \textbf{(Equation A2.3)}$$

Now assume the amplifier and attenuator were connected in series in a small system. The system gain would be

Total system gain (dB) = amplifier gain + attenuator gain

$$= 9.03 \text{ dB} + (-6.02 \text{ dB}) = 3.01 \text{ dB system gain} \quad \textbf{(Equation A2.4)}$$

The same result could have been obtained by multiplying the gains.

EXAMPLE A2.3
$$\text{Total system gain} = (4 \text{ watts/0.5 watt}) \times (3 \text{ mW/12 mW}) = 2.0$$
$$\text{Total system gain (dB)} = 10 \log_{10}(2.0) = 3.01 \text{ dB}$$

A2.2 dBm or Decibels Referenced to One MilliWatt

As we have seen, decibels are a ratio of powers and are therefore unitless. To make our calculations easier engineers have devised a scheme to express power levels in a decibel format. All the following power levels are referenced to 1 milliwatt of power. That is, the denominator in the decibel equation is 1 milliwatt. The units of power are decibels referenced to 1 milliwatt, or **dBm.**

EXAMPLE A2.4 What is the power level in dBm of an oscillator with an output power of 20 mW?

$$\text{Output power (dBm)} = 10 \log_{10}\left(\frac{20 \text{ mW}}{1 \text{ mW}}\right) = 10 \log_{10}(20) = 13 \text{ dBm}$$

A2.2.1 Receiver Sensitivities

Receiver sensitivities are expressed in dBm. Fiber optic detectors might have a sensitivity of -40 dBm, while a cellular radio receiver could have a sensitivity of -115 dBm.

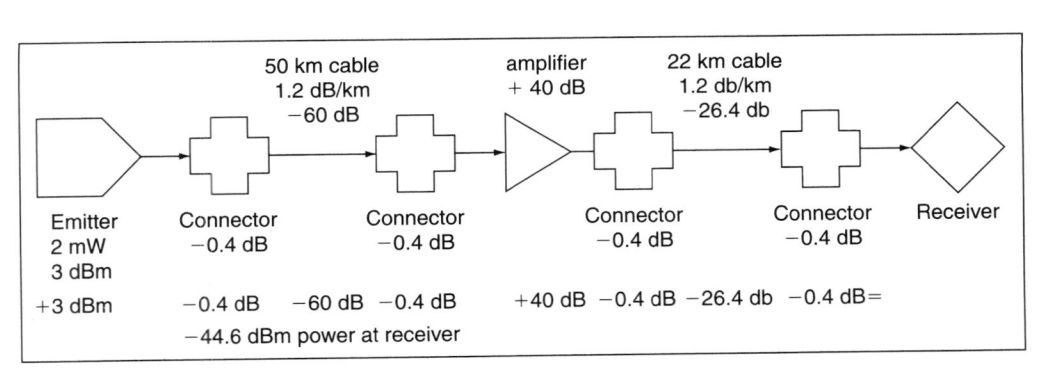

FIGURE A2.1
Optical fiber communications systems power budget. Power at receiver = antilog (−44.6 dBm/10) = 34.7 × 10^{-6} mW = 34.7 nW. The signal required at the receiver for adequate BER is −49 dBm. The signal margin is −44.6 dBm − (−49 dBm) = + 4.4 dB.

The greater the minus number, the greater the sensitivity, or the less power needed for an adequate signal.

EXAMPLE A2.5   The power level of the fiber optic detector mentioned above is −40 dBm. The absolute sensitivity is

$$\text{Power level (mW)} = \text{antilog}_{10}\left(\frac{-40 \text{ dBm}}{10}\right) = 10^{-4}\text{mW} = 0.1 \ \mu\text{W}$$

EXAMPLE A2.6   The power level of the cellular receiver mentioned above is −115 dBm. The absolute sensitivity is

$$\text{Power level (mW)} = \text{antilog}\left(\frac{-115 \text{ dBm}}{10}\right) = 3.16 \times 10^{-12} \text{ mW} = 3.16 \text{ aW (attowatt)}$$

EXAMPLE A2.7   In the communications system of Figure A2.1, the transmitter output is 2 mW or +3 dBm. The transmitter output goes through a connector, into a 50-Km cable, into a second connector, and into a 40-dB amplifier. The amplifier output passes through a connector into a 22-Km cable, and hence through a connector to the receiver. The receiver sensitivity is −49 dBm. The connector losses are −0.4 dB, and the cable loss is 1.2 dB/km.
    Will enough energy get to the receiver to be above the threshold? If not, how much amplification is required to get the incident energy up to the receiver threshold? As we see from the example, we have enough signal to have a 4.4-dB margin.

A2.2.2 Decibels and Voltage

In most communications systems power is easier to measure than either voltage or current. However oscilloscopes are often used in audio systems, and they measure voltage. Decibels are handled differently using voltage rather than power. Remember the formulas for power.

$$P = VI = I^2R = \frac{V^2}{R} \qquad \textbf{(Equation A2.5)}$$

Notice the voltage squared term in the last equation. That means we have to modify our decibel equation as shown.

$$dB = 2 \times 10 \log_{10} \frac{V\,out}{V\,in} = 20 \log_{10} \frac{V\,out}{V\,in} \qquad \textbf{(Equation A2.6)}$$

Notice we must multiply the logarithm of the ratios by 20 instead of 10, because of the voltage squared term.

EXAMPLE A2.8

Given an amplifier with 0.5 mV input and 12 volts output, what is its gain in dB?

$$\text{Gain (dB)} = 20 \log_{10} \frac{12}{0.5 \times 10 - 3} = 20 \log (24{,}000) = 87.6 \text{ dB}$$

EXAMPLE A2.9

There is one "gotcha" using voltage ratios to calculate dB gain. Remember $P = \frac{V^2}{R}$. The resistance R must be the same at the input and the output. Many communications systems operate with the input load and output load the same value. A common value is 50 ohms. However some amplifiers transform impedances.

Given an amplifier with an input impedance of 2K ohms and an output impedance of 50 ohms, the input voltage is 0.5 mV and the output voltage is 12 volts. What is the power gain in dB?

In this case it is best to convert the input and output voltages to power and proceed with the original dB formula.

$$P_{out} = \frac{12^2}{50} = 2.88 \text{ watts}$$

$$P_{in} = \frac{(0.5 \times 10^{-3})^2}{2 \times 10^3} = 1.25 \times 10^{-10} \text{ W}$$

$$\text{Gain (dB)} = 10 \log_{10} \left(\frac{2.88 \text{ W}}{1.25 \times 10^{-10} \text{W}} \right) = 10 \log_{10} (2.3 \times 10^{10}) = 103.6 \text{ dB}$$

A2.3 Final Comments

The "Bel" was named in honor of Alexander Graham Bell, the patent holder on the original telephone. In practice the Bel was too small a unit, and therefore the multiplier "10" was added.

A2.4 Problems

A2.4.1 Given the following power input and outputs, find the gain (or loss −negative gain) in dB, or the missing power:

Power In	Power Out	Gain (dB)
1 watt	12 watts	
0.5 watt	220 watts	
2 mW	2.2 watts	
1.2 watts	22 mW	
	3 watts	23
0.5 mW		28

A2.4.2 Given the following dBm and power, find the missing dBm or power.

dBm	Power
16.4	
33.3	
−33.3	
	2,200 mW
	0.4 mW
	42 μW

A2.4.3 Find the missing gain in dB, or the missing voltage.

V_{in}	V_{out}	Gain dB
0.5 V	23.5 V	
2.2 V	5,020 V	
22 μV	456 mV	
	25 V	42
28 mV		−21.2

A3

QUEUE THEORY

OBJECTIVES

In this appendix we will discuss:

   I. Why we use queue theory or traffic theory.

  II. The Erlang is a measure of traffic intensity or density.

     A. One must use the same time units when computing the traffic density.

     B. Erlang traffic theory depends on a Poisson arrival rate.

 III. Another measure of traffic density is the **Hundred Call Seconds (CCS) per hour.**

     A. The time units are more convenient.

     B. Arrival rate is the number of calls during a busy time in seconds (NCBH).

     C. Often used by telcos.

  IV. There are 36 CCS in 1.0 Erlang.

   V. In Erlang C, requests are put into a queue and all calls will eventually be serviced.

  VI. In Erlang B, if the system is unable to handle a call request, the call is blocked (not serviced).

 VII. AT&T's traffic policy in times of disaster.

A3.1 How many?

How does a telco, LAN, or WAN provider decide how many lines or trunks or multiplexers to install? How do they analyze the potential traffic to neither have too few lines and trunks and not be able to take advantage of the market, nor overbuild and have too many expensive lines and trunks not earning their keep? The answer is **queue theory.** The term *queue* is used in England and most of the world. The American equivalent is "line," or to "wait in line." The British say "in queue."

A3.2 Traffic Intensity

A3.2.1 Erlangs

A measure of traffic is the **Erlang,** named in honor of the Danish mathematician A. K. Erlang.

$$E = \lambda H \qquad \text{(Equation A3.1)}$$

where E is the traffic in Erlangs, λ is the arrival time in arrivals (new calls) per unit time, and H is the holding time. H and λ must use the same time units. Some authors use

$$\mu = \frac{1}{H} \text{ or } H = \frac{1}{\mu}$$

The net effect is certainly not to clarify but to further confuse the long-suffering student. This new equation is

$$E = \frac{\lambda}{\mu} \qquad \text{(Equation A3.1.1)}$$

We will use H is this book.

EXAMPLE A3.1

Given an arrival time of 7 calls per hour and a holding time of 4 minutes (240 seconds, or 1 / 15 hour), what is the traffic in Erlangs? There are 3,600 seconds in 1 hour.

$$E = \frac{7 \text{ calls}}{\text{hour}} \times \frac{\text{hour}}{60 \text{ minutes}} \times \frac{4 \text{ minutes}}{\text{call}} = 0.4666 \text{ Erlang}$$

or

$$E = \frac{7 \text{ calls}}{\text{hour}} \times \frac{\text{hour}}{3,600 \text{ seconds}} \times \frac{240 \text{ seconds}}{\text{call}} = 0.4666 \text{ Erlang}$$

Note that the same time units were used in both examples.

If a channel is completely occupied by one call for an entire hour ($\lambda = 60$ minutes), the traffic intensity is 1.0 Erlang.

EXAMPLE A3.2

$$E = \frac{1 \text{ call}}{\text{hour}} \times \frac{1 \text{ hour}}{\text{call}} = 1.0 \text{ Erlang}$$

A3.2.2 Hundred Call Seconds (CCS) per Hour

Telcos often use the Hundred Call Seconds (CCS) per hour to measure traffic intensity.

$$CCS = NCBH \times \frac{H}{100} \qquad \text{(Equation A3.2)}$$

where NCBH is the number of calls during a busy time in seconds, or arrival rate. NCBH is the same as the arrival rate λ as discussed in the previous section.

EXAMPLE A3.3 Given an arrival time of 7 calls per hour and a holding time of 4 minutes (240 seconds), what is the traffic in CCS? There are 3,600 seconds in 1 hour.

$$CCS = \frac{7 \text{ calls}}{\text{hour}} \times \frac{240 \text{ seconds}}{\text{call}} \times \frac{1}{100} = 16.8 \text{ CCS}$$

EXAMPLE A3.4 If a channel is completely occupied by one call (NCBH = 1.0) for an entire hour (holding time is 3,600 seconds), the traffic intensity is 36.0 CCS.

$$CCS = 1.0 \text{ NCBH} \times \frac{3,600 \text{ seconds}}{100} = 36.0 \text{ CCS}$$

Thus the conversion between Erlangs and CCS is 36 CCS = 1.0 Erlang.

A3.3 Poisson Distribution

Rarely does the traffic arrive at a uniform rate. In 1887 the French mathematician Simon Denis Poisson formulated his famous distribution

$$P(k,t) = \frac{(\lambda t)^k}{k!} e^{-\lambda t} \qquad \textbf{(Equation 8.3)}$$

where $P(k,t)$ is the probability of k calls arriving during a fixed time of t seconds. As before λ is the call arrival rate. k is an integer. Note that there are three parts to the equation: the numerator being raised to the k power and increasing, the denominator growing larger factorially as k increases thus reducing the probability, and the negative exponential also decreasing the probability. When k is small, the function increases, but eventually the denominator grows larger and the exponential term grows larger, reducing the probability as k grows larger. The function is zero when $t = 0$, passes through a peak, and finally approaches zero, as shown in Figure A3.1. Figure A3.1 shows the probability of k arrivals in a certain time. The arrival rates are 3, 10, and 15, respectively.

Of course the calls rarely come at an exact Poisson rate, but often this probability function is a good approximation.

A3.4 Erlang B and Erlang C

A3.4.1 Erlang C

Erlang C is a formula for call requests put into a queue so that all calls will eventually be serviced. An example is a queue waiting for bank tellers. There may be more than one teller (server). A packet network would be another example.

A typical queue would be an M/M/1 queue, which has Poisson arrival rate, exponential service rate, and one server. The queue size would be

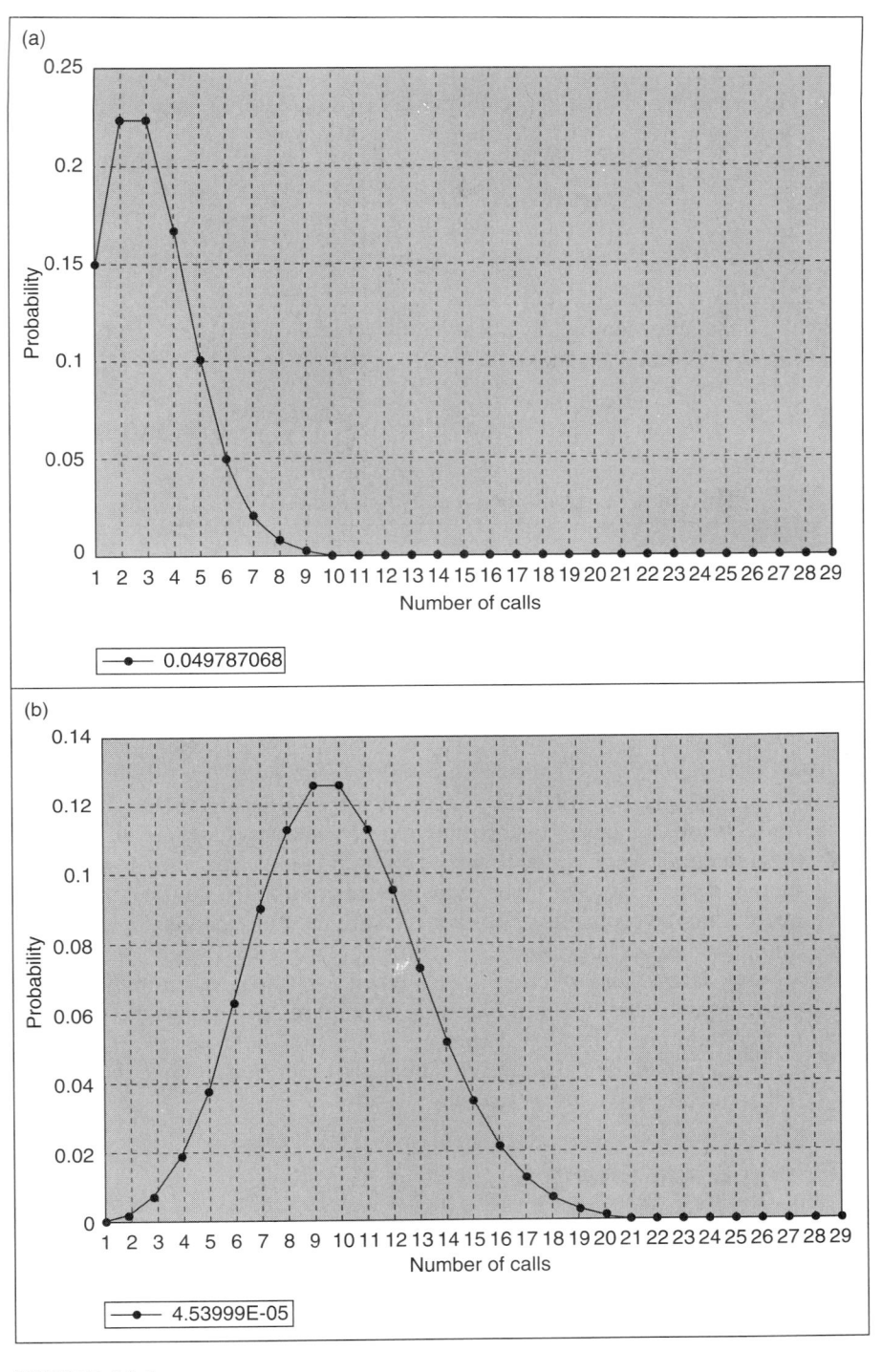

FIGURE A3.1
Poisson distribution. (a) Arrival rate = 3, (b) arrival rate = 10, and (c) arrival rate = 15.

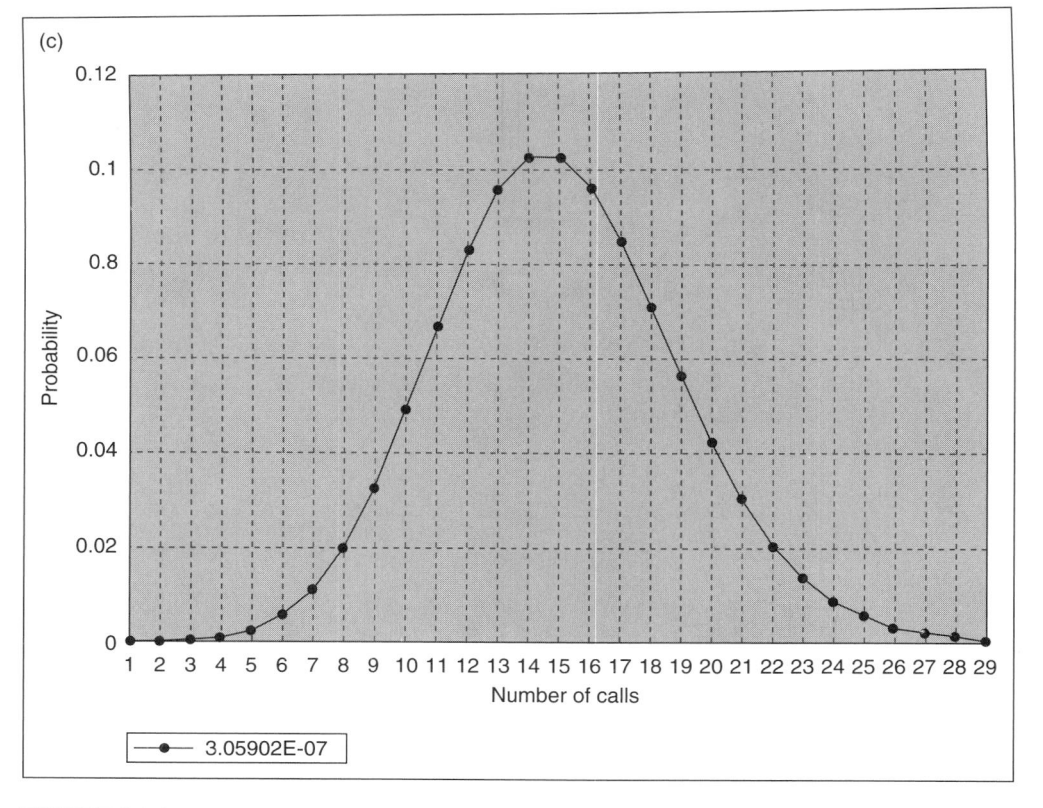

(c)

FIGURE A3.1
Continued

$$N = \frac{p}{1 - p} = \frac{\lambda H}{1 - \lambda H} \qquad \textbf{(Equation A3.3)}$$

where N is the size of the queue, and p is the probability the server is being utilized. $p = \lambda H$. Figure A3.2 shows the queue size for $0.0 \le p \le 1.0$. Note that the queue size is zero at $p = 0$ and approaches infinity as p approaches 1.0.

The delay waiting in the queue to be serviced is given by

$$\frac{1}{1 - p} = \frac{1}{1 - \lambda H} \qquad \textbf{(Equation A3.4)}$$

Figure A3.3 shows the waiting time in queue as $0.0 \le p \le 1.0$. Note that the waiting time in queue is zero at $p = 0$ and approaches infinity as p approaches 1.0.

A3.4.2 Erlang B

The telephone system does not work this way and is analyzed with Erlang B. If the telephone system is unable to handle a call request, the call is blocked. A blocked call returns

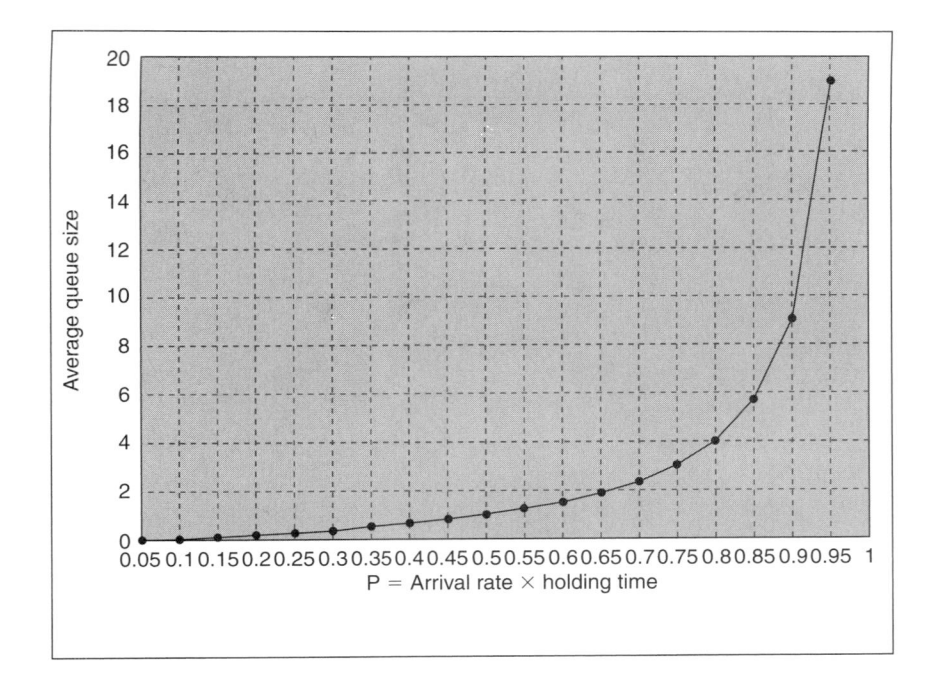

FIGURE A3.2
Average queue size.

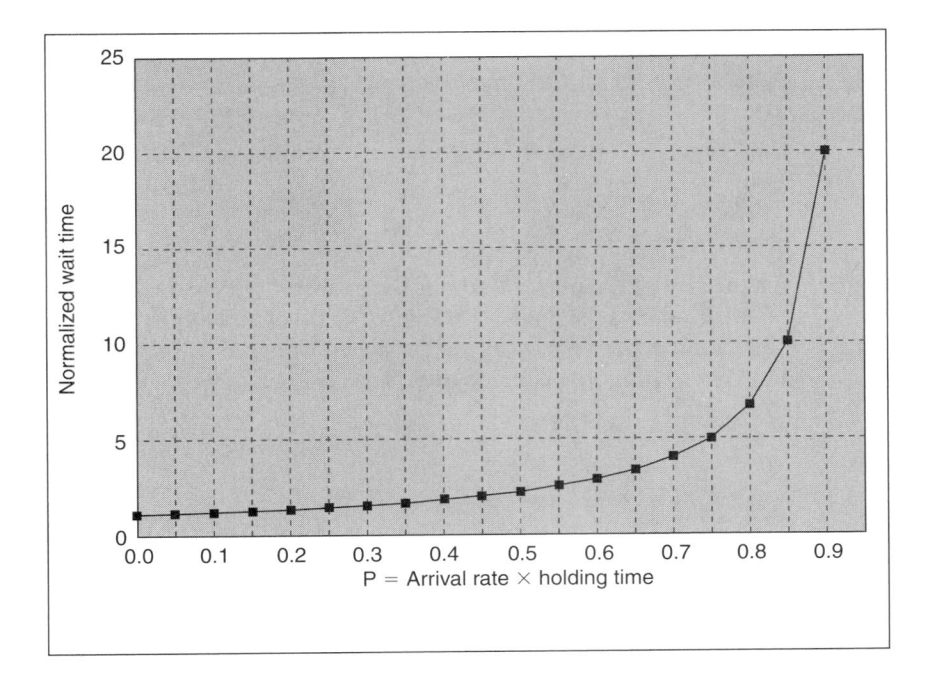

FIGURE A3.3
Normalized queue wait time.

a busy signal or the infuriating "all circuits are busy, please try later" recording. The user is not put into a queue and must try again to complete the call. There may be more than one channel. Let us examine the Erlang B in Table A3.1.

The leftmost column is the number of channels N or trunks available to handle the traffic. The topmost row is the "grade of service," or GOS. The GOS is expressed in the probability of a blocked call occurring. Typical GOS in the United States is 0.02, or 2 percent probability of a call being blocked or uncompleted. Only 2 calls out of every 100 attempted will not be completed. For example, assume that 12 channels are available and the GOS is 0.02. The maximum traffic intensity possible is 6.61 Erlangs. Any greater traffic intensity will cause the GOS to decrease and may require additional channels. The arrival rate is assumed to be Poisson.

A3.4.3 Blocking Probability

Another way of expressing the probability that a call will be blocked is the definition of Erlang B.

$$P(C) = \frac{\dfrac{E^C}{C!}}{\displaystyle\sum_{N=0}^{C} \dfrac{E^N}{N!}}$$ **(Equation 8.4)**

where E is the traffic intensity in Erlangs and C is the number of channels available.

EXAMPLE A3.5

Given a system with two channels or trunks, assume that 20 callers per hour are accessing the system and have an average holding time of 6 minutes for a traffic intensity of

$$E = \frac{20 \text{ calls}}{\text{hour}} \times \frac{6 \text{ minutes}}{\text{call}} \times \frac{\text{hour}}{60 \text{ minutes}} = 2 \text{ Erlangs}$$

$$P(C) = \frac{\dfrac{E^C}{C!}}{\displaystyle\sum_{N=0}^{C} \dfrac{E^N}{N!}} = \frac{\dfrac{2^2}{2!}}{\displaystyle\sum_{N=0}^{2} \dfrac{2^N}{N!}} = \frac{\dfrac{4}{2}}{\displaystyle\sum_{N=0}^{C} \dfrac{E^N}{N!}} = \frac{2}{\dfrac{1}{1} + \dfrac{2}{1} + \dfrac{4}{2}} = \frac{2}{1 + 2 + 2} = 0.4$$

AT&T and other long distance carriers monitor the news organizations and networks for fast-breaking events that could affect long distance traffic. For instance when a natural disaster—such as a tornado, hurricane, or earthquake—occurs, the carrier will give priority to outgoing calls from the affected area over incoming calls. Of course people outside the affected area will be most concerned about their loved ones and want to call into the affected area. The communications systems in the affected area are almost certainly affected, and the people calling in have no clue as to what is or is not working. The people in the area are better able to judge the situation and can be expected to call to their loved ones as soon as possible.

TABLE A3.1
Blocking Probability $P(S, A)$ for Erlang B Load ($S = 1$ to $S = 50$)

N	A in Erl												
	B												
	0.01%	0.02%	0.03%	0.05%	0.1%	0.2%	0.3%	0.4%	0.5%	0.6%	0.7%	0.8%	0.9%
1	.0001	.0002	.0003	.0005	.0010	.0020	.0030	.0040	.0050	.0060	.0070	.0081	.0091
2	.0142	.0202	.0248	.0321	.0458	.0653	.0806	.0937	.105	.116	.126	.135	.144
3	.0868	.110	.127	.152	.194	.249	.289	.321	.349	.374	.397	.418	.437
4	.235	.282	.315	.362	.439	.535	.602	.656	.701	.741	.777	.810	.841
5	.452	.527	.577	.649	.762	.900	.994	1.07	1.13	1.19	1.24	1.28	1.32
6	.728	.832	.900	.996	1.15	1.33	1.45	1.54	1.62	1.69	1.75	1.81	1.86
7	1.05	1.19	1.27	1.39	1.58	1.80	1.95	2.06	2.16	2.24	2.31	2.38	2.44
8	1.42	1.58	1.69	1.83	2.05	2.31	2.48	2.62	2.73	2.83	2.91	2.99	3.06
9	1.83	2.01	2.13	2.30	2.56	2.85	3.05	3.21	3.33	3.44	3.54	3.63	3.71
10	2.26	2.47	2.61	2.80	3.09	3.43	3.65	3.82	3.96	4.08	4.19	4.29	4.38
11	2.72	2.96	3.12	3.33	3.65	4.02	4.27	4.45	4.61	4.74	4.86	4.97	5.07
12	3.21	3.47	3.65	3.88	4.23	4.64	4.90	5.11	5.28	5.43	5.55	5.67	5.78
13	3.71	4.01	4.19	4.45	4.83	5.27	5.56	5.78	5.96	6.12	6.26	6.39	6.50
14	4.24	4.56	4.76	5.03	5.45	5.92	6.23	6.47	6.66	6.83	6.98	7.12	7.24
15	4.78	5.12	5.34	5.63	6.08	6.58	6.91	7.17	7.38	7.56	7.71	7.86	7.99
16	5.34	5.70	5.94	6.25	6.72	7.26	7.61	7.88	8.10	8.29	8.46	8.61	8.75
17	5.91	6.30	6.55	6.88	7.38	7.95	8.32	8.60	8.83	9.03	9.21	9.37	9.52
18	6.50	6.91	7.17	7.52	8.05	8.64	9.03	9.33	9.58	9.79	9.98	10.1	10.3
19	7.09	7.53	7.80	8.17	8.72	9.35	9.76	10.1	10.3	10.6	10.7	10.9	11.1
20	7.70	8.16	8.44	8.83	9.41	10.1	10.5	10.8	11.1	11.3	11.5	11.7	11.9
21	8.32	8.79	9.10	9.50	10.1	10.8	11.2	11.6	11.9	12.1	12.3	12.5	12.7
22	8.95	9.44	9.76	10.2	10.8	11.5	12.0	12.3	12.6	12.9	13.1	13.3	13.5
23	9.58	10.1	10.4	10.9	11.5	12.3	12.7	13.1	13.4	13.7	13.9	14.1	14.3
24	10.2	10.8	11.1	11.6	12.2	13.0	13.5	13.9	14.2	14.5	14.7	14.9	15.1
25	10.9	11.4	11.8	12.3	13.0	13.8	14.3	14.7	15.0	15.3	15.5	15.7	15.9
26	11.5	12.1	12.5	13.0	13.7	14.5	15.1	15.5	15.8	16.1	16.3	16.6	16.8
27	12.2	12.8	13.2	13.7	14.4	15.3	15.8	16.3	16.6	16.9	17.2	17.4	17.6
28	12.9	13.5	13.9	14.4	15.2	16.1	16.6	17.1	17.4	17.7	18.0	18.2	18.4
29	13.6	14.2	14.6	15.1	15.9	16.8	17.4	17.9	18.2	18.5	18.8	19.1	19.3
30	14.2	14.9	15.3	15.9	16.7	17.6	18.2	18.7	19.0	19.4	19.6	19.9	20.1
31	14.9	15.6	16.0	16.6	17.4	18.4	19.0	19.5	19.9	20.2	20.5	20.7	21.0
32	15.6	16.3	16.8	17.3	18.2	19.2	19.8	20.3	20.7	21.0	21.3	21.6	21.8
33	16.3	17.0	17.5	18.1	19.0	20.0	20.6	21.1	21.5	21.9	22.2	22.4	22.7
34	17.0	17.8	18.2	18.8	19.7	20.8	21.4	21.9	22.3	22.7	23.0	23.3	23.5
35	17.8	18.5	19.0	19.6	20.5	21.6	22.2	22.7	23.2	23.5	23.8	24.1	24.4

B												
1.0%	1.2%	1.5%	2%	3%	5%	7%	10%	15%	20%	30%	40%	50%
.0101	.0121	.0152	.0204	.0309	.0526	.0753	.111	.176	.250	.429	.667	1.00
.153	.168	.190	.223	.282	.381	.470	.595	.796	1.00	1.45	2.00	2.73
.455	.489	.535	.602	.715	.899	1.06	1.27	1.60	1.93	2.63	3.48	4.59
.869	.922	.992	1.09	1.26	1.52	1.75	2.05	2.50	2.95	3.89	5.02	6.50
1.36	1.43	1.52	1.66	1.88	2.22	2.50	2.88	3.45	4.01	5.19	6.60	8.44
1.91	2.00	2.11	2.28	2.54	2.96	3.30	3.76	4.44	5.11	6.51	8.19	10.4
2.50	2.60	2.74	2.94	3.25	3.74	4.14	4.67	5.46	6.23	7.86	9.80	12.4
3.13	3.25	3.40	3.63	3.99	4.54	5.00	5.60	6.50	7.37	9.21	11.4	14.3
3.78	3.92	4.09	4.34	4.75	5.37	5.88	6.55	7.55	8.52	10.6	13.0	16.3
4.46	4.61	4.81	5.08	5.53	6.22	6.78	7.51	8.62	9.68	12.0	14.7	18.3
5.16	5.32	5.54	5.84	6.33	7.08	7.69	8.49	9.69	10.9	13.3	16.3	20.3
5.88	6.05	6.29	6.61	7.14	7.95	8.61	9.47	10.8	12.0	14.7	18.0	22.2
6.61	6.80	7.05	7.40	7.97	8.83	9.54	10.5	11.9	13.2	16.1	19.6	24.2
7.35	7.56	7.82	8.20	8.80	9.73	10.5	11.5	13.0	14.4	17.5	21.2	26.2
8.11	8.33	8.61	9.01	9.65	10.6	11.4	12.5	14.1	15.6	18.9	22.9	28.2
8.88	9.11	9.41	9.83	10.5	11.5	12.4	13.5	15.2	16.8	20.3	24.5	30.2
9.65	9.89	10.2	10.7	11.4	12.5	13.4	14.5	16.3	18.0	21.7	26.2	32.2
10.4	10.7	11.0	11.5	12.2	13.4	14.3	15.5	17.4	19.2	23.1	27.8	34.2
11.2	11.5	11.8	12.3	13.1	14.3	15.3	16.6	18.5	20.4	24.5	29.5	36.2
12.0	12.3	12.7	13.2	14.0	15.2	16.3	17.6	19.6	21.6	25.9	31.2	38.2
12.8	13.1	13.5	14.0	14.9	16.2	17.3	18.7	20.8	22.8	27.3	32.8	40.2
13.7	14.0	14.3	14.9	15.8	17.1	18.2	19.7	21.9	24.1	28.7	34.5	42.1
14.5	14.8	15.2	15.8	16.7	18.1	19.2	20.7	23.0	25.3	30.1	36.1	44.1
15.3	15.6	16.0	16.6	17.6	19.0	20.2	21.8	24.2	26.5	31.6	37.8	46.1
16.1	16.5	16.9	17.5	18.5	20.0	21.2	22.8	25.3	27.7	33.0	39.4	48.1
17.0	17.3	17.8	18.4	19.4	20.9	22.2	23.9	26.4	28.9	34.4	41.1	50.1
17.8	18.2	18.6	19.3	20.3	21.9	23.2	24.9	27.6	30.2	35.8	42.8	52.1
18.6	19.0	19.5	20.2	21.2	22.9	24.2	26.0	28.7	31.4	37.2	44.4	54.1
19.5	19.9	20.4	21.0	22.1	23.8	25.2	27.1	29.9	32.6	38.6	46.1	56.1
20.3	20.7	21.2	21.9	23.1	24.8	26.2	28.1	31.0	33.8	40.0	47.7	58.1
21.2	21.6	22.1	22.8	24.0	25.8	27.2	29.2	32.1	35.1	41.5	49.4	60.1
22.0	22.5	23.0	23.7	24.9	26.7	28.2	30.2	33.3	36.3	42.9	51.1	62.1
22.9	23.3	23.9	24.6	25.8	27.7	29.3	31.3	34.4	37.5	44.3	52.7	64.1
23.8	24.2	24.8	25.5	26.8	28.7	30.3	32.4	35.6	38.8	45.7	54.4	66.1
24.6	25.1	25.6	26.4	27.7	29.7	31.3	33.4	36.7	40.0	47.1	56.0	68.1

TABLE A3.1

Continued

N	A in Erl												
	B												
	0.01%	0.02%	0.03%	0.05%	0.1%	0.2%	0.3%	0.4%	0.5%	0.6%	0.7%	0.8%	0.9%
36	18.5	19.2	19.7	20.3	21.3	22.4	23.1	23.6	24.0	24.4	24.7	25.0	25.3
37	19.2	20.0	20.5	21.1	22.1	23.2	23.9	24.4	24.8	25.2	25.6	25.9	26.1
38	19.9	20.7	21.2	21.9	22.9	24.0	24.7	25.2	25.7	26.1	26.4	26.7	27.0
39	20.6	21.5	22.0	22.6	23.7	24.8	25.5	26.1	26.5	26.9	27.3	27.6	27.9
40	21.4	22.2	22.7	23.4	24.4	25.6	26.3	26.9	27.4	27.8	28.1	28.5	28.7
41	22.1	23.0	23.5	24.2	25.2	26.4	27.2	27.8	28.2	28.6	29.0	29.3	29.6
42	22.8	23.7	24.2	25.0	26.0	27.2	28.0	28.6	29.1	29.5	29.9	30.2	30.5
43	23.6	24.5	25.0	25.7	26.8	28.1	28.8	29.4	29.9	30.4	30.7	31.1	31.4
44	24.3	25.2	25.8	26.5	27.6	28.9	29.7	30.3	30.8	31.2	31.6	31.9	32.3
45	25.1	26.0	26.6	27.3	28.4	29.7	30.5	31.1	31.7	32.1	32.5	32.8	33.1
46	25.8	26.8	27.3	28.1	29.3	30.5	31.4	32.0	32.5	33.0	33.4	33.7	34.0
47	26.6	27.5	28.1	28.9	30.1	31.4	32.2	32.9	33.4	33.8	34.2	34.6	34.9
48	27.3	28.3	28.9	29.7	30.9	32.2	33.1	33.7	34.2	34.7	35.1	35.5	35.8
49	28.1	29.1	29.7	30.5	31.7	33.0	33.9	34.6	35.1	35.6	36.0	36.4	36.7
50	28.9	29.9	30.5	31.3	32.5	33.9	34.8	35.4	36.0	36.5	36.9	37.2	37.6
51	29.6	30.6	31.3	32.1	33.3	34.7	35.6	36.3	36.9	37.3	37.8	38.1	38.5
52	30.4	31.4	32.0	32.9	34.2	35.6	36.5	37.2	37.7	38.2	38.6	39.0	39.4
53	31.2	32.2	32.8	33.7	35.0	36.4	37.3	38.0	38.6	39.1	39.5	39.9	40.3
54	31.9	33.0	33.6	34.5	35.8	37.2	38.2	38.9	39.5	40.0	40.4	40.8	41.2
55	32.7	33.8	34.4	35.3	36.6	38.1	39.0	39.8	40.4	40.9	41.3	41.7	42.1
56	33.5	34.6	35.2	36.1	37.5	38.9	39.9	40.6	41.2	41.7	42.2	42.6	43.0
57	34.3	35.4	36.0	36.9	38.3	39.8	40.8	41.5	42.1	42.6	43.1	43.5	43.9
58	35.1	36.2	36.8	37.8	39.1	40.6	41.6	42.4	43.0	43.5	44.0	44.4	44.8
59	35.8	37.0	37.6	38.6	40.0	41.5	42.5	43.3	43.9	44.4	44.9	45.3	45.7
60	36.6	37.8	38.5	39.4	40.8	42.4	43.4	44.1	44.8	45.3	45.8	46.2	46.6
61	37.4	38.6	39.3	40.2	41.6	43.2	44.2	45.0	45.6	46.2	46.7	47.1	47.5
62	38.2	39.4	40.1	41.0	42.5	44.1	45.1	45.9	46.5	47.1	47.6	48.0	48.4
63	39.0	40.2	40.9	41.9	43.3	44.9	46.0	46.8	47.4	48.0	48.5	48.9	49.3
64	39.8	41.0	41.7	42.7	44.2	45.8	46.8	47.6	48.3	48.9	49.4	49.8	50.2
65	40.6	41.8	42.5	43.5	45.0	46.6	47.7	48.5	49.2	49.8	50.3	50.7	51.1
66	41.4	42.6	43.3	44.4	45.8	47.5	48.6	49.4	50.1	50.7	51.2	51.6	52.0
67	42.2	43.4	44.2	45.2	46.7	48.4	49.5	50.3	51.0	51.6	52.1	52.5	53.0
68	43.0	44.2	45.0	46.0	47.5	49.2	50.3	51.2	51.9	52.5	53.0	53.4	53.9
69	43.8	45.0	45.8	46.8	48.4	50.1	51.2	52.1	52.8	53.4	53.9	54.4	54.8
70	44.6	45.8	46.6	47.7	49.2	51.0	52.1	53.0	53.7	54.3	54.8	55.3	55.7

1.0%	1.2%	1.5%	2%	3%	5%	7%	10%	15%	20%	30%	40%	50%
25.5	26.0	26.5	27.3	28.6	30.7	32.3	34.5	37.9	41.2	48.6	57.7	70.0
26.4	26.8	27.4	28.3	29.6	31.6	33.3	35.6	39.0	42.4	50.0	59.4	72.1
27.3	27.7	28.3	29.2	30.5	32.6	34.4	36.6	40.2	43.7	51.4	61.0	74.1
28.1	28.6	29.2	30.1	31.5	33.6	35.4	37.7	41.3	44.9	52.8	62.7	76.1
29.0	29.5	30.1	31.0	32.4	34.6	36.4	38.8	42.5	46.1	54.2	64.4	78.1
29.9	30.4	31.0	31.9	33.4	35.6	37.4	39.9	43.6	47.4	55.7	66.0	80.1
30.8	31.3	31.9	32.8	34.3	36.6	38.4	40.9	44.8	48.6	57.1	67.7	82.1
31.7	32.2	32.8	33.8	35.3	37.6	39.5	42.0	45.9	49.9	58.5	69.3	84.1
32.5	33.1	33.7	34.7	36.2	38.6	40.5	43.1	47.1	51.1	59.9	71.0	86.1
33.4	34.0	34.6	35.6	37.2	39.6	41.5	44.2	48.2	52.3	61.3	72.7	88.1
34.3	34.9	35.6	36.5	38.1	40.5	42.6	45.2	49.4	53.6	62.8	74.3	90.1
35.2	35.8	36.5	37.5	39.1	41.5	43.6	46.3	50.6	54.8	64.2	76.0	92.1
36.1	36.7	37.4	38.4	40.0	42.5	44.6	47.4	51.7	56.0	65.6	77.7	94.1
37.0	37.6	38.3	39.3	41.0	43.5	45.7	48.5	52.9	57.3	67.0	79.3	96.1
37.9	38.5	39.2	40.3	41.9	44.5	46.7	49.6	54.0	58.5	68.5	81.0	98.1
38.8	39.4	40.1	41.2	42.9	45.5	47.7	50.6	55.2	59.7	69.9	82.7	100.1
39.7	40.3	41.0	42.1	43.9	46.5	48.8	51.7	56.3	61.0	71.3	84.3	102.1
40.6	41.2	42.0	43.1	44.8	47.5	49.8	52.8	57.5	62.2	72.7	86.0	104.1
41.5	42.1	42.9	44.0	45.8	48.5	50.8	53.9	58.7	63.5	74.2	87.6	106.1
42.4	43.0	43.8	44.9	46.7	49.5	51.9	55.0	59.8	64.7	75.6	89.3	108.1
43.3	43.9	44.7	45.9	47.7	50.5	52.9	56.1	61.0	65.9	77.0	91.0	110.1
44.2	44.8	45.7	46.8	48.7	51.5	53.9	57.1	62.1	67.2	78.4	92.6	112.1
45.1	45.8	46.6	47.8	49.6	52.6	55.0	58.2	63.3	68.4	79.8	94.3	114.1
46.0	46.7	47.5	48.7	50.6	53.6	56.0	59.3	64.5	69.7	81.3	96.0	116.1
46.9	47.6	48.4	49.6	51.6	54.6	57.1	60.4	65.6	70.9	82.7	97.6	118.1
47.9	48.5	49.4	50.6	52.5	55.6	58.1	61.5	66.8	72.1	84.1	99.3	120.1
48.8	49.4	50.3	51.5	53.5	56.6	59.1	62.6	68.0	73.4	85.5	101.0	122.1
49.7	50.4	51.2	52.5	54.5	57.6	60.2	63.7	69.1	74.6	87.0	102.6	124.1
50.6	51.3	52.2	53.4	55.4	58.6	61.2	64.8	70.3	75.9	88.4	104.3	126.1
51.5	52.2	53.1	54.4	56.4	59.6	62.3	65.8	71.4	77.1	89.8	106.0	128.1
52.4	53.1	54.0	55.3	57.4	60.6	63.3	66.9	72.6	78.3	91.2	107.6	130.1
53.4	54.1	55.0	56.3	58.4	61.6	64.4	68.0	73.8	79.6	92.7	109.3	132.1
54.3	55.0	55.9	57.2	59.3	62.6	65.4	69.1	74.9	80.8	94.1	111.0	134.1
55.2	55.9	56.9	58.2	60.3	63.7	66.4	70.2	76.1	82.1	95.5	112.6	136.1
56.1	56.8	57.8	59.1	61.3	64.7	67.5	71.3	77.3	83.3	96.9	114.3	138.1

TABLE A3.1

Continued

	A in Erl												
N	B												
	0.01%	0.02%	0.03%	0.05%	0.1%	0.2%	0.3%	0.4%	0.5%	0.6%	0.7%	0.8%	0.9%
71	45.4	46.7	47.5	48.5	50.1	51.8	53.0	53.8	54.6	55.2	55.7	56.2	56.6
72	46.2	47.5	48.3	49.4	50.9	52.7	53.9	54.7	55.5	56.1	56.6	57.1	57.5
73	47.0	48.3	49.1	50.2	51.8	53.6	54.7	55.6	56.4	57.0	57.5	58.0	58.5
74	47.8	49.1	49.9	51.0	52.7	54.5	55.6	56.5	57.3	57.9	58.4	58.9	59.4
75	48.6	49.9	50.8	51.9	53.5	55.3	56.5	57.4	58.2	58.8	59.3	59.8	60.3
76	49.4	50.8	51.6	52.7	54.4	56.2	57.4	58.3	59.1	59.7	60.3	60.8	61.2
77	50.2	51.6	52.4	53.6	55.2	57.1	58.3	59.2	60.0	60.6	61.2	61.7	62.1
78	51.1	52.4	53.3	54.4	56.1	58.0	59.2	60.1	60.9	61.5	62.1	62.6	63.1
79	51.9	53.2	54.1	55.3	56.9	58.8	60.1	61.0	61.8	62.4	63.0	63.5	64.0
80	52.7	54.1	54.9	56.1	57.8	89.7	61.0	61.9	62.7	63.3	63.9	64.4	64.9
81	53.5	54.9	55.8	56.9	58.7	60.6	61.8	62.8	63.6	64.2	64.8	65.4	65.8
82	54.3	55.7	56.6	57.8	59.5	61.5	62.7	63.7	64.5	65.2	65.7	66.3	66.8
83	55.1	56.6	57.5	58.6	60.4	62.4	63.6	64.6	65.4	66.1	66.7	67.2	67.7
84	56.0	57.4	58.3	59.5	61.3	63.2	64.5	65.5	66.3	67.0	67.6	68.1	68.6
85	56.8	58.2	59.1	60.4	62.1	64.1	65.4	66.4	67.2	67.9	68.5	69.1	69.6
86	57.6	59.1	60.0	61.2	63.0	65.0	66.3	67.3	68.1	68.8	69.4	70.0	70.5
87	58.4	59.9	60.8	62.1	63.9	65.9	67.2	68.2	69.0	69.7	70.3	70.9	71.4
88	59.3	60.8	61.7	62.9	64.7	66.8	68.1	69.1	69.9	70.6	71.3	71.8	72.3
89	60.1	61.6	62.5	63.8	65.6	67.7	69.0	70.0	70.8	71.6	72.2	72.8	73.3
90	60.9	62.4	63.4	64.6	66.5	68.6	69.9	70.9	71.8	72.5	73.1	73.7	74.2
91	61.8	63.3	64.2	65.5	67.4	69.4	70.8	71.8	72.7	73.4	74.0	74.6	75.1
92	62.6	64.1	65.1	66.3	68.2	70.3	71.7	72.7	73.6	74.3	75.0	75.5	76.1
93	63.4	65.0	65.9	67.2	69.1	71.2	72.6	73.6	74.5	75.2	75.9	76.5	77.0
94	64.2	65.8	66.8	68.1	70.0	72.1	73.5	74.5	75.4	76.2	76.8	77.4	77.9
95	65.1	66.6	67.6	68.9	70.9	73.0	74.4	75.5	76.3	77.1	77.7	78.3	78.9
96	65.9	67.5	68.5	69.8	71.7	73.9	75.3	76.4	77.2	78.0	78.7	79.3	79.8
97	66.8	68.3	69.3	70.7	72.6	74.8	76.2	77.3	78.2	78.9	79.6	80.2	80.7
98	67.6	69.2	70.2	71.5	73.5	75.7	77.1	78.2	79.1	79.8	80.5	81.1	81.7
99	68.4	70.0	71.0	72.4	74.4	76.6	78.0	79.1	80.0	80.8	81.4	82.0	82.6
100	69.3	70.9	71.9	73.2	75.2	77.5	78.9	80.0	80.9	81.7	82.4	83.0	83.5
102	70.9	72.6	73.6	75.0	77.0	79.3	80.7	81.8	82.7	83.5	84.2	84.8	85.4
104	72.6	74.3	75.3	76.7	78.8	81.1	82.5	83.7	84.6	85.4	86.1	86.7	87.3
106	74.3	76.0	77.1	78.5	80.5	82.8	84.3	85.5	86.4	87.2	87.9	88.6	89.2
108	76.0	77.7	78.8	80.2	82.3	84.6	86.2	87.3	88.3	89.1	89.8	90.5	91.1
110	77.7	79.4	80.5	81.9	84.1	86.4	88.0	89.2	90.1	90.9	91.7	92.3	92.9

1.0%	1.2%	1.5%	2%	3%	5%	7%	10%	15%	20%	30%	40%	50%
57.0	57.8	58.7	60.1	62.3	65.7	68.5	72.4	78.4	84.6	98.4	115.9	140.1
57.0	58.7	59.7	61.0	63.2	66.7	69.6	73.5	79.6	85.8	99.8	117.6	142.1
58.9	59.6	60.6	62.0	64.2	67.7	70.6	74.6	80.8	87.0	101.2	119.3	144.1
59.8	60.6	61.6	62.9	65.2	68.7	71.7	75.6	81.9	88.3	102.7	120.9	146.1
60.7	61.5	62.5	63.9	66.2	69.7	72.7	76.7	83.1	89.5	104.1	122.6	148.0
61.7	62.4	63.4	64.9	67.2	70.8	73.8	77.8	84.2	90.8	105.5	124.3	150.0
62.6	63.4	64.4	65.8	68.1	71.8	74.8	78.9	85.4	92.0	106.9	125.9	152.0
63.5	64.3	65.3	66.8	69.1	72.8	75.9	80.0	86.6	93.3	108.4	127.6	154.0
64.4	65.2	66.3	67.7	70.1	73.8	76.9	81.1	87.7	94.5	109.8	129.3	156.0
65.4	66.2	67.2	68.7	71.1	74.8	78.0	82.2	88.9	95.7	111.2	130.9	158.0
66.3	67.1	68.2	69.6	72.1	75.8	79.0	83.3	90.1	97.0	112.6	132.6	160.0
67.2	68.0	69.1	70.6	73.0	76.9	80.1	84.4	91.2	98.2	114.1	134.3	162.0
68.2	69.0	70.1	71.6	74.0	77.9	81.1	85.5	92.4	99.5	115.5	135.9	164.0
69.1	69.9	71.0	72.5	75.0	78.9	82.2	86.6	93.6	100.7	116.9	137.6	166.0
70.0	70.9	71.9	73.5	76.0	79.9	83.2	87.7	94.7	102.0	118.3	139.3	168.0
70.9	71.8	72.9	74.5	77.0	80.9	84.3	88.8	95.9	103.2	119.8	140.9	170.0
71.9	72.7	73.8	75.4	78.0	82.0	85.3	89.9	97.1	104.5	121.2	142.6	172.0
72.8	73.7	74.8	76.4	78.9	83.0	86.4	91.0	98.2	105.7	122.6	144.3	174.0
73.7	74.6	75.7	77.3	79.9	84.0	87.4	92.1	99.4	106.9	124.0	145.9	176.0
74.7	75.6	76.7	78.3	80.9	85.0	88.5	93.1	100.6	108.2	125.5	147.6	178.0
75.6	76.5	77.6	79.3	81.9	86.0	89.5	94.2	101.7	109.4	126.9	149.3	180.0
76.6	77.4	78.6	80.2	82.9	87.1	90.6	95.3	102.9	110.7	128.3	150.9	182.0
77.5	78.4	79.6	81.2	83.9	88.1	91.6	96.4	104.1	111.9	129.7	152.6	184.0
78.4	79.3	80.5	82.2	84.9	89.1	92.7	97.5	105.3	113.2	131.2	154.3	186.0
79.4	80.3	81.5	83.1	85.8	90.1	93.7	98.6	106.4	114.4	132.6	155.9	188.0
80.3	81.2	82.4	84.1	86.8	91.1	94.8	99.7	107.6	115.7	134.0	157.6	190.0
81.2	82.2	83.4	85.1	87.8	92.2	95.8	100.8	108.8	116.9	135.5	159.3	192.0
82.2	83.1	84.3	86.0	88.8	93.2	96.9	101.9	109.9	118.2	136.9	160.9	194.0
83.1	84.1	85.3	87.0	89.8	94.2	97.9	103.0	111.1	119.4	138.3	162.6	196.0
84.1	85.0	86.2	88.0	90.8	95.2	99.0	104.1	112.3	120.6	139.7	164.3	198.0
85.9	86.9	88.1	89.9	92.8	97.3	101.1	106.3	114.6	123.1	142.6	167.6	202.0
87.8	88.8	90.1	91.9	94.8	99.3	103.2	108.5	116.9	125.6	145.4	170.9	206.0
89.7	90.7	92.0	93.8	96.7	101.4	105.3	110.7	119.3	128.1	148.3	174.2	210.0
91.6	92.6	93.9	95.7	98.7	103.4	107.4	112.9	121.6	130.6	151.1	177.6	214.0
93.5	94.5	95.8	97.7	100.7	105.5	109.5	115.1	124.0	133.1	154.0	180.9	218.0

N							A in Erl B						
	0.01%	0.02%	0.03%	0.05%	0.1%	0.2%	0.3%	0.4%	0.5%	0.6%	0.7%	0.8%	0.9%
112	79.4	81.1	82.2	83.7	85.8	88.3	89.8	91.0	92.0	92.8	93.5	94.2	94.8
114	81.1	82.9	84.0	85.4	87.6	90.1	91.6	92.8	93.8	94.7	95.4	96.1	96.7
116	82.8	84.6	85.7	87.2	89.4	91.9	93.5	94.7	95.7	96.5	97.3	98.0	98.6
118	84.5	86.3	87.4	89.0	91.2	93.7	95.3	96.5	97.5	98.4	99.2	99.9	100.5
120	86.2	88.0	89.2	90.7	93.0	95.5	97.1	98.4	99.4	100.3	101.0	01.7	102.4
122	87.9	89.8	90.9	92.5	94.7	97.3	98.9	100.2	101.2	102.1	102.9	103.6	104.3
124	89.6	91.5	92.7	94.2	96.5	99.1	100.8	102.1	103.1	104.0	104.8	105.5	106.2
126	91.3	93.2	94.4	96.0	98.3	100.9	102.6	103.9	105.0	105.9	106.7	107.4	108.1
128	93.1	95.0	96.2	97.8	100.1	102.7	104.5	105.8	106.8	107.7	108.5	109.3	109.9
130	94.8	96.7	97.9	99.5	101.9	104.6	106.3	107.6	108.7	109.6	110.4	111.2	111.8
132	96.5	98.5	99.7	101.3	103.7	106.4	108.1	109.5	110.5	111.5	112.3	113.1	113.7
134	98.2	100.2	101.4	103.1	105.5	108.2	110.0	111.3	112.4	113.4	114.2	115.0	115.6
136	100.0	101.9	103.2	104.9	107.3	110.0	111.8	113.2	114.3	115.2	116.1	116.8	117.5
138	101.7	103.7	105.0	106.6	109.1	111.9	113.7	115.0	116.2	117.1	118.0	118.7	119.4
140	103.4	105.4	106.7	108.4	110.9	113.7	115.5	116.9	118.0	119.0	119.9	120.6	121.4
142	105.1	107.2	108.5	110.2	112.7	115.5	117.4	118.7	119.9	120.9	121.8	122.5	123.3
144	106.9	109.0	110.2	112.0	114.5	117.4	119.2	120.6	121.8	122.8	123.6	124.4	125.2
146	108.6	110.7	112.0	113.8	116.3	119.2	121.1	122.5	123.6	124.6	125.5	126.3	127.1
148	110.4	112.5	113.8	115.5	118.1	121.0	122.9	124.3	125.5	126.5	127.4	128.2	129.0
150	112.1	114.2	115.6	117.3	119.9	122.9	124.8	126.2	127.4	128.4	129.3	130.1	130.9
152	113.8	116.0	117.3	119.1	121.8	124.7	126.6	128.1	129.3	130.3	131.2	132.0	132.8
154	115.6	117.8	119.1	120.9	123.6	126.5	128.5	129.9	131.2	132.2	133.1	133.9	134.7
156	117.3	119.5	120.9	122.7	125.4	128.4	130.3	131.8	133.0	134.1	135.0	135.9	136.6
158	119.1	121.3	122.7	124.5	127.2	130.2	132.2	133.7	134.9	136.0	136.9	137.8	138.5
160	120.8	123.1	124.4	126.3	129.0	132.1	134.0	135.6	136.8	137.9	138.8	139.7	140.4
162	122.6	124.8	126.2	128.1	130.8	133.9	135.9	137.4	138.7	139.8	140.7	141.6	142.4
164	124.3	126.6	128.0	129.9	132.7	135.8	137.8	139.3	140.6	141.7	142.6	143.5	144.3
166	126.1	128.4	129.8	131.7	134.5	137.6	139.6	141.2	142.5	143.5	144.5	145.4	146.2
168	127.9	130.2	131.6	133.5	136.3	139.4	141.5	143.1	144.3	145.4	146.4	147.3	148.1
170	129.6	131.9	133.4	135.3	138.1	141.3	143.4	144.9	146.2	147.3	148.3	149.2	150.0
172	131.4	133.7	135.2	137.1	139.9	143.1	145.2	146.8	148.1	149.2	150.2	151.1	151.9
174	133.1	135.5	136.9	138.9	141.8	145.0	147.1	148.7	150.0	151.1	152.1	153.0	153.9
176	134.9	137.3	138.7	140.7	143.6	146.9	149.0	150.6	151.9	153.0	154.0	155.0	155.8
178	136.7	139.0	140.5	142.5	145.4	148.7	150.8	152.4	153.8	154.9	156.0	156.9	157.7
180	138.4	140.8	142.3	144.3	147.3	150.6	152.7	154.3	155.7	156.8	157.9	158.8	159.6

1.0%	1.2%	1.5%	2%	3%	5%	7%	10%	15%	20%	30%	40%	50%
						B						
95.4	96.4	97.7	99.6	102.7	107.5	111.7	117.3	126.3	135.6	156.9	184.2	222.0
97.3	98.3	99.7	101.6	104.7	109.6	113.8	119.5	128.6	138.1	159.7	187.6	226.0
99.2	100.2	101.6	103.5	106.7	111.7	115.9	121.7	131.0	140.6	162.6	190.9	230.0
101.1	102.1	103.5	105.5	108.7	113.7	118.0	123.9	133.3	143.1	165.4	194.2	234.0
103.0	104.0	105.4	107.4	110.7	115.8	120.1	126.1	135.7	145.6	168.3	197.6	238.0
104.9	105.9	107.4	109.4	112.6	117.8	122.2	128.3	138.0	148.1	171.1	200.9	242.0
106.8	107.9	109.3	111.3	114.6	119.9	124.4	130.5	140.3	150.6	174.0	204.2	246.0
108.7	109.8	111.2	113.3	116.6	121.9	126.5	132.7	142.7	153.0	176.8	207.6	250.0
110.6	111.7	113.2	115.2	118.6	124.0	128.6	134.9	145.0	155.5	179.7	210.9	254.0
112.5	13.6	115.1	117.2	120.6	126.1	130.7	137.1	147.4	158.0	182.5	214.2	258.0
114.4	115.5	117.0	119.1	122.6	128.1	132.8	139.3	149.7	160.5	185.4	217.6	262.0
116.3	117.4	119.0	121.1	124.6	130.2	134.9	141.5	152.0	163.0	188.3	220.9	266.0
118.2	119.4	120.9	123.1	126.6	132.3	137.1	143.7	154.4	165.5	191.1	224.2	270.0
120.1	121.3	122.8	125.0	128.6	134.3	139.2	145.9	156.7	168.0	194.0	227.6	274.0
122.0	123.2	124.8	127.0	130.6	136.4	141.3	148.1	159.1	170.5	196.8	230.9	278.0
123.9	125.1	126.7	128.9	132.6	138.4	143.4	150.3	161.4	173.0	199.7	234.2	282.0
125.8	127.0	128.6	130.9	134.6	140.5	145.6	152.5	163.8	175.5	202.5	237.6	286.0
127.7	129.0	130.6	132.9	136.6	142.6	147.7	154.7	166.1	178.0	205.4	240.9	290.0
129.7	130.9	132.5	134.8	138.6	144.6	149.8	156.9	168.5	180.5	208.2	244.2	294.0
131.6	132.8	134.5	136.8	140.6	146.7	151.9	159.1	170.8	183.0	211.1	247.6	298.0
133.5	134.8	136.4	138.8	142.6	148.8	154.0	161.3	173.1	185.5	214.0	250.9	302.0
135.4	136.7	138.4	140.7	144.6	150.8	156.2	163.5	175.5	188.0	216.8	254.2	306.0
137.3	138.6	140.3	142.7	146.6	152.9	158.3	165.7	177.8	190.5	219.7	257.6	310.0
139.2	140.5	142.3	144.7	148.6	155.0	160.4	167.9	180.2	193.0	222.5	260.9	314.0
141.2	142.5	144.2	146.6	150.6	157.0	162.5	170.2	182.5	195.5	225.4	264.2	318.0
143.1	144.4	146.1	148.6	152.7	159.1	164.7	172.4	184.9	198.0	228.2	267.6	322.0
145.0	146.3	148.1	150.6	154.7	161.2	166.8	174.6	187.2	200.4	231.1	270.9	326.0
146.9	148.3	150.0	152.6	156.7	163.3	168.9	176.8	189.6	202.9	233.9	274.2	330.0
148.9	150.2	152.0	154.5	158.7	165.3	171.0	179.0	191.9	205.4	236.8	277.6	334.0
150.8	152.1	153.9	156.5	160.7	167.4	173.2	181.2	194.2	207.9	239.7	280.9	338.0
152.7	154.1	155.9	158.5	162.7	169.5	175.3	183.4	196.6	210.4	242.5	284.2	342.0
154.6	156.0	157.8	160.4	164.7	171.5	177.4	185.6	198.9	212.9	245.4	287.6	346.0
156.6	158.0	159.8	162.4	166.7	173.6	179.6	187.8	201.3	215.4	248.2	290.9	350.0
158.5	159.9	161.8	164.4	168.7	175.7	181.7	190.0	203.6	217.9	251.1	294.2	354.0
160.4	161.8	163.7	166.4	170.7	177.8	183.8	192.2	206.0	220.4	253.9	297.5	358.0

TABLE A3.1
Continued

							A in Erl						
N							B						
	0.01%	0.02%	0.03%	0.05%	0.1%	0.2%	0.3%	0.4%	0.5%	0.6%	0.7%	0.8%	0.9%
182	140.2	142.6	144.1	146.1	149.1	152.4	154.6	156.2	157.6	158.7	159.8	160.7	161.6
184	142.0	144.4	145.9	147.9	150.9	154.3	156.4	158.1	159.5	160.6	161.7	162.6	163.5
186	143.7	146.2	147.7	149.8	152.8	156.1	158.3	160.0	161.4	162.5	163.6	164.5	165.4
188	145.5	148.0	149.5	151.6	154.6	158.0	160.2	161.9	163.3	164.4	165.5	166.5	167.3
190	147.3	149.8	151.3	153.4	156.4	159.8	162.1	163.8	165.2	166.4	167.4	168.4	169.3
192	149.1	151.6	153.1	155.2	158.3	161.7	163.9	165.6	167.0	168.3	169.3	170.3	171.2
194	150.8	153.4	154.9	157.0	160.1	163.6	165.8	167.5	168.9	170.2	171.2	172.2	173.1
196	152.6	155.2	156.7	158.8	161.9	165.4	167.7	169.4	170.8	172.1	173.2	174.1	175.0
198	154.4	156.9	158.5	160.7	163.8	167.3	169.6	171.3	172.7	174.0	175.1	176.1	177.0
200	156.2	158.7	160.3	162.5	165.6	169.2	171.4	173.2	174.6	175.9	177.0	178.0	178.9

A3.5 Problems

A3.5.1 Given the traffic parameter in the following two tables, fill in the missing data.

Arrival Time λ	Holding Time	Traffic—Erlangs
222/hour	0.05 hour	
222/hour	3 minutes	
23/hour	12 minutes	
	15 minutes	2.2
38/hour		0.5

						A in Erl							
						B							
1.0%	1.2%	1.5%	2%	3%	5%	7%	10%	15%	20%	30%	40%	50%
162.3	163.8	165.7	168.3	172.8	179.8	185.9	194.4	208.3	222.9	256.8	300.9	362.0
164.3	165.7	167.6	170.3	174.8	181.9	188.1	196.6	210.7	225.4	259.6	304.2	366.0
166.2	167.7	169.6	172.3	176.8	184.0	190.2	198.9	213.0	227.9	262.5	307.5	370.0
168.1	169.6	171.5	174.3	178.8	186.1	192.3	201.1	215.4	230.4	265.4	310.9	374.0
170.1	171.5	173.5	176.3	180.8	188.1	194.5	203.3	217.7	232.9	268.2	314.2	378.0
172.0	173.5	175.4	178.2	182.8	190.2	196.6	205.5	220.1	235.4	271.1	317.5	382.0
173.9	175.4	177.4	180.2	184.8	192.3	198.7	207.7	222.4	237.9	273.9	320.9	386.0
175.9	177.4	179.4	182.2	186.9	194.4	200.8	209.9	224.8	240.4	276.8	324.2	390.0
177.8	179.3	181.3	184.2	188.9	196.4	203.0	212.1	227.1	242.9	279.6	327.5	394.0
179.7	181.3	183.3	186.2	190.9	198.5	205.1	214.3	229.4	245.4	282.5	330.9	398.0

NCBH	H	CCS
8	300 s	
2	560	
	3,600	28.8
27		36

A3.5.2 How much traffic in Erlangs could 3 channels handle with a GOS of 2 percent? Assume the arrival rate is Poisson.

A3.5.3 Assume traffic of 9 Erlangs. How many channels would be needed for a 2 percent GOS?

A4

FOURIER SERIES

Jean Babtiste Fourier, a French mathematician and physicist, laid the groundwork for communication theory with his simple, yet elegant, expression of the relationship between a waveform's shape and frequency, and bandwidth. Simply stated

$$F(t) = A_0 + A_1 \sin (2\pi f + \Theta_1) + A_2 \sin [2\pi (2f) + \Theta_2] +$$

$$A_3 \sin [2\pi (3f) + \Theta_3] + A_4 \sin [2\pi (4f) + \Theta_4] + \ldots +$$

$$A_n \sin [2\pi (nf) + \Theta_n] \qquad \textbf{(Equation A4.1)}$$

where $F(t)$ is the waveform as a function of time, f is the fundamental frequency, and sin $[2\pi [nf) + \Theta_n]$ is the harmonics at frequency (nf) of the fundamental frequency f. Θ is any phase shift associated with that particular harmonic.

From Equation A4.1 we see that $F(t)$ is made up of many sine waves, each at an integer multiple n (harmonic) of the fundamental frequency f.

Let's look at an example of this in Figure A4.1.

In Figure A4.1a the period T of the square wave is 0.001 second. The fundamental frequency of this square wave is

$$f_1 = \frac{1}{T} = \frac{1}{0.001 \text{ second}} = 1{,}000 \frac{\text{cycles}}{\text{second}} = 1{,}000 \text{ Hz} \quad \textbf{(Equation A4.2)}$$

The unit for frequency is hertz, in honor of the German physicist Heinrich Hertz. Years ago the designation was cycles per second, but people would just say "cycles" instead of the proper "cycles per second." This lazy and definitely incorrect slang upset the purists, who prevailed upon the standards committees to give "cycles per second" the units of hertz.

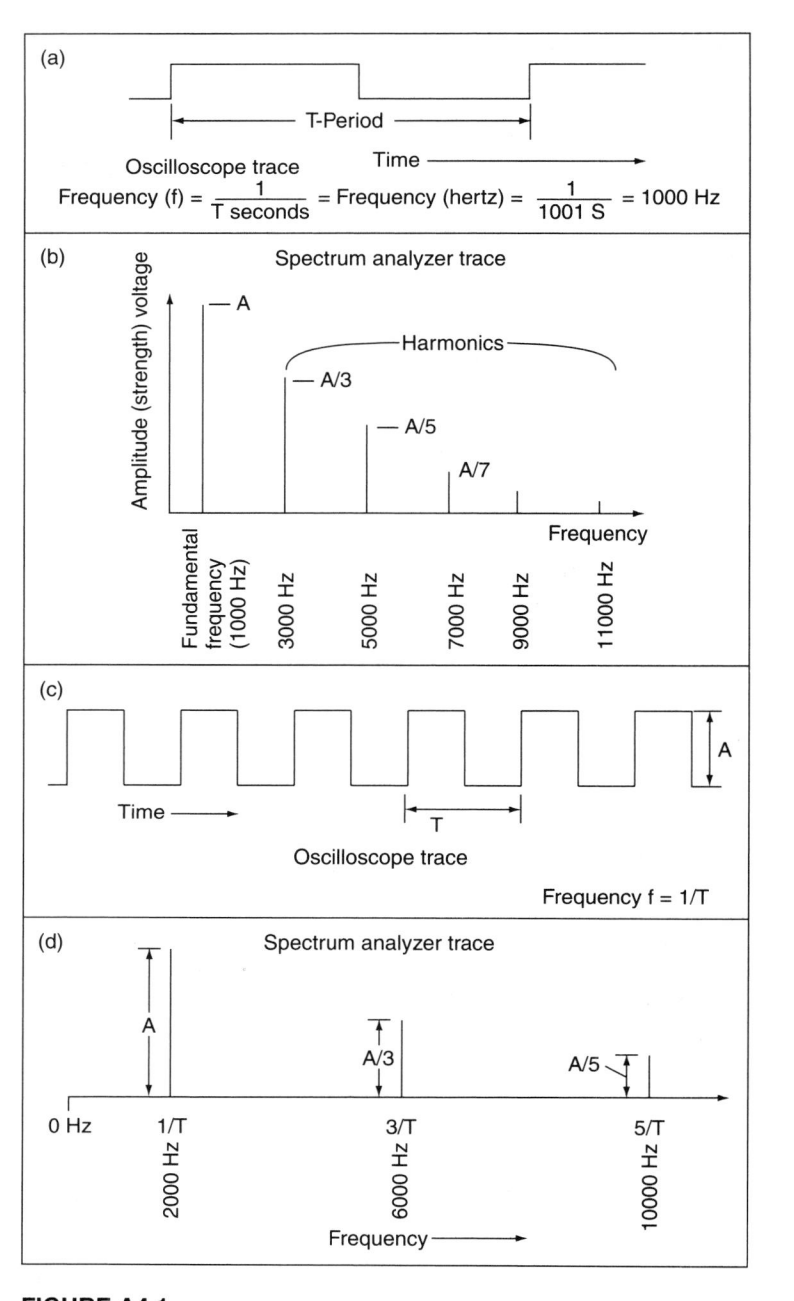

FIGURE A4.1
Fourier series.

Figure A4.1b shows how the spectrum of a square would look on a spectrum analyzer. A spectrum analyzer displays signal amplitude on the vertical scale and frequency on the horizontal scale.

The fundamental frequency is the lowest AC (alternating current) frequency of this waveform. Since the waveform is not symmetrical about zero volts (equal portions of the signal above ground [zero volts] and below ground), some DC (direct current) component exists. From Equation A4.1 this DC term is A_0. Please notice A_0 on the frequency plot of Figure A4.1.

From Equation A4.1 we also have the fundamental frequency given by the term A_1 sin $(2 \pi f + \Theta_1)$. Each harmonic A_n sin $[2 \pi (nf) + \Theta_n]$ is at an exact multiple frequency of the fundamental. Each harmonic decreases in amplitude as the harmonic increases in frequency. A_n decreases as the harmonic number increases. The calculation of A_n is beyond the scope of this text.

Let's construct a square wave from the sum of each harmonic. This is done in Figure A4.2. Figure A4.2a shows the fundamental frequency ($n = 1$), the third harmonic ($n = 3$), and their sums. The sum shows the "molar tooth" shape of a square wave.

Figure A4.2b shows the fundamental frequency ($n = 1$), the third harmonic ($n = 3$), the fifth ($n = 5$) harmonic, and their sums. The "molar" becomes more pronounced, and the edges become more steep.

Figure A4.2c shows the fundamental frequency ($n = 1$), the third harmonic ($n = 3$), the fifth ($n = 5$) harmonic, the seventh ($n = 7$) harmonic, and their sums. Figure A4.2d shows fundamental frequency ($n = 1$), the third harmonic ($n = 3$), the fifth ($n = 5$) harmonic, the seventh ($n = 7$) harmonic, the ninth ($n = 9$) harmonic, and their sums. As more harmonics are added, the waveform becomes more like a square wave and the edges become steeper.

Thus we see that the more harmonics in a signal, the better the reproduction or fidelity. Analog television signals take up 4 to 6 MHz of bandwidth for best resolution. High-fidelity music needs 16 kHz of bandwidth (the human hearing range is up to about 16 kHz).

The Public Switched Telephone Network (PSTN) bandwidth for voice is 300 to 3,400 Hz. This is adequate for voice transmission but completely inadequate for good musical reproduction. If a square wave with a fundamental frequency of 2,400 Hz entered the PSTN, it would let only the first harmonic (fundamental) frequency pass. Only a 2,400 sine wave would be received, and all harmonics (4,800 Hz, 7,200 Hz, 9,600 Hz, and so on) would be filtered out (not passed).

If a signal with fundamental frequency greater than 3,400 Hz were sent into the PSTN, nothing would be transmitted. This is a great problem when we try to send data faster than 2,400 bits per second (bps). Modems use clever techniques to circumvent this limitation.

Students desiring more information are encouraged to examine Chapter 7 on PSTN, Chapter 8 on multiplexing and Codecs, and Chapter 9 on modulation and modems.

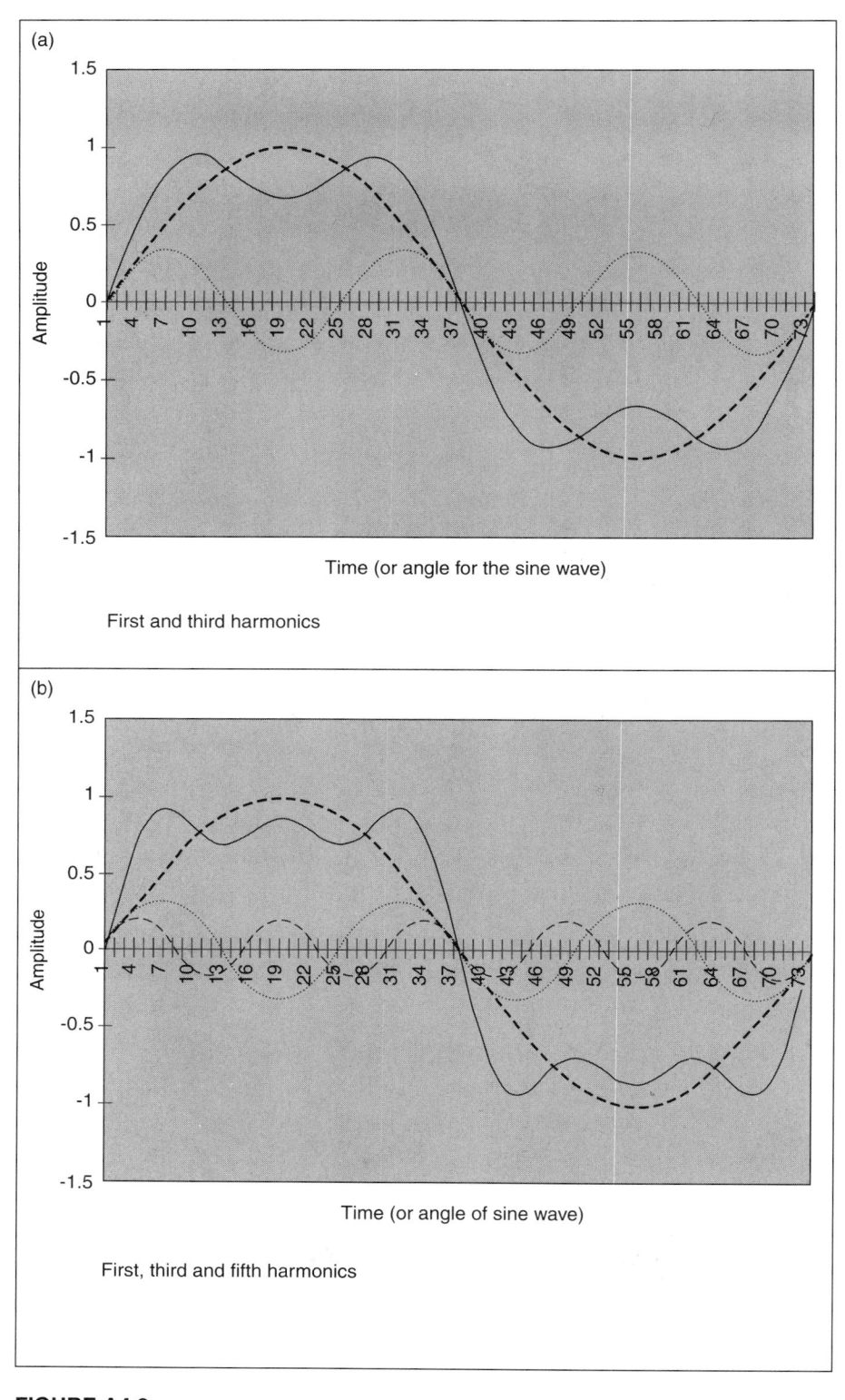

FIGURE A4.2
Fourier Series. (a) First and third harmonic, (b) Sin (X) + Sin (3X) + Sin (5X).

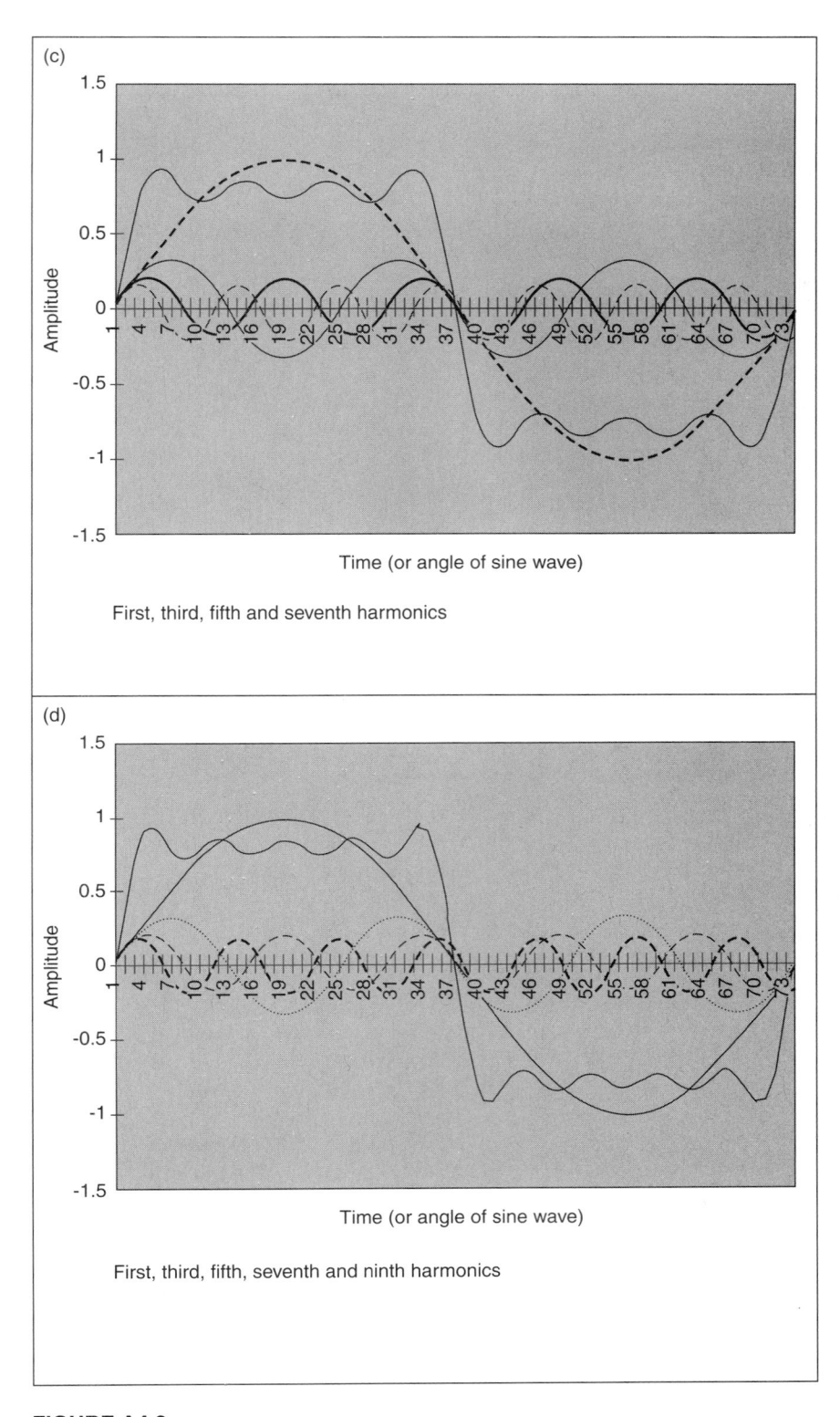

FIGURE A4.2

Fourier Series. (c) Sin (X) + Sin (3X) + Sin (5X) + Sin (7X), and (d) Sin (x) + Sin (3x) + Sin (5x) + Sin (7x) + Sin (9x).

A5

WIDE AREA PROTOCOLS (WAN)

OBJECTIVES

In this chapter we will discuss:

  I. A table comparing the protocols as they relate to WANs.
  II. Wide Area Networks (WANs). There are a lot of standards, and the student can easily feel overwhelmed. The purpose of this chapter is to prepare the student for these various protocols and hopefully reduce the confusion level.
  III. The protocols can be divided into two groups: lower level (levels 1 through 3) and upper level protocols (levels 3 and up). Most of the lower level protocols use only levels 1 and 2. The only level 3 protocol discussed is X.25.

A5.1   Lower Level Protocols

Table A5.1 summarizes the lower level protocols. It is suggested that the student refer to Table A5.1 while studying each protocol in order to relate that protocol to others.

The table lists seven WAN protocols. T-1 (T Carrier) and ISDN were discussed in Part III on the Public Switched Telephone Network (PSTN). Nevertheless it is appropriate to include these protocols in this chart because they are designed for wide area use and also cannot be properly included in any LAN discussion.

Table A5.1 gives the acronym for each protocol, its creator, and the reason for its creation. Note that the earliest created protocols, T Carrier and BiSync, are at the left and ATM, the latest, is at the right. It is important to understand that protocols were created to address a need using existing technology. The protocols were developed as the customer's needs changed from voice only to voice, video, and data. Technology improvements in noise levels, data rates, and voice and video conversions allowed newer standards to be developed. It is hoped that the student will be able to relate each protocol to the reason for its existence and the driving technology.

At this time it is quite understandable for the student to wail, "More protocols, why more protocols?" No, the profusion of protocols is not to vex the student, although at first glance this certainly appears to have been the designer's ulterior motive.

TABLE A5.1
WAN Protocols

Protocol	T Carrier, T-1, T-3, E-1, E-3	Binary Synchronous Control	One of many "X" protocols	Frame Relay	Integrated Systems Digital Network	Synchronous Optical NETwork	Asynchronous Transfer M code
Acronym	"T" = twisted pair; E = Europe	BiSync or BSC	X.25	FR	ISDN	SONET	ATM
Created by whom and when	AT&T, early 1960s	IBM, 1962	Rand Corp and CCITT; early 1960s	CCITT and others	CCITT; 1968–1984	Bellcore 1985	Various
Purpose	Increase capacity over twisted pair using digitized voice	Connect IBM products	Data over noisy quality and poor quality trunks	Data over good quality and low noise trunks; variation of X.25	Data and digitized voice and video from office/home to CO	Long haul, backbone, optical fiber, video	"Universal" for data, voice, video
Source/destination	Between COs and intra-LATA	Host to peripherals	Many possible	Many possible	Home/office to CO	High-capacity trunks, intra-LATA, between COs	Many possible
Routing	Usually fixed, not easily changed	Various	Many possible paths in PSN	Many possible paths in PSN	Via PSN and PSTN	Path rarely changed	One temporary per connection
Frame/cell size	T-1 has 24 channels, E-1 has 30 channels, and T-3 has 672 channels	Various sized frames	Various sized Packets	Various sized Packets	Various sized Packets	810-byte frame width 774-byte payload	53-byte cell Byte payload
Data Link protocol	D4, superframe, extended superframe	HDX	Link Access Procedure/Balanced (LAPB)	Similar to Link Access Protocol over D channel as per ISDN	Link Access Procedure over D channel (LAPD)		Convergent Segmentation Reassembly

Protocol	T Carrier, T-1, T-3, E-1, E-3	BiSync or BSC	X.25	FR	ISDN	SONET	ATM
Physical link	Twisted pair, later optical fiber	Various	Various	Various	Twisted pair	Optical fiber	Various
Speeds	T-1 has 1.544 Mbps; T-3 has 44.74 Mbps; E-1 has 2.048 Mbps	Various	Varies	Varies	BRI—2X64 kbps + 16 kbps = 144 kbps; PRI—23X64 kbps = 1.472 Mbps	n X 51.84 Mbps; Varies, but n is odd integer; works into rates up to 9.95 gbps	Various
OSI RM	Physical, DLL	DLL	Network, DLL	DLL	Physical, DLL	Physical, DLL	Physical, DLL
Error control	In ESF	Various	Between relay nodes, destination, and source	Between destination and source	In LAPD	Responsibility of upper layers	In last byte of header, for the response upper layer
Disadvantages	Best for constant rate data (voice); poor for "bursty" data	Half duplex, slow, "stop and wait"	Much error checking, overhead; expensive	Not good for voice	Limited availability; may be obsoleted by newer technology	Expensive, only for backbone, long haul	Standards in flux, delaying deployment, development

So please be patient as we traverse this sometimes confusing information. Hopefully, knowing the history of the protocol will help to understand how all these protocols fit together. Yes, I know many of you hate history. However I believe understanding the history of these myriad protocols is the only way one can understand them. As the protocols are discussed, please refer to Table A5.1. Hopefully this will aid in comparing and comprehending them.

Table A5.1 also compares the protocol's routing, source and destinations, level 2 differences, orientation, and error and flow control methods. Note that all the protocols in Table A5.1 are levels 1 and 2, except for X.25. X.25 is a level 3 (Network) protocol.

A5.2   Upper Level Protocols

The common upper level protocols, TCP/IP and SNA, are compared in Chapter 17 and then discussed separately in Chapters 18 and 19.

A6

DATA COMMUNICATIONS EXPERIMENTS

Bouktache, Essaid, "Computer Networking: Experiments for and Undergraduate Laboratory," Purdue University at Calumet, 1995 ASEE Annual Conference Proceedings.

CACI (3344 North Torrey Pines Ct., La Jolla, CA 92037) has COMNET III, a graphical network design program.

Feedback Inc., 437 Dimmocks Mill Road, P.O. Box 400, Hillsborough, NC 27278.

Frontline Test Equipment, Inc. (P.O. Box 7507, Charlottesville, VA 22906-7507) has a disk with an Ethernet LAN Analyzer, Serial data analyzer and serial Bit Error Rate Test demonstrations.

Hioki, Warren, "Laboratory Manual to Accompany Telecommunications," 3rd edition, Prentice Hall 1998.

Novell, Inc., Orem, Utah.

ScopeComm, Inc., 100 Otis Street, Northboro, MA 01532. Their FrameScope is a LAN analyzer demonstration program.

Tucson Amateur Packet Radio (TAPR) (8987-309 East Tanque Verde Road #337, Tucson, Arizona 85749-9399) has TCP/IP over AX.25 source code and object code discs available for a nominal fee.

Wade, Ian G3NRW, "NOSintro, TCP/IP over Packet Radio, An introduction to the KA9Q Network Operating System" describes TCP/IP over AX.25. See Tucson Area Packet Radio (TAPR).

GLOSSARY

2B1Q   2 Binary, 1 Quaternary is the signaling method for ISDN. Two bits of information are sent using four voltage states.

4ESS   A special-purpose switching computer.

5ESS   The successor to the 4ESS.

10Base2   An Ethernet CSMA/CD LAN using RG-58 coax.

10Base5   An Ethernet CSMA/CD LAN using RG-8 coax.

10BaseT   An Ethernet CSMA/CD LAN using twisted pair wire.

A-law   A Codec non-linear response curve used in Europe.

A/D   Analog-to-Digital conversion (or ADC) is the process of converting an analog signal (voice or modem tones) to digital numbers. See also **PCM.**

AAL   ATM Adaptation Layer roughly corresponds to the OSI RM DLL Layer 2. The AAL is divided into the Convergence Sublayer (CS) and the Segmentation And Reassembly (SAR) sublayer.

AC   Alternating Current. Electric current that flows in a conductor in one direction and then reverses direction. These reversals usually happen many times per second.

ADC   See **A/D.**

AMI   Alternate Mark Inversion is a signaling technique used in T-1 systems. AMI prevents "DC buildup," or capacitor charging and inductor saturation.

AMPS   Advanced Mobile Phone Service is the first cellular system used in the United States. AMPS uses analog techniques and is being replaced by digital systems.

Analog-to-Digital Conversion   A/D or ADC is the process of converting an analog signal (voice or modem tones) to digital numbers. See also **PCM.**

Analog signals   Signals that are continuous through time. By contrast digital signals can have only two stable values.

ANSI   American National Standards Institute is the main standards organization in the United States. ANSI is a member of the ISO. Data communication standards are only a small portion of ANSI responsibilities.

APPN   Advanced Peer-to-Peer Networking is a variation of SNA for smaller machines including AS/400 computers and personal computers.

ARP   Address Resolution Protocol is a subset of TCP/IP and maps (converts) an IP address to an e-mail or LAN (MAAC) address.

Byte   Eight bits. This is called an *octet* in Europe.

C/I   Carrier-to-Interference ratio is a measure of how much a cellular radio signal is being interfered with by a signal from a nearby cell. C/I determines how closely cells using the same frequency can be placed.

CAD   Computer Aided Design and graphic files are often very large and tax the limits of communications systems such as FTP of TCP/IP.

CCIS   Common Channel Interoffice Signaling uses one (common) channel for signaling (setup, maintenance, and teardown) of a voice circuit. The protocol is usually used in SS7.

CCITT   Comité Consultatif Internationale de Telegraphiqué et Telephonieqé is a part of the United Nations setting worldwide communications standards. It has been renamed the ITU-T.

CCS   Hundred Call Seconds per hour, a measure of traffic density used by Telcos. See also **Erlang.**

CDMA   Code Division Multiple Access is a direct sequence spread spectrum method of cellular communications. It can dramatically increase user capacity.

Cell   A hexagonally (usually) shaped geographical area that is served by a transmitter in a cellular mobile communications system.

Cell splitting   Dividing a cell into smaller parts to handle increased traffic.

Cellular system   Refers to a mobile communications system consisting of many cells controlled by an MTSO.

Class of service   The percentage of blocked calls permitted during the busiest traffic times.

CO   The Central Office receives the twisted pair cables from the user's home and/or office, converts the analog signal to a digital signal, and transmits the signal to other COs via high-speed trunk lines.

Coax   A transmission medium with a center conductor carrying the signal and a shield carrying the return signal. The two are separated by a non-conductive dielectric (insulator).

Co-channel interference   Interference from other users using the same channel in a cellular system. See C/I.

Codec   CODer / EnCoder converts the analog signal received at the CO from the customer into a digital signal. At the destination CO the Codec converts the digital signal into an analog signal to be sent to the customer destination.

Communications Act of 1934   Created the U.S. Federal Communications Commission.

Comparator   An electronic device that compares two voltages and outputs a logic signal according to which signal has the higher voltage.

Connectionless   Packets or datagrams sent containing the Destination Address and no routing information. The datagrams could take different routes to the final destination. No circuit setup or teardown is normally required. TCP/IP uses this method.

Constellation   A grouping of low earth orbiting satellites. The careful grouping is needed to provide continuous coverage to users on earth.

Constellation   A phase-amplitude pattern used for modems.

Control field   Part of the SDLC, X.25, Frame Relay, and other protocols. It contains frame or packet control information.

Corning Glass Works   A major producer of optical fiber.

CRC   Cyclic Redundant Code or Cyclic Redundant Check is an error detection system. Either 8, 16 or 32 bits of CRC generated data are added to the end of frames for error detection.

Cross talk   A form of interference where a portion of a signal passes from one wire to an adjacent wire.

CSMA/CD   Carrier Sense Multiple Access with Carrier Detection is used by Ethernet systems. It's "listen before talking, don't talk if someone else is talking."

D channel   The channel carrying control information in an ISDN system.

D-4   A type of T-1 frame.

DA   Destination Address is used in connectionless systems so that the destination node knows the frame is meant for itself. Also used for routing the frame to the final destination.

AS/400 A high-end mini-computer made by IBM.

ASCII American Standard Code for Information Exchange is an eight-bit code to transmit alphanumeric information. Originally the ASCII code was seven bits of data and one bit of parity. Pronounced "ask - eee."

Asynchronous Denotes signals that are not referenced to a clock or reference signal.

AT&T American Telephone & Telegraph, the original company founded by Alexander Graham Bell. In 1984 AT&T was forced by the U.S. Department of Justice to split into many smaller companies.

ATM Asynchronous Transfer Mode is a DLL protocol for carrying all types of digital information.

Attenuator A device to reduce signal power.

AWG American Wire Gauge is a measure of a wire's diameter. The larger the number, the smaller diameter the wire. AWG is often used to describe the size of twisted pair(s) of wire.

B8ZS Binary Eight Zero Substitution is a technique used in T-1 systems to prevent loss of receiver synchronization when a long string of zeros is sent.

B channel Bearer channels are the channels carrying data in an ISDN system.

Backhoe A trench and hole digging machine responsible for the majority of buried transmission line failures. The backhoe operators often fail to properly check for underground cables and pipelines. The former cause communications outages, and the latter cause severe explosions and considerable excitement. Always check before digging!

Baby Bells The ten companies providing local telephone service. The Baby Bells were created by the breakup (divestiture) of AT&T in 1984. Also called **RBOC.**

Bandwidth In digital communication systems, the maximum data rate possible in bits per second. In analog systems, bandwidth is the difference between the highest frequency and lowest frequency able to pass through the system. Bandwidth is often confused with the Baud rate.

Baud rate The rate the analog signal changes. Baud is often confused with the bit rate. They are not the same thing.

BECN Backward Explicit Congestion Notification is a bit in a Frame Relay packet to send congestion information back to the sender, asking the sender to slow the data rate.

Bell, Alexander Graham Received the first patent for the telephone in 1876. Bell went on to form AT&T. Bell is not the inventor of the telephone. That honor probably belonged to Philip Reise in 1854.

Bellcore Bell Communications Research is the former Bell Laboratories. Bell Labs became Bellcore after the breakup (divestiture) of AT&T in 1984.

BIOS Basic Input Output System is used on IBM PCs and compatibles to provide software control of input and output devices.

Bipolar Signaling with alternate positive and negative pulses. The bipolar AMI system is used in T Carrier systems.

Bit The smallest piece of digital information.

Blocked calls Calls arriving at the communications system and the system is not able to handle the call. The call is then said to be "blocked."

BOC Bell Operating Company refers to the ten "Baby Bells" providing local telephone service. The BOCs were created with the breakup (divestiture) of AT&T in 1984. Also see **RBOC.**

BRI Basic Rate Interface is two information (Bearer, or B) channels of 64 kbps each and one data (or D) channel of 16 kbps for a total of 144 kbps in an ISDN system.

Bridge Used to connect LANs together. A bridge operates at the DLL.

BSC Binary Synchronous Communications, or bisynchronous (or BiSync), was developed by IBM in the early 1960s. BSC is half duplex (HDX).

BT British Telecomm is the United Kingdom (Great Britain) equivalent of AT&T in the United States.

Bus A common wire over which some LANs communicate. The bus can be coax, twisted pair, or optical fiber.

DARPA   Defense Advanced Research Projects Agency oversaw the development of TCP/IP and the Internet.

Datagram   A digital frame sent with the Destination Address, but not any routing information. This "connectionless" packet could take any of several routes to its destination. TCP/IP uses this method.

dB   The decibel is a logarithmic notation of a ratio of two voltages, two currents, or two powers. The dB is used to express amplifier and system gains, and transmission line losses.

dBm   A measure of power relative to 1 milliwatt.

DC   Direct Current is a voltage or current that does not change flow direction or polarity.

DCE   Data Communications Equipment is hardware interfacing between a network and a DTE.

DE   Discard Eligibility is a bit within the Frame Relay control field. If the DE bit is set, the frame may be discarded if the network become congested.

DEC   Digital Equipment Corporation is a major manufacturer of digital computers.

De facto standards   Standards that are used but have not been formally approved by any agency.

Differential Manchester coding   Used by TRN LANs.

Digital signals   Have only two values through time. This makes digital signals easier to communicate and manipulate (perform mathematical operations or compute).

Diode   An electronic device. Current flow is much easier in one direction (forward direction) than the other direction (reverse). A forward biased (voltage across it) diode will have a relatively large current flow, while a reversed biased diode will have only a very small leakage current approximately 1 microampere or less.

DNS   Domain Name Service is a part of the TCP/IP protocol suite and converts e-mail addresses to IP addresses.

DOD   Department of Defense (United States).

DOS   Disk Operating System is an early operating system used on the IBM PC.

DQDB   Distributed Queue Dual Bus is a connectionless data transmission system designed to carry SMDS.

DS-0   Digital Signal, level 0 is a 64-kbps data rate.

DS-1   Digital Signal, level 1 is a 1,544-kbps data rate.

DS-3   Digital Signal, level 3 is a 44.736-Mbps data rate.

DSP   Digital Signal Processing uses a special-purpose computer to perform signal filtering, rather than by traditional analog techniques.

DSU   Digital Service Unit is an interface into a digital network.

DTE   Data Terminal Equipment is the hardware at the ends of a data network, such as mainframes, terminals, printer, and the like. A DTE is hardware that originates or terminates (destination) data.

DTMF   Dual Tone Multi-Frequency uses tones generated in the telephone set to send signaling (dialing) information to the CO. The CO converts the tones into numbers to set up the call switching.

DTV   Digital Television is a new standard for broadcasting digital television signals and will eventually replace the present analog system. DTV allows more channels to use the same spectrum and greatly reduces ghosts. DTV will use digital compression. See also **HDTV** and **SDTV.**

Echo   A situation in which the sender hears its own transmission.

Echo cancellation   The process of comparing the transmitted signal with the received signal. If a match is found, an echo is assumed and the echo is eliminated (canceled). This is used for voice transmissions but not data transmissions.

Echo suppression   Reduces echos by putting an attenuator in the signal return line.

EIA   Electronic Industries Association is a U.S. industrial group that sets standards for electronic equipment.

e-mail, or electronic mail   One of the features of the Internet. It often uses SMTP.

Encapsulation The process of putting something into a carrying device. One might put (encapsulate) a letter into an envelope. Also one might wrap a fragile object in a layer of protective cartons. In the data communications world it is the process of passing information down the OSI RM (or equivalent). When the information is passed from one layer to the layer below, the information is encapsulated into the lower layer's frame.

Enterprise computing Integrating LANs and WANs into a user friendly environment. Sorry Captains Kirk, Picard, and Janeway.

Erlang A measure of traffic density. See also **CCS.**

Error control The process of the communications system recovering from an error at the receiving node. Most communications systems detect the error(s) by a CRC process and then ask the node with the last good copy of the data for a re-transmission. A few systems have error correction built in.

ESF Extended Super Frame is used by T Carrier systems to send information and CRC error control.

ESN Electronic Serial Number is unique to each AMPS cellular phone and is sent over the airwaves to set up a call and for billing purposes.

ESS Electronic Switching System is a special-purpose computer designed for switching voice and data circuits.

FACCH Fast Associated Control CHannel is a part of the signaling in a cellular system.

Fast select A feature of X.25. It sends a packet with up to 128 bytes. It is often used for credit card verification.

FCC Federal Communications Commission is part of the Department of Commerce and regulates communications in the United States.

FCS Frame Check Sequence is used for error detection. FCS is either 8, 16, or 32 bits added to the end of a frame. It is also known as CRC.

FDDI Fiber Distributed Data Interface is a MAN with a dual ring topology, and uses tokens similar to TRN.

FDM Frequency Division Multiplexing is a technique to allow many users to share the same transmission medium. The frequency or radio spectrum space is divided among the users.

FDMA Frequency Division Multiple Access is a technique to allow many users to share the same transmission medium. The frequency or radio spectrum space is divided among the users.

FDX Full Duplex allows users at each end to transmit and receive simultaneously.

FEC Forward Error Control is an error correction method. The received data has extra bits enabling the data to be corrected even if corrupted by errors. These are Hamming codes or a derivation thereof. Reed-Solomon is a commonly used method.

FECN Forward Explicit Congestion Notification (pronounced "fek 'in") is used by Frame Relay to request the sender to reduce the data rate.

FEP Front End Processor is used by SNA systems to handle the communications for the host computer.

File server A computer configured to send and receive files from users. Usually used in LANs.

Flag A particular bit pattern used in synchronous transmissions to denote the beginning and end of a frame. The typical pattern is binary "0 1 1 1 1 1 1 0" or hexadecimal "7E."

Flow control The process of controlling the data reception rate so that the receiver does not receive data any faster than it is capable of processing, nor too slowly in order to preserve link efficiency.

FR Frame Relay is a level 2 data transmission protocol that error-checks only between sender and receiver, not between intermediate relay nodes as with X.25. This reduced error checking allows faster speeds and cheaper rates.

Frame A group of digital bits. The frame start and end are marked (delimited) with either a special bit (in T-1 systems) or specific bit pattern. Between the start and end delimiters there can be control information, data, error detection, and other information. The frame is created by the Data Link Level (DLL) at level 2 and transmitted by the Physical Layer.

Frequency   How often an alternating signal alternates, or how often a pulsating signal pulses. The units are cycles per second, or pulses per second, or more formally hertz.

Frequency reuse   Within a cellular communications system it allows the same frequency to be reused in nearby cells. This feature makes cellular systems possible.

Full duplex   See **FDX.**

Gateway   Broadly speaking it connects two systems together. It either converts one protocol to another or connects an SNA system to a LAN. It can also mean differing addresses on either side.

GFC   Generic Flow Control is a four-bit field within an ATM UNI cell header. The GFC allows equitable access for all data types into the ATM network.

Graded index   A type of optical fiber.

GSM   Global System for Mobile communications is a cellular system developed in Europe. It is the most widely used cellular system in the world.

Guard time   The time within a cellular communications frame needed to account for mobile units being different distances from the base station. The radio waves do not travel from the mobile to the base station instantly. The exact arrival times depend on the distance between the mobile and the base stations.

Handoff   The process of passing control from one base station to another as a cellular mobile unit leaves one cell and enters another. The MTSO controls the handoff.

Half duplex   Half duplex allows users to send information in only one direction at a time.

HDLC   High-level Data Link Control is a Data Link Level synchronous protocol.

HDTV   High-Definition Television will be broadcast by DTV and will allow much higher picture quality than the present analog system and use less spectrum space. Currently several formats exist, but one format will have over twice the scan lines of the present analog system. See also **DTV** and **SDTV.**

Hertz   A measure of an alternating or pulsing signal's frequency. It is named for a nineteenth-century German physicist, Heinrich Hertz. The units are cycles per second, or hertz.

IBM   International Business Machines was one of the first companies to enter the digital computer field. IBM is the world's largest computer company.

ICMP   Internet Control Message Protocol is used by IP for routing and flow control.

IEC   Inter Exchange Carriers are long distance carriers such as AT&T, MCI, Sprint, and Qwest. IXC is the same thing, just a slightly different acronym to further confuse the student.

IEEE   Institute of Electrical and Electronic Engineers is a professional organization that also writes the 802.X specifications for LANs.

IMPS   Improved Mobile Phone Service is an obsolete mobile telephone system.

Infrared light   Used for most optical fiber communications systems. Its wavelength is longer than visible light. Infrared light has the least attenuation in glass optical fibers.

Inmarsat   An international consortium to provide maritime satellite communications. It is based in London.

Intel   The company that invented the microprocessor.

Interface   The conversion process needed to transmit data between differing protocols or systems.

Internet   A collection of networks and gateways. The Internet connects private users, educational institutions from primary through universities, and government agencies in almost every country in the world. The Internet uses the TCP/IP protocol suite.

IP   Internet Protocol is a Network level protocol of the TCP/IP suite.

IS-54   Interim Standard-54 is a digital cellular TDMA (Time Division Multiple Access) communications standard used in North America.

IS-95   Interim Standard-95 is a digital cellular CDMA (Code Division Multiple Access) communications standard used in North America.

ISDN   Integrated Services Digital Network is a unified system for voice and data transmission at faster rates than telephone modems.

ISO   International Standards Organization writes standards for worldwide communications.

IXC   Inter eXchange Carriers are long distance carriers such as AT&T, MCI, Sprint, and Qwest. IEC is the same thing, just a slightly different acronym to further confuse the student.

Kingsbury Commitment of 1913   Stated that AT&T would not buy up any more independent telephone companies and would allow the independents to be connected to the AT&T long distance system.

LAN   Local Area Networks transmit data between nodes in a local (building or campus) area.

LAP/B   Link Access Protocol / Balanced is the Network level 3 protocol for X.25.

LAPD   Link Access Protocol over the D channel is the Data Link Level 2 protocol for ISDN.

LATA   Local Access and Transportation Areas approximate area codes.

LCI   Local Channel Identifier is routing information within the X.25 packet.

LED   Light Emitting Diodes are used as visual indicators, and emitters in optical fiber systems.

LLC   Logical Link Control is a sublayer within a LAN's level 2. It is specified by IEEE standard 802.2.

Loopback tests   Used to troubleshoot a communications system. The test signal is fed to a downstream node, and then the signal is "looped back" to the sending node. If the looped back signal is satisfactory, the transmission line and node are assumed to be functioning. The loopback point is then moved further downstream and the process repeated until the failed portion of the communications system is found.

LU   Logical Units are used to gain access into an SNA system.

MAC   Media Access Control is a sublayer of the DLL in a LAN system. The MAC address is the Physical address of the NIC (Network Interface Card).

MAC   The colloquial nickname for the Apple MacIntosh computer.

MAN   Metropolitan Area Network is a network covering an area such as a large city.

Manchester   Manchester encoding is the signaling method used with Ethernet LANs.

MAU   Media Access Unit (Ethernet) is the transceiver used to interface between a node and a 10Base5 or 10Base2 LAN.

MAU   Multiple Access Unit (TRN) or Multistation Access Unit is the center of the "hub" for a TRN LAN. Even though the topology looks like a star, the wiring within the MAU makes the topology a ring.

MCI   Microwave Communications, Inc., is the second largest long distance provider in the United States.

MF   Multi-Frequency.

MFJ   Modified Final Judgment was issued by Judge Harold Green and took effect in 1984. The MFJ ordered the breakup (divestiture) of AT&T into separate "Baby Bells" or RBOCs (Regional Bell Operating Companies).

Microwaves   Radio signals with a wavelength between 30 cm and 1 cm. These are much shorter than AM broadcasting wavelengths of 1,000 meters or more, hence the term *micro*.

Modem   MODulator / DEModulators convert digital pulses within a computer into tones suitable for transmission over the PSTN. At the receiving end the process is reversed.

MTSO   Mobile Telephone Switching Office is a special-purpose computer and facility used to handle mobile telephone calls.

Multi-mode   An optical fiber that allows many modes to exist within the fiber core. Multi-mode optical fiber is the lowest bandwidth optical fiber. Also called *step index*.

Mu-law   See μ-law.

NAU   Network Addressable Units are logical connection ports within an SNA system.

NCP Network Control Program controls the Data Flow Control, Transmission Control, and Path Control Layers of SNA.

Near-far problem of cellular systems The varying signal strengths of mobile units received at base stations. The signal strength can vary widely and cause many problems particularly in CDMA systems. These problems are reduced by the MTSO controlling the mobile's signal strength.

NetBIOS Network Basic Input Output System The software to interface a node to a LAN.

NIC Network Interface Card is a PCB card usually installed inside a computer interfacing between the computer and a LAN.

Nibble Four bits, one-half of a byte.

NNI Network-Network Interface is an ATM cell type sent between nodes within the ATM network.

NOS Network Operating Systems control LANs. Two major examples are NetWare from Novell and NT Server from Microsoft.

NRZI Non Return to Zero with Inversion on "ones" is the signaling system used with FDDI.

NSF The National Science Foundation was the first civilian user of the Internet. The NSF is part of the U.S. government but is a civilian (non-military) organization. Originally the Internet was exclusively for military use.

NT New Technology is a Microsoft operating system. NT Server is Microsoft's client/server LAN operating system. NT Windows for Workgroups is their peer-to-peer LAN operating system.

NT Northern Telecom (now Nortel) is Canada's largest telecommunications manufacturer.

NT1/2 Network Termination 1 or 2 are types of ISDN (Integrated Services Digital Network) terminations, or access into the ISDN system.

OC-X Optical Carrier and bit rate "X" is the optical bit rate sent over a SONET system. The bit rate is the number "X" times 51.84 Mbps.

Octet Eight bits, a European term. This is called a *byte* in the United States.

Open system A standard to which anyone can manufacture equipment or software.

OSI Open Systems Interconnect seven-layer Reference Model (RM) was developed by the ISO. The RM is based on SNA.

P(r) Packet number of the next frame expected.

P(s) Packet number of the frame transmitted.

Packet A message is divided into exact length blocks, namely, packets. Routing, control, and error detection information is added before transmission. Packet transmission is usually connection oriented and "reliable." Ordinarily a packet is encapsulated within a frame.

PAD A Packet Assembler/Disassembler is needed to interface a non-X.25 DTE (Data Terminal Equipment) to an X.25 network. A PAD is a converter from non-X.25 equipment to an X.25 network.

PBX Private Branch eXchanges are switches between lines in a building or campus and the connections to a CO (Central Office) via a trunk line.

PC Low-cost Personal Computers are largely responsible for the explosive growth of the data communications industry.

PCB Printed Circuit Board is the circuit board on which electronic components are mounted.

PCM Pulse Coded Modulation is the process of converting analog signals into digital numbers, or Analog-to-Digital conversion.

PDN Public Data Networks transmit data.

PDU Protocol Data Units are added to each frame by each communications layer. PDUs communicate with the equivalent layer at the destination.

P/F The Poll / Final bit in the packet or frame control field is used to demand a response from the destination (Poll) or indicate the last frame (Final).

Photon A light particle. Light exhibits characteristics of a wave and a particle. The photon is that particle. When a light photon interacts with a light detector, an electron is knocked loose from an atom within the detector. In a LASER or LED when an electron drops from a high-energy shell to a lower-energy shell, a photon is emitted.

Physical Layer The lowest layer of the OSI RM and the actual physical medium carrying the electrical or optical signals. The Physical Layer includes the transmitter and receiver.

PING   Packet InterNet Groper is used to check the availability of TCP/IP destinations.

POTS   Plain Old Telephone Service (or System).

PRI   Primary service of ISDN (Integrated Services Digital Network) is similar to T-1 or E-1 rates. Interfacing to T-1, PRI has twenty-three data channels and one control channel. While interfacing to E-1, PRI has twenty-nine data channels and one control channel. Each channel is 64 kbps.

Print servers   Computers to handle printing chores in a LAN. The printer is shared among the LAN users.

PSTN   Public Switched Telephone Network is the telephone network we all use.

PT   Payload Type is a three-bit field within an ATM header indicating what type of data the payload is carrying.

PU   Physical Units are software programs in Cluster Controllers within SNA systems.

PVC   Permanent Virtual Channels are similar to leased lines, but all the user's data is statistically multiplexed onto the network.

Queue   Potential users waiting to use a system. An example is customers waiting in queue (British) or line (American) to use a bank teller.

RBOC   Regional Bell Operating Company is the local "Baby Bell" company such as Bell South, US West, or Bell Atlantic. See also **BOC.**

Re-generation   The process of receiving a signal and re-transmitting the original signal. Strictly this can only be done with digital signals.

RIP   Routing Information Protocol resides at the Application Layer of TCP/IP and aids in routing the datagram.

RJ-45   The connector type used to connect to 10BaseT NICs and some ISDN equipment.

ROM   Read Only Memory.

Routers   Used to connect LANs. Routers look at the frame Destination Address and determine the best route to send the frame.

Schmidt trigger   An electronic device for recovering a digital signal containing electrical noise. The Schmidt trigger will recover the original digital signal, while a comparator will have difficulty eliminating the noise.

SDTV   Standard Definition Television is not the present analog system, but DTV allows several television channels to fit into the spectrum space of one analog system.

Server   See **file server.**

Setup   The process of establishing a connection.

Seven-Layer Model   The Open Systems International (OSI) Reference Model (RM) of the ISO used to describe a complete communications system. It is based on IBM's SNA.

Single mode   The highest bandwidth optical fiber.

SMTP   Simple Mail Transfer Protocol is used by TCP/IP to send e-mail over the Internet.

SNMP (Simple Network Management Protocol)   Used to manage TCP/IP networks.

SPC   Stored Program Control. SPC controls switching within the PSTN (Public Switched Telephone Network).

Step index   A form of optical fiber. It has the lowest bandwidth of any glass optical fiber.

Step-by-step switch   An electromechanical rotary switch used to route telephone calls. Current pulses from the user's telephone moved the switch arm. It is no longer used in developed countries. It is also called the Strowger switch after its inventor.

Strowger Switch   See **step-by-step switch.**

SVC   Switched Virtual Channel is set up and used only when needed by the customer and torn down after its use.

System Network Architecture (SNA)   A wide area data communications system designed by IBM. It is the basis of the OSI RM.

Teardown   The process of disconnecting a connection between the transmitting and receiving node.

Telco   The local telephone company, such as US West, Bell Atlantic, Bell South, or GTE.

Traffic   The flow of frames (bits) through a network.

Twisted pair (TP)   A pair of insulated wires (usually copper) twisted together. Used for voice and some data transmission systems.

μ-law   A non-linear Codec response used in North America and Japan.

UNI   User Network Interface is a type of ATM cell sent by the user to the ATM network. This is contrasted with the NNI (Network-Network Interface) cell used within the network.

VCI   Virtual Channel Identifier is routing information contained within an ATM cell header. ATM needs the VCI because it is a connection oriented protocol.

VPI   Virtual Path Identifier is routing information contained within an ATM cell header. ATM needs the VPI because it is a connection oriented protocol.

VSAT   Very Small Aperture Terminal is a satellite communications system designed for small size, portability, and low cost.

VTAM   Virtual Telecommunications Access Method is a part of SNA. It frees the operating system of communication responsibilities.

WAN   Wide Area Network is a network designed to communicate over wide (long distance) areas.

INDEX

BIBLIOGRAPHY

"AX.25 Amateur Packet Radio Link Layer Protocol," American Radio Relay League, Newington, CT.

Bates, Bud and Gregory, Donald, "Voice & Data Communications Handbook," 1995, McGraw-Hill, New York 0-07-005147-X.

Black, Uyless, "Data Networks; Concepts, Theory and Practice," Prentice Hall, Inc., Englewood Cliffs, NJ 07632, 1989, 0-13-198466-7.

Campbell, June, "What's All the Fuss About Wireless?" ComputerEdge, March 16, 1998, pp. 15–17, Englewood, CO 80115-5073.

Campbell, Larry L., "Broadband and SONET," 1990, Information Technologies.

Chien, Philip, "Inmarsat, the First PCS Satellite System," Satellite Times, September 1998, pp. 16–19.

Corner, Douglas E., "Internetworking with TCP/IP, Volume I," 1996, Prentice Hall, Inc.,

Englewood Cliffs, NJ 07632, 1989, 0-13-468505-9.

Digital Dave, "Digital Dave Defines: Digital Convergence," ComputerEdge, September 7, 1998, p. 14.

Forouzan, Behrouz A., "Introduction to Data Communications and Networking," 1988, McGraw-Hill, New York 0-256-23055-7.

Gareiss, Robin, "Bringing Flexibility to Frame Relay," November 1997, Data Communications, a McGraw-Hill publication, p. 36.

Gareiss, Robin, "Satellite Services; Down to Earth and Ready for Business," December 1997, Data Communications, a McGraw-Hill publication, pp. 83-92.

Gates, Harvey M., "Data Communications I," University of Colorado, Boulder, CO 1994. Class notes for TLEN 5330.

"ATM Testing and Verification," GN Nettest, Markham, Ontario L3R 8H3.

Held, Gil and Sarch, Ray, "Data Communications: a Comprehensive Approach," 3rd ed., 1995, McGraw-Hill, New York 0-07-028049-5.

"HP 8920B RF Communications Test Set/HP 8920B Option 800 for TDMA Test," Hewlett Packard, June 1996.

"HP 8921A Caell Site Test Set," Hewlett Packard, July 1996.

"HP 8924E CDMA Mobile Station Service Test Set," Hewlett Packard, February 1998.

"79000 ADSL Test Station System," Hewlett Packard, 1997.

"GSM Mobile Test Solutions," Hewlett Packard, 1996.

"HP Internet Advisor WAN—ISDN Test Solutions" Hewlett Packard.

"HP J2905B ISDN BRI S/T and U Interface Module," Hewlett Packard.

"SDH Network Testing," Hewlett Packard—Cerjac Division, Cerjac Telceom Operation. Westford, MA 01886-4113, 1997.

"SONET Testing Starts Here," Hewlett Packard—Cerjac Division, 1996, Cerjac Telceom Operation. Westford, MA 01886-4113.

"T-1 Test Advisor," Hewlett Packard—Cerjac Division, 1996, Cerjac Telceom Operation. Westford, MA 01886-4113.

"Testing ATM Interoperability—HP Solutions Note," Hewlett Packard, 1997.

"Testing Operations & Maintenance (OAM) Implementation for ATM—HP Solutions Note," Hewlett Packard, 1997.

"Testing ATM Signaling Performance—HP Solutions Note," Hewlett Packard, 1997.

"Functional Testing of ATM Signaling Protocols—HP Solutions Note," Hewlett Packard, 1997.

Hill Associates, Inc., Colchester, VT, "ATM Technology, Applications, and Services," April 1988.

Hill Associates, Inc., Colchester, VT, "DSL Technologies," January 1998.

Hill Associates, Inc., Colchester, VT, "Frame Relay," January 1998.

"ISDN Basics," 1989, Hewlett-Packard Company, Colorado Telecommunications Division, Colorado Springs, CO 80919, part number 18356-98201.

Hioki, Warren, "Laboratory Manual for Tele-communications," 3rd ed., Prentice Hall.

Hioki, Warren, "Telecommunications," 3rd ed., Prentice Hall, 1998.

"1992 Communications Test Symposium and Exhibition Technical Paper," Hewlett Packard, Colorado Telecommunications Division, Colorado Springs, CO 80919.

Johnson, Bobby (Foundry Networks, Inc.) and Jotwani, Kishore (IBM), "Cells vs. Frames; Which Wins on the Backbone?" December 1997, Data Communications, a McGraw-Hill publication, pp. 99–124.

Kushal, Dave, "Feel the Power," ComputerEdge, Englewood, CO 80115-5073, March 16, 1998, p. 24.

Layland, Robin, "Is the FEP Finished?" Data Communications, a McGraw-Hill publication, November 21, 1994, pp. 25–26.

Martin, James with Kavanagh, Kathleen, and Leben, Joe, "Local Area Networks," 1994,

Prentice Hall, Inc., Englewood Cliffs, NJ 07632.

Miller, Mark A., PE, "Internetworking; A Guide to Network Communications LAN to LAN; LAN to WAN," 1995, M&T Book, 115 West 18th Street, New York 10011, 1-55851-436-8.

Motorola, Inc., "The Basics of Frame Relay," 1993, Corporate and Professional Publishing Group, Addison-Wesley, One Jacob Way, Reading, MA, 1988, 0-20156377-0.

"Moving Your Enterprise to TCP/IP," 1997, WRQ, Inc., 1500 Dexter Avenue North, Seattle, WA 98109.

"Novell's LANalyzer for Windows 2.1" by Novell, Inc. Provo, Utah 94606-6194.

"Networking Standards," Data Communications, a McGraw-Hill publication, March 1997, pp. 62–65.

Newman, David; Melson, Brent; Kimar, Siva S., "DLSw Routers: Scaling to New Heights," July 1996, Data Communications, a McGraw-Hill publication, p. 69.

Peterson, Larry L., and Davie, Bruce S., "Computer Networks: A Systems Approach," 1996, Morgan Kaufmann Publishers, San Francisco, CA 1-55860.

Pooch, Udo W.; Macheul, Denis; McCahn, John, "Telecommunications and Networking," CRC Press, Inc., 2000 Corporate Blvd., N.W., Boca Raton, FL 0-493-7172-4.

"Racal's High Speed Dial-up Modem Handbook," Racal-Datacom, Inc., Fort Lauderdale, FL 33340-7044.

Ramos, Emilio; Schroeder, Al; Beheler, Ann, "Computer Networking Concepts," 1996, Prentice Hall, Inc., Englewood Cliffs, NJ 07632, 0-02-408031-4.

Ramteke, Timothy, "Networks," 1994, Prentice Hall, Inc., Englewood Cliffs, NJ 07632, 0-13-958059-X.

Ranade, Jay & Sackett, George, "Introduction to SNA Networking," 2nd ed., a Professionals Guide to, McGraw-Hill, 1994, 0-07-051506-9.

Roddy, Dennis, "Satellite Communications," 2nd ed. 1995, McGraw-Hill, New York 0-07-053370-9.

Russell, Travis, "Telecommunications Protocols," McGraw-Hill, 1997, 0-07-057695-5.

Schwartz, Mischa, "Telecommunications Networks, Protocols, Modeling and Analysis," 1988, Addison-Wesley, One Jacob Way, Reading, MA 0-201-16423-X.

Sexton, Mike and Reid, Andy, "Broadband Networking: ATM, SDH and SONET," Artech House, Inc., 685 Canton Street, Norwood, MA 02062, 0-89006-578-0.

Sherman, Ken, "Data Communications: a User's Guide," 3rd ed., Prentice Hall, Inc., Englewood Cliffs, NJ 07632, 1990, 0-13-199092-6.

Stallings, William, "Communications," IEEE Spectrum, January 1997, pp. 27–37.

"T-1/E1 Primer and Basic Applications," 3rd ed., 1992, Racal-Datacomm, Inc., Fort Lauderdale, FL 33340-7074.

Taylor, Ed, "Demystifying SNA," Wordware Publishing, Inc., 1506 Capital Avenue, Plano, Texas 75074, 1993, 1-55622-404-4.

Taylor, Ed, "The McGraw-Hill Internetworking Handbook," McGraw-Hill, 0-07-063263-4.

Thorpe, Nicolas M., "X.25 Made Easy," Prentice Hall, Inc., Englewood Cliffs, NJ 07632, 1992, 0-13-972183-5.

Trulove, James, "LAN Wiring, an Illustrated Guide to Network Cabling," 1997, McGraw-Hill, New York 0-07-065302-X.

Veeneman, Daniel, "Introduction to Personal Communications Service Satellites," Satellite Times, Volume 4 Number 9, July 1998, pp. 60–61.

Veeneman, Daniel, "Personal Communications Systems—Anywhere, Anytime," Satellite Times, Volume 5 Number 1, September 1998, pp. 10–15.

Walrand, Jean, "Communications Networks: A First Course," 1991, Aksen Associates/Irwin, Hometown, IL 60430 & Boston, MA 02116, 0-256-08864-0.

Walrand, Jean & Pravin, Varaiya, "High-Performance Communication Networks," Morgan Kaufmann Publishers, San Francisco, CA 1-55860-341-7.